11/05

W9-CEW-282

UFO

The Definitive Guide
to
Unidentified Flying Objects
and
Related Phenomena

UFO

The Definitive Guide
to
Unidentified Flying Objects
and
Related Phenomena

David Ritchie

Facts On File®

AN INFOBASE HOLDINGS COMPANY

To Betsy Ryan

UFO: The Definitive Guide to Unidentified Flying Objects and Related Phenomena

Copyright © 1994 by David Ritchie

Facts On File, Inc.
460 Park Avenue South
New York NY 10016

Library of Congress Cataloging-in-Publication Data
Ritchie, David, 1952 Sept. 18–
    UFO: the definitive guide to unidentified flying objects and
related phenomena / David Ritchie.
      p.   cm.
    Includes index.
    ISBN 0-8160-2894-X
    1. Unidentified flying objects—Encyclopedias. I. Title.
TL789.R57 1994
001.9'42—dc20   93-31037

Jacket design by Steven Brower
Printed in the United States of America

VC VB 10 9 8 7 6 5 4 3 2 1

This book is printed on acid-free paper.

Preface

Several principles have guided the research for, and writing of, this book. Readers should be aware of those principles before using this work, so as to avoid possible misinterpretations and to understand the intellectual framework and belief system into which the author places his treatment of the UFO phenomenon.

I reject the hypothesis that UFOs represent visitations by corporeal beings from other planets and star systems, traveling in material spacecraft. This particular hypothesis is widely known as the "extraterrestrial hypothesis." It strikes me as mere fantasy. At the very least, it is unsupported by evidence. After approximately half a century of UFO reports, including numerous alleged close encounters, there is no incontrovertible (nor even reasonably solid) evidence in favor of this hypothesis. Moreover, there is abundant evidence against the extraterrestrial hypothesis, such as the reported behavior of UFOs themselves, which often have been seen performing maneuvers that cannot be accomplished by a material object subject to the known laws of motion. Perhaps the word "fraud" is too strong to use in this context, but I believe that many backers of the extraterrestrial hypothesis are afflicted by wishful thinking, if not responsible for self-deception and/or intentional deception of others.

Despite the lack of persuasive evidence for the extraterrestrial hypothesis, one must admit that the modern UFO phenomenon is real nonetheless. Something very much out of the ordinary appears to have happened to large numbers of eyewitnesses over a period of about the last 50 years. These events are too numerous and too detailed, and exhibit too many close resemblances to one another and to certain other phenomena, to be dismissed in their entirety as imagination, hallucination, error and deceit.

The "other phenomena" mentioned in the previous sentence are those commonly called "paranormal." The spectrum of paranormal activity includes a wide variety of phenomena, from so-called extrasensory perception (ESP) to "hauntings" and poltergeist activity. I believe that the UFO phenomenon is linked closely to many other forms of paranormal activity, up to and including reports of demonic activity and diabolical possession of individuals. Indeed, it is impossible to separate UFOs from the realm of the paranormal. No other interpretation of the UFO phenomenon, in my opinion, fits the known evidence better.

The UFO phenomenon is essentially occult in character. Involvement in occultism precedes or accompanies close encounters in many individual cases, and various aspects of the UFO phenomenon—such as "channeling" of extraterrestrial entities—are virtually identical to occult practices outside the realm of UFO studies. Also, one finds numerous links between certain prominent "contactees" and practitioners of occultism.

In treating UFOs as a paranormal, occult phenomenon, one also must consider them as a spiritual phenomenon. Some students of UFOs may prefer to dismiss the thought that UFOs might have a spiritual dimension. Yet a pronounced spiritual element has been part of UFO contact reports from the very start. Messages relayed through these alleged contacts have encouraged humankind to embrace a syncretic faith centered on a highly imprecise conception of "God." Moreover, a strong element of

Hinduistic thinking pervades the UFO phenomenon. This evidence alone, I believe, justifies treating UFOs as spiritual phenomena. Much other evidence is also available, as various entries in this book demonstrate.

The public is coming to believe in UFOs as a possible agency of salvation for human civilization. This strange conviction is reinforced by popular entertainment, which has replaced traditional fantasies of hostile aliens invading Earth with a new mythology of benevolent extraterrestrials who supposedly are waiting to swoop down and rescue us from ourselves if and when human civilization reaches the point of self-destruction. An alternative belief is that extraterrestrials have been involved in the evolution of the human species from lower animal forms and stand ready to guide us along, at the proper time, to the next higher level in evolutionary progress. In either case, humans, in increasing numbers, look for superhuman intervention from the skies to deliver us from the problems of our modern era.

Even if one accepts the premise that extraterrestrials are watching Earth closely and are prepared to interfere in its "evolution," there is no reason to presume that such beings are benevolent. On the contrary, there are numerous reports of hostile action on the part of UFOs; and in many abduction reports, the aliens subject their human captives to procedures that would qualify as torture.

As Jacques Vallee has suggested, UFOs appear to constitute a control system for human belief. The aim of UFO "contacts" and other communications is evidently to redirect human thinking. Among the techniques used to reshape human belief systems is what Vallee has called "metalogic," a pattern of confusing, seemingly nonsensical behavior and communications that leaves witnesses bewildered and seeking explanations. Thus the human mind is prepared for whatever explanation eventually is provided.

In which direction exactly is the UFO phenomenon redirecting human belief? There are many opinions on that subject. None of them can be proven conclusively true or untrue just yet. Nonetheless, certain elements of belief appear so frequently in UFO contact reports that one must suspect that they form part of a belief system or systems that the UFO phenomenon is engineered (if one may use that word) to encourage. Those elements include collectivism; the unification of human society into some kind of global regime; veneration, bordering on worship, of nature and of natural objects; faith in occult principles and practices, such as mediumism or "channeling"; discouragement of traditional Judaeo-Christian religious beliefs, such as the doctrine of the divinity, crucifixion and resurrection of Christ; and a syncretic set of religious beliefs with identifiable parallels in Buddhism, Hinduism and shamanism. These elements also are all part and parcel of the so-called New Age movement, and one may view the modern UFO phenomenon as a companion to that movement.

Another curious and often disturbing parallel between the UFO phenomenon and the New Age movement, with all its prominent occult elements, is the speed with which both belief systems can take over the human mind. Various commentators have noted that interest in UFOs quickly can become an obsession that displaces virtually everything else in an individual's life. (This obsession was dramatized in the famous motion picture about UFOs, *Close Encounters of the Third Kind*.) The same is true of occultism and other New Age beliefs. Once admitted to the mind, they have a remarkable way of expanding and, in some cases, controlling the individual's life completely. This virulence can make deep interest in the UFO phenomenon hazardous in the extreme, and would-be believers in the extraterrestrial hypothesis and in the occult components of UFO lore have been warned in emphatic language to avoid such involvement with the UFO phenomenon and all its related phenomena. Those who say UFO lore is harmless, a mere hobby comparable to stargazing or bird-watching, are mistaken. The author's investigation of UFOs has turned up abundant evidence of the dangers of involvement with the UFO phenomenon; and the author's wish is that persons deeply interested in UFO study will exercise the greatest caution in its pursuit.

• • •

Because thousands of individual UFO sightings have been reported in detail, and many of those sightings have been publicized widely, it was possible to select only a comparatively few individual sightings for inclusion in this volume. These cases, as a rule, have been chosen because they were especially well-publicized; because they had particular significance to the history, psychology and sociology of the UFO phenomenon; or because they illustrated some prominent element of the UFO phenomenon. The author apologizes to readers whose favorite encounter story may have been omitted.

The selection of illustrations was a difficult matter. There are, to put it politely, few or no convincing photographs of UFOs and related phenomena. Most of the so-called photographic evidence for UFOs is obviously fabricated, in many cases with laughable clumsiness. The author and editor decided that artists' conceptions would be more useful to the reader, and so this volume relies heavily upon such illustrations. Unless noted otherwise, all illustrations are from the author's collection.

A

Abbiate Guazzone incident, Italy At 10:00 P.M. on April 24, 1950, one Bruno Facchini reportedly encountered a dark UFO and, near it, a humanoid dressed in close-fitting clothing and a helmet. This individual appeared to be making repairs to the craft. Three other humanoids also allegedly were seen. Light was seen shining out through a hatch in the craft. Eventually, the hatch was closed, and the craft departed. In one respect, this report resembles many others from the UFO literature of the late 19th through the mid-20th centuries: a humanoid apparently making repairs to a landed UFO.

See also ENCOUNTER PHENOMENA; REPAIRS.

abductions Reports of abduction of humans by "extraterrestrials" have become prominent features of UFO lore. Many different phenomena have been reported in abduction cases. Entities described as "aliens" have allegedly appeared to abductees in various forms, including small humanoids, celebrities and deceased relatives of abductees. The aliens may conduct an abductee out of his or her body or enter and take control of a human body. Some kind of indoctrination may be involved in an abduction story. The aliens may predict an imminent time of great turmoil and destruction on Earth. The abductee may be subjected to painful operations involving probes inserted into the anus or the genital area. Forced sexual activity, with aliens or with other abductees, may be reported. "Missing time," an inability to account for one's activities during a period of hours or even days, may accompany a reported abduction. Many different explanations have been put forward to account for abduction reports and the phenomena associated with them. Hoaxes are one

possibility, as are various mental disorders. UFO abduction reports also resemble in many ways reported incidents from the literature on demonology.

See also DEMONOLOGY; ENCOUNTER PHENOMENA; HILL INCIDENT; HUMANOIDS; MISSING TIME; SEXUAL ENCOUNTERS; WALTON INCIDENT.

absurdity As a prominent element of the UFO phenomenon, absurdity occurs in many forms, from non sequiturs to inconsistencies in behavior. For example, UFOs violate known physical laws. Though "aliens" may claim their spacecraft are made of steel, as in the Bethurum incident, the ships behave as no material object could, maneuvering in a manner inconsistent with Newtonian laws of motion. Alleged space people say they have mastered "magnetic force" (by which, apparently, they mean they can neutralize gravity by means of electromagnetism), but their vehicles, in many cases, shoot out fiery exhaust in the manner of ordinary chemical rockets—a much less advanced mode of propulsion.

Many more examples can be cited. The UFOs' "advanced" technology seems ridiculously unreliable, requiring frequent landings for "repairs." The behavior of alleged aliens often is inconsistent with their professed motives. The "benevolent" space folk often say they have the best interests of humankind at heart, but many close encounters reportedly involve hostile action on the visitors' part. The aliens supposedly wish to keep their presence hidden from humankind for the moment, yet do all they can to advertise their presence. The putative visitors from space also offer unconvincing "wisdom," which often is incoherent and sounds almost like the ramblings of schizophrenics.

Notably absurd is the pattern of reported contacts between aliens and humans. If, as has been suggested, the purpose of face-to-face contacts between alien visitors and selected humans is to make the visitors' presence known to Earth's "power elite" (to use C. Wright Mills's term), then the aliens appear to have chosen a highly indirect and ineffective method. These encounters tend to occur in isolated areas and involve men and women far removed from the centers of intellectual, political and military power.

The element of absurdity in the UFO phenomenon extends far beyond mere descriptions of "extraterrestrials" and their behavior in encounter cases. Whole genres of literature on UFOs have arisen to defend preposterous hypotheses such as the existence of UFO bases inside a hollow Earth, with flying saucers traveling between the planet's surface and interior through portals at the North and South Poles. Religious cultists also have tried to build extravagant "theologies" around the UFO phenomenon.

It has been suggested that absurdity in many UFO reports is an attempt to reshape human belief systems by confusing observers with preposterous and contradictory information, so as to leave their minds more receptive to implantation of new beliefs.

See also BETHURUM INCIDENT; HOLLOW EARTH HYPOTHESIS; METALOGIC; MYTHOLOGY; RELIGION, UFOS AND; VALLEE, JACQUES.

acoustical effects

Although many UFO sightings appear to occur in silence, numerous sounds also have been reported in connection with UFOs, including voices (sometimes speaking in colloquialisms), explosions, hissing, humming, laughter and the sound of heavy machinery. On rare occasions, music has been associated with UFOs. In motion pictures, a droning noise is commonly associated with UFOs in flight. This association may be seen in the opening sequence of the 1951 motion picture *The Day the Earth Stood Still*, which depicts a classic flying saucer landing in Washington, D.C. A notable feature of some UFO encounter incidents, as noted earlier, is the apparent absence of sound. The percipient reports later that some influence seemed to absorb or suppress sound in the UFO's vicinity during the encounter. As a result, the percipient feels oddly isolated from his or her immediate environment and may report later that time seemed to slow down or stop in the UFO's presence. This combination of silence and perceived "timelessness" has been called the "Oz factor," after the prolonged dream sequence that makes up most of the famous motion picture *The Wizard of Oz*.

See also AIRSHIPS; DEMONOLOGY; ENCOUNTER PHENOMENA; OZ FACTOR.

Adamski, George (1891–1965)

An American UFO cultist and author, George Adamski became famous after his report of a meeting with an alien astronaut in the California desert on November 20, 1952. A Polish immigrant, Adamski was 61 years old at the time of his first reported encounter with an extraterrestrial. Adamski said the visitor (apparently in his late twenties) was handsome, had shoulder-length hair and wore what looked like a brown ski suit. Adamski said his visitor was capable of reading images in his mind.

The alien claimed to be from Venus. He and his fellow space travelers, he indicated, were here on friendly business and were worried about radiation emanating from Earth as a result of testing nuclear weapons. A vague conversation about God followed. Adamski understood that the aliens believed in a Creator and lived according to the Creator's will. Exactly what the aliens believed about this "Creator," however, seemed uncertain.

The alien also indicated that space travel was commonplace, that people from other worlds were visiting Earth often, and that some aliens had been killed on missions to our planet. On further questioning, Adamski was told that humans had caused some of these deaths.

Venus, seen here in radar image, turned out to be much less hospitable to life than "contactee" George Adamski imagined. (NASA)

This was not Adamski's only reported encounter with aliens. He claimed that visitors from space had also taken him on a trip to the Moon, on the far side of which he said he had seen alien settlements.

In his final years, some details of Adamski's conversations with extraterrestrials were proven incorrect by unmanned space probes to the Moon and Venus. Far from being an inhabitable world, Venus turned out to have extremely high surface temperatures and crushing atmospheric pressure, which virtually ruled out the possibility that the planet could support life such as the handsome humanoid described by Adamski in his 1952 desert meeting. Likewise, the far side of the Moon, made visible at last by photographs taken by a Soviet space probe, showed no trace of habitation.

Although Adamski was a formidable and controversial presence in the UFO phenomenon for more than a decade, much of his life and activities remains mysterious. He contributed to popular belief in a great conspiracy called the "Silence Group" that was thought to operate far from public scrutiny. The Silence Group was supposed to be an organization bent on keeping the "truth" about UFOs from reaching the public. Later, belief in an alleged (though vaguely defined) conspiracy became an outstanding feature of faith in UFOs.

See also ABSURDITY; CONSPIRACY THEORIES; HUMANOIDS; SILENCE GROUP; VENUS.

Adamski saucer   This term refers to a particular kind of "saucer" design resembling the UFO that early "contactee" George Adamski reportedly encountered in the southwestern desert of the United States. The Adamski saucer has a shallow, cylindrical cabin with a domed top and a flared "skirt" below, with portholes in the cabin wall and three hemispherical protuberances on the bottom of the craft. It has been suggested that the Adamski saucer bears a strong resemblance to certain overhead lamps that have three exposed light bulbs in the same positions as the hemispheres beneath the Adamski saucer. Although the Adamski saucer is widely believed to have been a crude hoax, UFOs of almost identical design have been reported seen in other parts of the world. Some or all of these reports are also suspected of being hoaxes. The Adamski saucer appears to have exercised a strong influence on UFO "designers" on Earth; a variation on the Adamski saucer was seen, for example, on the closing credits of the American television series "The Invaders."

See also ADAMSKI, GEORGE; INVADERS, THE; TECHNOLOGY.

Adamski saucer, shown here in oblique top and bottom views, was characterized by a cabin with portholes, and by "three-ball" landing gear. Adamski's "spaceship" may actually have been an overhead lamp. (D. Ritchie)

Aetherius Society   A British organization, the Aetherius Society was founded in 1954, after a London taxi driver named George King allegedly was contacted by some kind of extraterrestrial intelligence and told that he was to serve as the voice, on Earth, of an interplanetary "parliament." Reportedly named after an alleged inhabitant of Venus, the organization is widely considered to be a cult group.

See also CULTS.

Afghanistan   UFO reports such as the widely publicized Kandahar incident have come out of Afghanistan on occasion, but there is reason to think these reports most likely represent missile tests or sightings of other explicable phenomena such as clouds of vapor released by spacecraft.

See also KANDAHAR INCIDENT.

Agobard incident, France   Agobard, who served as archbishop of Lyons in the early part of the 9th century, denounced as "folly" the popular conception of "Magonia" as a foreign land served by flying ships. He added that he once had encountered three men and a woman being kept in captivity and exhibited as curiosities after reportedly having fallen from one of the aforementioned flying vessels. Plans called for the prisoners to be stoned, but apparently they were spared.

See also MAGONIA.

aircraft, UFOs and   Many reported encounters with UFOs involve aircraft. In many cases, UFOs are merely reported seen from aircraft, but in some instances the UFO allegedly interacts with the aircraft and its pilot. The UFO may approach the aircraft, match its speed and pace it for a time, seemingly copying the maneuvers of the plane. In other cases, UFOs reportedly have flown directly toward aircraft, forcing the aircraft into violent maneuvers to avoid collision. The size, shape, appearance and behavior of UFOS involved in such encounters may vary greatly from one incident to another. In the "foo fighter" phenomenon of World War II, for example, aircraft appeared to be accompanied in flight by small lights that flew along with the planes for a time, then departed. At the other extreme of size, aircraft are said to have encountered UFOs the size of aircraft carriers or even larger. This latter category includes a widely publicized report of a Japan Air Lines Boeing 747 that encountered a walnut-shaped UFO vastly larger than the aircraft during a flight over Alaska on November 17, 1986.

There appears to be no proven, documented case of a UFO actually doing any harm to an aircraft or anyone on board the aircraft, but instances of seemingly hostile action by UFOs toward aircraft, notably military interceptors, have been reported. The death of U.S. Air Force Captain Thomas Mantell in 1948, on a flight to intercept a UFO seen over Kentucky, is sometimes cited as evidence of hostility on the part of UFOs, but it is widely believed that Mantell exceeded a safe altitude while trying to close in on a high-altitude weather balloon, became unconscious from lack of oxygen and crashed as a result.

UFO sightings by aircraft pilots are often taken seriously as evidence that UFOs are not merely hallucinations or misidentifications of actual phenomena, on the grounds that pilots are skilled judges of the character, behavior, size and distance of airborne objects, and that a pilot officially approved to fly an aircraft is hardly likely to suffer from hallucinations. UFO "debunkers" have pointed out, however, that it is not always easy to identify objects in flight, and that even a sincere, experienced and observant pilot may err in identifying a familiar celestial object such as a star or planet, and claim to have seen a UFO. During World War II, American B-29 aircrews in the Pacific theater reported being pursued by searchlight-bearing aircraft, when in fact the crews had seen and misidentified the bright planet Venus. Various atmospheric phenomena also may be mistaken for UFOs when observed from aircraft.

Interference with the electrical and communications systems of aircraft has also been reported on occasion.

See also FOO FIGHTERS; SALANDIN INCIDENT.

Air Force, U.S.   The Air Force took a major role in investigating the UFO phenomenon in the 1950s and 1960s, notably through Project Blue Book. Although the Air Force apparently concluded that UFOs did not represent any direct threat to national security, official Air Force studies of the UFO phenomenon are viewed widely as a cover-up of sorts, designed to calm the public's fears of UFOs and to discredit the so-called extraterrestrial hypothesis. There is reason to think that the U.S. government, in the years immediately after World War II, did see an indirect threat to national security from public interest in flying saucers. Spurious calls reporting flying saucer sightings, the government evidently feared, might be used to help overwhelm U.S. air defenses in the event of an air attack from the Soviet Union. Viewed in this context, the Air Force studies appear to have been efforts to minimize the aforementioned risk to air defenses by persuading the public that there was nothing to fear from UFOs.

See also BLUE BOOK, PROJECT; CONSPIRACY THEORIES; GRUDGE, PROJECT; ROBERTSON PANEL.

Air Force Regulation 200-2   Shortly after the Robertson Panel met in January of 1953, the Air Force implemented Regulation 200-2, which said that the number of unidentifieds in UFO reports must be reduced as much as possible. The directive allegedly was linked to another regulation, JANAP-146, which made release of information about UFOs by military personnel a criminal act, punishable by 10 years in prison and a $10,000 fine.

See also ROBERTSON PANEL.

airships   In the late 19th and early 20th centuries, numerous Americans—notably Californians—claimed to have seen strange aircraft in the skies and, in some cases, to have had face-to-face meetings with the crews of these vehicles. The airships shared many characteristics with UFOs of the late 20th century. They reportedly manifested themselves both as lights in the evening sky and as apparently material craft (complete with propellers) during the day. Descriptions differed on details but generally agreed that the craft were ovoid or oblong; carried propellers or fans that appeared to move the airships against the wind; and had either a cockpit atop the fuselage or a cabin beneath the main body of the craft.

Airships, fanciful flying machines, were reportedly seen over the United States in the 1890s. (D. Ritchie)

The strange vehicles, as seen in California starting in 1896, often were said to move approximately in a north-south direction, to fly close to the ground (as if trying to maximize the ship's visibility to eyewitnesses) and to have a peculiar, undulating flight path that looked as if the crew were having trouble controlling the vehicle's altitude. Some accounts of encounters with the airships included reports of hearing voices from the alleged airship, including songs and laughter.

In 1897, the wave of airship sightings spread from the Pacific coast of the United States to other parts of the country. The details of sightings also changed, bringing the airship phenomenon much nearer in character to the UFO sightings of half a century later. The airships often were witnessed in the form of nocturnal lights apparently attached to large, vaguely seen, dark forms. The altitude also appears to have increased; one airship was reported seen flying at about 1,000 feet, much higher than in earlier sightings. Explanations of sightings of nocturnal lights in the skies during this early UFO wave also resemble those put forward by the scientific commu-

nity in the 20th century, such as the view that the lights were merely stars.

The airship sightings of the 1890s may be interpreted in various ways. Hoaxes are a strong possibility. It would have required little imagination to produce a convincing story of aerial craft in the late 19th century. The technology suitable for building airships (or at least the rudiments of it) had become public knowledge by 1896, when the airship sightings began, and science fiction writers had used the emerging technology of powered flight in their stories. French science fiction author Jules Verne, in his 1886 novel *Robur le conquerant* (translated into English in 1887 as *Robur the Conqueror*), related the adventures of a brilliant inventor and his airship, the *Albatross*. Verne's imaginary aircraft resembled in many ways the airships allegedly seen over America after the novel was published. It is conceivable that a large number of readers in the United States were familiar with Verne's novel and modeled their reports on it.

See also ENCOUNTER PHENOMENA; PRECEDENTS.

Alamogordo incident, New Mexico, United States

An Air Force sergeant reportedly was watching meteors near Alamogordo on August 13, 1975, when he sighted a discoid UFO. Later he allegedly professed to recall, without hypnosis, meeting humanoids who communicated with him by telepathy and placed him on an examination table where some kind of instrument was placed upon his back. The entities reportedly said they planned to have only restricted contact with humankind in the future.

See also ABDUCTIONS.

Alamosa incident, United States

One of the earliest incidents of animal mutilations linked tentatively with the UFO phenomenon, the Alamosa incident involved a colt discovered dead near Alamosa, Colorado, on September 9, 1967. Allegedly, all flesh had been removed from the animal's head, and the brain, spine, heart, lungs and thyroid gland were absent. No evidence of blood or tire tracks could be found near the body, but a set of 15 circular marks were reported found on the ground some 40 feet away from the corpse. Each mark was said to be approximately four inches in diameter and three to four inches deep. Evidence of radioactivity was reported in the vicinity of the marks. A pathologist who examined the body of the colt reported that the flesh looked as if it had been "cauterized" surgically along an incision running from the neck to the base of the chest. Later, a microscopic examination of tissue from the "cauterized" edge of the cut revealed damage consistent with burning, the pathologist reported. Equipment to perform such a cut is available now but apparently was not widely available in 1967, when the incident was reported.

The Alamosa incident attracted widespread attention and followed the same pattern as many other reported animal mutilations in later years, namely removal of flesh and organs; seemingly cauterized incisions; and absence of blood and vehicle tracks in the vicinity of the corpse.

See also ANIMALS, UFOS AND.

Alençon incident, France   Early on the morning of June 12, 1790, an incident similar to modern UFO encounters reportedly occurred near Alençon, France. According to the story, farmers in the area saw a huge globe, described as big enough to contain a carriage and apparently surrounded by fire, flying through the air with a whistling noise, at high velocity. Then it decelerated and settled on a hilltop. The object gave off so much heat that trees and grass beneath it began to burn. Area residents managed to control the fire. That evening, the story goes, they examined the globe and found it was still warm. It appeared to be undamaged after its fiery flight and landing. From a door that opened in the side of the object, a humanoid wearing tight-fitting clothing emerged. The entity said something that the spectators did not understand, and then escaped into the nearby woods. The onlookers backed away in fear. Soon afterward, the globe exploded and sent fragments flying all around. The fragments allegedly burned themselves to powder. No trace was found of the humanoid.

See also HUMANOIDS; SPHERES.

Algonquin flying basket   A legend from the Algonquin people of North America involves a "basket" that descends from the sky bearing 12 beautiful maidens. When a hunter tries to approach them, they fly away in the basket. Eventually, he captures one of the maidens, marries her and has a son by her. She pines for the company of the other maidens, however, and one day makes a basket for herself. Taking the child with her, she climbs into the basket and uses it to fly away into the skies by singing a charm. After two years back in her faraway homeland on another star, she is told to return to Earth and retrieve her husband, along with specimens of the game he kills. She brings her husband back with her from Earth, and they attend a great banquet where the game is served.

Astronomer and UFO investigator Jacques Vallee, who has performed an intensive study of parallels between UFO stories and folklore, notes that significant similarities exist between the Algonquin legend and modern UFO lore, including the account of intermarriage between the "alien" and the human; the exchange of food and drink; and the extraterrestrial folk's interest in terrestrial fauna, namely the game killed by the hunter. Also, the beautiful maidens mentioned in the Algonquin story are reminiscent of attractive female "aliens" in modern UFO contact tales, such as Captain Aura Rhanes and Semjase. Another possibly significant element of the Algonquin legend, in light of modern UFO lore, is the musical charm the maiden uses to propel her basket into the skies. Some UFO encounter stories in our own time emphasize the musical qualities of "extraterrestrial" speech, and UFOs themselves are sometimes described as playing "music" to witnesses. In the 1977 motion picture *Close Encounters of the Third Kind*, for example, the fictional extraterrestrials communicate with humans by means of a five-note musical theme.

See also ABDUCTIONS; ACOUSTICAL EFFECTS; BETHURUM INCIDENT; CLOSE ENCOUNTERS OF THE THIRD KIND; ENCOUNTER PHENOMENA; INTERMARRIAGE; MUSIC; SEMJASE; SEXUAL ENCOUNTERS.

Allen, Kirk   A case from the annals of psychiatry, the story of "Kirk Allen" appears to demonstrate how a detailed vision of extraterrestrial worlds, such as that related by certain UFO "contactees," can originate within the human mind. "Kirk Allen" is the name assigned to the patient by the psychiatrist who treated him, Dr. Robert Lindner. Afterward, Lindner related the details of the case in his 1955 book *The Fifty-Minute Hour: A Collection of True Psychoanalytic Tales*. An employee at a U.S. government installation in New Mexico (Jacques Vallee, in his book *Revelations*, says Allen worked at a facility where thermonuclear weapons research was being conducted), Allen was referred to Lindner after his superiors became distressed by his bizarre behavior. The efficiency of Allen's department was suffering, and Allen had promised them he would try to spend more time on Earth. At government expense, Allen was flown to Baltimore to meet with Lindner. Although Allen himself was well-dressed and well-mannered, he told a bizarre story and produced masses of written documentation for it. Apparently, Allen had come to believe that a series of science fiction stories, featuring a character with the same name as his own, were really accounts of Allen's own life. The stories were set on distant worlds. Allen had produced voluminous accounts of life on these other planets. In trying to resolve what he considered to be inconsistencies in the stories, Allen became convinced that he could travel by psychic means to the fictional worlds.

Lindner asked to see the documents Allen used to support his fantasy. Allen produced a typescript biography of himself some 12,000 pages long, with 200 chapters. Allen also supplied approximately 20 pages of handwritten notes, as well as various other notes written on scraps of paper in Allen's own cryptic shorthand. Also among this material were an extensive glossary of terms and names, dozens of colored maps of other worlds, more than 60 architectural sketches, a set of genealogical tables and astronomical charts and star maps made from the perspectives of various planets in the system that the fictional Allen supposedly inhabited. Allen even supplied a history, some 200 pages long, of the empire that he thought he ruled. A set of more than 40 folders contained information on various planets in this imaginary realm. The reports had titles such as "The Fauna of Srom Olma I," "The Transportation System of Seraneb" and "The Application of Unified Field Theory and the Mechanics of the Star Drive to Space Travel."

Lindner knew this would be a difficult case to treat. He ruled out shock therapy as too extreme, and decided against hypnosis because he thought the procedure might harm Allen further. Lindner chose to enter the fantastic world that Allen had created and try to cure Allen's madness that way. Lindner studied Allen's documents carefully, found points that seemed to need clarification, and asked Allen to retrieve the information by psychic methods.

Lindner became increasingly absorbed in Allen's fantasy and almost became trapped in it himself. At the same time, however, Allen took progressively less interest in the fantasy. Finally, Allen admitted to Lindner that the whole imaginative world he had created was "nonsense," and his psychic travels there were "foolishness." Cured of his fantasy, Allen went back to his government work. Evidently, the fantasy Allen invented could not be shared by two individuals. There was room in it (so to speak) for only one; and when Lindner entered it, Allen was displaced and returned to health. Lindner admitted years later that he remained fascinated with Allen's fictional worlds and thought of them often.

It has been suggested that Allen's case bears some similarity to the life and work of Paul Myron Anthony Linebarger (1913–1966), who became famous as a science fiction writer under the pseudonym Cordwainer Smith. His stories are set in the context of a vast interstellar civilization called the "Instrumentality," which he reportedly imagined at or before age 15. Elements of UFO close-encounter cases, such as apparent animal-human hybrids, appear in Smith's stories.

See also FANTASY-PRONE PERSONALITY; HOMEWORLDS.

Allende letters Beginning in 1956, a series of mysterious letters was sent to astronomer Morris Jessup, author of several books on UFOs, from a man known as "Carlos Allende" or "Carl Allen." Allende claimed to have witnessed an experiment during World War II that teleported a Navy vessel from a shipyard in Philadelphia to another shipyard in the Hampton Roads area of Virginia, and then back again. (This alleged incident has come to be known as the "Philadelphia experiment" and is said to have been engineered with the help of extraterrestrials.) Allende claimed the experiment was successful but had left many of the men on the ship deranged. Jessup showed the letters to the Office of Naval Research (ONR) in Washington, D.C., which had received a hand-annotated copy of Jessup's book *The Case for the UFO*. The book, mailed anonymously from Texas, contained notes that indicated the annotators—known as Mr. A, Mr. B, and Jemi—possessed extensive knowledge about UFOs, including their origin and means of propulsion. The annotations were bizarre and nonsensical in places but contained so much seemingly technical knowledge that the annotators appeared to know what they were talking about. According to some accounts of the case, the Navy had a special edition of the book printed, incorporating the annotations, with the letters to Jessup included as an appendix.

See also JESSUP, MORRIS; TELEPORTATION.

Allingham case In 1954, only a few months after American "contactee" George Adamski claimed to have met an extraterrestrial in the southwestern desert of the United States, one "Cedric Allingham" published a book titled *Flying Saucer from Mars*, his account of an alleged encounter in Britain with aliens from Mars. The Martians were said to travel in a spacecraft much like the one Adamski described. Allingham said he had encountered the Martians while on a trip to Scotland. The extraterrestrial he allegedly encountered resembled Adamski's putative visitor from Venus, except that the Martian was said to be wearing some kind of breathing equipment.

Despite efforts to contact "Allingham," he avoided speaking with the press. Soon after his book appeared, the author was reported to have died. Rumors circulated that "Allingham" was actually a celebrated British astronomer writing under a pseudonym, but those rumors remain unsubstantiated. The Allingham case is widely considered to have been a hoax.

See also ADAMSKI, GEORGE; ENCOUNTER PHENOMENA; HOAXES; MARS.

amber gambler A reputed variety of UFO, the amber gambler is a small, luminous sphere that hovers near the ground or close to the horizon, and is visible for a few seconds or minutes before vanishing. The name is evidently English in origin and is said to have come from Warminster, U.K., where the phenomenon was reported in the 1960s. This appears to be one of the most common varieties of UFO reported, accounting for more than 20 percent of UFO sightings. Several possible explanations have been put forward for amber gamblers. One is an optical illusion associated with the sun. Another is moonlight shining through mist or clouds. Ball lightning is also a possibility, as are certain manmade phenomena, such as parachute flares near military installations.

See also BALL LIGHTNING.

anchors One curious element of UFO lore involves anchors allegedly dropped by UFOs. A report of a UFO dropping an anchor dates from 1211, when an aerial vehicle reportedly snagged its anchor on the roof of a church in Cloera, Ireland. In 1897, an "airship" reported flying over Merkel, Texas, allegedly caught its anchor on a fence. In both cases, the anchors reportedly were cut free and preserved. If the anchors really existed, however, their whereabouts today appear to be unknown. The reports of UFO anchors are sometimes cited as evidence of the "cultural factor" in UFO reports. Numerous students of UFO lore have observed that the technology described in UFO reports tends to reflect the technological knowledge of the land and time in which a report is made. Just as modern UFO reports may describe UFO technology in terms of lasers, "force fields" and the like, witnesses of supposed UFO encounters in earlier centuries apparently described the technology in terms of hardware familiar to them, such as anchors.

See also AIRSHIPS; CULTURAL FACTOR; TECHNOLOGY.

ancient astronauts In the 1970s, popular imagination was captured by the so-called ancient astronauts hypothesis. According to this hypothesis, the "gods" of human mythology were actually extraterrestrial astronauts who supposedly visited Earth in prehistoric times and performed such marvelous feats of technology that humans accepted the visitors as deities. Although this hypothesis had circulated for many years beforehand in works of science and pseudoscience, the best-selling books of Swiss author Erich von Däniken brought the idea of "gods" as ancient astronauts to a mass audience in the late 1960s and early 1970s. The commercial success of von Däniken's works led to a proliferation of books on the ancient astronauts hypothesis and similar subjects. The result was an international enthusiasm for UFOs and the possibility of extraterrestrial life in general that lasted for several years and coincided roughly with a widely publicized wave of UFO sightings in the early 1970s, including the famous alleged encounter case in Pascagoula, Mississippi. Eventually, the ancient astronauts fad ran its course and subsided, but it left its mark on the thinking of a generation and helped to encourage the belief that UFOs represented visitations by corporeal beings from other worlds, traveling in material spacecraft.

See also MYTHOLOGY; PASCAGOULA INCIDENT; PSEUDOSCIENCE; VON DÄNIKEN, ERICH.

ancient civilizations One prominent theme in UFO lore is that UFOs represent remnants of technology from ancient, supposedly lost, civilizations— either on this planet or on other worlds. Atlantis and Lemuria are examples of these mythical ancient civilizations on Earth. In some accounts, the ancient cultures were destroyed by warfare; according to other stories, natural calamities wrecked the ancient civilizations and forced their people to flee. These myths may be extremely elaborate and may represent a desire on the part of myth-makers to recapture the imagined innocence of earlier ages in history or of the myth-makers' own early lives.

See also ANCIENT ASTRONAUTS; ATLANTIS; LEMURIA; TELOS; VON DÄNIKEN, ERICH.

Anders incident, Sweden The Anders incident reportedly involved a man, given the pseudonym "Anders," who was allegedly taken aboard a UFO on the night of March 23, 1974, and subjected to an apparent medical examination that involved inserting a probe into his head. After this alleged experience, Anders was said to be capable of influencing a compass needle by putting his hands near it and of seeing "auras" around objects and people. Although details of this case appear dubious, it matches the overall pattern of many other reported instances of UFO abductions from the United States and other countries, including the levitation of the abductee into a UFO; the "medical" exam; and the insertion of a probe into the subject's body. The incident was part of a "wave" of UFO sightings that occurred in the Vallentuna region near Stockholm, Sweden, in 1974.

See also ABDUCTIONS; ENCOUNTER PHENOMENA; WAVES.

Andreasson case Among the most famous cases in the literature on UFO encounters, this case involves Mrs. Betty Andreasson Luca, an American "contactee" who reportedly had a series of encounters with extraterrestrials having oversized heads and capable of passing unimpeded through walls. She reported contacting an extraterrestrial named Quazgaa and experiencing a quasi-medical examination that included having a needle inserted into her abdomen, in the manner of alleged contactee Betty Hill. The religious element of the Andreasson case was extremely prominent. Betty Andreasson Luca said she had heard God's voice and had exchanged her Bible for a religious text supplied by the extraterrestrials. (This book was later reported lost.) Her account of seeing a city of crystal during her encounters is reminiscent of certain "near-death" experiences in which a person may report having seen a magnificent city.

See also ABDUCTIONS; CHRIST AND CHRISTIANITY; HILL INCIDENT; HUMANOIDS; NEAR-DEATH EXPERIENCE; RELIGION, UFOS AND.

Andrée expedition One of the most famous expeditions into the Arctic, the balloon flight of Swedish aeronaut Salomon August Andrée in 1897 illustrates how easily false reports of aerial objects can be generated.

Riding a hydrogen-filled balloon launched from Spitsbergen on July 11, 1897, Andrée and two companions intended to ride the balloon to the north geographic pole. Instead, the balloon came down far short of its goal, at White Island, a small island east of Spitsbergen. The balloon had spent only three days aloft and had been forced down by the weight of accumulated ice. All three men on the expedition died on White Island, where their bodies were discovered in 1930.

Soon after Andrée's departure from Spitsbergen, numerous reports similar to those of modern UFO sightings circulated concerning Andrée and his craft. One report placed the balloon over Canada several days before Andrée had actually left Spitsbergen. Other reports from Canada indicated Andrée had passed that way in August. Reports from Russia also were numerous; one sighting of Andrée's balloon

was reported from Sakhalin in far eastern Russia in September, long after the balloon had crashed. Another sighting of the balloon was reported from the southwestern coast of Greenland in August 1897, weeks after the balloon had gone down hundreds of miles away. A psychic in Iowa claimed to have made contact with Andrée's party and suggested that Swedish authorities search a location in northeastern Greenland for the aeronauts. Faked "messages" from Andrée started turning up soon after his disappearance. One such message, written in French, was reportedly found along a railroad in Russia's Ural Mountains and stated that Andrée's craft had crossed the Urals.

The many erroneous sightings of Andrée's balloon and the fabricated messages from his expedition bear a close resemblance to elements of the UFO phenomenon and demonstrate how easily misleading information can be generated.

See also HOAXES.

angel hair A fine, fibrous, light-colored material, "angel hair" is said to have dropped from UFOs on numerous occasions. As in other cases of UFOs leaving behind physical evidence, the existence of angel hair is questionable, since no samples of it appear to have endured long enough to be analyzed.

See also EJECTA.

angels Angels are commonly defined as created intelligences, more powerful and clever than humans, and capable of appearing in many forms and performing seemingly impossible deeds. In traditional Christian doctrine, angels are believed to occupy two separate categories: the righteous angels, obedient to God's commands and often assigned to protect humans from harm, and the evil or "fallen" angels—which took Satan's side in his rebellion against God and were cast out of heaven with Satan, thus forming his demonic host.

The similarity of certain UFO encounter cases to traditional accounts of angelic apparitions has been noted frequently in the literature on UFOs. Although some elements of UFO encounter cases resemble biblical descriptions of the appearances of righteous angels—notably intense light effects—various commentators have observed that the reported behavior of UFOs in many cases (including lying to, assaulting and even torturing human subjects) is consistent with descriptions of demonic activity. The celebrated Eastern Orthodox monk and theologian Father Seraphim Rose, in his 1978 book *Orthodoxy and the Religion of the Future*, argued that the UFO phenomenon must represent demonic activity. Various other commentators, citing the many reports of hostile, cruel and deceptive activity on the part of alleged extraterrestrials, have reached the same conclusion as Father Seraphim.

See also ABDUCTIONS; DEMONOLOGY; ENCOUNTER PHENOMENA; ROSE, FATHER SERAPHIM; VALENS INCIDENT.

Angelucci case, Soon after George Adamski's published account of his meeting with an extraterrestrial, Orfeo Angelucci published in 1955 his own book on his alleged meetings with aliens, entitled *Secret of the Saucers.* Angelucci reportedly encountered the extraterrestrials in California (as in the Adamski case), met with them on several occasions and was taken aboard their spacecraft for a tour of the solar system. As in the case of "contactee" Truman Bethurum, one of the aliens was a beautiful woman (named "Lyra"). Angelucci reported meeting with the aliens in public on occasion. The "revelations" supposedly made to Angelucci included his previous existence as an extraterrestrial called "Neptune." Angelucci also was told that unless the inhabitants of Earth improved their behavior, the world could expect a great catastrophe in 1986. That year turned out to be no more calamitous than many others in the 20th century, despite the fact that human behavior continued to be as reprehensible as ever.

See also ADAMSKI, GEORGE; BETHURUM INCIDENT; ENCOUNTER PHENOMENA; LYRA; PRECEDENTS.

animals, UFO and In many so-called close-encounter incidents, domestic animals are said to experience strong reactions of anxiety. The literature on UFOs is full of descriptions of animals, especially dogs, behaving strangely and even violently when confronted with UFOs. Similarities have been noted between reports of animal behavior during UFO encounters and accounts of animals' reactions to other "paranormal" phenomena. In both situations, animals may cower, flee, howl and injure or even kill themselves.

Animal mutilations—that is, the mutilation and killing of domestic animals, particularly of cattle—are widely associated in the public mind with UFOs following a series of heavily publicized incidents in the United States during the 1970s. In the western United States, bodies of cattle were found drained of blood and mutilated. Much has been written in the popular press about the possibility of UFO occupants performing such acts on domestic animals as a means of gathering tissue samples for analysis. Attacks by predators remain a questionable theory, since predators are not likely to drain blood.

Animal deaths and mutilations have been reported in connection with other UFO incidents in the late 19th and early 20th century. The "Egryn lights" phenomenon coincided approximately with reports of mysterious animal deaths in England, and at least one animal mutilation was associated with "airship" sightings over the United States in the 1890s.

See also AIRSHIPS; EGRYN LIGHTS.

Ansett-ANA incident, Australia/New Guinea
On May 28, 1965, an Ansett-ANA DC-6b airliner in flight from Brisbane, Australia, to Port Moresby, New Guinea, was reportedly accompanied by a UFO described as an oblate object emitting some kind of exhaust. The object flew along with the airliner for 10-to-15 minutes in the vicinity of Bougainville Reef, off the coast of Queensland. According to one account of the incident, the airliner's captain contacted ground control and said he was taking photographs of the object; but the captain received orders not to have the film processed, and the film was confiscated along with the flight recorder when the aircraft returned to Australia. The UFO sighting also was reportedly witnessed by a stewardess and the airplane's co-pilot.

See also AIRCRAFT, UFOS AND; AUSTRALIA, UFOS IN.

Antarctica The ice-covered southernmost continent occupies a peculiar place in UFO lore. Because it is remote and seemingly lifeless, it has become a convenient place for UFO enthusiasts to locate imagined bases for extraterrestrial spacecraft. Albert Bender, a prominent figure in the early history of the UFO phenomenon in America, thought Antarctica was the site of a vast installation under the ice, where aliens extracted some mysterious but valuable substance from sea water. Bender claimed to have visited this base and gone aboard a spacecraft parked there. Antarctica was also the location of "Rainbow City," another imagined community of extraterrestrials under the ice. In the hollow Earth hypothesis, which played a small but colorful part in UFO lore, Antarctica was supposed to be the site of a great portal into the interior of a hollow Earth. Another portal was supposed to be located in the Arctic. Flying saucers from an advanced civilization within the planet were said to use the portals for travel to and from the surface. A wave of UFO sightings near Antarctica, at Deception Island in the South Shetland Islands, was reported in 1965. Argentine, British and Chilean personnel stationed there reported seeing UFOs, including a noiseless, luminous, round or oval object that moved from east

SOUTH POLAR REGIONS

EARTH

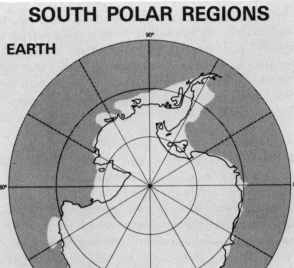

MARS

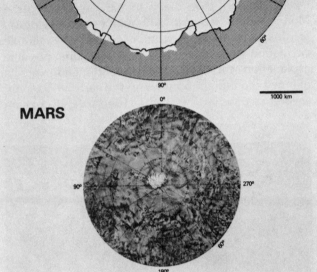

1000 km

Antarctica has been the site of notable UFO reports. (NASA)

to west and exhibited "oscillations" in its trajectory. The object reportedly had a red center and borders of changing colors.

See also BASES; BENDER MYSTERY; HOLLOW EARTH HYPOTHESIS; RAINBOW CITY.

Anthony, Saint, the Great (4th century A.D.)

Saint Anthony once reportedly met a "satyr," or a being that appears to resemble those described in certain UFO encounter cases in our own time. The entity allegedly claimed to live in woods, fields, and remote areas, and said he and his people were worshipped as gods by pagans. The being then admitted that he and his kind were mortal, and he asked Saint Anthony to pray to God on their behalf. The creature bowed down to Anthony, writes translator Montague Summers in his introduction to an En-

glish-language edition of *De Daemonialite* by Lodovico Maria Sinistrari.

See also DEMONOLOGY; SINISTRARI, LODOVICO MARIA.

Antichrist   This evil figure, who according to the traditional Christian belief will attain world domination at the end of the present age of history, immediately before Christ's anticipated return, figures in some religious commentaries on the UFO phenomenon. Citing a prophecy that "signs and wonders" in the skies would precede Christ's return, some commentators have argued that this prophecy refers to UFOs, and that the UFO phenomenon prefigures the rise of the Antichrist. The 20th-century Eastern Orthodox theologian Father Seraphim Rose, for example, argued that the UFO phenomenon was essentially diabolical in character, and that it might constitute one of the means that evil spirits would use to effect the advent of the Antichrist. Rose added that one New Testament prophecy says the Antichrist will have the ability to call down fire from heaven (Rev. 13:13). "Fire from heaven" is a reasonably accurate description of luminous objects seen in the skies, and Rose speculated that demonic "humanoids" might land in UFOs one day to pay homage to their diabolical master, the Antichrist. Another link between the UFO phenomenon and expectations of the Antichrist is that, according to some commentators, the Antichrist will perform "miracles" by illusion, persuading observers to see what actually is not there. Likewise, the illusory and deceptive element of the UFO phenomenon has received considerable attention from its investigators.

See also DECEPTION; DEMONOLOGY; ROSE, FATHER SERAPHIM.

anti-gravity   One of the great chimeras of pseudoscience and the UFO phenomenon, anti-gravity may be defined as any method proposed to counteract the influence of gravitation without using suspension (as by a rope or cable), a reaction engine (a rocket, for example), an explosive device (such as a cannon or rifle), isostatic lift (from a lighter-than-air balloon) or dynamic lift (the effect that supports an airplane in flight) to elevate and maintain a heavier-than-air object above the ground. Schemes for anti-gravity systems have occupied some of the most prominent figures in fantastic literature. The 17th-century French fabulist Cyrano de Bergerac conceived of several schemes for counteracting gravitation, including one clever but unworkable plan for a spacecraft driven by electromagnetism. British science fiction author H.G. Wells, in his 1901 novel *The*

First Men in the Moon, conceived of a material called "cavorite" (named after its inventor, one Mr. Cavor) that could block gravitation in much the same way that a window shade blocks light. The protagonists of Wells's story mount panels of cavorite on a glass sphere and travel to the Moon by neutralizing the Earth's gravitation. They steer their craft by manipulating panels of cavorite on the outside of the hull.

Anti-gravity technology has been a significant interest of UFO enthusiasts, who have seen it as perhaps the only way for huge, material spacecraft to perform the hovering and other feats of flight attributed to certain kinds of UFOs. The fallacy behind many proposals for anti-gravity is that gravitation is not strictly comparable to radiation, which can be blocked by some physical object, but rather is an intrinsic property of all matter and therefore cannot be neutralized by shielding.

The crackpot literature on this subject is huge and often invokes electromagnetism as the energy source for anti-gravity technology. Electromagnetism can neutralize gravitation on a small scale by suspending objects a short distance above the ground, but a strong electromagnetic field is required, and this approach is not suitable for levitating any object of substantial weight more than a few inches. Wilhelm Reich, to name only one prominent figure in the field of UFO phenomenon, devoted himself to the problem of anti-gravity and reportedly thought he had devised equations for it but refused to divulge them. Famed "contactee" George Adamski also speculated about the possible use of electromagnetism in spacecraft propulsion. Anti-gravity has a parallel in occult literature in "levitation," the raising of persons or objects off the ground as if by unseen hands. Levitation also figures in certain UFO close-encounter reports as an alleged means of carrying persons onto UFOs.

See also ADAMSKI, GEORGE; LEVITATION; PSEUDOSCIENCE; REICH, WILHELM.

anti-matter

A favorite topic of speculation where possible propulsion systems for extraterrestrial spacecraft are concerned, anti-matter consists of matter having reversed electrical charges from ordinary matter. When anti-matter encounters ordinary matter, they annihilate each other in a burst of radiation. According to one speculation, a substantial piece of anti-matter caused the mysterious midair Tunguska explosion that devastated several hundred square miles of the Siberian wilderness early in the 20th century. Interactions between anti-matter and ordinary matter have been observed on a small scale. Although a reasonably large quantity of anti-matter would be required to harness such interactions in order to supply power for a spacecraft's propulsion, such interactions could release tremendous amounts of energy. It has been suggested that anti-matter reactors might provide power for extraterrestrial spacecraft visiting Earth, but there is no evidence to support this speculation.

See also TUNGUSKA EVENT.

Apollo 11

One of the more colorful (though unsubstantiated) rumors in UFO lore concerns *Apollo 11*, which made the first manned lunar landing, in 1969. According to the rumor, menacing extraterrestrial spacecraft landed near *Apollo 11* soon after the lunar module touched down. The extraterrestrials allegedly made it clear that a human presence on the Moon was not desirable. Although no solid evidence for this story exists, the rumor has had considerable circulation and is widely viewed as one possible explanation for America's discontinuation of its manned moonflight program in the early 1970s, only several years after the *Apollo 11* landing. It appears

The *Apollo 11* mission encountered aliens on the Moon, according to one colorful but unsubstantiated story. (NASA)

more likely, however, that political and budgetary problems on Earth—not intimidation by extraterrestrials—were responsible for the withdrawal of the United States from the Moon. The rumor of *Apollo 11*'s encounter with alien spacecraft is one of many such stories involving astronauts and UFO sightings attributed to them.

See also ASTRONAUTS, UFO REPORTS ATTRIBUTED TO; RUMORS.

apparent motion This illusion, which may account for certain reports of UFOs in flight at night, involves an observer's interpretation of two lights seen at different positions. When the observer sees a light appear and disappear at point A, followed by the appearance and disappearance of another similar light at point B, he may conclude that the two lights represent a single object moving from the first position to the second. The observer presumes that a single object is passing across his field of view, when it is possible that two distinct, motionless light sources are involved instead. The illusion of apparent motion is a familiar example of how the human mind may create a perception of a phenomenon that actually does not exist. Such illusions may be responsible for many reports of luminous UFOs moving across the night sky.

See also PERCEPTION.

apparitions Broadly defined as "supernatural" manifestations of persons, spirits, objects or animals, apparitions are an important component of the UFO phenomenon. Although apparitions generally are associated with ghosts and other phenomena traditionally considered supernatural, apparitions are essentially identical with many reported encounters involving UFO entities. Apparitions share many characteristics with such encounters, including humanoid figures appearing to the witness; a perception of cold; unusual (often unpleasant) odors; "psychokinetic" movement of objects (that is, movement supposedly by power of thought); the ability of apparitions to pass through material objects such as walls; and the communication of messages, such as warnings of events to come. There is no universally accepted explanation for apparitions. Hypotheses include hallucinations, manifestations of demonic activity and actual visitations by spirits of the dead.

See also COMMUNICATIONS; DEMONOLOGY; ENCOUNTER PHENOMENA; HALLUCINATIONS; HUMANOIDS; MESSAGES; ODORS; TEMPERATURE EFFECTS.

Aquarius, Project An alleged top-secret U.S. government study of UFOs conducted in the late 1970s and early 1980s, Project Aquarius is said to remain under top-secret classification. An effort to obtain documents related to Project Aquarius under the Freedom of Information Act in 1986 reportedly failed because the National Security Agency said that release of the material might cause "grave" harm to America's national security.

aquatic objects A curious category of sightings, related to and in some cases overlapping with UFO reports, concerns mysterious objects seen in, entering or rising from the waters. Numerous cases in this category have been reported, including the mysterious "ghost rockets" seen over Scandinavia in the 1940s. Although incidents of unusual objects in, rising from or falling into the waters have been reported from many different parts of the world, Janet and Colin Bord, in their book *Unexplained Mysteries of the Twentieth Century* (1989), describe an unusual concentration of sightings off the coast of Argentina. Inland bodies of water such as lakes and rivers also have been the sites of similar reports, especially in Scandinavia. Information on this particular aspect of the UFO phenomenon is less than reliable in many cases, however, and should be viewed with at least a normal degree of skepticism. Also, it should be noted that reports of mysterious submarine activity off the coasts of northern Europe in recent years may be explained by military operations. Aquatic objects also play a small but colorful part in motion pictures, notably the Japanese classic *The Mysterians*.

See also GHOST ROCKETS; MOTION PICTURES; MYSTERIANS, THE.

Area 51 This alleged military UFO test site, also known as "Dreamland," is located at Nellis Air Force Range and Nuclear Test Site in Nevada and is famous in UFO lore as a testing ground for UFOs and related technology. Rumor also has it that a secret U.S. government project code named Red Light, involved with the reconstruction and test-flying of crashed UFOs, has operated at Area 51. Some rumors of activities at Area 51 involving alleged UFOs are highly detailed, but such rumors remain unsubstantiated.

See also RUMORS; TECHNOLOGY.

Arezzo incident, Italy A widely cited incident in UFO lore, this encounter case reportedly occurred one morning in the Italian province of Arezzo, when one Signora Rosa Lotti was walking barefooted through the woods. She carried her shoes and stockings, along with carnations that she planned to place on her sister's grave. According to one account, she

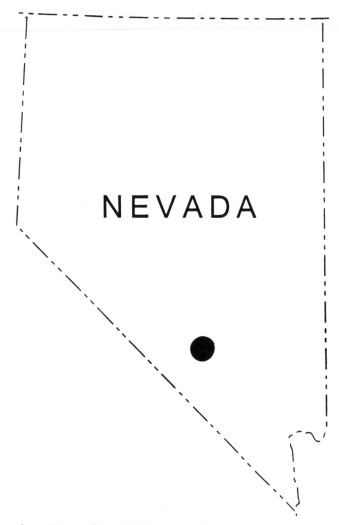

NEVADA

Area 51, an alleged UFO test site, is part of military facilities in Nevada. (U.S. Geological Survey)

saw, in the woods beside a clearing, a spindle-shaped object about six feet tall and three feet in diameter, covered in what appeared to be leather. From behind the object appeared two small, cheerful humanoids wearing gray overalls, doublets and cloaks. The humanoids were the size of young children but had the faces of aged men, with slightly protruding teeth. They conversed in a language reminiscent of Chinese. Inside the object, Signora Lotti thought she could see seats and controls. The humanoids relieved Signora Lotti of her carnations and one of her stockings, and she fled.

See also HUMANOIDS.

Argentina Argentina has been identified as a saucer "window," or area where large numbers of UFO reports originate. Among the widely reported UFO encounter cases to come out of Argentina is the Mendoza incident of September 1, 1968, in which

two men reportedly were paralyzed and given, in effect, a lecture by three humanoid entities standing near a hovering UFO at Mendoza, near the Chilean border. The Argentine armed forces are said to have taken strong interest in UFO activity, and the Argentine Air Force reportedly set up its own UFO study division in 1964 to cope with the large numbers of UFO sightings being reported.

See also MENDOZA INCIDENT.

Armageddon Identified in the Bible as the site of the climactic battle of human history, where numerous armies are expected to meet in a valley near Mount Megiddo in the Middle East immediately before the return of Christ, "Armageddon" now is commonly used as a synonym for global nuclear warfare. The threat of Armageddon is cited in alleged messages from extraterrestrials concerned about the danger of such warfare on Earth. Extraterrestrials in so-called contactee cases often are portrayed as warning humans to adopt a less belligerent attitude or else face obliteration in an atomic holocaust. This theme is treated in various ways in UFO lore. Sometimes the aliens are depicted as benevolent bystanders, or as figures prepared to intervene and halt any nuclear exchange that appears about to occur. Famed contactee George Adamski, for example, claimed that friendly aliens from Venus were worried about atomic testing on Earth. The alleged aliens in other contact cases seem less favorably disposed toward humankind, however, and may even threaten to set off Earth's stockpile of nuclear warheads if humans interfere with the aliens' business (whatever it may be) on our planet. This particular threat was part of communications relayed by alleged contactee Albert Bender.

See also ADAMSKI, GEORGE; BENDER MYSTERY; WARFARE.

Armed Services hearing At the urging of then-Congressman Gerald Ford of Michigan, Congressman L. Mendel Rivers of South Carolina, chairman of the House Armed Services Committee, held a meeting of the committee on April 5, 1966, to investigate the UFO phenomenon. The meeting lasted less than two hours. Only three individuals were called to address the committee. These were Air Force Secretary Harold Brown; Major Hector Quintanilla, head of Project Blue Book, the Air Force UFO study group; and Dr. J. Allen Hynek, astronomer and consultant to Project Blue Book. Brown pointed out that the vast majority of UFO reports investigated by the Air Force had been identified as phenomena such as stars, planets, comets and meteors.

In the few remaining cases, Brown said, information was insufficient for analysis. Hynek called for a more thorough and open-minded study of the UFO phenomenon than the Air Force had seemed willing to undertake. Although Hynek admitted that it was "productive" to work from the presumption that a "conventional explanation" existed for UFO reports, he said that such an approach did not work in every case. Hynek added that he had been unable to explain 20 UFO reports by "conventional" means such as hoaxes, hallucinations and misidentification of familiar objects. The hearing took place several weeks after the widely publicized "swamp gas" incident in Michigan.

See also BLUE BOOK, PROJECT; HYNEK, J. ALLEN; SWAMP GAS INCIDENT.

Arnold, Kenneth   See ARNOLD INCIDENT.

Arnold incident   The sighting that set off the "flying saucer" phenomenon in the 20th century is

Mount Rainier, seen here from U.S. Skylab space station, was the site of the Arnold incident. (NASA)

the so-called Arnold incident, in which a pilot named Kenneth Arnold, flying his private aircraft near Mount Rainier in Washington state on June 26, 1947, reported seeing nine shiny objects flying nearby. Although he apparently was too far away to discern details, he described the motion of the shiny objects as resembling that of saucers skipped over water. This description was misinterpreted in press accounts as saying that the objects themselves resembled saucers, and so the expression "flying saucer" entered the English language. (The expression "UFO," for "Unidentified Flying Object," originated with Air Force Captain Edward Ruppelt, who worked with Project Blue Book on the study of UFO sightings and allegedly coined the term UFO to differentiate plausible sightings from those that seemed less so.)

Various explanations have been put forward for what Arnold actually saw, or thought he saw, that day. According to one hypothesis, he witnessed, from a distance, test flights of early jet aircraft. This hypothesis gains some weight when one considers that the Boeing aircraft production facilities are located in nearby Seattle. Arnold later came in contact with Ray Palmer, an editor of occult and science fiction magazines, and played a part in what has come to be known as the Maury Island incident.

See also MAURY ISLAND INCIDENT; MYTHOLOGY; PALMER, RAYMOND.

Ashtar   An alleged extraterrestrial, Ashtar supposedly communicated with humankind through early "contactee" George Van Tassel. In 1952, Van Tassel claimed to have received a message from Ashtar, who identified himself as commandant of something called the "quadra sector" and indicated he was assigned to a "patrol station" named Schare. The message, he added, came to humankind, courtesy of the "Council of the Seven Lights." This being's alleged communications emphasized several themes that would become prominent in the UFO lore of the late 20th century, including some vaguely defined but sweeping change affecting the entire planet prior to the advent of some new spiritual age. The message of "Ashtar" is comparable in many ways to information supposedly imparted to other "contactees" of the 1950s, such as George Adamski and Daniel Fry. Even the name "Ashtar" is consistent with the pattern of childish, two-syllable names assigned to alleged extraterrestrial entities in such contacts.

The mythological aspect of this story is interesting. The name "Ashtar" appears to refer to the Syrian fertility goddess Astarte, also known as Ishtar, Ashteroth and Ashtoreth. As Ashteroth, Astarte was worshipped by the Phoenicians in biblical times. She was known as the "queen of heaven" and is mentioned as an "abomination" in II Kings 23:13. It appears possible that Van Tassel, if he did not simply make up the story of his communications with "Ashtar," may have been in contact with a spiritual being by that name. Another connection involving Astarte has to do with her identity as Ishtar, or Venus. The "Venus connection" in UFO lore has been extremely prominent, starting with Adamski's alleged meeting with a space traveler from Venus.

See also ADAMSKI, GEORGE; CHANNELING; DEMONOLOGY; FRY INCIDENT; MEDIUMISM; MESSAGES; MYTHOLOGY; NAMES.

Asket   An imagined extraterrestrial female entity from the Pleiades, supposedly involved in the case of Swiss "contactee" Eduard Meier, Asket claimed to come from a different universe existing "parallel" to our own. Messages from Asket, reportedly encouraged the young Meier to go out and explore other parts of the world. Meier allegedly engaged in many different jobs, ranging from catching snakes to prospecting for gold, under Asket's direction. Asket is said to have told Meier that he had been chosen to offer truth to the world and that he was expected to accumulate more knowledge than any other human of his time. Asket added that Meier had been "destined" for this role from the moment of "procreation." She had also reportedly told Meier that his ancestors had come from the constellation Lyra, and that the descendants of those ancestors one day would reveal more information to him. Later, Meier allegedly made contact with the "Pleiadean" woman Semjase.

See also ERRA; MEIER CASE; PLEIADES; SEMJASE.

astrology   A widely practiced pseudoscience, astrology is based on the premise that the apparent motion of the Sun, Moon and planets through the constellations of the zodiac embodies a symbolism that bears on the traits, interests and activities of humans on Earth. Astrological symbolism figures in certain UFO abduction reports. In one famous report, for example, a woman in southern California claimed to have been marked on her back with a glyph resembling the astrological symbol for the planet Jupiter. The symbol for the planet Saturn also has turned up from time to time in the recollections of alleged abductees questioned under hypnosis. An indirect connection between astrology and the UFO phenomenon involves the anticipated advent of the "Aquarian age," a time of peace, love and har-

mony. In the belief system of the New Age movement, UFOs are suspected of having some role to play in the opening of the Aquarian age. Connections between astrology and UFOs illustrate the numerous occult associations bearing on UFO phenomenon.

See also ABDUCTIONS; HYPNOSIS; JUPITER; OCCULTISM; TUJUNGA CANYON CASE.

astronauts, UFO reports attributed to   Since the early days of manned space flight, rumors have circulated concerning UFOs supposedly seen by American astronauts in outer space and even on the Moon. NASA and some astronauts have gone to considerable lengths to refute these rumors, but the stories have proven impossible to stop. "Santa Claus" is reportedly the expression American astronauts used to refer to UFOs near spacecraft. According to one of the most colorful rumors, *Apollo 11*, the first manned mission to land on the Moon, encountered other spacecraft, much larger than the Apollo lander and described as "menacing," on the lunar surface. Similar stories have been told of Soviet cosmonauts encountering UFOs in space. The

Numerous UFO sightings have been attributed to astronauts, but such reports are questionable at best. (NASA)

cosmonauts aboard the *Voskhod I* spacecraft in October of 1964 are said to have been overtaken by flying disks, British UFO investigator Timothy Good says. He adds that *Voskhod II* reportedly was harassed by an unknown object in space, but that the Soviets would admit only to having seen an "unmanned" satellite approximately half a mile from their spacecraft on March 19, 1965. Soon afterward, the capsule lost contact with ground control and had to make an emergency landing several hundred miles from the anticipated recovery site. Although entertaining, UFO reports ascribed to astronauts and cosmonauts are viewed with skepticism by responsible UFO investigators.

See also RUSSIA; STOLYAROV COMMITTEE.

astronomy Discrepancies between accounts of "extraterrestrial" homeworlds and actual knowledge of astronomy are gross and numerous in UFO lore. When alleged space travelers have reportedly spoken in detail about conditions on their homeworlds, the information they provided has been hard to reconcile with data from space probes and observations made from Earth. George Adamski's alleged visitor from Venus, for example, looked all but indistinguishable from a human, although intense heat and atmospheric pressure known to exist on Venus would make human life there impossible. Likewise, conditions on Mars, as described by "Captain Aura Rhanes" to American "contactee" Truman Bethurum, bore little resemblance to actual conditions on that planet as revealed by American space probes; pictures returned by the probes showed no sign of the industrial facilities that Rhanes described. In the celebrated Meier case, humanoid extraterrestrials from the Pleiades are said to have contacted a Swiss pensioner; yet what is known of the Pleiades—a collection of young, hot stars that produce a high-radiation environment—appears virtually to rule out the possibility of life as we know it existing there. Defenders of the extraterrestrial hypothesis have proposed that humanoids might exist on seemingly hospitable worlds in some other, "parallel" universe where conditions are more favorable to life. This speculation, however, is little more than fantasy.

Supporters of the "ancient astronauts" hypothesis have argued that extraterrestrials may have visited Earth in centuries past and imparted to humans some of their advanced astronomical knowledge, which then was passed down as tradition. The so-called Dogon mystery, involving the star Sirius, has been cited as evidence in favor of this hypothesis. Here again, however, there are great discrepancies

Astronomy has contributed to certain UFO reports and helped demolish others. (NASA)

between ancient tradition and modern knowledge of astronomy.

See also ADAMSKI, GEORGE; ANCIENT ASTRONAUTS; BETHURUM INCIDENT; CLARION; DOGON MYSTERY; HOMEWORLDS; MARS; MEIER CASE; PLEIADES.

Atlantis The mythical "lost continent" of Atlantis, which supposedly occupied part of what is now the Atlantic Ocean basin, is sometimes cited in UFO literature as a possible origin for flying saucers. According to myth, Atlantis sank beneath the sea and was destroyed for its corrupt society. The story of Atlantis and its destruction was recorded in the *Dialogues of Plato* around 350 B.C., specifically his *Timaeus* and *Critas*. The crank literature on the subject of Atlantis and "lost continents" is tremendous and includes the 1882 book *Atlantis: The Antediluvian World*, by Ignatius Donnelly. The Atlantis myth and its associated beliefs constitute a link between the

UFO phenomenon and occultist belief in "lost" lands and civilizations.

See also LEMURIA; MYTHOLOGY; OCCULTISM.

Atlas incident, United States

A UFO reportedly was caught on film as it flew near an Atlas F missile during a test on September 15, 1964. The missile was launched from Vandenberg Air Force Base in California and was tracked by a television camera attached to a telescope. The UFO allegedly flew around the missile and emitted several brilliant flashes of light. Moments later, the missile went out of control at an altitude of approximately 60 miles. The Atlas was a liquid-fuel rocket intended for military use and was used as a booster on several early American space missions. As in other reports of hostile activity by UFOs, this story has little or no solid evidence to confirm it. This report of alleged anti-missile activity by a UFO has been cited in connection with another story from the former Soviet Union, about the destruction of guided missiles fired at a UFO near Rybinsk, about 90 miles from Moscow, in the summer of 1961.

See also RYBINSK INCIDENT.

atmospheric phenomena

Numerous atmospheric phenomena are commonly thought to be UFOs, notably clouds and ball lightning. Certain atmospheric conditions may produce, for example, "lenticular," or lens-shaped clouds that resemble the classic configuration of multiple flying saucers. Ice crystals or water droplets in the atmosphere may produce a variety of effects, by reflection or refraction of sunlight or moonlight, that also may be mistaken for UFOs. UFO debunkers frequently cite such phenomena as explanations for UFO sightings.

See also BALL LIGHTNING; CLOUDS AND VAPOR; DEBUNKERS; NATURAL PHENOMENA, UFOS AND.

aurora

(1) Luminous natural displays in the skies at high latitudes, caused by interactions between the Earth's atmosphere and charged particles directed by the planet's magnetic fields. On some occasions, the aurora have been clearly visible in the temperate latitudes. Aurora in high northern latitudes are called the "aurora borealis" or "northern lights," while in the extreme southern latitudes the aurora are called the "aurora australis." Some widely reported UFO sightings have been attributed to the aurora. (2) An extremely fast military reconnaissance aircraft said to be under development by the United States to replace its recently retired SR-71 Blackbird. Aurora is said to be based in the southwestern United States, and mysterious "skyquakes" reported

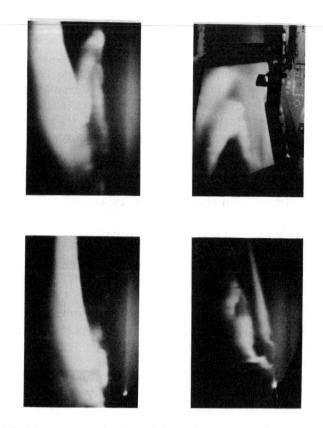

Aurora are among natural phenomena that may be mistaken for UFOs. (NASA)

in recent years have been attributed tentatively to shock waves from Aurora's passage.

See also SKYQUAKES.

Austin, Texas, incident, United States

One of the unidentified phenomena mentioned in the files of Project Blue Book is an encounter that reportedly occurred on June 24, 1967, near the Mansfield Dam in the vicinity of Austin, Texas. A motorist driving in the area at around 3:00 A.M. noticed another automobile stop and appear to signal with its headlights to a bright blue UFO moving near the horizon. The observer then tried signaling to the UFO with his flashlight. He signaled the mathematical value of *pi*, or 3.14, the ratio between the circumference and diameter of a circle. After he had signaled this value several times, the UFO hung stationary, and its luminosity faded for a moment. Then its brightness returned, and the UFO resumed moving on its previous course. The motorist examined the object through binoculars and saw it was shaped like a cigar. The UFO vanished into low clouds after it had been in sight for about eight minutes. In reporting the incident later to the Air Force, the man said he had the impression that something like mental telepathy had affected him during the sighting, giving him a feeling of being watched. Later, the Air Force declared that the data in this case were insufficient for scientific analysis.

See also BLUE BOOK, PROJECT; TELEPATHY.

Australia, UFOs in   The Australian continent has been the site of several notable UFO incidents and has a number of outstanding "window areas" where sightings appear to be concentrated. The Bass Straits, a narrow stretch of water separating Australia from the island of Tasmania to the south, was the site of the reported disappearance of pilot Frederick Valentich and his private aircraft on October 21, 1978. Unidentified aircraft were reported to have been seen along the northern shore of the Bass Straits in 1930, but official investigation was unable to identify them definitely as aircraft at all, much less identify their nationality. A Royal Australian Air Force (RAAF) pilot flying his aircraft off the Tasman Peninsula one afternoon in 1942 reportedly sighted an unusual "airfoil," bronze-colored and approximately 50 feet wide by 150 feet long, surmounted by a reflective dome. This UFO reportedly kept pace with the RAAF pilot's aircraft for some minutes, then departed rapidly and descended into the sea. Another sighting in 1944 involved a Beaufort bomber that allegedly was joined in flight while over the Bass Straits by a UFO described as a "shadow" with flame emanating from its rear. This object reportedly approached to within 100 to 150 feet of the bomber

Australia is known for numerous UFO sightings. (U.S. Geological Survey)

and remained alongside it for perhaps 20 minutes, while radio equipment and certain instruments on the bomber went out of order. At last, the object was said to have departed, at a speed estimated at approximately 700 miles per hour, or some three times that of the bomber.

Tasmania has also been the site of "crop circle" reports and of alleged interference with the operation of motor vehicles.

The Nullarbor region between Perth and Adelaide, along the southern coast of Australia, was the location of British nuclear bomb tests in the 1950s. At one test site, following a series of tests, several witnesses reportedly saw a discoid UFO appear in November of 1957. The UFO allegedly was tilted at an angle and reflected light as from a metallic surface. The report said that windows and plates of metal could be seen on the object, which hung stationary above the site for a quarter of an hour, then departed and vanished. (This event coincided with a widely reported UFO incident at Levelland, Texas, on November 2, 1957.) Another UFO sighting in the Nullarbor region reportedly occurred on February 4, 1973, when a man and woman driving along the Eyre Highway observed, in a field beside the road, a rectangular orange glow in which stood a white, humanoid figure. The observers did not stop to investigate, but they did look behind them as they departed, and noticed that the glow appeared to have extended across the highway. A later investigation of the incident is said to have located other witnesses who alleged that they also had been driving along the highway at that location at the same time and had seen, in the field, some phenomenon similar to that described by the aforementioned witnesses. A third widely publicized UFO incident in the Nullarbor region reportedly occurred along the Eyre Highway on January 21, 1988. A family traveling by car at night near the border of South Australia and West Australia claimed to have been attacked by an ovoid UFO that lifted the vehicle from the road and then dropped the car, causing it to burst a tire on landing. There were other reports that night of vehicles being buffeted by some force along the highway and of observers seeing unusual lights. These incidents have been explained tentatively, however, as the result of meteorological conditions.

The Kempsey region in New South Wales, Australia, along the MacLeay River valley, was the site of a reported incident on July 21, 1975, involving a very bright light that appeared to be moving rapidly westward across the sky. The light reportedly hovered above the horizon and changed color before descending out of sight. Although this sighting was categorized as a misidentification of the planet Venus, that interpretation is not supported by the alleged behavior of the object, specifically its rapid motion. A report of vehicle interference in the early morning of March 22, 1976, described how a yellow-green light allegedly descended from the sky, enveloped an automobile in which a family was returning home from a vacation, and caused the car first to swerve, then to lose power and stop. The cloud reportedly changed color, from yellow-green to white, and persisted around the car for a couple of minutes. On departing, the cloud is said to have left behind a deposit of white powder on the outside of the automobile. When power returned to the automobile, the family drove away.

Northeastern Australia contains a rainforest in which some of the first "crop circles," a phenomenon now linked with UFOs, were reported. The circles, described as "saucer nests," were found among reeds near Cairns. The reeds had been flattened in a circular pattern. Reeds at the edge of the circle remained vertical. UFO sightings were associated with the "saucer nests."

See also ANSETTA-ANA INCIDENT; CROP CIRCLES; GEOGRAPHICAL DISTRIBUTION OF UFO SIGHTINGS; HORSESHOE LAGOON INCIDENT; HUMANOIDS; LEVELLAND INCIDENT; MARALINGA INCIDENT; PENNINES; VALENTICH CASE; VEHICLE EFFECTS; WINDOWS.

autokinetic effect   This effect, described by prominent UFO "debunker" Donald Menzel, occurs when someone stares at a stationary, small light source such as a star or planet and imagines the light is moving. Menzel described how a nonmoving, pinpoint light source can be perceived (incorrectly) to move within several seconds of one's starting to gaze at it. The light may appear to move through an arc, maneuver rapidly, or swing back and forth,

Autokinetic effect: stare at a stationary light source long enough, and it may appear to move, in the manner of a classic UFO. (D. Ritchie)

though the light in fact remains stationary. The autokinetic effect is magnified if the observer is in a moving vehicle, according to UFO researcher Philip Klass.

See also DEDUCTIVE-PSYCHOLOGICAL EFFECT; VENUS.

automatic writing   One small but significant element of the UFO phenomenon is its association with the occult practice of automatic writing. Defined as writing produced while a human subject is in an altered or "dissociated" state (commonly known as a "trance"), automatic writing is used to contact what the practitioner considers to be either spirits of the dead, or discarnate, "higher" entities possessing special wisdom.

Automatic writing was used widely in the spiritualist movement of the 19th century. One practitioner of automatic writing was the American Judge John Worth Edmonds, who said he had taken down written communications from Francis Bacon, the 16th-century English philosopher, and from Swedish occultist Emanuel Swedenborg. In the 20th century, a practitioner of automatic writing, an American housewife named Pearl Curran, reportedly produced some four million words, including several historical novels and thousands of poems, through automatic writing. Curran was said to be in contact with the spirit of one Patience Worth, who claimed to have been born in England in 1649 and killed by Native Americans in a massacre in the colonies.

On occasion, a practitioner of automatic writing has claimed to have delivered messages from entities from another planet. George Hunt Williamson, an associate of George Adamski, described a variety of messages supposedly delivered through automatic writing from inhabitants of "Masar," which Williamson and his companions presumed to be the planet Mars. Williamson reported using several different methods of intercepting and recording messages. The initial method was simply using a pencil and a sheet of paper. A later approach was to take a sheet of wrapping paper and write on it the letters of the alphabet, as well as the numbers 1 through 10. Eventually, Williamson and company appear to have re-invented the Ouija board, using an inverted glass tumbler as a "locator" to deliver messages.

A message from "Masar" arrived on August 2, 1952. The speaker identified himself (or itself) as "Nah-9." The semi-coherent message indicated that the salvation of our world depended on "organization." As in George Adamski's exchange with an alleged visitor from Venus in the California desert, the message from Nah-9 contained vague and puzzling

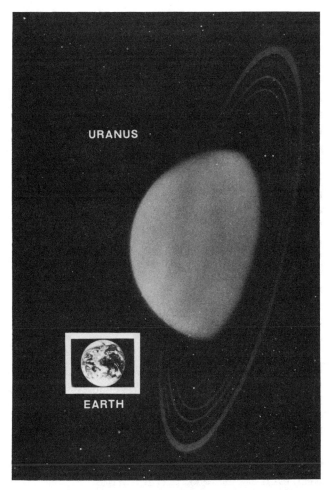

Uranus was alleged homeworld of "Affa," a being reportedly contacted through automatic writing. (NASA)

ent and confusing in many places, and tend to be demonstrably false when their information can be checked against other sources.

The potential for fraud is, of course, tremendous in cases of automatic writing. Moreover, there appears to be very little chance that such "contacts" (if they actually occur) involve the spirits of departed humans. Another interpretation of automatic writing is that messages delivered through this practice originate not with spirits of deceased humans, nor with inhabitants of other planets, but rather with demons. This interpretation is consistent with the numerous falsehoods contained in the messages. Severe emotional and spiritual damage has been associated with automatic writing.

See also ABSURDITY; ADAMSKI, GEORGE; DEMONOLOGY; METALOGIC; OCCULTISM; SWEDENBORG, EMANUEL; TELEPATHY; UMMO; WORTH, PATIENCE.

Aviano incident, Italy A report of UFO activity associated with a widespread power failure came in 1977 from Italy, where the North Atlantic Treaty Organization (NATO) base at Aviano allegedly underwent a blackout early on the morning of July 1, as a luminous UFO was seen hovering over the facility. The UFO reportedly was seen poised above an area where military aircraft were kept.

See also POWER FAILURES, UFOS AND.

AVRO The AVRO machines of the 1950s were two Earth-built "flying saucers" that were essentially primitive hovercraft. They proved to be unstable and work on them was abandoned. In the early 1950s, rumors circulated that the AVRO machines were actual flying saucers under development by the Royal Canadian Air Force and the Toronto, Canada, firm of A. V. Roe Ltd. Rumors still surround the AVRO devices. According to one story, the AVRO craft were built as a cover for the alleged test-flying of a genuine alien spacecraft, presumably under U.S. Air Force direction.

Aylan Also known as A-Lan or Alan, this being reportedly communicated with American "contactee" Daniel Fry on several occasions, starting with a meeting at White Sands, New Mexico, in 1950. Aylan allegedly took Fry on a cross-country trip in a remote-controlled "vimana," or spacecraft. At his first meeting with Fry, Aylan used American colloquialisms such as "pal," but later adopted a professorial style of speaking. At his reported meetings with Aylan, Fry received lengthy dissertations about the physics of space travel and was told to write up his experiences with Aylan for publication in book

references to God. Nah-9 also pointed out the danger of great destruction from nuclear weapons. A week later, on August 9, Williamson reported another communication from Masar. This time the speaker was one "Regga." Part of the message was a set of nonsensical statements about the Sun and solar radiation. A message on August 17, from one Zo, described as an inhabitant of Neptune, urged the people of Earth to remain calm and reassured the contactees that the aliens had only love for humankind. The message warned again about the danger from nuclear weapons and indicated that "rites" would save the people of Earth. Also contained in the message was a seemingly meaningless proverb about apples and salt; Zo said that humans eventually would understand what the saying meant. Later messages contained spurious information about conditions on other planets in our solar system. The messages relayed by Williamson are consistent with other such information allegedly delivered by extraterrestrials. That is to say, they are vague, incoher-

form. The aim of global unification—"One World," in Aylan's words—was part of Aylan's message.

One small but interesting element of Aylan's communications was a reference to Tibet. There, Aylan said, representatives of his people had met in ancient times, following a tremendous war on Earth, to hold a council. The council meeting according to this story, determined that some of Aylan's people should leave Earth and travel into space to escape the destruction caused by warfare. The "Tibetan connection" is a subtle but significant element of UFO lore as well as traditional occultism.

See also COMMUNICATIONS; FRY INCIDENT; OCCULTISM; TIBET; VIMANA.

Aztec incident   An alleged UFO crash in which bodies of extraterrestrials were recovered by the United States military, the Aztec incident reportedly occurred in 1948 near Aztec, New Mexico, where the bodies of 14 to 16 aliens were said to have been recovered from their crashed but undamaged saucer. The disc was said to be about 100 feet in diameter and made of a lightweight material that was highly resistant to heat and drilling. According to the story, a porthole in the cabin was cracked, and the crack allowed investigators to reach inside with a pole and push a control that opened a hatch. The extraterrestrials were reported to be about three to four feet in height, with large, slanted eyes; small mouths and noses; and heads very large in proportion to the rest of their bodies. The bodies allegedly weighed about 40 pounds each and had thin necks and torsos. The fingers were said to be long and slender and have webbing between them. Autopsies reportedly revealed no alimentary tract or digestive system, nor any reproductive system. In place of blood, the extraterrestrials supposedly had a clear liquid with a peculiar smell.

Rumor has it that the craft was inspected by a team of distinguished scientists including Dr. Robert Oppenheimer, director of the U.S. A-bomb project at Los Alamos, New Mexico, during World War II; and Dr. John von Neumann, the Hungarian-born U.S. mathematician who helped develop the first electronic computers. The craft allegedly carried control panels that had no wiring, as well as a "book" with leaves of a plastic-like material, bearing unfamiliar characters reminiscent of Sanskrit. According to one report, the craft was disassembled and taken to Los Alamos, then moved to another location several months later.

Although the Aztec incident makes an entertaining story, there is little or no solid evidence to support it, and the story is widely considered to be a hoax. The Aztec incident often is confused with the so-called Roswell incident, the report of another alleged UFO crash near Roswell, New Mexico.

See also CRASHES; ENCOUNTER PHENOMENA; EXTRATERRESTRIAL BIOLOGICAL ENTITIES; HUMANOIDS; ROSWELL INCIDENT; SANSKRIT; TECHNOLOGY.

B

Bahio Blanca incident, Brazil Early on the morning of October 28, 1973, a truck driver stopped in the vicinity of Bahio Blanca, Brazil, to replace a flat tire and allegedly encountered a UFO accompanied by three humanoids in silvery outfits. Under hypnosis, he claimed to recall an abduction in which the "extraterrestrials" said they had a mission to study the human species. The alleged abductee reportedly was completely unable to recall what happened during a period of approximately two hours.

See also ABDUCTIONS; MISSING TIME.

Balearic Islands, Spain Located in the Mediterranean Sea, the Balearics are known as a "window" for UFO sightings. One notable UFO report that came from here occurred on November 11, 1979, when two red lights reportedly accompanied a TAE Airlines jet in flight. Radar contact also was reported.

See also WINDOWS.

ball lightning A curious and poorly understood phenomenon of meteorology, ball lightning reportedly takes the form of luminous spheres slightly less than a foot in diameter, resembling certain UFOs. The spheres may take on various colors and be surrounded by a corona, or "halo." A manifestation of ball lightning may last for a minute or longer before it disappears. The manner of disappearance varies. In some cases, the ball lightning explodes dramatically, and in other instances it merely fades out. Ball lightning has been known to occur within enclosed spaces, such as the cabins of aircraft. Acoustical effects such as crackling and hissing also are reported in certain cases, as is a sulfurous odor.

See ACOUSTICAL EFFECTS; AMBER GAMBLER; FOO FIGHTERS; ODORS.

balloons Various kinds of balloons are released into the air on a regular basis, and under certain conditions a balloon may be identified as a UFO. Balloons have played a part in certain well-known UFO incidents. A high-altitude balloon, for example, is suspected of having been the alleged UFO that U.S. Air Force Captain Thomas Mantell was trying to intercept in his jet aircraft when he crashed and was killed in 1948; and the so-called Roswell incident, in 1947, is said to have involved the recovery of debris not from an extraterrestrial spacecraft (as legend has it), but rather from a balloon-borne payload. A large balloon at high altitude can take on a spherical, ovoid or discoid appearance, like that of a classic UFO, when seen from the ground, as diminished air pressure at that altitude allows gas inside the balloon to expand and give the balloon a rounder configuration. Also, a high-altitude balloon near dusk may catch the sun's rays and appear to be glowing, in the manner of a luminous UFO, when darkness prevails already on the ground below. This set of circumstances may be responsible for some sightings of large, glowing UFOs in the early evening. Deliberate hoaxes involving balloons are, of course, possible, and in some cases probably have resulted in alleged UFO sightings. For a small sum of money, one can devise a primitive hot-air balloon, a couple of feet in height, that can carry a light or be made to glow from within by the light of its own heat source, after the fashion of a paper lantern. Such a device may float through the air for considerable distances at night and generate reports of a lu-

Balloons like the one shown here may be mistaken for UFOs. (NASA)

minous UFO flying overhead. Balloon technology also has provided an intriguing insight into the mystery of the Nazca lines, patterns created on Peru's Nazca plain centuries ago. The Nazca lines, which include geometric formations and representations of animals, can be seen clearly only from the air. The Nazca lines attained a certain fame during the "ancient astronauts" enthusiasm of the 1960s and 1970s, when the patterns were presented as evidence that extraterrestrials had visited Earth in the distant past and used the formations as markings, so to speak, on a landing field for their spacecraft. A more realistic interpretation of the lines is that they were designed to be viewed from the air, but by observers in an early hot-air balloon. Such a balloon could have been constructed from light fabric and attained an altitude of perhaps 500 feet, or enough to bring the patterns on the ground into clear view from above, perhaps as some kind of religious ceremony.

See also ANCIENT ASTRONAUTS; HOAXES; MANTELL INCIDENT; NAZCA LINES; ROSWELL INCIDENT.

bases   If one accepts the proposition that extraterrestrial spacecraft are visiting Earth, then there also is reason to presume that these vehicles operate from bases comparable to airfields and naval facili-

ties on our planet. Within the community of UFO enthusiasts, it is widely believed that UFOs utilize bases on Earth, perhaps located in remote areas, under the sea or even within the planet itself. A bizarre literature, for example, has developed around the concept of a hollow Earth, within which (according to some speculations) UFOs supposedly have their bases. During the "ancient astronauts" phenomenon of the 1960s and 1970s, certain features of the Earth's surface were interpreted as possible bases for extraterrestrial spacecraft that supposedly visited our world in the distant past. The Nazca lines of Peru, a set of geometric figures drawn on a plain by displacing rocks and exposing the relatively light-colored soil underneath, were presented for a time as an ancient "landing field" for extraterrestrial spacecraft, but this hypothesis was soon discredited.

Among believers in the so-called extraterrestrial hypothesis of UFO origins, it is also permissible to think that UFOs operate from installations on other celestial bodies, such as the Moon, Venus or Mars, or from some point in space near Earth. Astronomer Morris Jessup argued that UFOs originated from a point in space within the Earth–Moon system. Finding evidence of postulated bases on other planets has occupied the minds of numerous UFO enthusiasts. Although early "contactee" George Adamski was persuaded that flying saucers came from Venus, he apparently believed that space people maintained a base on our Moon as well. Adamski once claimed to have seen these lunar facilities on a trip he took to the Moon aboard a flying saucer. After detailed photographs of the Martian surface were returned by American space probes later in this century, some of those pictures were interpreted as evidence of an extraterrestrial base on Mars, supposedly built by spacefaring aliens who visited our solar system hundreds of thousands of years ago. Among the proponents of this hypothesis is Richard Hoagland, who imagines that the ruins of a great city exist on Mars near the so-called Face on Mars, a formation that resembles a giant human face. Other speculations about extraterrestrial bases on Mars have focused on the two Martian moons, Phobos and Deimos, which at one time were imagined to be huge artificial satellites.

Photographs of other worlds have generated much speculation (usually based on the flimsiest of evidence) about alleged alien bases in our solar system. An imagined artificial "bridge" was spotted on photographs of the lunar surface in 1953 by H. Percy Wilkins, a Briton. Other photographs were presented as evidence of spires and towers—imagined to be rockets or radio masts—on the lunar surface. Such speculations flourished in both the United States and the Soviet Union before photographs returned by U.S. Apollo missions to the Moon showed the apparent structures to be purely figments of the imagination, created by effects of light and shadow. The "spires," for example turned out to be unremarkable rocks that cast long shadows when the sun's rays struck them at very low angles. Nonetheless, claims of extraterrestrial "engineering" on the Moon continued at least into the mid-1970s. Hard evidence of extraterrestrial UFO bases, however, has eluded even the most diligent investigators.

See also ADAMSKI, GEORGE; ANCIENT ASTRONAUTS; ANTARCTICA; BENDER MYSTERY; EXTRATERRESTRIAL HYPOTHESIS; FACE ON MARS; HOLLOW EARTH HYPOTHESIS; JESSUP, MORRIS; MARS; MOON; NAZCA LINES; RAINBOW CITY; VENUS; VON DÄNIKEN, ERICH.

Battle of Los Angeles

Unidentified aircraft were sighted over Los Angeles, California, in the early morning of February 25, 1942, and provoked a vigorous response from anti-aircraft defenses, which fired 1,430 rounds of ammunition. No bombs were reported dropped, nor do any enemy planes appear to have been shot down. One large UFO in particular is said to have hung stationary as anti-aircraft shells

Los Angeles, shown here, was site of World War II "battle" with alleged UFOs. (NASA)

exploded on and near it. The object then moved slowly along the coast between Santa Monica and Long Beach at a speed of about 6 miles per hour, then vanished. Highly maneuverable red lights were also reported seen in the skies, moving in zigzag patterns and maneuvering around bursting shells. Three persons, none of them armed forces personnel, were reported killed in the incident, and three others allegedly died of heart attacks related to the shelling. According to an official statement from the secretary of the navy, no enemy aircraft had appeared over Los Angeles, and the incident was declared a false alarm. The Battle of Los Angeles has never received a conclusive explanation.

Bauru incident, Brazil

Workers at Bauru, near Pitanga, on July 23, 1947, reportedly saw a discoid UFO land only 150 feet away. This incident allegedly involved an encounter with two tall (more than six feet) humanoids dressed in shiny clothing, with large bald heads and oversized eyes without eyebrows or eyelashes. The beings reportedly drew a diagram of the solar system and indicated the planet Uranus as if to show they had originated from it. Similar entities, though much smaller in stature, would become familiar in close-encounter cases in the United States in the late 20th century.

See also GRAYS; HUMANOIDS.

Beijing incident, China

On April 25, 1981, a luminous, bullet-shaped, multicolored UFO was re-

Beijing incident involved the sighting of a multicolored, bullet-shaped UFO over China's capital. (U.S. Geological Survey)

ported seen over Beijing. The UFO allegedly remained in view for almost half an hour. The sighting is remarkable for its resemblance to another that occurred in Britain some four months earlier.

See also CHINA; LONDON–KENT SIGHTING.

Belgian incidents   A set of several thousand UFO reports starting in November of 1989, these incidents concern large, triangular or rectangular UFOs sighted over Belgium. Reports in 1990 indicated that the UFOs were capable of sudden, dramatic changes in velocity, from a near-standstill to thousands of feet per second. When confronted by military fighter aircraft, the UFOs reportedly descended quickly to altitudes below 750 feet, then returned slowly to their previous, higher altitudes. The triangular shape of the reported UFOs is reminiscent of other large UFOs reported in the ongoing Hudson Valley sightings in the United States.

See also HUDSON VALLEY SIGHTINGS.

belief systems   Many different belief systems have been formulated to accommodate the UFO phenomenon. These belief systems are subject to frequent change as more information on UFOs becomes available and as popular thinking about the phenomenon changes. Indeed, UFO investigator Jacques Vallee has suggested that the UFO phenomenon itself constitutes a "control system" for human beliefs, although he has not said conclusively who or what appears to be exercising that system.

According to the so-called extraterrestrial hypothesis, UFOs are thought to be material spacecraft occupied by "extraterrestrial biological entities" (EBEs) that are traveling to Earth from other planets. The theoretical velocity limit—that of light—imposed by relativity theory for space travel has made a literal interpretation of the extraterrestrial hypothesis difficult, so that some exponents of EBEs now hypothesize that the alleged aliens exist in some "parallel universe" to our own and visit us through some vaguely defined mechanism for transition. Another device used by supporters of the extraterrestrial hypothesis to permit (in theory) alien visitations to Earth is the "black hole/wormhole" hypothesis, according to which either or both of those two astrophysical phenomena might allow space travelers to cover vast distances outside of "real time," thus permitting journeys of tremendous length to be made in reasonably short duration.

Another belief system is based on the assumption that the "extraterrestrials" actually are entities indigenous to Earth: possibly inhabitants of some postulated ancient civilization inside a hollow Earth, shuttling to and from the surface in luminous UFOs. Although belief in a hollow Earth was once popular and has persisted, in some circles, well into this century, the hollow Earth hypothesis has only a few defenders and is viewed mainly as a curiosity of pseudoscience.

The UFO "debunker's" belief system is generally to dismiss all UFO reports as hoaxes, hallucinations, misidentifications of natural phenomena such as clouds or ball lightning, or almost anything other than visits by extraterrestrials. This critical attitude has helped to expose numerous hoaxes and to dispel delusions based on fraud or honest error. The debunker's belief system, however, is deficient in some respects, notably in that it does not usually address the spiritual aspect of the UFO phenomenon.

From the beginnings of the "contactee" phenomenon in the years immediately after World War II, one article of belief in extraterrestrials is that they are benevolent and are prepared to intervene in human history, to save our civilization if and when we approach self-destruction through war, pollution or whatever other cause. George Adamski was among the first proponents of this belief, which has gained so many adherents that large numbers of UFO believers now apparently look forward to some kind of deliverance from extraterrestrials in the not too distant future. Some entire cults have arisen around that faith in salvation from space, especially in the United States.

The spiritual element of the UFO phenomenon is large and growing in importance. Reported messages from "extraterrestrials" increasingly emphasize the significance of UFOs to the spiritual life of humankind. The spiritual side of the phenomenon is essentially occultist in character, as demonstrated by the numerous "channelers" and other occultists who purport to deliver messages from the "space people." Not everyone sees a benevolent influence in the spiritual component of UFO-related belief systems. Although some students of UFOs interpret UFOs and their communications as manifestations of divine power, skeptics may take the opposite view and interpret the UFO phenomenon as diabolical in character, intended to lead humankind into embracing demonic deception. This latter view was expounded eloquently by the Russian Orthodox theologian Father Seraphim Rose.

See also ADAMSKI, GEORGE; BLACK HOLES; CHANNELING; CHRIST AND CHRISTIANITY; COMMUNICATIONS; CULTS; DEBUNKERS; EXTRATERRESTRIAL BIOLOGICAL ENTITIES; EXTRATERRESTRIAL HYPOTHESIS; HOLLOW EARTH HYPOTHESIS; MESSAGES; METALOGIC; OCCULTISM; PSYCHOLOGICAL EFFECTS; REAL TIME; RELIGION, UFOS AND; ROSE, FATHER SERAPHIM; WORMHOLE.

Bender mystery

The Bender mystery centers on the alleged experiences of Albert Bender, a supervisor at an industrial firm in Bridgeport, Connecticut, in the 1950s. After becoming interested in UFOs, Bender reported being contacted by three mysterious men, dressed in black, with eyes that glowed like flashlight bulbs. The visitors supposedly delivered a message to Bender through telepathy, advising him that their people should not be disturbed while carrying out their business on Earth. The beings also allegedly said that their people had carried away humans from Earth in order to use their bodies as disguises. The visitors gave Bender a small metal disk with a thickened center. To contact the aliens, he was told to hold the disk tightly in his hand, turn on his radio and say the word "Kazik."

Later Bender tried to contact the aliens by this method, and allegedly found himself suddenly in a large, circular room surmounted by a transparent dome. There he was shown a series of pictures, including what he was told was the home of the extraterrestrials. He heard a vague and puzzling explanation of how star systems were formed by a great, luminous object. He was given to understand that the aliens' world had formed billions of years before Earth, and that Earth had been "cursed" by problems that did not affect other worlds, such as divisions among nations. The aliens, he was told, visited Earth to extract a valuable chemical from its ocean water. He also was informed that the aliens had numerous agents stationed on Earth, notably in the Pentagon. When shown an image of nuclear weapons stockpiled on Earth, Bender was informed that the extraterrestrials could make all those weapons explode at any time they chose. He was reassured that the aliens would do so, however, only if humankind tried to stop them. During this presentation, Bender saw what he described as a "monster." A being who addressed him seemed to speak from the monster's mind. (The monster resembled a creature reported seen in a close encounter case at Flatwoods, West Virginia, Bender said.) He was told that the aliens had three sexes: male, female and a third that was neither male nor female. Individuals of that third kind were described as "exalted ones," for they allegedly served as the aliens' rulers. Bender perceived terrific coldness for a moment, then found himself back in his bed on Earth.

On another occasion, Bender reported, the three mysterious men returned and took him to a tremendous cavern of ice in Antarctica. There he allegedly boarded a spaceship the size of an ocean liner, filled with mysterious equipment that appeared to be distilling some clear liquid. He also encountered a monster like the one he had seen earlier. The monster said that Bender had just seen sea water being processed, as had been explained to him before. Bender noticed a smell of sulfur.

On this visit, Bender claimed to have met a handsome, nine-foot-tall humanoid who was identified as one of the "exalted ones." The being had white hair and darkened skin, as if he had a heavy suntan, and was surrounded by what Bender described as a blue haze. Bender had the impression that this being commanded the base and possibly the aliens' entire operation on Earth. The "exalted one" reportedly told Bender that the aliens had been on Earth since 1945 and admitted that the aliens had brought about the deaths of some humans. The being added that humans had been carried off from Earth to the aliens' world, some for experimentation and some to be placed on exhibit, but that no humans had survived the relocation. The alien allegedly explained to Bender that star systems supposedly were formed by a great, central, luminous object. This central mass was so hot that one could not approach within billions of light-years of it, Bender was told. There also was a great black area in which the aliens had lost many of their craft.

Eventually, Bender reported, the conversation turned to matters of belief. Bender said he had asked if the aliens believed in God, and was told that God was merely a "creation" of humans. When Bender inquired about Christ, the being replied that Christ had been merely a "great believer" in God, and implied that Christ's reputation had been exaggerated. Bender inquired about the resurrection and ascension into heaven of Christ. After remarking on the "primitive" state of humankind, the extraterrestrial supposedly said that Christ's resurrection had not occurred, but that Christ's body had been hidden or stolen instead. Bender allegedly tried to clarify the aliens' beliefs and asked if they worshipped a god on their world. According to Bender's story, the alien replied that his people did not worship anything; the alien emphasized, however, that the great central object mentioned earlier had created his people.

At the end of the alleged interview, Bender was told that the aliens would stage a demonstration of their powers in several days. One of their craft would project a fireball that would damage some object of little value in Bender's community. No one would be harmed, but the incident would generate great excitement. Then the interview was over, and the alien departed. Bender left the spacecraft, again felt a sensation of intense cold, and found himself once more back at home. Soon afterward, on August 20, 1953, a mysterious flying object reportedly punched a hole through a signboard in New Haven, Connecticut, only a few miles from Bender's home in Bridgeport. An investigation of the incident reportedly revealed that one witness detected an offensive odor like that of rotten eggs or burning sulfur after the unidentified object had damaged the sign.

Bender interpreted his encounter with the "exalted one" in terms reminiscent of traditional Christian doctrine. He imagined that the great central entity described by the extraterrestrials was their God and Creator, and the black void of which the "exalted one" spoke was their hell. This interpretation receives some support from the New Testament. The dark void resembles the "Abyss," thought by many Christians to be a place of intense darkness and torment that terrifies evil spirits. If one applies to the Bender mystery the framework of traditional Christian teaching about evil spirits and their activities, the alleged extraterrestrials bear a strong resemblance to demons, both in their appear-

ance and in their capabilities. In most cases, they have a sinister and terrifying appearance, but they are capable of taking on beautiful forms if necessary. In this case, the "exalted one" discouraged belief in Christ's resurrection and tried to present Christ as merely a believer in God, rather than as God. The alien also described God as only a creation of humankind. These are arguments that one would expect from evil spirits in opposition to God. Other attributes of the aliens are consistent with what is known of diabolical activity, including the foul odors and coldness associated with them. There also is a strong resemblance between Bender's alleged experience and accounts of diabolical possession of individuals. At one point, Bender writes, his sinister visitors told him that they could take control of his body.

An occult connection exists in the Bender mystery as well. Bender was fascinated with the occult before his alleged contacts with extraterrestrials began. He writes that he even transformed part of his home into a "chamber of horrors" and used it playfully to frighten guests. Occultism provides a substantial link between UFO activity and various other paranormal phenomena, including diabolical activity.

See also ABDUCTIONS; CHRIST AND CHRISTIANITY; DEMONOLOGY; FLATWOODS INCIDENT; MEN IN BLACK; OCCULTISM; RELIGION, UFOS AND.

Ben MacDhui, Scotland This Scottish mountain is a focus for paranormal incidents that bear a striking resemblance to many UFO close-encounter reports. Perhaps the most famous of these incidents on the mountain involves the "Gray Man," a gigantic humanoid figure that reportedly was seen approaching two crystal hunters.

A very tall humanoid resembling the "Bigfoot" of North American legend, but much larger (reportedly some 20 feet in height) has also been reported seen on Ben MacDhui. The being allegedly stood erect and was covered in what looked like short brown fur. Another apparition reported seen on Ben MacDhui is said to be that of the Devil: a tall humanoid figure in a black robe, waving his arms in a threatening manner. Not all apparitions reported on Ben MacDhui have been obviously sinister. Sir Hugh Rankin, a baronet, was traveling with his wife through the Lairig Ghru pass when they experienced a sensation of intense cold (though it was July). They perceived a strange presence near them and, when they turned to look, saw a large man with olive skin and long hair, wearing a robe and sandals. The Rankins, both Buddhists, recognized the figure as a "Bodhisattva," one of several powerful beings who, according to Buddhist thinking, govern the world. The being reportedly addressed the Rankins in Sanskrit.

These strange phenomena exhibit close parallels with UFO "contactee" reports, including temperature effects (the chill experienced by the Rankins); encounters with large humanoids; and visions of a diabolical character. The apparition of an Eastern religious figure, the so-called Bodhisattva, also resembles elements of certain UFO encounters and is consistent with the supposed occult influence in UFO encounter cases.

See also BIGFOOT; DEMONOLOGY; HUMANOIDS; MOTHMAN; TEMPERATURE EFFECTS.

Bentwaters incident, United Kingdom A famous radar/visual contact, the Bentwaters incident reportedly occurred on August 13, 1956, at the Bentwaters/Lakenheath facility operated by the Royal Air Force and the United States Air Force, in Suffolk. Ground-based radar reportedly tracked at least one UFO. Airborne radar contact and visual contact also were reported. Such radar/visual contacts are rare in UFO literature.

See also RADAR.

Bermuda Triangle Coinciding with the "ancient astronauts" enthusiasm in the United States during the 1970s, the Bermuda Triangle captured the public's imagination with reports of ships and aircraft that supposedly were lost in this area of the Atlantic Ocean bounded approximately by Bermuda, Florida and Puerto Rico. The Bermuda Triangle has been linked with UFO activity and has a reputation for mysterious, seemingly paranormal occurrences. The Bermuda Triangle also has been tied to the legend of Atlantis, which in turn has played a small but significant part in UFO lore. Careful analysis of various legends associated with the Bermuda Triangle, however, has produced convincing explanations, such as bad weather, that do not involve the paranormal. The Bermuda Triangle is one of a number of sites around the globe that have been linked with supposedly mysterious disappearances of ships and aircraft.

See also ANCIENT ASTRONAUTS; ATLANTIS.

Bethurum incident, United States A well-publicized case of contact with "extraterrestrials," following closely on George Adamski's reported meeting with a spaceman in California, concerned Truman Bethurum, a mechanic who allegedly had numerous encounters with space travelers in the western United States in the early 1950s. Bethurum

was living in Santa Barbara, California, in 1952 when an acquaintance in Nevada invited him to come there and work on a highway construction project near a formation called Mormon Mesa. One Sunday evening, Bethurum reportedly encountered on the mesa a group of eight to 10 men who stood less than five feet tall. They had black hair, clean-shaven faces and olive skin that appeared to be stretched tightly over their bones. The small men wore jackets and trousers of a blue-gray color. One of the men addressed Bethurum in English. Then Bethurum saw a disk-shaped spacecraft some 300 feet wide standing a few yards away. He was supposedly ushered into the craft and introduced to the ship's captain, a beautiful woman—even shorter than the little men Bethurum had just met—with a very high-pitched voice, olive skin and dark hair. She wore a red-and-black outfit consisting of a beret, blouse and skirt, and gave an evasive response when Bethurum asked where the visitors came from. Bethurum was escorted out of the ship and told that the aliens would return soon. Then the disc flew away.

In an alleged series of further encounters over the next several months, Bethurum met with the captain repeatedly aboard the ship and learned that her name was "Captain Aura Rhanes." She claimed to be from the planet Clarion, located at some unspecified point on the far side of the Moon. She described Clarion in sketchy terms but indicated that it was free of the ills that afflicted Earth. Among the few specifics she volunteered about Clarion were that the Clarionites loved dancing and were familiar with polkas and ballet. She added that Clarion was "beautiful" and said she hoped visitors from Earth might have a chance to travel to Clarion someday. She reacted strangely to a request from Bethurum to take her picture. The cabin was brightly illuminated, and Bethurum brought a camera with him on one occasion. The captain, however, refused to let herself be photographed.

Aura Rhanes's final two visits with Bethurum occurred at his home. In the first of these visits, Rhanes emphasized the need for peace on Earth and assigned Bethurum to found a "Sanctuary of Thought," a meeting place where humans could discuss their differences in the interest of achieving mutual understanding. On Bethurum's next and last visit with Rhanes, she encouraged him to keep trying to set up the "Sanctuary."

Bethurum's accounts of his meetings with the Clarionites came to the attention of George Adamski, who visited Bethurum and discussed the encounters with him. Bethurum's tale is similar in many ways to Adamski's encounter stories.

See also ABSURDITY; ADAMSKI, GEORGE; CLARION; ENCOUNTER PHENOMENA; METALOGIC.

Bible, alleged UFOs in the

Although the expression "UFO" is a 20th-century invention and appears nowhere in the Bible, some readers of the Bible have professed to see in it references to UFOs. The most famous of such alleged references is in the book of Ezekiel, in which the Old Testament prophet describes a vision that has been construed as a description of a spacecraft landing on Earth. The imagery used in Ezekiel's account parallels that used in other portions of the Bible, however, and the "UFO" interpretation of the vision has been discredited. In the New Testament, Christ's prophecy of "signs and wonders" to be sighted in the heavens during the last days of the current age has been interpreted as a possible reference to UFO sightings, and Saint Paul predicts that the Antichrist will be able to summon fire from heaven.

See also ANTICHRIST; CHRIST AND CHRISTIANITY; EZEKIEL; ISRAEL; RELIGION, UFOS AND; ROSE, FATHER SERAPHIM.

Bigfoot

Part of the lore of America's Pacific Northwest, Bigfoot (also known as the Sasquatch) is reported to be a tall, powerful, hairy, foul-smelling humanoid and is said to haunt the forests and to be associated in some way with UFO sightings. Numerous huge footprints said to be those of the monster have been reported, although many of these are suspected of being hoaxes. Bigfoot has counterparts in the lore of other lands, notably the Yeti, or "Abominable Snowman," of the Himalayas. A Bigfoot-like being also has been reported at Ben MacDhui in Scotland, a site of frequent paranormal incidents. As a staple of tabloid stories, Bigfoot has become a figure of fun in the American media. What links Bigfoot sightings to UFOs is not clear. Small, hairy humanoids like Bigfoot in miniature also have been reported in UFO close encounters. In some respects, the Bigfoot phenomenon resembles that of the "tulpa," an occult phenomenon also known as a "thought form."

See also BEN MACDHUI; HUMANOIDS; TULPA.

biolocation

Practiced in Russia to determine the landing sites of alleged UFOs, biolocation is similar to the practice of dowsing and involves much the same equipment. In dowsing, a forked stick, a length of stiff wire or other such indicator is held at arm's length, and a downward motion of the unsecured end is supposed to indicate the presence of whatever one is seeking, often underground water. Biolocation appears to operate on similar principles. Biolocation was used to study one notable set of close-encounter reports in Russia, namely the Voronezh sightings. There is no accepted scientific explanation for dowsing or for biolocation, and both phenomena appear to belong to occultism.

See also OCCULTISM; VORONEZH SIGHTINGS.

birds

Among the most frequently cited explanations for UFO sightings is misidentification of birds in flight. Birds flying in **V** formation at night, with their light-colored breast feathers reflecting illumination from the ground, might be mistaken for a boomerang-shaped formation of UFOs; or so some UFO "debunkers" argue. This birds-in-flight explanation was invoked as a natural phenomenon that would account for the mysterious "Lubbock lights" UFO sightings in Texas.

See also DEBUNKERS; LUBBOCK LIGHTS; NATURAL PHENOMENA, UFOS AND.

black dogs

In a small but significant number of UFO encounter reports, witnesses may report seeing a large black dog in the company of alleged extraterrestrials. This element of UFO lore constitutes a close parallel with reports of such dogs in the literature on the supernatural.

Britain, for example, has a legend about "Black Shuck," a gigantic black dog with glowing eyes. According to superstition, anyone who sees Black Shuck will die within a year. The name "Shuck" is thought to be derived from the Anglo-Saxon expression "scucca" or "scoecca," meaning a demon or Satan. The spectral dog is said to haunt lonely roads and graveyards and to be accompanied by an intense feeling of cold.

Black Shuck resembles closely certain descriptions of UFO-related beings, such as the sinister men in black, whose eyes in some cases are said to glow. The cold sensation associated with Black Shuck is another parallel with alleged UFO occupants, encounters with whom are said to leave witnesses deeply chilled. As in the lore of Black Shuck, witnesses to UFO encounters may report some kind of illness, oppression or tribulation soon after seeing the UFO.

The black dog also appears in stories about Agrippa (1486–1535), the European occultist whose full name was Henry Cornelius Agrippa von Nettesheim. Agrippa was said to be accompanied everywhere by a "familiar," or evil spirit, that appeared in the form of a big black dog. Just before his death,

Agrippa allegedly blamed the familiar for his destruction and banished the demon dog from him. According to one account, the dog ran out of Agrippa's room, plunged into a river and drowned, in a manner reminiscent of the biblical story of the Gerasene swine (Mark 5:13).

See also ANIMALS, UFOS AND; EYES; MEN IN BLACK; OCCULTISM; TEMPERATURE EFFECTS.

black hands   The literature on UFOs and the paranormal contains strange reports of disembodied black hands and arms that appear out of thin air, grab hold of an individual, and then let go. One such incident allegedly occurred along France's Loire River in 1950. Two black hands reportedly appeared, seized a young woman and dragged her through bushes and fields.

The black hands phenomenon resembles another set of reports from the British Isles. In these stories, large, disembodied, hairy hands appear, seemingly from nowhere. On Dartmoor in Devon, for example, there have been several recorded sightings of such hands. One woman in her late 20s was driving along the road between Two Bridges and Postbridge when she had car trouble and stopped her vehicle. She reported that a sensation of cold came over her, and when she looked up, she saw a pair of very large, hairy hands pressed against the windshield. They disappeared when she screamed. After this incident, the car started with no difficulty. (There is a strong resemblance here to certain features observed in many UFO encounter reports. The encounter is accompanied by problems with the operation of an automobile and by strange temperature effects.) Later, she learned that similar phenomena had been reported along this particular section of road for decades. Starting early in the 20th century, travelers along the road were vexed by unexplained interference with transportation. One motorcyclist reported that the handlebars of his cycle were torn from his grasp, causing him to hit a wall; and an army officer allegedly saw a pair of huge hands covered with dark hair grasp his steering wheel. Perhaps the most dramatic case involved a couple who stopped for the night in the area with their caravan (what Americans would call a trailer or mobile home). The woman was awakened by a scratching noise that sounded as if it were coming from outside the caravan. When she got up to investigate, she noticed a pair of gigantic, hairy hands moving across a window over the bunk where her husband slept. When she made the sign of the cross, the hands disappeared. These are not, strictly speaking, incidents involving UFOs, but

are included here because they follow a pattern observed in many UFO close-encounter cases: the abrupt and unexpected appearance, in an isolated location, to an individual, of an entity or entities that reportedly inflict physical and/or emotional harm on that person, then dematerialize. Such "hairy hands" reports also bear some likeness to cases in which UFOs are said to have taken physical control of motor vehicles and redirected their movement.

See also ABDUCTIONS; DEMONOLOGY; ENCOUNTER PHENOMENA; TEMPERATURE EFFECTS; VEHICLE EFFECTS.

black holes   These phenomena of astrophysics result when a massive star collapses and produces a tremendously dense "singularity" known as a black hole, from which not even light can escape. It has been suggested that the physics of black holes might allow for rapid travel between universes and between distant portions of this universe. In theory, such effects might eliminate one of the principal objections to the hypothesis that UFOs are spacecraft from other star systems. Our knowledge of physics indicates that no moving object can exceed the velocity of light. This limitation means that interstellar travel would take many years, even millennia, and thus would be impractical for a craft and occupants traveling at velocities much slower than light. If black holes permitted a "shortcut," however, then interstellar voyages might be reduced to a fraction of the period required at sub-light speeds. Such ideas, however, remain in the realm of speculation. Meanwhile, there is considerable evidence that UFOs represent a phenomenon confined to Earth and to the space immediately around the planet.

Blavatsky, Helena Petrovna, Russian occultist, (1831–1891)   Founder of Theosophy, a 19th-century occult phenomenon that gave rise to much of the modern New Age movement, Blavatsky is credited with inventing a minor but colorful piece of UFO lore involving the so-called *Book of Dzyan*, an alleged ancient Indian chronicle of how extraterrestrials arrived on Earth in a metal vehicle and set up a colony here. According to this account, dissension among the aliens led to civil war and an attack using a weapon reminiscent of modern ballistic missiles equipped with nuclear warheads. The story, which bears a strong likeness to elements of the "ancient astronauts" enthusiasm of the 1960s and 1970s, appears to be entirely imaginary but has been cited in numerous books about UFOs. It is related in Blavatsky's 1886 book *The Secret Doctrine*. Blavatsky's work provides a small but significant link between the modern UFO movement and occultism.

See also ANCIENT ASTRONAUTS; HOAXES; MYTHOLOGY; OCCULTISM.

Blue Bolt, Project Sometimes called Project Bluebolt, this alleged Air Force effort is said to have involved anti-gravity research, but little information beyond the project's name is available. Project Blue Bolt is not to be confused with Project Blue Book, the Air Force study of UFOs.

See also ANTI-GRAVITY; BLUE BOOK, PROJECT.

Blue Book, Project Starting in 1952 and ending in 1969, Project Blue Book was a U.S. Air Force investigation of the UFO phenomenon. Under the leadership of Captain Edward Ruppelt, Blue Book developed procedures for analyzing sightings. Staffers distributed questionnaires to witnesses of UFO sightings; analyzed photos of alleged UFOs; and interviewed eyewitnesses. Staff members also studied meteorological records, astronomical data and aircraft flight information to see if they could help account for UFO sightings. Blue Book explained most reported sightings as hoaxes, hallucinations or misidentifications, but had trouble accounting for a small percentage of investigated sightings. The project came under strong criticism for its alleged bias against non-traditional explanations of UFOs and for conducting a superficial study. Dr. J. Allen Hynek worked on Project Blue Book but concluded that there was indeed a mystery in the UFO phenomenon that required deeper investigation.

See also GRUDGE, PROJECT; HYNEK, J. ALLEN; RUPPELT, EDWARD; SIGN, PROJECT.

bodily effects Close encounters with UFOs reportedly have resulted in a wide range of effects on the bodies of contactees. These effects allegedly range from burns and scars to the death of the contactee. Notable cases in this category include the so-called Andreasson incident, in which "abductee" Betty Andreasson Luca reportedly discovered a "scoop mark" on her left calf; the Cash–Landrum incident, in which a woman is said to have been admitted as a burn victim at a hospital following a close encounter with a UFO; and the Falcon Lake, Canada, incident, in which an observer of a landed UFO allegedly suffered burns in a pattern matching that of an exhaust outlet seen on the UFO, as well as other symptoms apparently consistent with exposure to large amounts of X-rays or gamma radiation over the whole body. In numerous cases, "abduc-

tees" have reported, under hypnosis, having had small, metallic objects resembling BB shot placed inside their bodies, commonly in the nasal region. Although such "implants" are widely reported, there appears to be little or no solid evidence that they actually exist.

See also ANDREASSON CASE; CASH–LANDRUM INCIDENT; DR. X INCIDENT; FALCON LAKE INCIDENT; IMPLANTS.

bolides Bright meteors that may explode, bolides have long been associated with UFO reports and may account for some alleged UFO sightings. A 1902 report made by the French astronomer Lucien Libert describes a bolide as bright as Venus traveling in a looped trajectory through the constellations Perseus and Taurus, starting near the star Capella, looping around the star Beta Persei and swinging toward the star Aldebaran. Near Aldebaran, the bolide split into several objects. The entire observation lasted approximately 12 seconds, and the bolide left behind a trail that lingered for more than a minute.

See also ASTRONOMY; METEORS.

boomerangs These are UFOs described as having the configuration of a shallow **V**, like a boomerang. They are commonly reported seen at night and are said to carry numerous lights set on what appears to be a dark, solid body. The "boomerangs" figured prominently in the Hudson Valley UFO sightings of the 1980s. Boomerangs the size of football fields have been reported, but a boomerang may be comparatively small, perhaps only 25 feet from tip to tip. The **V** shape of some boomerangs, similar

Boomerang UFO like those reported in Hudson Valley sightings. (D. Ritchie)

to that of a flock of migrating birds, has led to speculation that some boomerangs actually have been flocks of birds, seen in flight with lights from the ground reflected on their undersides. This explanation has been applied to the "Lubbock lights" phenomenon in Texas, where lights in such a configuration were seen and photographed.

See also HUDSON VALLEY SIGHTINGS; LUBBOCK LIGHTS.

border phenomena This expression refers to phenomena that occur on the border (so to speak) between "ordinary" reality and some other kind of reality, and sometimes is applied to UFO abduction experiences. Border phenomena supposedly are perceived in some state of consciousness that alters ordinary consciousness and perception.

See also ABDUCTIONS; IMAGINAL REALM.

boundary deficit disorder In psychology, a "boundary" is a concept that helps the individual distinguish between fantasy and reality. A boundary deficit means an absence of such concepts and a corresponding inability to tell the difference between the real and the unreal. In UFO abduction cases, one may be dealing with individuals having boundary deficits, one therapist, Dr. William Cone of Newport Beach, California, has suggested. Cone noticed parallels in character structure between persons who claim to have undergone Satanic abuse and individuals who recall being abducted by extraterrestrials. From a clinical viewpoint, Cone suggested that both populations had boundary deficits. Cone also explained that the boundary deficit disorder was related to another condition known as the "nightmare personality," in which the sufferer has vivid, upsetting dreams and has trouble distinguishing between the dreams and real life. Cone did not go so far as to propose a direct cause-and-effect relationship between these psychological characteristics and UFO abduction cases, but he did note that a person suffering from such psychological problems may have difficulty telling actual experience apart from disturbing dreams. (The 15th-century demonologists Heinrich Kramer and James Springer, in their text on witches and witchcraft, *Malleus Maleficarum*, made a similar observation when they noted that a person may imagine having been molested by an incubus, a "male" demon capable of having sexual activity with women, when in fact no such event has occurred.) Cone also said he had observed, in both groups, a large proportion of individuals who had not only histories of sexual abuse, but also disorders of sexual identity. According to psychodynamic theory, the article pointed out, problems with sexual identity and sexuality are tied to a failure to conclude a "healthy" separation from the parent during childhood. Even in the absence of overt abuse, either physical or sexual, boundary problems arise from such an unsuccessful separation, because the sufferer cannot discern a boundary between self and parent. Cone linked boundary problems with paranormal occurrences such as alleged UFO abductions. If the boundaries can be strengthened in an individual, that change should put an end to the "abduction" problem, he suggested. He emphasized that long-term therapy is required.

See also ABDUCTIONS; CRYPTOMNESIA; INCUBI AND SUCCUBI; PSYCHOLOGICAL EFFECTS.

Bracewell probe Suggested in 1960 by R.N. Bracewell, professor of astronomy at Stanford University, a Bracewell probe would be an unmanned spacecraft designed for contact with extraterrestrial civilizations. The probe would be sent out to a nearby star system that seems likely to have planets capable of supporting intelligent life. The probe would go into orbit in that system and wait until it detected electromagnetic signals that indicated the presence of a civilization using radio technology. When the probe received such signals, it would return them, as apparent "echoes," to their source. If the probe then received a response that indicated an intelligent agency was responsible for the signals, the probe would start a "conversation" aimed at setting up an eventual exchange of communications by radio between the two civilizations involved. Bracewell suggested that signals received from such a probe would resemble echoes with delays of some seconds or minutes. A set of signals matching this pattern was indeed reported from Norway in the 1920s. Later analysis of these signals led some observers to suspect that the "echoes" came from an extraterrestrial Bracewell probe in orbit around Earth at the same distance as the Moon. This interpretation, however, has been discounted.

See also COMMUNICATIONS; EPSILON BOOTIS.

Brazil So many UFO reports have originated in Brazil that the country's armed forces and civilian government have taken the UFO phenomenon seriously, and the government established a special agency, the Air Force's UFO Study Division, to investigate the UFO Phenomenon. Although UFO reports have been reported and discussed widely in

Brazil's government reportedly has taken the UFO phenomenon seriously. (U.S. Geological Survey)

Brazil, some degree of government censorship on the subject has been alleged.

See also CHUPAS; MATLES-BARBOSA INCIDENT; MORRO DE VINTEM INCIDENT; PEROPAVA RIVER INCIDENT; VILLAS-BOAS INCIDENT.

Broadlands incident, United Kingdom The Broadlands incident was remarkable in that it involved Lord Louis Mountbatten, a cousin of the queen. A UFO reportedly landed on Mountbatten's estate at Broadlands in Hampshire. The observer was one Frederick Briggs, a bricklayer working at the estate. Briggs said he was riding his bicycle to work at Broadlands from the nearby community of Romsey on the morning of February 23, 1955, just after 8:30 A.M., when he saw the UFO hovering over a field. The UFO was reportedly shaped like a child's top and was 20 to 30 feet in diameter. Briggs compared its luster to that of a dull aluminum sauce-

pan and said the object had "portholes" like those of a steamship. Briggs stopped to watch. He saw a "column" about as wide as a man's body extend downward from the object. At the end of the column stood a humanoid figure that appeared to be wearing overalls and a helmet or close-fitting hat. The object was less than 300 feet from Briggs. As he watched, a bright "bluish" light like that of a mercury-vapor lamp appeared in one of the portholes. At this point Briggs felt something push him over. He fell with the bicycle on top of him, then found himself unable to get up. He felt as if something were pinning him down. The tube was retracted into the craft, which then took off rapidly and vertically. Mountbatten later visited the site of the alleged encounter and provided a statement to the effect that he considered Briggs "sincere" and not given to hallucinations.

See also ENCOUNTER PHENOMENA; HUMANOIDS; PARALYSIS.

Brooksville, Florida, incident, United States The Brooksville incident reportedly occurred on March 2, 1965, when a retired longshoreman took a walk in woods near his home and encountered a UFO resting on four landing legs. A being resembling a robot, wearing a silvery outfit, was walking toward the object. The robot raised an object to its face, a bright flash occurred, and the man had the impression he had been photographed. Then the being boarded the vehicle, the landing legs retracted and the craft departed with a whistling noise and a roar. As the story has it, after the UFO departed, the man examined the site and found two pieces of paper bearing symbols resembling hieroglyphics. Air Force investigators later interviewed the man and took the papers with them. Some weeks afterward, the Air Force reportedly returned the papers to him, claiming to have deciphered the message. Supposedly, it originated from Mars and was a summons for a space traveler to come home. Another landing allegedly occurred later at the same site as the earlier incident. This time footprints were reported seen, and several small pieces of metal were found, including a wire.

The case is of particular interest because a sheriff's deputy reportedly claimed that the documents returned by the Air Force were not the same as those provided by the witness. The original documents were said to have had different markings on them than the papers returned by the Air Force. Also, a small piece of the original papers reportedly was set afire and burned quickly and brightly, with little smoke and residue; the papers returned by the Air

Brooksville, Florida, incident reports involved a small robot. (U.S. Geological Survey)

Force allegedly did not have those same characteristics.

The Brooksville incident contains a strong element of the absurd, specifically the suggestions that a visitor from Mars would have to have a written order for his return delivered to him; that the Air Force would know how to translate such a document from the original "Martian"; and that intelligent life would exist on Mars, which appears to be a lifeless world. Controversy over this case has continued for years, and the alleged landing site became a popular camping ground for UFO enthusiasts.

See also ABSURDITY; EVIDENCE.

brownies In the fairy lore of Britain, brownies bear a strong resemblance to beings reported in close encounters with UFO occupants. The brownie was often described as a small humanoid, perhaps three feet tall, with no discernible nose, though having some kind of nostrils. In some accounts, however, brownies were said to have prominent noses. At night, brownies would perform chores around a human household in return for food. They were said to be attracted to bodies of water. Holy water and Christian symbolism were thought to drive brownies away. Often brownies were reported seen on an individual basis, but sometimes they were said to congregate in small groups. The brownies' work allegedly included the mowing of grain.

Parallels between brownie legends and various elements of the UFO phenomenon are plain. Like brownies, the "extraterrestrials" in UFO encounter cases often are described as little humanoids with either nonexistent or very outstanding noses. Food plays an important part in contacts between humans and brownies, as in alleged encounters between humans and extraterrestrials. Both the legendary brownies and modern UFOs are said to be attracted to bodies of water such as pools and reservoirs. The grain-mowing activities of brownies also resemble the alleged link between UFOs and "crop circles" in the 20th century. Similarities between the brownie legends and modern UFO encounters also include the beings' aversion to Christian symbols.

See also CROP CIRCLES; DEMONOLOGY; ENCOUNTER PHENOMENA; FOOD AND DRINK; MYTHOLOGY; WATER.

Brush Creek incident, California, United States
Early in the evening of May 20, 1953, two miners reportedly saw a silvery object some eight feet in diameter and six feet thick land on a sandbar some 150 feet from them. The object had tripod landing gear. From the UFO emerged a broad-shouldered humanoid, considerably shorter than an average man, who filled a pail with water from the creek and passed the pail back inside the UFO. Then the entity apparently noticed he was being watched. He climbed quickly into the UFO, which took off with a hissing noise. This incident is one of many reports in which UFO occupants are said to take an interest in bodies of water. See also AQUATIC OBJECTS; WATER.

Burton, Robert (1577–1640) The 17th-century English scholar Robert Burton, in his *Anatomy of Melancholy*, cites numerous anecdotes describing incidents much like modern accounts of sexual encounters with "aliens." He attributes the incidents to the work of fallen spirits, to whom he ascribes "aerial bodies," and whose capabilities—essentially the same as those of the "aliens" mentioned in many close encounters—he describes as follows: "[If] their bodies be cut, with admirable celerity they come together again. . . . [Many] ancient fathers of the church [affirm] that in their fall their bodies were changed into a more aerial and gross substance. . . . [They are thought to be] of some shape, and that absolutely round, like Sun and Moon, because that is the most perfect form, which has no roughness, angles . . . [or] prominences, but is the most perfect among perfect bodies; therefore all spirits are . . . in their proper shapes round." He adds the speculation that "they can assume other aerial bodies, all manner of shapes at their pleasures, appear in what likeness they will themselves, that they are most swift in motion, can pass many miles in an instant, and so likewise transform bodies of others into what shape they please, and with admirable celerity remove them from place to place . . . that they can represent castles in the air, palaces, armies, spectrums, prodigies, and such strange objects to mortal men's eyes, cause smells, savours, [and] deceive all the senses, most writers [on] this subject credibly believe; and that they can foretell future events, and do many strange miracles. . . . [They] can be seen when, in what shape, and to whom they will . . . and use carnal copulation . . . with women and men."

See also APPARITIONS; DECEPTION; DEMONOLOGY; ENCOUNTER PHENOMENA; "SECRET COMMONWEALTH"; SEXUAL ENCOUNTERS; SPHERES.

Burtoo incident, United Kingdom   One of the most colorful tales in the literature on UFOs is that of Alfred Burtoo, an elderly angler who reportedly was taken aboard a UFO that landed on August 12, 1983, beside a canal in Aldershot, Hampshire. Burtoo was 78 years old at the time of the encounter. Shortly after 1:00 A.M., Burtoo was fishing alongside the canal, in the company of his dog. Burtoo saw a bright light pass overhead. Soon afterward, Burtoo saw two figures dressed in green coveralls approaching him. The figures stood approximately four feet tall. He was taken aboard a shiny metallic craft some 40 to 45 feet in diameter. He was directed to stand beneath an amber light. He obeyed. When asked his age, he said he was 78 years old. Then he was told to turn around. Several minutes later, he was informed that he was too aged and "infirm" for the beings' purposes and was free to leave. He left the craft and returned to the spot where he had left his dog and fishing equipment. Burtoo is said to have experienced none of the bodily effects (nausea, paralysis, and so forth) reported by some persons in close-encounter cases, but Burtoo did appear to lose his appetite for a while and have trouble getting to sleep. Although there appear to have been no other witnesses to Burtoo's encounter, Burtoo's wife claimed that he spent the remaining two years of his life without ever confessing that the report had been a hoax. Burtoo died in 1986 at age 80.

See also ENCOUNTER PHENOMENA; HUMANOIDS; ODORS.

Byland Abbey incident, England   This incident was said to have occurred in 1290 A.D. when a silver, disk-shaped UFO flew over Byland Abbey in Yorkshire. According to the story, the monks were about to have dinner when one Brother John came in to tell Abbot Henry that something highly unusual was happening outside. Then the monks went outside to investigate and were terrified by the sight of the UFO. The story has been exposed as a hoax devised in modern times by two British high-schoolers and presented in a letter to the *Times* of London.

See also HOAXES.

C

Cabo Rojo incident, Puerto Rico One of the most famous in modern UFO literature, this incident allegedly occurred in the Cabo Rojo area on December 28, 1988, when two F-14 jet fighters reportedly "disappeared" during an encounter with a large, triangular UFO. After "capturing" the two aircraft, the UFO allegedly altered its form to a less angular shape and split in half to form two separate, triangular UFOs. These two objects then were said to have departed at high velocity. Rumors have circulated that the encounter was observed on radar, but no evidence has been produced to substantiate this claim.

See also AIRCRAFT, UFOS AND; MISSING PERSONS AND AIRCRAFT.

Canada, UFOs in Like its neighbor to the south, Canada has been the site of numerous UFO reports, which appear to have followed largely the same pattern as similar incidents in the United States. The Canadian reports often have occurred in remote areas, to small numbers of witnesses, and have involved alleged sightings of small humanoids engaged in work on or outside their craft, such as drawing water from lakes. One widely publicized UFO close-encounter report from Canada involved a man who allegedly approached a landed saucer near Falcon Lake, Ontario, and was burned in a pattern reminiscent of an exhaust grill when the UFO took off. According to UFO lore, the Canadian and U.S. governments have collaborated on UFO investigations over the years.

See also ENCOUNTER PHENOMENA; FALCON LAKE INCIDENT; STEEP ROCK LAKE INCIDENT.

Canary Islands Located off the northwestern coast of Africa, the volcanic Canary Islands have been the site of notable UFO reports. One such incident reportedly occurred on June 22, 1976, when a doctor traveling by taxi reported seeing a transparent sphere perhaps 20 feet in diameter hovering just above the ground ahead. Inside the sphere were two very tall humanoids, about nine to 10 feet in height, apparently operating controls. When the driver of the taxi turned on the headlights, the sphere started rising. The UFO expanded to about 10 times its original diameter (although the figures inside did not change in size), emitted a high-pitched whistling noise and sailed off in the direction of Tenerife. Other widely publicized UFO reports from the Canary Islands include a June 22, 1976, incident in which the Spanish naval corvette *Atrevida* spotted a yellow light rising from near Punta Lantilla. The object allegedly produced what was described later as a "curtain" of light, bright enough to illuminate both land and sea, extending toward the ground. This incident appears to have coincided with the aforementioned sighting involving very large humanoids. On March 5, 1979, an unidentified object reportedly arose from the ocean and left a luminous trail that persisted for half an hour. That incident may have been attributable to the firing of a missile from a submarine.

See also AQUATIC OBJECTS; ATLANTIS.

Cape Race incident, North Atlantic Ocean Witnesses aboard the ship *Siberian* reportedly saw a great luminous sphere arise from the ocean off Cape Race, Newfoundland, at around midnight on November 12, 1887. The UFO reportedly climbed to an altitude of about 10 miles, moved against the wind and departed at high speed in a southeasterly direction.

See also AQUATIC OBJECTS.

Captain Aura Rhanes   One of the most famous figures in UFO lore, Captain Aura Rhanes was the female commander who allegedly spoke with American "contactee" Truman Bethurum in a series of encounters in 1952. Most of Bethurum's meetings with Aura Rhanes reportedly occurred at night in lonely places where Bethurum was the only human witness. According to Bethurum, Aura Rhanes's final two visits with him occurred at his home. In the first of these visits, Rhanes emphasized the need for peace on Earth and assigned Bethurum to found a "Sanctuary of Thought," a meeting place where humans could discuss their differences in the interest of achieving mutual understanding. On Bethurum's next and last visit with Rhanes, she encouraged him to keep trying to set up the "Sanctuary."

Bethurum's accounts of his meetings with the Clarionites came to the attention of George Adamski, who visited Bethurum once and discussed the encounters with him. Bethurum's tale is similar in many ways to Adamski's encounter stories. The captain and her crew look human but are short of stature. The visitors deliver a vague message in favor of peace and understanding. They reveal next to nothing about themselves and their society. The visitors refuse to pose for pictures, and they evidently prefer to avoid being seen by large numbers of witnesses at once. Moreover, they tend to manifest themselves at night, often when their human contact is in bed, either preparing for or emerging from sleep. In that last respect, Bethurum's reported encounters with Captain Aura Rhanes and her crew would appear to match the pattern of hypnogogic and hypnopompic hallucinations.

See also ABSURDITY; ADAMSKI, GEORGE; BETHURUM INCIDENT; ENCOUNTER PHENOMENA; HALLUCINATIONS; HUMANOIDS; METALOGIC.

Cardan incident, Italy   The mathematician Jerome Cardan reports in his book *De Subtilitate* an incident in 1491 that his father, Facius Cardan, described to him. On August 13, 1491, Facius Cardan allegedly was visited by seven men dressed in garments resembling togas. Their garments were impressive, and the men appeared no older than 30. They said they were made of "air," lived much longer than humans (up to 300 years) and underwent birth and death just as humans do. When

asked about the immortal nature of the soul, the visitors apparently implied that nothing "peculiar" to an individual survives the death of the body. The men disagreed on whether or not God had created the Earth. One denied that God had created the world, but another maintained that divine creation was the only thing that sustained the world. This incident resembles certain reports from the literature on modern UFO close encounters. The visitors wear unusual and impressive garments, claim to be superior to humans in some way or another (in this case, longevity), and deliver a strange metaphysical message (about the immortality of the soul and about God's creation of the world).

See also ENCOUNTER PHENOMENA; MESSAGES.

Casa Blanca, California, incident, United States   In August 1955, children playing in a garden in Casa Blanca, near Riverside, allegedly noticed a discoid object above them, then saw what appeared to be a group of specters approaching them. The figures were partly transparent and apparently humanoid, with heads, eyes, mouths and arms. Some of the apparitions also wore belts. Other UFOs appeared, and one of them landed in a nearby field. At one point, a disembodied arm appeared. Frightened, the children retreated into the house and told adults, but no specters were visible when they came back to the garden. This incident, especially the detail about the disembodied arm, resembles other reports from Britain, France and Russia of mysterious arms and hands that have appeared out of thin air.

See also BLACK HANDS.

Casablanca incident, Morocco   A minor incident in UFO lore, this case is nonetheless interesting for its reported temperature effect in connection with a UFO sighting. On September 18, 1954, a small gray discoid UFO allegedly flew over an automobile at extremely high speed, with cold currents of air following. Although a jet aircraft might be mistaken for a UFO such as the one described here, the cold air accompanying the UFO's passage is not what one ordinarily would expect to follow the overflight of a jet aircraft. Possibly some localized source of cold wind was involved. See also TEMPERATURE EFFECTS.

Cash–Landrum incident, United States   The story of Betty Cash and Vickie Landrum and their alleged encounter with a UFO has been cited to support the argument that aerospace technology is advancing to the point where it may become difficult to tell the difference between terrestrial technology and genuine UFOs. The incident reportedly occurred near Houston, Texas, on the night of December 29, 1980. Cash and Landrum were driving at around 9:00 P.M. when a luminous object appeared in the sky, descended to the level of the treetops and hovered before them, approximately 135 feet distant. The two women provided different descriptions of the object. Cash perceived it as a brilliant light with no definite shape, but Landrum saw it as an oblong shape with a pointed bottom and rounded top. Outbursts of flame from the object were accompanied by a noise like that of a flame thrower. The object reportedly emitted a roar and a beeping sound throughout the encounter. Temperature effects were noted: the door of the car reportedly became so hot that Cash could not bear to touch it with her bare hand. Cash and Landrum followed the UFO in their automobile and saw more than 20 twin-rotor helicopters accompanying the object, at a distance of perhaps three-quarters of a mile. The women stopped several times to observe the UFO, then drove home.

Cash and Landrum later developed serious medical problems and sued the U.S. government for $20 million in damages, but their case was dismissed on the ground that the government claimed to own and operate no device such as that the women reportedly encountered. The mysterious helicopters mentioned in this incident figure also in other UFO encounter reports. It has been suggested, though with little or no solid evidence to support the hypothesis, that the Cash–Landrum UFO was a nuclear-powered vehicle being test-flown under Project Snowbird, said to be an attempt to put a recovered extraterrestrial craft through test flights.

See also BODILY EFFECTS; HELICOPTERS; SNOWBIRD, PROJECT; TEMPERATURE EFFECTS.

catastrophes One prominent element of UFO lore is the vaguely defined set of catastrophes that alleged extraterrestrials are said to predict for Earth. The calamities include global nuclear warfare, environmental disasters, and various other horrors including the reversal of Earth's magnetic or geographic poles. In the 1950s nuclear warfare apparently was much on the minds of the "aliens," for their messages to alleged contactees such as George Adamski emphasized the risk that humankind would destroy itself in a worldwide nuclear exchange unless humans made major changes in their way of life. In the 1970s, as environmental concerns became major news, the character of the warnings from "space" changed to emphasize the threat from degradation of the environment. The environmental

Catastrophes often are associated with UFO reports. (Earthquake information Bulletin/U.S. Geological Survey)

emphasis of "extraterrestrial" warnings appears to have subsided in the 1990s, in favor of messages about the spiritual crisis of humankind. This change in emphasis has accompanied the rise of the so-called New Age movement. The overall pattern is that the alleged messages from extraterrestrials appear to reflect the major worries of the developed countries on Earth at any given time. This changing emphasis may originate partly with the interests of "contactees," but also appears consistent with UFO researcher Jacques Vallee's suggestion that the UFO phenomenon constitutes a mechanism for modifying the belief systems of humankind.

See also ADAMSKI, GEORGE; BELIEF SYSTEMS; MESSAGES; VALLEE, JACQUES.

Central Intelligence Agency, United States

America's Central Intelligence Agency (CIA) has long been suspected of harboring "secret" information about UFOs, including the whereabouts of crashed saucers and remains of their alleged extraterrestrial occupants. Documents released under the Freedom of Information Act, however, indicate that the CIA, soon after the start of the "flying saucer" phenomenon immediately after World War II, concluded that UFOs apparently had no extraterrestrial origin nor represented any direct threat to America's national security. Despite rumors to the contrary, there is no proof that this attitude on the CIA's part has changed since that time. UFO debunker Philip Klass, in a study of declassified CIA documents concerning UFOs, points out that fewer than 200 pages of official CIA documents concerning UFOs have actually been withheld from the public following requests for them. Klass suggests that if UFOs truly were a matter of major concern to the CIA, then the agency would have generated, and withheld, far more information than those few pages.

See also CHADWELL MEMORANDUM; CONSPIRACY THEORIES; CRASHES; KLASS, PHILIP; ROBERTSON PANEL; RUMORS.

Chadwell memorandum

This Central Intelligence Agency (CIA) memorandum, written by H. Marshall Chadwell, assistant director for scientific intelligence and dated September 24, 1952, allegedly discussed the UFO phenomenon at length and concluded that UFOs did have "national security implications" for the United States, though not in the sense of imminent invasion from outer space. Instead, concern focused on the potential for psychological warfare waged by the Soviet Union against the United States, using the UFO phenomenon to create unrest in America, as well as the possibility that UFO sightings might interfere with America's air defenses against Soviet bomber attack.

Chadwell explained: "The flying saucer situation contains two elements of danger which, in a situation of international tension, have national security implications. . . . With world-wide sightings reported, it was found that, up to the time of the investigation, there had been in the Soviet press no report or comment, even satirical, on flying saucers. . . . With a State-controlled press, this could only result from an official policy decision. The question, therefore, arises as to whether or not these sightings: (1) could be controlled, (2) could be predicted, and (3) could be used from a psychological warfare point of view, either offensively or defensively. The public concern with the phenomena . . . indicates that a fair proportion of our population is mentally conditioned to the acceptance of the incredible. In this fact lies the potential for the touching-off of mass hysteria and panic."

The memorandum addressed the vulnerability of air defenses as follows: "The United States Air Warning System . . . [depends] upon a combination of radar screening and visual observation. The U.S.S.R. is credited with the present capability of delivering an air attack against the United States, yet at any given moment now, there may be current a dozen official unidentified sightings plus many unofficial ones. At any moment of attack, we are now in a position where we cannot, on an instant basis, distinguish hardware from phantom, and as tension mounts we will run the increasing risk of false alerts and the even greater danger of falsely identifying the real as phantom." The report recommended taking three actions:

(a) Immediate steps should be taken to improve identification of both visual and electronic phantom[s] so that, in the event of an attack, instant and positive identification of enemy planes or missiles can be made.

(b) A study should be instituted to determine what, if any, utilization could be made of these phenomena by United States psychological warfare planners and what, if any, defenses should be planned in anticipation of Soviet attempts to utilize them.

(c) In order to minimize risk of panic, a national policy should be established as to what should be told the public regarding the phenomena. . . .

The memorandum also listed several "intelligence problems" that required investigation, including the then current level of Soviet knowledge about the UFO phenomenon; the Soviets' possible intentions and capabilities to use the UFO phenomenon to harm American security interests; and why the Soviet press had been silent about flying saucers.

Chadwell added, "I consider this problem to be of such importance that it should be brought to the attention of the National Security Council in order that a community-wide coordinated effort towards its solution may be initiated."

Chadwell's memorandum shows that the CIA's concern with UFOs centered on their potential for disrupting air defenses in hostilities between the United States and the Soviet Union, not on any military threat that UFOs might present directly, such as an "invasion from Mars" scenario. Noted UFO debunker Philip Klass, who has examined the declassified CIA documents quoted here, points out that a small portion of the Chadwell memorandum, specifically the previous paragraph, has been quoted out of context to give the impression that the CIA saw UFOs as extraterrestrial spacecraft that might endanger the national security of the United States.

In another memorandum dated December 2, 1952, however, Chadwell said that "the reports of incidents convince us that there is something going on that must have immediate attention. . . . Sightings of unexplained objects at great altitudes and traveling at high speeds in the vicinity of major U.S. defense installations are of such nature that they are not attributable to natural phenomena or known types of aerial vehicles." Chadwell said his office was proceeding to set up a "consulting group" to study UFOs. This group became the Robertson panel, which recommended that American national security agencies start a campaign to remove the "aura of mystery" surrounding the UFO phenomenon.

See also CENTRAL INTELLIGENCE AGENCY; ROBERTSON PANEL; SOVIET UNION.

Chaleix incident, France   One of the strangest incidents in European UFO lore, the Chaleix incident reportedly occurred on October 4, 1954, when a farmer saw a craft about as big as a carriage land in his field. Two men of normal human height got out of the craft through a sliding door, shook hands with the farmer and allegedly asked about their whereabouts. *"Paris?"* they asked. *"Nord* [north]?" They patted the witness's dog on the back and then departed at great velocity. This case would appear to be an exception to the pattern of dogs and other domestic animals responding with terror to encounters with UFOs and alleged extraterrestrials. This report was one of many from France in 1954.

See also ANIMALS, UFOS AND.

changeling   In a fairy myth that contains elements of the modern UFO phenomenon, the changeling was said to be a fairy child that was left in place of a human baby abducted by fairies. Sometimes, pregnant women and nursing mothers also were abducted. The fairy abductors in such cases were believed to steal children to preserve and improve the fairy race. From pregnant women and nursing mothers, the fairies supposedly wished to obtain human milk to care for fairy children. Modern UFO encounter reports include numerous allegations of "extraterrestrials" seeking to kidnap human children, or trying to obtain from women ova or even newborn infants, in addition to unspecified genetic material for breeding "hybrid" babies, half human and half alien. This parallel between traditional fairy lore and modern UFO encounter stories indicates the two mythologies may have a common origin.

See also ABDUCTIONS; FAIRIES; GENETIC MANIPULATION.

channeling   Also known as mediumism, this occult practice may be defined as the delivery through a human medium of verbal messages, images or other information from some other, non-incarnate source. Channeling has become an element of the UFO phenomenon. Various practitioners of channeling, known as "channels" or "channelers," claim to have made contact with extraterrestrials and delivered messages from them. These messages may include some or all of the following elements. Humankind is not alone in the universe, but rather is in the company of extraterrestrials who have come

to Earth to contact and educate humans in advanced learning, with the aim of bringing our species into some kind of spiritual association. This change will be made by elevating humans to a higher level of "vibration." Should humans fail to start vibrating at the proper rate, great cataclysms will befall the world and destroy all who have not vibrated themselves into whatever condition the extraterrestrials have in mind. The contactee may be told that he or she is really a native of some other planet and has been living on Earth since childhood. Another story is that the contactee is really the reincarnation of some celebrity of the past.

Channeling has been practiced for thousands of years and may take place under various circumstances. It may occur spontaneously or may be induced. Inducing an episode of channeling may involve use of meditation, self-hypnosis, mind-altering drugs or other techniques. The channeler may remain aware of the channeling process as it happens, or may enter a "full-trance" state, in which the channeler's personality is pushed aside, so to speak, and the channeler is possessed temporarily by another entity. Information may come through spoken messages, delivered in the channeler's own voice or that of the possessing entity, or through imagery or feelings. Various hypotheses have been put forward to explain the channeling phenomenon. It appears likely that many so-called channelers are mere frauds playing on the gullibility of the public. Another explanation is that channelers are drawing on some "higher" level of consciousness that ordinarily cannot be tapped for information. A third explanation is that channelers, or at least some of them, have made temporary, direct contact with evil spirits that feed disinformation through the medium about conditions in the afterlife, with the aim of misleading contactees and their disciples. This last interpretation of channeling, UFO-related and otherwise, is consistent with an analysis by the American 20th-century Eastern Orthodox theologian Father Seraphim Rose, who argued that the UFO phenomenon represents a manifestation of demonic activity. In any event, the occult origins of channeling are indisputable, and channeling supplies one of many links between UFOs and other occult phenomena.

See also AUTOMATIC WRITING; COMMUNICATIONS; DEMONOLOGY; OCCULTISM; ROSE, FATHER SERAPHIM.

Charleston incident, South Carolina, United States   In a case similar to the Walton incident in Arizona some years later, a mechanic reported being abducted by aliens in the vicinity of Charleston, South Carolina, on March 18, 1978. The mechanic

Charleston, S.C., incident reports involved small, pale entities. (U.S. Geological Survey)

they apparently have been dismissed as fantasy by all but a few extremists in UFO studies.

In popular entertainment, children often are presented as the playmates, protectors or other special companions of extraterrestrials on Earth. A case in point is the 1982 American motion picture *E.T.: The Extraterrestrial*, in which an alien is "adopted" by a group of children to protect him from capture by scientists.

A possible parallel between the UFO phenomenon and European ghost lore is the literature on "radiant boys," apparitions of male children murdered by their mothers. Sightings of such apparitions are said to mean that violent death will soon occur. A famous report from the literature on radiant boys concerns Lord Castlereagh, the 19th-century British statesman, who allegedly saw a radiant boy and committed suicide some years later. Radiant boys are said to appear in witnesses' bedrooms, as extraterrestrials are said to do in modern UFO reports. Also, such UFO reports resemble the "radiant boys" phenomenon in that both phenomena involve small humanoids. Still another parallel may be seen in the calamities, including emotional disorders, that are said to befall witnesses to UFOs and radiant boys following the sightings.

See also ENCOUNTER PHENOMENA; E.T.: THE EXTRATERRESTRIAL; HUMANOIDS; REGRESSIVE HYPNOSIS; SEXUAL ENCOUNTERS.

later said he had undergone an examination by three small entities with pale skin and features resembling those of a human fetus. The alleged abductee in this case was told that three distinct races of extraterrestrials were visiting Earth to study the human species.

See also HUMANOIDS; WALTON INCIDENT.

children, UFOs and Children figure prominently in the UFO phenomenon, especially in abduction reports. In many cases, alleged extraterrestrials are said to concentrate their attention on children, for purposes that sometimes reportedly include sexual abuse or even torture. An adult "recalling" childhood abduction experiences under regressive hypnosis may describe being taken aboard a UFO and undergoing a forced sexual encounter with an extraterrestrial or with another, older abductee. What actually is recalled in such cases is uncertain. A less exotic explanation than abduction by aliens is that the person under hypnosis is relating a distorted memory of sexual abuse by a human adult.

Some abduction reports include descriptions of "hybrid" children, half human and half alien, supposedly produced by genetic engineering from ova extracted from abducted women. There is no solid evidence to support such reports, however, and

Chiles–Whitted incident, Alabama, United States At 2:45 A.M. on July 23, 1948, Captain J.S. Chiles and his co-pilot, J.B. Whitted, were flying an Eastern Airlines transport aircraft from Houston,

Chiles–Whitted UFO: Artist's conception, after a drawing from Project Blue Book files, of the Chiles–Whitted UFO. (D. Ritchie)

Texas, to Boston, Massachusetts. In the vicinity of Montgomery, Alabama, Chiles and Whitted reportedly encountered a luminous object that approached them and passed at such close range that the aircraft had to maneuver drastically to avoid collision. The men estimated that the UFO passed less than 100 feet from their right wing and was flying at approximately 700 miles per hour, or about the speed of sound. The witnesses described the object as cigar-shaped, with brightly glowing rows of windows. The UFO allegedly went into a climb after passing the aircraft, accompanied by an emission of orange flame from the tail. Although this sighting was widely reported and has become a classic in the literature on UFOs, the Chiles–Whitted incident has been dismissed as the misidentification of a meteor, with details added by the witnesses' imaginations.

See also AIRCRAFT, UFOS AND; NEAR MISSES; PERCEPTION.

China Concern at the official level over UFO sightings appears to have arisen considerably later in China than in the West, although it is difficult to determine the degree of interest in UFOs in China because of the secrecy that has characterized the Communist government in Beijing. Early postwar sightings in China appear to have followed approximately the same timetable as in the United States and Europe; one UFO described as having the shape of a "platter" was reported seen in China in July 1947, soon after the sighting of the first "saucers" by Kenneth Arnold in Washington state that same year. Chinese government interest in the UFO phenomenon appears to have intensified in the mid-1960s following the reported sighting of two discoid UFOs in Beijing in 1965, followed two years later by another alleged UFO sighting in the capital, this time involving a globular UFO that was said to have moved at great velocity, halted in flight and hovered for a time, and finally departed toward the horizon. It is understandable that China's leaders would view UFOs as potential threats to their country's defenses, as the United States government interpreted UFOs in the years immediately after World War II. UFO close-encounter reports from China generally have resembled reports from the West in their particulars, including, in some cases, radar contacts, power failures and sightings of small humanoids.

See also BEIJING INCIDENT; POWER FAILURES, UFOS AND.

Chipping Warden incident, United Kingdom

A widely publicized case involving a near miss between a helicopter and a reported UFO, the Chipping Warden incident allegedly occurred on February 21, 1988, when the helicopter's pilot saw a red, luminous object approaching the aircraft at high velocity. The object then flew on a course parallel to the helicopter's at a distance estimated at perhaps 800 yards. The object was described as having a bright red light and two less luminous white lights and was about 300 feet long. Its precise shape was not determined. The object reportedly moved too fast and changed course too rapidly for a known terrestrial aircraft, and appeared to be too bright to be an anti-collision light on another aircraft. As the UFO departed, its velocity was said to be about 500 knots relative to the helicopter's. The pilot's wife was with him in the helicopter at the time of the sighting and kept the object under observation. The Chipping Warden incident appears difficult to explain as a sighting of another aircraft or of a meteor.

See also NEAR MISSES.

Christ and Christianity Numerous attempts have been made to identify Christ as an "extraterrestrial" visiting Earth from another planet and performing "miracles" with the aid of supposedly superior technology. Such an interpretation is of course inconsistent with the traditional Christian belief in Christ as the Son of God, the Messiah, who came to Earth to redeem fallen humankind and, while on Earth, performed numerous genuine miracles.

Christ has been the target of exceptionally pointed attacks in the literature on UFOs. Early "contactee" Albert Bender, for example, described a meeting with an extraterrestrial "exalted one" who claimed that Christ was merely a believer in God, not the Son of God. The "exalted one" also claimed that Christ's reputation had been exaggerated.

Christian students of the UFO phenomenon have suggested that such incidents as that described by Bender actually represent meetings between humans and demons who aim to undermine faith in Christ and Christianity and replace it with a demonic, UFO-related religion designed to prepare society for the coming of the Antichrist, as prophesied in the New Testament.

Although some such warnings come from extremist elements in the Protestant camp, more mainstream writers concur in the belief that some UFO encounters represent attempts at indoctrination by evil spirits hostile to Christ and the Christian faith. The distinguished Orthodox Christian monk and theologian Father Seraphim Rose wrote an extensive analysis of the UFO phenomenon based on this assumption. Father Seraphim suggested that the UFO phenomenon was among the celestial "signs and wonders" that Scripture tells believers to anticipate in the final days before the rise of the Antichrist and the subsequent return of Christ to Earth. This interpretation receives considerable support from numerous reported similarities between alleged extraterrestrials and evil spirits as described in the spiritual literature of Christianity.

The portrayal of Christ as a "spaceman" has become increasingly popular since the late 1960s, as traditional Christian faith has waned and left the public open to other, non-traditional belief systems. More recently, certain UFO "contactees" have tried not to refute the tenets of traditional Christianity outright, but instead to incorporate faith in UFOs into the belief system of the so-called New Age movement.

See also ANCIENT ASTRONAUTS; ANTICHRIST; BELIEF SYSTEMS; BENDER MYSTERY; DEMONOLOGY; EXALTED ONES; NEW AGE MOVEMENT; ROSE, FATHER SERAPHIM; "SIGNS AND WONDERS."

chupas   These alleged UFOs, reported from remote areas of Brazil's Amazon basin, have been associated with numerous deaths of hunters in the region. The chupas are described as box-like objects that direct intense rays of light at their victims, who then suffer intense and puzzling illness, followed by death. UFO investigator Jacques Vallee visited the Amazon to study such reports and was told that the objects resemble flying ice boxes and emit a hum like that of a refrigerator. An unpleasant odor and a perception of cold also are associated in some cases with alleged chupa attacks. Although the stories of chupa encounters are detailed and frightening, there appears to be no proof that the alleged UFOs actually caused the deaths of any hunters in the Amazon basin. Nonetheless, the chupa reports are consistent with an observed pattern of violence versus non-violence in UFO close-encounter reports: violent encounters are thought to be more likely in less developed nations than in the more developed countries.

See also BRAZIL; ODORS; TEMPERATURE EFFECTS.

cigars   Some UFOs are described as cigar-shaped or cylindrical, and there has been considerable speculation about what such a shape might signify. Some students of the UFO phenomenon, drawing an analogy with naval technology, have suggested that the "cigars" might be large "mother ships" that carry smaller, discoid "saucers" on board, in the same manner that jet aircraft ride aboard a modern aircraft carrier. Early "contactee" George Adamski

Cigar-shaped "vunu" releasing smaller UFOs. (D. Ritchie)

apparently was among the first to propose this "mother ship" model. This view is based on the assumption that UFOs represent material spacecraft visiting Earth: a view that is less than universally accepted. Two basic kinds of "cigars" have been reported. One is a solid-looking object that is said to have a dull metallic luster and, in certain cases, some kind of insignia. Another category is the "cloud cigar," a peculiar, cigar-shaped cloud formation that allegedly emits small, luminous UFOs. The cigar-shaped, silvery UFOs have been designated "vunus" in one classification system based on the Sanskrit language.

See also ADAMSKI, GEORGE; CLOUD CIGARS; DISCS; MOTHER SHIPS; SANSKRIT; VUNU.

circles   The figure of the circle is prominent in UFO lore. UFOs themselves are described in many cases as circular, spherical or discoid. Even when a UFO is described as cigar-shaped or cylindrical, it appears to have a circular cross section. The alleged spacecraft from Venus described by famed "contactee" George Adamski had a circular form when viewed from below, as did the extraterrestrial "saucers" depicted in many early science fiction movies about the UFO phenomenon.

Many interpretations are possible for the circular shape of UFOs. From the standpoint of aerodynamics, the disc or sphere is not necessarily a good choice for flight within the atmosphere, where a standard airfoil shape is better. It has been argued, however, that a spherical hull is best for a spacecraft because it would distribute most evenly the pressure of air inside the vehicle.

In many cases, the perceived circular shape of UFOs may have something to do with the similar shape of the Sun's or Moon's disc, which may be reflected or refracted by various atmospheric phenomena to generate an image of a luminous circular object in flight. Some UFOs also may have been misidentifications of high-altitude balloons, which expand in the upper atmosphere to a spherical or nearly spherical shape, thus presenting a round image to observers on the ground.

Psychiatrist Dr. Carl Jung, in his analysis of the UFO phenomenon, interpreted the round UFOs as symbols of "totality," or completeness, that reflect the human desire for greater security and harmony in the world. Jung compared the circular shape of UFOs to the mandala, a circular emblem with religious connotations, particularly in Buddhism and Hinduism. Jung also thought it significant that this expression of the mandala form should occur in our time as a vision of alien technology, because technology makes the vision of UFOs more acceptable to modern minds than would a "personification" from mythology.

The circle also has manifested itself in other UFO-related phenomena, notably "saucer nests" and "crop circles," circular patches of flattened, swirled crops found in various parts of the world in the late 20th century. Although many of these formations have taken the form of simple circles, either single or concentric, others have an elaborate geometry.

The round configuration of many UFOs bears a likeness to the round shapes attributed to spirits, notably by 17th-century English scholar Robert Burton, who suggested that spirits in the air were "absolutely round" and exhibited many other characteristics commonly ascribed to UFOs.

See also ADAMSKI, GEORGE; BALLOONS; BURTON, ROBERT; CROP CIRCLES; JUNG, DR. CARL GUSTAV; SPHERES.

Cisco Grove, California, incident, United States An incident reportedly involving humanoids and a "robot," this case allegedly occurred on the night of September 4, 1964, when a hunter became separated from the rest of his party just before nightfall. After dark, he saw a light in the sky and presumed it was a helicopter searching for him. The light was silent, however, and so the hunter recognized it as something out of the ordinary. He climbed into a tree for better observation. The light flew around the tree. There was a flash of light, and the hunter thought he saw a dark object fall to the ground. Then the man reportedly saw two humanoid figures, each slightly more than five feet tall, approaching him. They wore silvery garments and were accompanied by what appeared to be a small robot. To keep the humanoids at a distance, the

hunter tossed flaming bits of paper and clothing at them. They appeared to be afraid of the fire. The robot then allegedly emitted smoke that made the man lose consciousness. Bizarre as this incident may appear, it includes numerous elements common to other UFO close-encounter cases, including the strange, soporific vapor released by the robot. Some close-encounter reports mention the release of a gas or vapor that has some effect on the witness, such as causing drowsiness or nausea.

See also CLOUDS AND VAPORS; ROBOTS.

Clarion The alleged homeworld of "Captain Aura Rhanes," the extraterrestrial whom American "contactee" Truman Bethurum reported meeting, Clarion was said to be a world much like Earth, only more orderly and attractive. The "Captain" provided glimpses of life on Clarion; for example, the Clarionites allegedly enjoyed dancing polkas. Clarion supposedly was located in our solar system, but in a location that kept it always hidden from view from Earth.

See also BETHURUM INCIDENT; HOMEWORLDS.

Close Encounters of the Third Kind (1) an expression coined by UFO investigator Dr. J. Allen Hynek to describe UFO encounters involving animated entities. (2) A 1977 motion picture by Steven Spielberg depicting the arrival of an extraterrestrial spacecraft at Devil's Tower, Wyoming. The film concerns a man who witnesses several UFOs, becomes obsessed with them and eventually makes contact with extraterrestrial beings when their huge craft arrives at Devil's Tower. The film portrays the extraterrestrials as large-headed, pale-skinned beings comparable to the "grays" of popular UFO literature. The movie was released by Columbia and starred Richard Dreyfuss.

clothing UFO encounter reports mention many different kinds of clothing supposedly worn by extraterrestrials. In many cases, the aliens' attire is said to consist of coveralls or some kind of skin-tight clothing. The material often is said to be silvery or iridescent. Exceptions to this rule, however, are numerous. Some humanoids in close-encounter stories reportedly wear outfits resembling diving suits or even armor. The classic "space suit" worn by aliens in such accounts may have a transparent helmet enclosing the head. "Crash helmets" or similar headgear also are described in many accounts of alien encounters.

A wide range of stylishness may be seen in descriptions of extraterrestrials' garments. "Captain

Aura Rhanes," the extraterrestrial friend of "contactee" Truman Bethurum, allegedly dressed in a red-and-black outfit topped off by a beret. The sinister "men in black" are said to wear black suits, either rumpled or very neatly pressed.

Various accessories also have been reported, including pouches carried at the extraterrestrials' side and a flashing light or other such apparatus on the chest. In some reports, witnesses say they cannot distinguish extraterrestrials' clothing from skin. Emblems such as a winged serpent sometimes are reported seen on the clothing of aliens.

Some encounter cases reportedly involve the removal of abductees' clothing. A famous case in point is the Villas-Boas incident, in which a male abductee allegedly was stripped naked before having a sexual encounter with what appeared to be a humanoid, female extraterrestrial. A similar case from the literature on demonology involves an Italian woman who allegedly was left standing unclothed in public one day when an incubus removed her garments and carried them away.

See also BETHURUM INCIDENT; DEMONOLOGY; EMBLEMS; INCUBI AND SUCCUBI; KELLY–HOPKINSVILLE INCIDENT; SINISTRARI, LODOVICO MARIA; VILLAS-BOAS INCIDENT.

cloud cigars   This category of UFO sightings was reportedly named by French researcher Aime Michel and consists of peculiarly shaped clouds, in many cases elongated or cigar-shaped, and sometimes associated with a radar return. The "cigar" may assume a vertical position and possess its own luminosity. Smaller, more clearly defined objects may emanate from the cloud and, in some cases, return to it. Cloud cigars have been described as accompanied by huge formations of UFOs and have been witnessed by hundreds of observers at a time.

clouds and vapors   One commonly reported element of UFO close-encounter cases is a cloud or mass of vapor that is said to occur around or near a UFO or a contactee. The origin and purpose of the vapor is not certain. A whole category of UFO sightings, "cloud cigars," consists of elongated clouds from which UFOs are reportedly seen emerging. A curious atmospheric phenomenon called a lenticular cloud resembles a classic flying saucer and may be mistaken for a UFO. In various other ways, clouds and other atmospheric phenomena may create conditions in which sunlight produces effects that may be mistaken for UFOs, such as an apparent ball of light keeping pace with an aircraft. In some

UFO encounter cases and related incidents, clouds and vapors associated with UFOs are linked with temperature effects, specifically a feeling of cold, and even with bodily illness.

See also BODILY EFFECTS; CLOUD CIGARS; MOTOVILOV INCIDENT; TEMPERATURE EFFECTS.

collective delusion   Sometimes applied to the UFO phenomenon, collective delusion is the term for a situation in which large numbers of people in a given area become persuaded that some unusual and (for the moment) inexplicable event or process is occurring. "Mass hysteria" is another commonly used expression for this condition.

The concept of collective delusion has been applied specifically to the "mystery" of animal mutilations. It has been suggested that UFOs are associated in some way with numerous and widely publicized cases of cattle and other domestic animals found dead in various areas of the United States. The animals' bodies were reported mutilated in peculiar ways, such as the removal of tongues, genitalia, eyes and other organs, allegedly with surgical precision. The killing and mutilation were attributed to hypothetical alien visitors from other worlds, as well as to Satanists and to operatives of the U.S. government. Apparently, collective delusion also may be seen at work in other elements of the UFO phenomenon, such as abduction experiences. Collective delusion is of course strongly supportive of UFO-related conspiracy theories, in which huge and shadowy organizations, including but not limited to the national government, are accused of "covering up the truth" about the UFO phenomenon.

See also ANIMALS, UFOS AND; CONSPIRACY THEORIES; PARANOIA.

colors   Perceptions of color are an important part of the UFO phenomenon. For example, witnesses in UFO close-encounter cases may report a curious absence of color in alleged extraterrestrials and their surroundings. The small, humanoid "grays" widely reported in abduction cases from the United States illustrate how some alleged aliens are said to be virtually devoid of color. In other reports, witnesses may report highly unusual perceptions of color, as in the famous Douglas incident. UFOs themselves are said to exhibit a wide range of colors. Although the classic "flying saucer" is a metallic, silvery disk or a white or yellow luminous object, UFOs have been reported in almost every conceivable color. Multicolored UFOs with red, green and white lights have been reported widely, although there is reason to think some or all such reports are actually misinterpreted sightings of lights on aircraft.

See also DOUGLAS INCIDENT; GRAYS.

communications Alleged communications from extraterrestrials may take many different forms. Some contactees, such as George Adamski, report having met aliens in remote locations and had face-to-face conversations with them. In some cases, a contactee may report having spoken with extraterrestrials aboard their spacecraft during an abduction. The contactee may claim the extraterrestrials addressed him in his native language, but some reports also include descriptions of aliens speaking to one another in what appeared to be their own language. Reported communications with putative aliens also may be conducted through mediumism ("channeling"), dreams, telepathy, letters, radio messages, telephone calls, and patterns impressed in soil or standing crops. Because such so-called communications are easy to arrange as hoaxes, they deserve to be treated with extreme skepticism. Moreover, even a sincere individual may simply be exercising his or her imagination when claiming to have received a communication from extraterrestrials.

Some communications are said to have been retrieved from contactees under hypnosis. Although the potential for conscious fraud on the contactee's part may be slightly less under such circumstances than otherwise, skepticism again is necessary on the investigator's part, because hypnosis is known as a notoriously fallible means of retrieving memories.

Alleged communications from aliens may serve as the basis for cults.

See also ABDUCTIONS; ADAMSKI, GEORGE; CHANNELING; CROP CIRCLES; CULTS; DROP-IN COMMUNICATOR; HOAXES; HYPNOSIS; MESSAGES; OTTO INCIDENT; TELEPATHY; TELEPHONE CALLS.

Condon report, United States In 1966, the United States government commissioned a team of scientists under the direction of Dr. Edward U. Condon at the University of Colorado to investigate the UFO phenomenon. The committee's report was released in 1968 and concluded that UFOs could be explained as familiar phenomena and therefore did not deserve further scientific study. Although Condon was a respected physicist, questions have been raised about his objectivity in this study. The report itself has been criticized because its conclusion—that UFOs did not merit further scientific study—appeared to be at odds with the results of its actual investigations, which left a large percentage of investigated sightings unexplained.

cones One of the several basic shapes of UFOs, the cone has been reported in many sightings. The cone may resemble a spindle, like two cones joined at their rims, or have an "ice cream cone" configuration, with its apex pointed earthward and wire-like projections extending from its top.

See also CYLINDERS; DISCS; FLYING TOP; SPHERES.

confabulations This expression refers to fantasies devised by a subject under regressive hypnosis. Confabulations may occur when a hypnotized subject is asked a leading question.

See also HYPNOSIS.

conspiracy theories Whenever a deeply held set of beliefs becomes the subject of intense controversy, accusations of conspiracy to suppress "the truth" are apt to arise. Such is the case with the UFO phenomenon. Supporters of the "alien astronauts" hypothesis—in which UFOs are thought to represent the presence of living, corporeal extraterrestrials visiting Earth in actual, material spacecraft—have accused the United States government of trying to conceal "proof" that this hypothesis is correct. There are many examples of theories alleging a government role in conspiracies surrounding the UFO phenomenon. In one such scenario, the government allegedly is aware that UFOs are extraterrestrial vehicles occupied by intelligent beings, but has agreed to cooperate with the aliens and permit abductions in return for access to the aliens' technology; meanwhile, the government spreads disinformation to prevent the public from learning the true situation. In another scenario, the government may or may not be aware of what UFOs really are, but is interested in the UFO phenomenon mainly to gather information on the development and spread of belief systems—information that could prove useful in manipulating public opinion. A third scenario has it that the government may use disinformation about UFOs to conceal the testing of new high technology, which may or may not have originated with extraterrestrials.

The controversy over such conspiracy theories is colorful and has done much to increase public interest in UFOs, partly because the debate is fueled by widespread suspicion of public authorities, especially the armed forces, which repeatedly have been cast in the role of villain by defenders of the alien astronauts hypothesis.

The rumored evidence in such cases takes many forms. Perhaps the most famous case in point is the so-called Roswell incident, in which the bodies of several extraterrestrial visitors are said to have been recovered, along with the remains of their wrecked spacecraft, following a crash in the southwestern United States in 1947. It also has been suggested that various government-sponsored studies of UFOs were intended merely to diminish controversy rather than enlighten the public as to the "true" character of the UFO phenomenon.

One commonplace weakness of UFO conspiracy theories, particularly those directed against government authorities, is the lack of a creditable motive for cover-ups. For example, it has been suggested that the government possesses material evidence of visitations by extraterrestrial astronauts but is afraid to make that evidence known officially to the public because the knowledge might cause widespread panic, as did Orson Welles's famous 1938 radio dramatization of H.G. Wells's novel of a Martian invasion of Earth. Rumors of such evidence already appear to be widely accepted as fact, however, and yet there has been no sign of mass panic. Moreover, and perhaps more significantly, the government evidently does little or nothing to suppress lurid UFO reports in the tabloid press, although such papers reach a large audience. It is difficult to see how acknowledging the existence of material evidence of aliens visiting Earth would hurt the government any more than do the wild and persistent rumors of such evidence and its suppression. It is conceivable that government authorities do have a compelling reason to keep secret the actual existence of the very evidence that UFO enthusiasts suspect them of holding. For now, however, conspiracy theories concerning the government's possible role in suppressing important evidence related to the UFO phenomenon remain questionable at best, and seem likely to remain so indefinitely.

See also BLUE BOOK, PROJECT; CONDON REPORT; DECEPTION; HANGAR 18; HYNEK, J. ALLEN; KEYHOE, DONALD; MEN IN BLACK; PARANOIA; PENTACLE; ROSWELL INCIDENT; SILENCE GROUP.

constructive perception   This expression has been applied to witnesses' tendency to apply a highly elaborate perception to a given stimulus. In the UFO phenomenon, constructive perception may involve interpreting aircraft lights (for example) as extraterrestrial spacecraft, complete with all manner of accessories. Constructive perception is thought to account for many UFO sightings.

See also APPARENT MOTION; DEDUCTIVE-PSYCHOLOGICAL EFFECT; PERCEPTION.

contactees   In the UFO phenomenon, a contactee is a person who claims to have made personal contact with extraterrestrials. The reported contact may involve face-to-face meetings with the alleged aliens, or encounters through telepathy, radio, telephone calls or other long-distance means of communication. The contactee often claims to deliver a specific message from the alleged aliens, although such messages tend to be vague or banal at best, and nonsensical or incoherent at worst. Among the most famous contactees in the history of the UFO phenomenon are George Adamski, who claimed to have met a visitor from Venus in the southwestern desert of the United States; Betty and Barney Hill, whose reported encounter with extraterrestrials has generated extensive discussion among UFO enthusiasts and skeptics alike; and Albert Bender, a Connecticut man who reported terrifying encounters with sinister aliens. Although many reported contacts are described as friendly, contactees may report a wide variety of unpleasant experiences in their meetings with alleged aliens, up to and including torture and rape. Proof of such meetings is nonexistent, although some contactees have argued that curious scars on, and alleged "implants" within, their bodies constitute solid evidence to support their stories of contact with extraterrestrials. Contactees may found cults to promote their beliefs.

See also ADAMSKI, GEORGE; BENDER MYSTERY; BODILY EFFECTS; COMMUNICATIONS; CULTS; HILL INCIDENT; IMPLANTS; MESSAGES.

Conway incident, South Carolina, United States   On January 29, 1953, a farmer reportedly heard a disturbance in his barn and saw an object resembling a halved egg, about 20 feet long and 12 feet wide, at the level of the treetops. The UFO was allegedly gray and illuminated from within. The farmer fired a gun at the UFO. Much livestock reportedly died under mysterious circumstances in the vicinity after this incident.

See also ANIMALS, UFOS AND.

Copiago incident, Chile   Reminiscent in certain ways of the "airship" sightings reported in the United States some 30 years later, this incident reportedly occurred in July 1868 when an airborne device was sighted over the town of Copiago. Witnesses said it resembled a huge bird covered with scales and emitted a "metallic" sound. Though evidently unexplained, the report represents one of the earliest close sightings of a low-flying UFO in the 1800s.

See also AIRSHIPS.

correlations

correlations   Although discernible patterns may appear to be few and far between in UFO lore, some correlations have been noted among individual reports. These correlations include the alleged "channeling" by several independent practitioners of the same "extraterrestrial" being, as in the case of "Spectra," said to be a highly advanced alien intelligence from the future. Numerous correlations also have been observed in messages allegedly delivered from extraterrestrials. Themes included in many such messages, for example, include warnings of an imminent calamity that is expected to befall Earth; the ability of extraterrestrials to save humankind from such catastrophe; reassurances that the alleged aliens are trustworthy, even when their behavior incorporates deceit and betrayal; strong criticism of traditional Judeo-Christian beliefs; and admonitions to adopt an occultist and/or pantheistic belief system. Many close correlations also have been noted between UFO-related phenomena and descriptions of demonic activity, as reported in the spiritual literature of Christianity over the past 1,900 years. Numerous UFO encounter reports also agree on certain physical attributes of aliens, such as large dark eyes and disproportionately large heads in the case of "grays," as well as foul odors and a perception of intense coldness in the presence of the alleged extraterrestrials. Even certain elements of the appearance and behavior of "spacecraft" have shown correlations in large numbers of sightings. These correlations include the famous "falling leaf motion" and configurations such as the "mushroom" and "Saturn" shapes. Correlations in abduction reports include paralysis of the human subject, a quasi-medical "examination" aboard the alien craft, and the "tagging" of individuals, supposedly for tracking and study.

See also ABDUCTIONS; BELIEF SYSTEMS; CHANNELING; CHRIST AND CHRISTIANITY; COMMUNICATIONS; DEMONOLOGY; FALLING LEAF MOTION; GRAYS; MESSAGES; MUSHROOMS; ODORS; SATURN SHAPE; SPECTRA; TEMPERATURE EFFECTS.

Council of Seven Lights

Council of Seven Lights   An early example of imagined extraterrestrial communities and authorities, the Council of Seven Lights figured in the alleged contacts of George Van Tassel, an American airport manager who claimed to be in communication with aliens starting in the years immediately after World War II. The Council was said to be made up of former Earth-dwellers now inhabiting a spaceship in orbit around the planet. Later "contactees" would report receiving communications from other alleged extraterrestrial "councils" and potentates. The "seven lights" in this case bear a certain resemblance to the seven lampstands that are mentioned in the biblical book of Revelation and symbolize the seven churches to which Christ speaks. Conceivably, Van Tassel, or whoever invented the story of the Council of Seven Lights, intended it as a parody of the biblical symbolism. Van Tassel became a prominent figure in the community of UFO enthusiasts and organized a series of quasi-religious meetings called the Giant Rock Space Conventions.

See also ASHTAR; AUTOMATIC WRITING; CHANNELING; COMMUNICATIONS; GIANT ROCK SPACE CONVENTIONS; INTEGRATON; PSEUDOSCIENCE.

Cradle Hill hoax, Warminster, England

Cradle Hill hoax, Warminster, England   To demonstrate how unreliable eyewitness reports of UFOs can be, even when more than one witness reports a particular sighting, a hoax was arranged on the night of March 28, 1970, at Cradle Hill in Warminster, England, a well-known UFO "window." At 11:00 P.M. a bright purple spotlight was aimed from a nearby hill toward a group of witnesses about three-quarters of a mile away. The lamp was turned on for periods of various duration, with 5-second intervals in between. During one period, the alarm on a phony magnetic field detector, operated by a hoaxer among the observers, went off and appeared to indicate the presence of a strong magnetic field. There was in fact no magnetic field present; the sensor merely was synchronized with the purple light to make it appear that a magnetic field was somehow associated with the purple light. The hoax also included faked photographs that had been taken months earlier but purported to show the strange purple "UFO." The photos clearly showed a saucer-shaped object, as distinct from the purple light actually seen; moreover, the photos showed the "saucer" in two different locations rather than in the single location the purple light really occupied, and were photographed at different levels of magnification. Further discrepancies existed between the photographs and conditions on the night of the observed "UFO": between the time the photos were made and the purple light was spotted, repairs to streetlights seen in the photos had produced a different pattern of lights than was observed on the night of March 28. Despite this weight of evidence that the photographs were faked, the pictures were pronounced genuine on investigation. The difference in appearance between the object in the photos and the purple light seen on the hill was "explained" as the result of a monochromatic "halo" produced around the alleged UFO by ionization. The Cradle Hill hoax demonstrated how unreliable eyewitness testimony in UFO sightings can be and how easily hoaxes can mislead investigators.

See also CONSTRUCTIVE PERCEPTION; HOAXES.

crashes   On numerous occasions, extraterrestrial spacecraft are rumored to have crashed on Earth. Hard evidence for such reports is lacking, but "eyewitness" testimony is abundant. That testimony may include descriptions of saucer-shaped craft with unfamiliar control apparatus inside the cabin; living or dead extraterrestrials (usually small humanoids with oversized heads) strewn about the crash area; and sudden action by the armed forces to seize the spacecraft, its occupants and their remains. Among the most famous alleged crashes in UFO lore are the Roswell and Aztec incidents in the United States. Other countries also have reported UFO crashes, notably in the Peropava River incident in Brazil.

Such reports tend to be questionable in many ways. Material evidence supposedly disappears ("confiscated" by the military, in many cases) after the crash. Alleged eyewitness testimony also may be contradictory, vague and confusing. Finally, it is difficult to reconcile the frequent reports of saucer crashes with the "advanced" technology that the spacecraft are said to represent. Some reports would have the reader believe that extraterrestrial vehicles from a civilization far advanced over ours in technology could be knocked out of the sky by ordinary terrestrial storms. Nonetheless, a vast mythology about crashes and "captured" alien spacecraft has arisen, especially in the United States, where UFO lore contains numerous rumors of government efforts to test-fly such vehicles. Saucer crashes also are rumored to have provided certain widely used components of electronic technology such as transistors.

See also AZTEC INCIDENT; CASH–LANDRUM INCIDENT; CONSPIRACY THEORIES; HOAXES; PEROPAVA RIVER INCIDENT; ROSWELL INCIDENT; RUMORS; SNOWBIRD, PROJECT.

crisis   An element of pre-existing personal crisis figures prominently in many UFO sightings reported by individuals, and it is widely believed that the sightings (especially in abduction reports) reflect stresses the individual is undergoing at the time of the alleged UFO encounter. This same connection between crisis and UFO sightings also may apply on the level of society as a whole. A society under significant stress—from warfare, economic distress or political turmoil—may embrace belief in extraterrestrial visitors in "flying saucers" as a distraction from earthly troubles. The UFOs also may represent the society's real or imagined foes, or faith in the existence of some more tranquil and "advanced" society beyond Earth. It may be worth noting that since the fall of communism and the breakup of the former Soviet Union, increasing popular interest in UFOs has been observed in Russia, as political, economic and social uncertainties and instabilities have arisen and intensified.

crop circles   Also known as "crop glyphs" and "corn circles," these peculiar phenomena consist of areas of cropland that are flattened under mysterious circumstances at night, in various geometrical patterns, with no visible agency at work producing them. Crop glyphs have appeared each summer since the early 1980s, with numerous cases reported from the British Isles, particularly from the vicinity of Stonehenge. The incidence of crop glyphs is thought to have increased greatly starting in the late 1980s, with some 400 glyphs appearing in 1990 alone.

The patterns vary greatly in size, from only a few feet in diameter to perhaps as much as a quarter mile in length. To describe these formations as "circles" is slightly misleading, for the formations do not always consist of simple circles. Instead, intricate designs may appear. One of the most impressive examples of a crop circle is the Barbury Castle glyph, which appeared in a field of wheat near the ruins of Barbury Castle in England on July 17, 1991. A central, circular flattened area was surrounded by two concentric circles. Superimposed on the set of circles was an equilateral triangle, at each point of which another circular pattern was found. One of these patterns was a simple circle; the second, a six-armed pinwheel design; and the third, an exotic "stepped" spiral with strange offsets at 90-degree intervals along its course. The entire formation measured some 300 feet wide.

Numerous explanations, few of them persuasive, have been put forward to account for the origins of crop circles. Highly anomalous weather conditions have been suggested as one mechanism for their creation. Hoaxes are another possible explanation, although some of the formations are so intricate and sophisticated in design that it is hard to imagine how they could be crafted in a field, at night, by anyone with access to the ordinary tools that are likely to be available to prospective hoaxers. Crop circles also have been interpreted as manifestations of so-called psychic phenomena, and even as evidence of some vaguely defined "intelligence" inhabiting the planet itself.

Crop circles have been linked tentatively with UFO activity with little or no firm evidence to support such an association, although peculiar lights have reportedly been observed in the skies before the crop circles appeared. There is evidence of intelligent design and execution behind the crop glyphs, but to attribute them to the action of extraterrestrial visitors in spacecraft is premature.

See also CIRCLES; INSECTOGRAMS; MOWING DEVIL INCIDENT.

Crowley, Aleister, British occultist (1875–1947)

Known as the "Great Beast" for his involvement in occultism and Satanism, Crowley and his bizarre career illustrate the link between occultism and the UFO phenomenon. On several occasions, Crowley attempted communication with what he believed to be extraterrestrial intelligence. Crowley believed he actually had received several communications, by psychic means, from extraterrestrial sources. There is a close parallel between Crowley's efforts to contact "extraterrestrials" and the modern practice of "channeling" alleged alien intelligences. Some observers of Crowley's life see possible significance in the fact that his death in 1947 coincided with the beginnings of the modern UFO phenomenon; apparently, his invocations of unseen powers were merely one aspect of an occult phenomenon that continues, under various names, as part of the modern UFO phenomenon.

In 1919, Crowley claimed to have contacted an extraterrestrial entity called Lam. Crowley depicted Lam as resembling the large-headed, hairless "extraterrestrials" commonly mentioned in UFO contactee stories today.

One particular alleged incident in Crowley's career bears remarkable parallels with modern UFO encounters. With the help of an assistant, Crowley tried to summon up a being called Choronzon, said to be the guardian of the Abyss, and described by the Elizabethan occultist Edward Kelly as a "mighty devil." Crowley's attempt to call up Choronzon involved drawing a large "mystic" triangle in the sand and stepping inside the triangle. At one point, a voice could be heard crying out the word "Zazas" or "Zasas." Then Crowley's assistant saw several entities appear in succession within the triangle. One was a seductive woman; another was an elderly man; yet another was a snake. The assistant pre-

sumed these were merely illusions created by the shape-changing demon. At one point, the demon allegedly attacked the assistant but was driven back. At last the demon vanished.

In similar fashion, attributes of "extraterrestrials" in modern UFO lore include shape-shifting (that is, the ability to appear in many different forms); the triangle, used by Crowley and his assistant in the ritual to call up Choronzon, is a prominent symbol in the UFO phenomenon; and the word "Zazas" or "Zasas," if a proper name, matches the pattern of curious two-syllable names associated with beings and places in UFO lore, such as UMMO and Masar.

See also AUTOMATIC WRITING; CHANNELING; DEMONOLOGY; E.K. INCIDENT; NAMES; OCCULTISM; POLYMORPHY; TRIANGLE.

cryptomnesia   In this mental operation, a person incorporates a memory from a motion picture, television show, rumor, or whatever other source and uses that recollection as the basis for a personal memory. This process may be involved in cases where a UFO "abductee," for example, relates "memories" of the abduction similar to events seen dramatized earlier in a work of entertainment. Parallels have been noted between the release or broadcast of certain UFO-related dramas and subsequent reports of "abductions" and other incidents resembling events in those dramas. There is reason to think this process may have been active in the United States in the late 19th century, because of similarities between reports of "airship" sightings and the story of French science fiction author Jules Verne's previously published novel *Robur the Conqueror*, about an inventor and his fantastic airship.

See also AIRSHIPS; PRECEDENTS.

cults   Numerous cults have arisen around the UFO phenomenon. Most are small, but some have sizable memberships and may be international in extent. Cults generally center around the person and activities of a leader who claims to have established communication with extraterrestrials. Messages allegedly delivered to the cult by extraterrestrials may concern some anticipated but vaguely defined deliverance of humankind (or at least the cultists) by space-traveling aliens in the not-too-distant future. Cultists may believe they have a mission to deliver messages from extraterrestrials to humankind. Those messages may involve vast cataclysms that are expected to devastate the globe. The cult may develop an elaborate mythology of extraterrestrial life and civilization, and may utilize bizarre, quasi-mystical "technology" based on occultist theories of energy. Cult activity has been an element of the modern UFO phenomenon from the beginning. Early "contactee" George Adamski, for example, led a religious cult called the Royal Order of Tibet before his rise to prominence in the UFO phenomenon.

See also ADAMSKI, GEORGE; AETHERIUS SOCIETY; BELIEF SYSTEMS; MESSAGES; OCCULTISM; TECHNOLOGY; TIBET.

cultural factor   In many cases, reports of close encounters with UFOs and their occupants tend to reflect the culture of the witnesses. For example, witnesses of alleged UFO phenomena in Ireland in the 12th century A.D. described one UFO as having an anchor that snagged on a church's roof; the mysterious "airships" reported over the United States in the 1890s allegedly were equipped with large propellers; and 20th-century UFO reports from the United States and other developed countries may describe UFOs and their activities in terms of laser beams and other modern technologies. In less developed countries, such as 19th-century Japan, these encounters may be described in the imagery of spirit lore, as in the alleged meetings of the young Japanese spellcaster Torakichi with tengu, or mountain goblins, in the early 19th century.

There are several interpretations of this cultural factor in UFO reports. It has been suggested that some intelligent entity or entities managing the UFO phenomenon may "tailor" manifestations to suit the cultural and technological environment of the human witnesses. Another explanation is that the witnesses simply interpret an observed phenomenon in light of technologies they know already, such as lasers, rockets or propeller-driven aircraft. In some cases, hoaxers may extrapolate from known technologies to provide a fanciful description of an imagined spacecraft or aircraft.

Likewise, the reported "messages" delivered by alleged extraterrestrials tend to refer to preoccupations of people on Earth. In the 1950s, for example, many messages from "aliens," such as those described by American "contactee" George Adamski, referred to the threat of nuclear warfare, which was a major concern at that time. Today, with the danger of full-scale nuclear warfare diminished, such messages are more likely to deal with the spiritual condition of humankind, which has become a major element of the so-called New Age movement. In similar fashion, the condition of Earth's environment has become a major element of alleged messages from space folk as it has grown in importance as a scientific, social and political issue in the mass media.

See also AIRSHIPS; COMMUNICATIONS; NEW AGE MOVEMENT; TECHNOLOGY; TENGU.

cultural tracking   This term describes an effort to relate certain aspects of the UFO phenomenon, such as "alien" technology described in close-encounter reports, to cultural characteristic of societies from which the reports originate.

See also CULTURAL FACTOR.

cydonia   A region of the planet Mars about 41 degrees north of the planet's equator, Cydonia is the location of the "Face on Mars" and the so-called pyramids of Mars. These features have been widely interpreted as possible evidence of intelligent life on Mars at some time in the distant past. Some analysts of NASA photos of the Martian surface have claimed to see the "Face" and pyramids as structures bearing abundant evidence of intelligent design. Similar natural formations have been found on Earth, however, and the case for intelligent life on Mars remains dubious at best.

See also FACE ON MARS; MARS; PYRAMIDS.

cylinders   Many UFOs are said to take the shape of cylinders. This shape is, of course, convenient for hoaxers, because numerous cylindrical objects can be given, through photography, the appearance of UFOs in flight, although such photos tend to be easily exposed as hoaxes. The vunu, or alleged mother ship, reported in various sightings is said to be essentially a cylinder with tapered ends. Cylindrical components of UFOs also have been reported, as in the case of "mushrooms," discoid UFOs said to rest upon a vertical cylinder while in their landing position. The cylinder is one of several basic shapes of UFOs.

See also CONES; DISCS; HOAXES; MUSHROOMS; SPHERES; VUNU.

Cyprian the former sorcerer, Saint (3rd century A.D.)   The spiritual literature of Eastern Orthodox Christianity includes the life of Saint Cyprian the former sorcerer, who was converted through the influence of Saint Justina and was martyred with her. While still practicing sorcery, Cyprian reportedly taught his students how to fly through the air and how to sail in vessels on clouds. Cyprian also reported a personal encounter with the Devil, whom Cyprian described as wearing a phantom crown, apparently made of gold and "brilliant" gems, that illuminated the surrounding area. In the presence of the demonic legions, the Devil praised Cyprian and pledged to help him in all the sorcerer did. Later, Cyprian abandoned the Devil's service and drove away the evil spirit by making the sign of the cross. Cyprian's description of the display of light surrounding the Devil resembles many modern UFO encounter reports, as does the story of Cyprian instructing others in how to make ships sail among the clouds.

See also DEMONOLOGY; VIANNEY, JEAN-MARIE-BAPTISTE.

D

Dai-el-Aouagri incident, Morocco The witness to this encounter reportedly saw a luminous UFO about 60 feet in diameter on the ground. As the UFO took off, it allegedly emitted flashes of blue light and an odor of burning sulfur. The report is questionable because of uncertainty about the date, which apparently was near July 20, 1952. The incident is interesting, however, for its mention of a sulfurous odor associated with the UFO. A similar odor was reported in American "contactee" Albert Bender's accounts of his alleged meetings with extraterrestrials, and a smell of sulfur is a well-known element in reports of demonic activity.

See also BENDER MYSTERY; DEMONOLOGY; ODORS.

data streams This element of the UFO phenomenon exerts a powerful psychological effect on observers and can be used to manipulate investigators of UFOs. When an investigator enters a data stream—that is, starts receiving information from a particular source—the investigator may feel constrained to remain in that data stream even when it appears to be unreliable. UFO investigator Jacques Vallee cites a hypothetical case in point. Imagine that someone calls a UFO investigator and says, supposedly in confidence, that a flying saucer will land at a given location the following week; but the UFO does not show up as promised. Despite the unreliability of the information, the recipient may feel he or she must remain in this particular data stream (in other words, stay in contact with the source of the information) for fear of losing contact with that stream. Contact with the source provides some kind of gratification to the investigator, and it does not matter how often the "confidential" source is in error, provided that the source continues to pass along interesting stories, Vallee explains.

See also HOAXES; RUMORS; VALLEE, JACQUES.

Day the Earth Stood Still, The One of the most famous science fiction films, released in 1951 by 20th Century Fox, *The Day the Earth Stood Still* concerns the fictional arrival of an extraterrestrial visitor in Washington, D.C. The visitor, Klaatu (played by Michael Rennie), emerges from a flying saucer, accompanied by a giant humanoid robot named Gort. Klaatu has come to warn the people of Earth that their aggressive way of life, combined with the destructive power of nuclear weaponry, poses a threat to interplanetary peace and stability and will not be tolerated. Klaatu is shot immediately upon arrival. Taken to a hospital, he escapes and lives for a while in Washington under the assumed name of Mr. Carpenter, as the armed forces hunt for him. He returns briefly to the spaceship at one point to arrange a demonstration of his power, by stopping machinery all around the globe. Eventually, he is betrayed and shot again, this time fatally. Gort the robot retrieves Klaatu's body, carries it into the spacecraft and brings Klaatu back to life. Klaatu delivers a final warning to the people of Earth—renounce violence or be destroyed—and then departs with the robot in his saucer.

The motion picture was one of the first to deal with the UFO phenomenon and did so in a more subtle and intelligent way than many other films in the science fiction genre. The film also incorporates many elements of close-encounter reports that would become commonplace years later, including a humanoid robot and the spacecraft's ability to halt the operation of machinery. There is also an abduction scene in which a young widow who befriends Klaatu is seized by the robot and taken into the spacecraft, where she witnesses Klaatu's return to life. (Klaatu explains to her that the robot does not have the power of life and death. That power, Klaatu says, is reserved for what he calls the "Almighty Spirit." What she has just witnessed is merely a technique that can restore life for an indeterminate period.) The saucer's interior, an oval or circular room with a cot or table on which Klaatu's body is placed, resembles what various "abductees" have mentioned seeing inside alleged spacecraft during their abductions. Even Klaatu's vague reference to the "Almighty Spirit" has parallels in many reports of contact with extraterrestrials.

The film also starred Patricia Neal, Hugh Marlowe and Sam Jaffe, and was directed by Robert Wise. The screenplay by Edmund North was based on Harry Bates's short story "Farewell to the Master."

See also ABDUCTIONS; ENCOUNTER PHENOMENA; MOTION PICTURES; PRECEDENTS; ROBOTS.

deals UFO lore includes numerous stories of "deals" allegedly arranged between imagined extraterrestrials and the United States government to allow the aliens to abduct and monitor individuals in return for supplying extraterrestrial technology to the government. According to one version of this story, animal mutilations were permitted as a part of the "deal," allowing the extraterrestrials to extract valuable enzymes or hormones from the animals' bodies. One such "deal" is said to have been concluded between extraterrestrials and United States authorities around 1970. Among UFO enthusiasts, it is also thought that "deals" with the aliens and governments on Earth include permission for the visitors to steal genetic material from humans, in the form of ova or semen extracted from alleged abductees.

There is no solid evidence for such fanciful tales of "deals," and in any case the alleged rationale for such pacts does not bear close examination. As various commentators have pointed out, a species capable of interstellar flight probably would have no need to reach any kind of agreement with a terrestrial government to carry out operations of the kinds described here; more likely, the aliens would be in a position simply to take what they desired, with no concern for the government's views. (The "ocean liner analogy" sometimes is used to illustrate this principle: would an ocean liner's captain take time to negotiate a treaty with the monarch of a tiny island his ship happened to pass? Probably not.) Also,

the postulated need for the aliens to extract biological materials from animals on Earth is scarcely believable. Humans—supposedly at a much lower stage of technological development than space-traveling extraterrestrials—can synthesize complex organic molecules without great difficulty. Presumably, the aliens' technology would be much more sophisticated and capable of synthesizing organic chemicals of great complexity. Why, then, would the alleged extraterrestrials need to visit Earth on such a mission? Such arguments are strong evidence against the kind of "deals" described above, although such speculations probably will continue for the indefinite future.

See also ABDUCTIONS; ANIMALS, UFOS AND; CONSPIRACY THEORIES; GENETIC MANIPULATION; TECHNOLOGY.

deaths Although most reported UFO sightings involve no bodily harm to the witness or witnesses, numerous deaths have been reported or presumed in connection with UFO encounters. U.S. Air Force Captain Thomas Mantell, for example, was killed in the crash of his jet interceptor while investigating an alleged UFO sighting; pilot Frederick Valentich was lost along with his private aircraft during an apparent encounter with a UFO over the Bass Straits between Australia and Tasmania; and the Kinross incident involved the disappearance of a military jet sent up from a base in Michigan to investigate a UFO over Lake Superior. UFO investigator Jacques Vallee has studied reports of alleged UFO-related deaths in South America, notably the Morro de Vintem incident and a number of other reports from Brazil. In the Amazon basin, box-like UFOs called "chupas," equipped with bright lights resembling automobile headlamps, have been implicated in certain mysterious deaths of hunters.

See also BRAZIL; CHUPAS; KINROSS INCIDENT; MANTELL INCIDENT; VALENTICH CASE; VALLEE, JACQUES.

debunkers Some commentators on the UFO phenomenon have taken such a critical view of it, specifically by attributing most or all UFO reports to already known geophysical and technological phenomena such as clouds and aircraft, that they are known as "debunkers." The debunkers generally reject, or at least are skeptical of, the hypothesis that UFOs represent a manifestation of extraterrestrial intelligence. The debunking mentality also is inclined to consign some UFO reports, such as abductions, to categories including hoaxes and hallucinations. Among the most prominent debunkers in the history of the UFO phenomenon are American aerospace journalist Philip Klass, University of Colorado professor Dr. Edward Condon and Harvard University professor Donald Menzel.

See also CONDON REPORT; EXTRATERRESTRIAL HYPOTHESIS; HOAXES; KLASS, PHILIP; MENZEL, DONALD.

deception Many students of the UFO phenomenon have noted the important role that deception plays in it. Disinformation appears to be as common as reliable information in the UFO phenomenon and occurs on several levels. Information supposedly given by "extraterrestrials" commonly has been found to be inaccurate, as in accounts of cities to be found on other planets of our solar system. Alleged contactees may add their own disinformation to accounts of their communications with "aliens." Hoaxers may add to confusion and disinformation by fabricating phony tales of UFO contacts. Private organizations with their own agendas are suspected of disseminating untruths about the UFO phenomenon in an attempt to discredit and discourage investigation. Finally, major disinformation campaigns are said to have been conducted on the official level, with governments allegedly spreading falsehoods about UFOs. Whatever the origin of the many deceptions surrounding the UFO phenomenon, they have made serious research on UFOs needlessly difficult through notoriety and ridicule.

See also ABSURDITY; CONSPIRACY THEORIES; METALOGIC.

deductive-psychological effect UFO "debunker" Philip Klass describes the deductive-psychological effect as a thought process that presumes an unidentified object is a UFO. This effect, Klass believes, accounts for many instances in which observers mistake a star or planet, such as Mars or Venus, for a UFO. He cites examples including reports from World War II involving U.S. Air Force flight crews on B-29 missions against Japan. The aircraft crews reported that enemy aircraft bearing bright searchlights were following them, to direct their lights on the B-29s and make the bombers easier for Japanese interceptors to see and attack. Some gunners actually tried, unsuccessfully, to shoot down the searchlight planes. Later the searchlight aircraft were identified as the planet Venus. Klass also cites another case from his own experience, of a woman who related how she and her husband had been pursued by a UFO while driving. As they drove toward the UFO, the woman said, it moved away from them; when they stopped, the UFO also appeared to halt; and when they turned to go home, the UFO followed them, always maintaining the same distance from them. The alleged UFO in this case was the planet Mars, transformed by the deductive-psychological effect into a UFO. Klass adds that the deductive-psychological effect can combine with the "autokinetic effect," in which a stationary light source is imagined to be moving, to produce the illusion of a moving UFO.

See also AUTOKINETIC EFFECT.

Delarof incident, Aleutian Islands, Alaska, United States In March 1945, sailors aboard the transport *Delarof* reportedly watched as a dark, spherical UFO arose from the ocean, circled their ship and finally flew away. This incident is one of many involving sightings of UFOs that rise from the ocean or from other bodies of water.

See also AQUATIC OBJECTS.

Del Rio incident, Texas, United States Rumors have circulated about a saucer crash and recovery of an "extraterrestrial" body or bodies from a site in Mexico just across the border from Del Rio in 1950. This story resembles rumors concerning the so-called Roswell incident.

See also CRASHES; ROSWELL INCIDENT; RUMORS.

demonology Numerous parallels have been noted between UFO-related phenomena and alleged manifestations of demonic activity. Some students of the UFO phenomenon, such as the American-born Russian Orthodox theologian Father Seraphim Rose, have gone so far as to say that certain UFO encounter cases actually represent the activity of evil spirits. Although this hypothesis is beyond proof, at least for the moment, the similarities between the UFO phenomenon and incidents from the literature on demonology are impressive. For example, temperature effects like those reported in many UFO encounter incidents—specifically, an intense perception of cold—are elements also of numerous reports of contact with demons. As the Devil is described in the Bible as a liar and the "father of lies," the beings mentioned in UFO encounter cases often practice deception. Moreover, the UFO phenomenon in its entirety is characterized by multiple levels of deception, as investigator Jacques Vallee has commented. Unpleasant odors, another widely reported feature of UFO encounter cases, figure also in reports of demonic visitations. "Contactee" Albert Bender, for one, described a smell of sulfur in the presence of the extraterrestrials he claimed to have met. Other traits thought to be common to alleged extraterrestrials and evil spirits are telepathy; the ability to appear in various shapes, to fly through the air at great speed and to make themselves invisible; a tradition of appearing in fiery, airborne, "chariots" virtually identical to modern descriptions of luminous UFOs; and an aversion to things associated with the name and person of Christ, including the sign of the cross. Messages allegedly delivered by certain "extraterrestrials" appear to be attempts at undermining belief in Christ's divinity; Bender, again, reported an extensive message from an "exalted one"—supposedly a member of the aliens' ruling class—denying Christ's divinity and resurrection.

The alleged parallels between demonic activity and UFO encounter reports are especially pronounced in the literature on sexual encounters. "Extraterrestrials" frequently are said to perform forced sexual acts with abductees in such cases. These acts are essentially identical with the reported behavior of incubi and succubi, evil spirits said to be capable of having sexual intercourse with humans. As in accounts of diabolical possession, "aliens" in abduction reports are said to exhibit intense interest in the human reproductive and excretory systems.

Some commentators have seen in the modern UFO phenomenon a fulfillment of biblical prophecies that the Antichrist, the evil world ruler expected to arise in the years immediately before the anticipated return of Christ, would call down "fire from heaven." A similar fulfillment of prophecy has been seen in the biblical prophecy that "signs and wonders" in the skies would precede the Antichrist's coming and the subsequent end of this age. Such speculations form part of a large literature, much of it written by evangelical Protestants, on the alleged role of UFOs in such prophecies. Some authors have suggested that the Antichrist might arrive in a UFO. More subtle interpretations of the parallels between UFOs and biblical prophecy point out that messages supposedly delivered by "extraterrestrials" appear to encourage a syncretic belief system that (certain authors argue) could serve to prepare unbelieving humankind to accept the Antichrist as lord and master. Some authors also see significance in the confluence of numerous occult beliefs and practices, such as "channeling," with the UFO phenomenon in our time. Believers in the diabolical origins of occultism have suggested that UFOs and occultism may constitute part of the syncretic faith expected to make the Antichrist's advent possible. It should be emphasized, however, that much of the prophetic literature in the Bible remains mysterious and open to many different interpretations, in which UFOs are only one of many elements.

See also ABDUCTIONS; ANGELS; ANTICHRIST; BENDER MYSTERY; BIBLE, ALLEGED UFOS IN THE; BLAVATSKY, HELENA PETROVNA; CHANNELING; CHRIST AND CHRISTIANITY; COMMUNICATIONS; CROWLEY, ALEISTER; CYPRIAN THE FORMER SORCERER, SAINT; ENCOUNTER PHENOMENA; INCUBI AND SUCCUBI; MARTIN OF TOURS, SAINT; MESSAGES; MOTOVILOV INCIDENT; OCCULTISM; ODORS; RELIGION, UFOS AND; ROSE, FATHER SERAPHIM; SEXUAL ENCOUNTERS; SHAMANISM; SYNCRETISM; TEMPERATURE EFFECTS; VALENS INCIDENT; VALLEE, JACQUES.

Devil's footprints   On the morning of February 8, 1855, residents of the village of Topsham in Devon, England, reportedly found a curious set of tracks in the snow that had fallen during the night. The tracks are said to have resembled the marks of tiny horseshoes arrayed in single file and appeared to have been made by heat rather than by the weight of an animal. The prints allegedly were found along an erratic path some 40 miles long. According to descriptions, the single-file arrangement of the tracks was not their only curious spatial feature; at one location, the tracks were seen on both sides of a wall, although snow on top of the wall had not been disturbed. Elsewhere, the tracks allegedly led up to a haystack, then continued on the opposite side of the haystack, without any sign than an animal had climbed the haystack itself. Various explanations for this phenomenon were advanced, ranging from an animal hopping on one foot to an escaped balloon dragging the ground, but without notable success. In the absence of any better explanation, the strange prints were attributed to diabolical activity and went down in history as the case of the "Devil's footprints." This incident features in the case of the "Allende letters," in which the U.S. Office of Naval Research received an annotated copy of Morris Jessup's book *The Case for the UFO*. One annotation in the book explains that the "footprints" were made when something called the "Measure-Marker" was left idling by accident.

See also ALLENDE LETTERS.

dimensions   Much discussion of UFOs and their operation involves the physics of multiple dimensions. The three dimensions familiar to everyone are those of length, width and height. The fourth dimension is time, through which the three-dimensional world moves. It has been suggested that UFOs represent "time machines" that visit our world and era after traveling backward through the fourth dimension from some point or points in our future, or perhaps forward from our distant past. Such an explanation would account for the reported ability of certain UFOs to "materialize" and "dematerialize" in a given location, without visibly traveling to that location from somewhere else. There is no solid evidence for such activity, however, and therefore speculation about "time-traveling" UFOs appears to be completely unsubstantiated.

See also TIME TRAVEL.

discs   The classic "flying saucer" is a disc ranging in diameter from perhaps three to more than 100 feet. Many reports describe such a disc as looking like a lens, convex on both sides, or like two dinner plates inverted atop each other. The disc may have a hemispherical or cylindrical "cabin" on top, and sometimes on the bottom as well. Apparent antennae or other protuberances, such as landing legs, may be reported also. Some students of the UFO phenomenon have tentatively classified certain small discs (up to perhaps 30 feet in diameter, and presumably manned) as scout ships, or "vimanas," according to one UFO classification system based on the Sanskrit language. It has been suggested that some discoid UFOs may be short-range "scout craft" or "shuttlecraft" carried about much larger "mother ships" comparable in function to aircraft carriers. Discoid UFOs are said to have a wide variety of characteristics. They may be brightly luminous, or have a dull metallic luster; their hulls may appear seamless, or show clearly visible seams between plates; and they may have prominent portholes, or appear windowless. In some cases, transparent "bubble" canopies have been reported seen, with humanoid occupants visible inside.

The disc or lens shape has a symbolic meaning, according to psychologist Carl Jung. He suggested that the discoid shape attributed to many UFOs represented a vision of completeness, as symbolized by the shape of the circle.

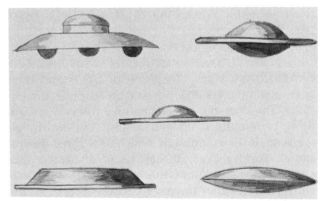

Discoid saucers, seen here in profile, are the Adamski saucer (top left), Saturn shape (top right), domed disc (center), pie pan (bottom left), and lens (bottom right). (D. Ritchie)

See also CIGARS; JUNG, CARL GUSTAV; MANDALA; SANSKRIT; VIMANA; VUNU.

dissociative states   Also known as "dissociative phenomena," these psychological conditions are part of a continuum extended between normal mental health and multiple personality, and have been proposed as possible explanations for the experiences of certain alleged UFO abductees. A dissociative state also has been proposed as the explanation for the "visions" of the celebrated medium Helene Smith, who claimed to have relayed images of a civilization to be found on Mars.

See also SMITH, HELENE.

divining rod   This implement, which sometimes consists merely of a forked stick held in both hands, has been used for many years in an occult exercise known as "water witching." A pronounced downward motion of the tip of the stick is said to indicate the presence of water underground, near the surface. Such devices also have been used to search for buried treasure. In the late 20th century, a device similar to the divining rod has been introduced to UFO studies, notably in the former Soviet Union. In a procedure called "biolocation," a looped wire, equivalent to a divining rod, is used to search for areas that UFOs are thought to have visited.

See also BIOLOCATION; OCCULTISM; RUSSIA; VORONEZH SIGHTINGS.

Dogon mystery   Widely circulated in the 1970s, the Dogon "mystery" is part of UFO lore and concerns the alleged astronomical knowledge of the Dogon, an African people living in Mali. Dogon lore was said to include a detailed knowledge of the Sirius star system. This information was supposed to be so accurate, yet to have been part of Dogon tradition for so long, that "ancient astronauts"—extraterrestrials visiting Earth in the distant past—were invoked as the explanation for the Dogons' knowledge. Dogon tradition also was said to include an account of an "ark" or vessel, reminiscent of a modern spacecraft or aircraft, arriving from the sky. Close study of Dogon traditions, however, revealed that the "ark" of legend actually was said to be a bridge or arch: something quite different from a flying machine. The Dogon model of Sirius also was found to be deficient in essential information about the Sirius system, such as the number of objects in the system. After careful investigation, the Dogon knowledge of Sirius has been attributed to contact with Western visitors in the early 20th century, because such contact did occur then, and because the

Dogon model of the system is consistent with what Western astronomers knew of Sirius at that time.

See also ANCIENT ASTRONAUTS; ASTRONOMY; HOMEWORLDS.

Douglas incident, Argentina   The close-encounter report of Eugenio Douglas on October 12, 1963, involves many commonly cited elements of such encounters. While driving during a rainstorm between Monte Maiz and Isla Verde, Argentina, Douglas reportedly saw a single, extremely bright light on the road in front of him. Then the light vanished. He stopped his truck and got out to investigate. Reportedly, he saw a circular UFO approximately 35 feet high, with a metallic appearance. From the object emerged three very large humanoids, described as being more than 12 feet tall and wearing what appeared to be headpieces with antennae on them.

A beam of red light shone on him and allegedly burned him. He fired several time at the tall entities with a revolver and fled on foot to Monte Maiz for help. The red light, accompanied by a sharp odor, allegedly pursued him to the village and caused street lights there to change color, to green and purple. Douglas sought help at a house where candles were burning indoors. As Douglas arrived, the candle flames reportedly changed color to a greenish hue.

After Douglas proceeded to the police station, his burns were examined and were found to be consistent with exposure to ultraviolet radiation. The police allegedly said they had been informed about the mysterious color changes but had attributed the effect to problems at a power plant. Extremely large footprints allegedly were found in mud near the site of the encounter but were later obliterated by rain. The encounter on the highway, and the disagreeable odor, large humanoids, huge footprints, mysterious ray and burns are all widely reported elements of UFO close-encounter cases.

One peculiar detail of this case, UFO investigator Jacques Vallee pointed out, was the color change reported in the candle flames at the house Douglas visited. According to Vallee, it is difficult to explain that effect as a result of problems with a local power plant, if one presumes the change in the flames' color was not merely an illusion.

Another curious element of this case involves the character of Douglas's burns and the color of the beam of light that allegedly struck him. Although his burns were described as resembling those caused by ultraviolet light, the beam was described as red. This would appear to be a discrepancy, because ultraviolet radiation is found toward the opposite end of the visual and near-visual spectrum from red wavelengths.

See also BODILY EFFECTS; ENCOUNTER PHENOMENA.

Dover demon   An encounter case with a strong similarity to reports of humanoids associated with UFO sightings, the Dover demon incidents occurred in 1977 near Dover, Massachusetts. The first encounter with the so-called demon occurred on the evening of May 21 when three male teenagers were driving along a road. The headlights reportedly shone on a humanoid figure three-to-four feet in height, with a large head, slender body, and long, thin limbs and digits. The skin was allegedly rough in texture and the color of a peach. The being was seen along a stone wall near the road, at about 20 feet distance. The sighting is said to have lasted for only several seconds. Only one of the young men actually reported seeing the entity; his companions had not noticed it. Although the single witness was frightened, the young men returned to the site for a second look; but they found no trace of the mysterious being. That same night, another young man walking along a road within a mile of the aforementioned encounter site saw a being similar to the big-headed entity approach him on the road, then scurry into the woods when challenged. His description of the being was essentially the same as that given by the earlier witness. The following night, yet another encounter with the Dover demon, as the being came to be known, took place when a teenage boy and girl, driving at around midnight, reported passing within several feet of the being. Both witnesses saw the entity, although the girl appears to have had the clearer view of it. She described essentially the same being that was seen by the earlier witnesses.

A hoax is possible in this case, but there is no proof of such. The description of the Dover demon matches that of many another nocturnal, big-headed, spindly limbed humanoid in UFO encounter stories, although there appears to have been no mention of UFO activity associated with the Dover demon sightings.

See also HUMANOIDS.

dreamland   See AREA 51.

drop-in communicator   An occult phenomenon, the drop-in communicator is thought to be an unknown spiritual being that appears without warning during a seance or other such event. The alleged being may communicate through automatic speech or automatic writing. UFO lore contains numerous accounts of communications with "extraterrestrials" similar to drop-in communicators.

See also AUTOMATIC WRITING; BENDER MYSTERY; COMMUNICATIONS; OCCULTISM; WORTH, PATIENCE.

Dr. X incident, France   This case involves a close encounter that reportedly occurred on the night of November 2, 1968. A physician, Dr. X, was awakened at around 4:00 A.M. by the crying of his young son, whose was about 14 months old. When Dr. X went to the boy's room, the doctor observed flashes of light coming from outside. The child noticed them too and pointed toward the window. Dr. X went out onto the balcony to see what was happening. He saw two identical discs, oriented horizontally. Each disc was silver-white on top and the color of the setting sun on the bottom, and had both a tall vertical antenna on top and a shorter horizontal antenna on the side. Using familiar landmarks, the doctor was able to estimate the size of the discs at about 200 feet in diameter and 50 feet in thickness. The discs were about 700 feet from the doctor's house. Soon the discs joined to form a single UFO that moved toward Dr. X. The object directed a beam of white light at the doctor. Then with a loud noise, the object vanished. It left behind pale material similar to cotton candy, which the wind carried away. An object like a wire emerged from the object as the UFO vanished. The "wire" flew upward and exploded in the manner of a fireworks display. Shaken, the doctor went back inside and found that two injuries to his body—an injury to his foot, inflicted by accident three days before the sighting while chopping wood, and a war wound from his service in Algeria—had been healed by some mysterious process. Later, the doctor exhibited a red, triangular discoloration around his navel. A similar discoloration appeared on the body of his young son. This phenomenon occurred again years afterward.

Poltergeist activity occurred in the house after this incident. Dr. X also reported meetings with a mysterious man, described as tall and having blue eyes and brown hair, who tutored him in paranormal phenomena and subjected him to experiences including time travel and teleportation. Dr. X referred to this individual as Mr. Bied. On one occasion, Mr. Bied reportedly showed Dr. X strange landscapes on a road that the doctor knew did not exist. Once, Mr. Bied visited Dr. X's home, accompanied by a small humanoid who did not speak but seemed keenly ob-

servant. Another curious incident reportedly involved Mr. Bied. One day, as Dr. X and his wife were preparing to receive guests for lunch, the doctor said he was going outside to move the car out of the sunshine. When inside the car, Dr. X felt the urge to drive to town, where he encountered Mr. Bied and was told that the two of them had to take a trip. The next thing Dr. X knew, he was in Paris. Dr. X called his wife from Paris and then found himself back home, bewildered over what had happened.

The Dr. X incident helps to place close encounters with UFOs on a continuum of paranormal phenomena such as teleportation and poltergeist activity.

See also BODILY EFFECTS; HUMANOIDS; POLTERGEIST; TELEPORTATION.

dwarves   In European mythology, dwarves were said to be small, long-nosed, bearded humanoids who lived underground and engaged in mining. Beings similar to dwarves are reported seen in many UFO close-encounter cases. In some cases, the entities resemble the dwarves of mythology in numerous details, down to their beards and prominent noses. Some dwarves described in UFO lore, however, may differ greatly from the classical "dwarfish" set of characteristics. "Hairy dwarves," like miniature versions of the legendary Bigfoot, for example, have been reported in the UFO literature. In general, the expression "dwarf" in UFO lore applies to a variety of small humanoids.

See also BIGFOOT; HUMANOIDS.

Dyfed, Wales, United Kingdom   The Dyfed "window" has been the site of numerous UFO sightings, including one of the most prominent "waves" in British history, starting in February 1977 and lasting for several weeks. This wave included a significant close-encounter report on April 19, 1977, in which humanoid figures with unusually long arms were reported seen near a subterranean atomic bomb shelter. There is reason to believe, however, that at least some of the UFO reports from this area actually represent sightings of birds, which live in great numbers in outcrops of rock along the coast.

See also BIRDS; UNITED KINGDOM, UFOS IN; WALES; WAVES.

Dzyan   See BLAVATSKY, HELENA PETROVNA.

E

earth lights This phenomenon, also known as "spook lights," consists of mysterious balls or spots of luminosity that are reported seen in various remote areas of the world and bear a strong resemblance to certain kinds of UFOs. Because the lights are often seen near power lines and transmitting towers, they have been dismissed in many cases as luminous electrical phenomena. Earth lights, however, also allegedly are sighted near other, non-electrical facilities, such as railroad tracks, highways and remote buildings. In the manner of UFOs, the lights appear in a variety of colors and may change color while under observation; tend to be seen only in remote locations; appear to react by vanishing or retreating when subjected to noise or light, as from a flashlight or automobile headlights; and are associated with a hum or buzzing sound. Earth lights have been reported seen in the United States, notably near Joplin, Missouri, and in the Brown Mountains of North Carolina. The lights also have been reported seen in many other locations around the world, including the Himalayas in Asia and megalithic sites in Europe. Many explanations have been suggested for earth lights. According to one hypothesis, the lights merely represent vehicle lights. Another hypothesis is that the lights are related somehow to seismic activity or earthquakes.

See also EARTHQUAKE LIGHTS; MARFA LIGHTS; SPOOK LIGHTS.

earthquake lights Postulated as a possible natural explanation of some UFO sightings, earthquake lights are believed to be electrical phenomena, similar to ball lightning, that occur in the atmosphere near the epicenters of imminent earthquakes. (The "epicenter" is the point on the earth's surface directly above the underground center, or "focus," of the earthquake.) Earthquake lights are described as luminous spheres about the size of basketballs or large melons and may be orange or blue-white in color or have a greenish hue. Many UFO sightings in New Mexico in 1951 and 1952 were reported within 60 miles of the epicenters of three moderately powerful earthquakes that occurred only a few months after the sightings. After sightings with clear astronomical sources such as planets were eliminated, some 150 sightings on the list remained, and about 80 of these were concentrated in locality and time around the epicenters of the aforementioned earthquakes. The sightings were reportedly found to occur closer to the epicenter as the date of an earthquake drew near. Earthquake lights allegedly have occurred in other areas of high-intensity earthquake activity in the United States, including the Cascade Mountains of Oregon and Washington state; Texas; and the New Madrid fault zone, which runs along part of the Mississipi River valley near Memphis and was the site of a series of extremely powerful earthquakes during the winter of 1811–1812.

See also AMBER GAMBLER; BALL LIGHTNING.

earthquakes Some prominent UFO "windows," or areas of numerous reported sightings, are located in areas of frequent and/or powerful earthquake activity, such as California in the United States. What, if anything, links seismic activity to frequency of UFO sightings is not known for certain. It has been suggested, however, that electrical charges in the atmosphere in earthquake-prone areas may be involved in generating luminous atmospheric phe-

Earthquakes, shown here on seismograph recording, have been associated with the UFO phenomenon. (G.A. Mac Donald/U.S. Geological Survey)

nomena commonly identified as UFOs. Another possibility is that flammable methane arises from the Earth's interior in areas of intense earthquake activity and is ignited somehow, so that the gas burns with a glow that is identified as belonging to UFOs. A third hypothesis is based on the association between certain mountain ranges, such as the Rockies in North America and the Andean cordillera in South America, and luminous electrical phenomena such as mountain-top glows. These visible accumulations of static electricity have been observed on mountain peaks in seismically unstable, mountainous areas and may account for some associations between UFOs and earthquakes.

See also EARTHQUAKE LIGHTS; METHANE; MOUNTAIN-TOP GLOWS.

Earth Versus the Flying Saucers

American motion picture, 1956. Starring Hugh Marlowe (who also appeared in the UFO-related film *The Day the Earth Stood Still*) and Joan Taylor, *Earth Versus the Flying Saucers* depicts the invasion of Earth by aliens in large, lens-shaped spacecraft. Abductions play a role in the story. In it, the aliens are defeated by an invention that interferes with the propulsion of their spacecraft. The film is remembered for its spectacular special effects, devised by Ray Harryhausen. Flying saucers are seen falling out of the sky and crashing into prominent landmarks in Washington, D.C. The motion picture was directed by Fred Sears.

See also ABDUCTIONS; MOTION PICTURES.

Easter Island monuments

In the "ancient astronauts" phenomenon of the 1970s, the famous monuments of Easter Island—huge, stylized heads carved from volcanic rock—were cited as evidence of extraterrestrial visitations in ancient times. This interpretation of the giant figures owes much to the writings of Erich von Däniken, who suggested that aliens produced the monuments for their own amusement while stranded on the island. When rescued, the aliens left their unfinished work behind. The islanders tried to finish the project using their own, much inferior technology but soon gave up in frustration and left the monuments uncompleted. Thor Heyerdahl, the explorer who described the Easter Island monuments in his book *Aku-Aku*, issued a rebuttal to von Däniken's interpretation of the monuments. Heyerdahl explained that there was no mystery about the origin of the statues, and that the approximate date and the methods of their construction and erection were known, as was the reason for their existence. The statues, Heyerdahl claimed, were intended as memorials to deceased leaders and were produced in the 17th century A.D. The giant figures were carved from volcanic rock with basalt tools, transported on skids and set upright using a clever system of stone supports. Work on the statues was interrupted by a civil war on Easter Island. In short, advanced extraterrestrial technology was not needed for the statues' production.

See also ANCIENT ASTRONAUTS; PSEUDOSCIENCE; VON DÄNIKEN, ERICH.

Edwards, Frank (1908–1967)

American journalist Frank Edwards, author of two books on flying saucers, did much to popularize the UFO phenomenon in the 1960s. He was notably skeptical of reported abduction cases as well as UFO "debunkers." Edwards cited absurd tales of abductions, including one story in which an "abductee" claimed that Martians had made him a present of a large black dog. Edwards also criticized debunker Philip Klass's suggestion that corona discharges along power lines could be mistaken for UFOs. Edwards claimed to have challenged Klass to produce such a discharge, outside a laboratory, that could be construed as a UFO.

See also ABDUCTIONS; KLASS, PHILIP.

Egryn lights

A series of UFO reports from the British Isles in the winter of 1904–05, the Egryn lights reportedly were associated with one Mrs. Mary Jones, who lived on a farm near Egryn in Wales. Unusual lights allegedly would appear over a chapel where Jones was preaching after receiving a vision. Reporters from London covered the Egryn lights. One reporter from the *Daily Mail* (September 2, 1905) witnessed the appearance, about two miles away from him, of a very bright white light that sparkled in the manner of a diamond. The light would vanish, then reappear in a different location. Soon afterward, another light, this one blood-red, appeared to the same reporter. The mysterious lights are said to have accompanied Jones as she traveled to preaching engagements in other communities. On occasion, the lights reportedly appeared indoors. This phenomenon coincided approximately with reports of mysterious animal deaths in England, including livestock found drained of blood. This coincidence of UFO-like activity and mysterious deaths of livestock is reminiscent of animal mutilations linked tentatively with UFO activity in North America during the 1970s.

See also ANIMALS, UFOS AND.

Eisenhower incident According to one widely circulated rumor, U.S. President Dwight D. Eisenhower was taken on February 20, 1954, to Edwards Air Force Base, Muroc Dry Lake, California, to meet extraterrestrials and to examine their spacecraft being studied there. At the time, the president was visiting a friend's ranch in Palm Springs, California. The president is said to have "disappeared" for some four hours during this visit, then returned. An official explanation of this incident was that Eisenhower had lost the cap on a tooth while eating and had been taken to a local dentist. Although the Eisenhower incident remains merely rumor, it is typical of a substantial body of speculation about collaboration between the United States government and alleged extraterrestrials.

See also CONSPIRACY THEORIES; DEALS.

ejecta UFOs reportedly have dropped liquid or solid material on occasion. This material has included liquid metal, slag, metallic-looking foil, and a lightweight, fibrous substance known as "angel hair." In some cases, the ejecta have originated from "saucers" that were flying in an erratic manner and appeared to be in trouble. The descent of angel hair has been reported widely, notably in the 1954 UFO sightings over Rome. Ejecta also were reported in the Maury Island sightings in the United States in 1947. Samples of ejecta have seldom been recovered and subjected to careful analysis. When analysis has been performed, nothing has been found to prove an extraterrestrial origin for the material.

See also ANGEL HAIR; MAURY ISLAND INCIDENT; ROME INCIDENTS.

E.K. incident This event took place in the life of John Dee, the Elizabethan astrologer and occultist, and bears a strong resemblance to close-encounter cases in later centuries. Dee wrote in his diary on April 3, 1586, that "E.K." (Edward Kelly, a thief with whom Dee associated) was looking at a vineyard one day and saw what appeared to be a gardener at work there. The "gardener," however, at one point ascended in what Dee described as a pillar of fire. Kelly told Dee that an evil spirit appeared to be loose. Dee and Kelly went down to the vineyard and sat there for several minutes. Then Dee saw, under a nearby almond tree, what resembled a sheet of white paper blown to and fro by the wind. He investigated and found lying there three occult books that he said he had burned some days earlier. The books, Dee reported, showed no sign of having been set afire. A few minutes later, the "gardener" reappeared and said, "Kelly, follow me." Kelly departed with the entity, leaving Dee behind. Dee reported that the gardener's feet apparently were about 12 inches above the ground. The being conducted Kelly to a furnace where Dee's aforementioned books had been burned. A bright light shone from within the furnace. The being reached into the furnace and produced still more books. Kelly picked up these books and followed the being (which Dee said moved in a small "fiery cloud") away from the furnace. Kelly delivered the books to Dee, who was still waiting under the almond tree. With some details changed slightly, Dee's account of this incident might be a description of certain close-encounter cases of the 20th century. Dee's report of the humanoid being apparently floating several inches off the ground, and traveling either in a cloud or on a pillar of fire, is reminiscent of UFO contact reports in our own time.

See also DEMONOLOGY; ENCOUNTER PHENOMENA; HUMANOIDS; OCCULTISM.

electrical phenomena There have been numerous attempts to explain UFO sightings as mere misidentifications of natural electrical phenomena, such as ball lightning, in which a luminous ball of plasma may fly through the air and behave in apparently intelligent fashion. UFO debunker Philip Klass argues that ball lightning has been known to pass through a window without breaking the glass and can even display the wide range of colors attributed to certain luminous UFOs. Klass admits that the physics of ball lightning remains mysterious, but he points out that it is widely regarded as a mere phenomenon of atmospheric physics. Klass also argues that certain apparent UFOs actually may be produced by electrical equipment. He cites the case of a brilliant UFO reported seen on shore by crew members on a U.S. Coast Guard cutter off Freeport, Texas, in 1966. The UFO was described as a white glowing object 300 to 500 feet above the ground and reportedly appeared immediately after a brilliant flash of light lit up the sky. The incident accompanied an electrical power failure on shore. Klass says his investigation of the incident revealed that a transformer failed in a violent fashion, exactly at the spot where the UFO was seen. Apparently, a short circuit had caused the transformer's cover to blow off, releasing a ball of luminous plasma that was perceived as a UFO.

Klass also suggests that electrical phenomena may have been responsible for other mysterious sightings that, in the days before the expression "flying saucer" became popular, were attributed to ghosts. He cites the legend of "La Llorna," a tale from Spanish-American folklore concerning a woman who allegedly was cursed to wander on Earth as a ghost after murdering her children. The spectral lady was said to wear a white, flowing gown. La Llorna allegedly made an appearance in Aguilar, Colorado, one October night in 1946. A woman was found in hysterical condition after seeing what she described as a white, luminous object—presumably a ghost—moving along electric power lines. Another witness, recalling the sighting years later, said a white object resembling a woman had appeared near a power line. Klass interprets these reports as sightings of a corona, or luminous plasma, traveling along power lines. This incident took place just before the saucer sighting near Mount Rainier in Washington state in 1947, Klass points out, and so there was no such category in which to report the observed phenomenon. Consequently, the corona was misidentified as a wandering ghost. Had the sighting occurred after 1947, "flying saucer" or "UFO" would have been another possible way of describing it.

Another aspect of electrical phenomena in connection with UFO reports concerns the alleged failure of electrical equipment in the vicinity of UFOs. In the Freeport, Texas, incident mentioned above, lights in houses near the alleged UFO were seen flickering on and off, then went out just before the brilliant flash and the ball of light appeared. If the apparent UFO actually was the result of a transformer failure, then the strange phenomena seen just before the failure are easy to explain. UFO lore also contains numerous reports of automobile engines failing in the presence of UFOs. These incidents have been attributed to electromagnetic effects produced by the UFOs, when the reactions of the driver—specifically, to pull over and stop the car—may have been responsible. Whether or not these effects can be produced by extraterrestrial visitors, it is admitted that causes other than alien spacecraft can make an auto engine cease operating.

See also ARNOLD INCIDENT; ATMOSPHERIC PHENOMENA; KLASS, PHILIP; VEHICLE EFFECTS.

element 115   In UFO lore, this hypothetical element is said to be used in anti-matter reactors to supply power to UFOs. According to this story, element 115, when bombarded with protons, turns into element 116 and then decays, becoming element 115 again and releasing a small amount of anti-matter. This bit of anti-matter supposedly is directed toward a target of ordinary matter, with which it reacts to release energy. The existence of such an element and reactor is, of course, rumor.

See also ANTI-MATTER; RUMORS; TECHNOLOGY.

elementals   In occult lore, elementals are "nature spirits" of a lower order. Descriptions of them and their behavior bear a strong resemblance to certain reports of "extraterrestrials" in UFO encounter cases. Neoplatonic Greeks of the 3rd century A.D. classified elementals on the basis of the four classical elements of nature: earth, air, fire and water. Later scholars added two more categories, one of underground dwellers and another described as the lucifugum, a Latin expression meaning "fly-the-light." If one translates lucifugum as "flying light," it becomes an exact description of many UFOs. Elementals reportedly can appear in humanoid form and are said to be capable of comprehending human speech. Such spirits are believed to manifest themselves in a vast variety of shapes and sizes. This polymorphism is also a characteristic of the UFO phenomenon. Many different configurations of UFOs have been reported, and "extraterrestrials" in UFO encounters have been described as having a great range of sizes and shapes, from tiny, fetus-like humanoids to towering monsters. Some nature spirits have a reputation for mischievous and even hostile behavior. Here again, parallels exist with the UFO phenomenon, in which aliens may seem indifferent to the well-being of humans and even subject humans to torture.

See also DEMONOLOGY; ENCOUNTER PHENOMENA; HUMANOIDS; OCCULTISM; POLYMORPHY; TULPA.

Elidor   The British legend of Elidor (or Elidurus) resembles 20th-century accounts of contacts between humans and "extraterrestrials," although the legend predates the modern UFO phenomenon by some 800 years. An account of the Elidor legend, from a book published in 1850 by British mythologist Thomas Keightley, is worth quoting at length. The text is a translation of Giraldus Cambrensis's *Itinerarium Cambriae*, a story of Giraldus's travels in Wales in the late 12th Century A.D.:

A short time before our days, a circumstance worthy of note occurred in these parts, which Elidurus . . . most strenuously affirmed had befallen himself. When he was a youth of 12 years . . . and was following his literary pursuits, in order to avoid the discipline and frequent stripes inflicted on him by his preceptor, he ran away, and concealed himself under the hollow bank of a river; and, after [he had remained] in that situation for two days, two little men of pygmy stature appeared to him, saying, "If you will come with us, we will lead you into a country full of delights and sports." Assenting, and rising up, he followed his guides through a path, at first subterraneous and dark, into a most beautiful country, adorned with rivers and meadows, woods and plains, but obscure, and not illuminated with the full light of the sun. All the days were cloudy, and the nights extremely dark, on account of the absence of the moon and stars. The boy was brought before the king, and introduced to him in the presence of the court; when, having examined him for a long time, [the king] delivered him to his son, who was then a boy. These men were of the smallest stature, but very well proportioned for their size. They were all fair-haired, with luxuriant hair falling over their shoulders, like that of women. They had horses proportioned to themselves, of the size of greyhounds. They ate neither flesh nor fish, but lived on milk . . . made up into messes with saffron. They never took an oath, for they detested nothing so much as lies. As often as they returned from our upper hemisphere, they reprobated our ambition, infidelities, and inconstancies. They had no religious worship, being only, as it seems, strict lovers and reverers of truth.

The boy frequently returned to our hemisphere, sometimes by the way he had first gone, sometimes by another; at first in company with others, and afterwards alone, and confided his secret only to his mother, declaring to her the manners, nature, and state of that people. Being desired by her to bring a present of gold, with which that region abounded, he stole, while at play with the king's son, [a] golden ball . . . and brought it to his mother in great haste; and when he reached the door of his father's house, but not unpursued, and was entering it in a great hurry, his foot stumbled on the threshold, and, [as he fell] down into the room where his mother was sitting . . . two Pygmies seized the ball, which had dropped from his hand, and departed, spitting at and deriding the boy. On recovering from his fall, confounded with shame, and execrating the evil counsel of his mother, he returned by the usual track to the subterraneous road, but found no appearance of any passage, though he searched for it on the banks of the river for nearly the space of a year. Having been brought back . . . and restored to his right way of thinking and his literary pursuits, he attained in process of time the rank of priesthood. Whenever David the Second, bishop of St. David's, talked to him in his advanced stage of life concerning this event, he could never relate the particulars without shedding tears.

He also had a knowledge of the language of that nation [that is, the aliens], and used to recite words of it he had readily acquired in his younger days. These words . . . were very conformable to the Greek idiom. When they asked for water, they said, Udor udorum, which signifies "Bring water"; for Udor, in their language, as well as in the Greek, signifies water. . . .

The similarities between this legend and modern UFO close-encounter reports are both close and numerous. The boy is approached, in an isolated setting, by small humanoids who offer to conduct him to an alien world more agreeable than this one. The humanoids have long, beautiful hair, in the manner of the space traveler allegedly encountered by George Adamski in the southwestern desert of the United States. The alien land resembles Earth in many ways, but there is a curious quality to the light perceived in the alien country, as well as a difference in the skies and the celestial bodies in them. These discrepancies between our world and that of the aliens give the contactee's experience a degree of "high strangeness," a feature of many UFO contact reports in the 20th century. The young traveler is presented to a being of high rank, as in American UFO "contactee" Albert Bender's reported meeting with the "exalted one" during his visit with alleged extraterrestrials. Also as in the Bender case, the aliens profess no religious beliefs. The aliens make a point of chiding humans for various moral failings, however, just as "extraterrestrials" in modern UFO encounter cases often are said to point out the greed, short-sightedness, violence and rapacity of humankind. The boy visits the aliens repeatedly through some kind of gateway that they maintain between their world and ours. Likewise, modern "contactees" may report repeated visits with extraterrestrials. When the boy attempts to bring back a gold ball as evidence of his visit to the other world, however, the evidence is taken away from him, and he is denied further access to the other country. In similar fashion, alleged material evidence of modern UFO contacts has a way of "disappearing" before skeptical analysts can examine it closely. The aliens in Elidor's account speak a language different from, but translatable into, the contactee's own tongue. In like manner, aliens described in modern UFO contact cases may speak a language distinct from, but similar in many ways to, English or other widely spoken terrestrial languages. In short, the Elidor legend belongs to a tradition of alien-encounter stories that predates but also includes modern stories of visitations by "extraterrestrials."

See also ADAMSKI, GEORGE; BENDER MYSTERY; COMMUNICATIONS; ENCOUNTER PHENOMENA; EVIDENCE; HIGH STRANGENESS; HOMEWORLDS; HUMANOIDS; INTERDIMENSIONAL GATEWAYS; LANGUAGE; RELIGION, UFOS AND; UMMO.

emblems   Insignia and emblems of various kinds have been reported seen on UFOs and on the clothing of their alleged occupants. In the famous Vilvorde sighting, a UFO was reported seen bearing an emblem consisting of a dark circle with a cartoon-like lightning bolt through it. The occult symbol of the winged serpent also has turned up on occasion, as have astrological emblems such as the symbols for the planets Jupiter and Saturn. The significance of such emblems is not entirely clear, although those familiar with occult symbolism tend to emphasize the close connections between occultism and the UFO phenomenon.

See also ASTROLOGY; JUPITER; OCCULTISM; VILVORDE INCIDENT.

emotional responses   One might expect witnesses to a close encounter with a UFO to experience fear, curiosity and wonder; and indeed, these are feelings that many such witnesses report. In many cases, however, emotional responses to alleged UFO encounters are complex and seemingly contradictory. A witness may report feeling both fear of the "extraterrestrials" and a strong desire to accompany them at the same time. A peculiar feeling of peace and contentment may come over the witness, as in the case of French farmer Maurice Masse in the famous Valensole incident. "Abductees" may relate afterward how they were terrified of the alleged aliens during the abduction, yet also persuaded to cooperate with them, on the presumption that the aliens were "good" despite their cold manner and brutal treatment of the abductee. Recollections of emotional responses in such cases must be regarded with skepticism, however, because many alleged recollections are retrieved while the subject is under hypnosis, a notoriously questionable means of extracting information.

See also ABDUCTIONS; ENCOUNTER PHENOMENA; HYPNOSIS; VALENSOLE INCIDENT.

encounter phenomena   This expression covers a wide range of experiences involving UFOs, from sightings of airborne objects at a distance to reported face-to-face contacts between humans and "occupants" of alien "spacecraft." Of greatest interest to most students of the UFO phenomenon is the so-called close encounter, in which an observer witnesses UFO activity, or evidence of it, at close range, perhaps less than 500 feet. Dr. J. Allen Hynek, one of the most celebrated students of UFOs, classified close encounters in three categories:

- Close encounters of the first kind (CEI). Here, a UFO is observed at close range but shows no apparent interaction with the observers or with its environment. The reported object may be spectacular and perform dramatic maneuvers, but it leaves no traces of its presence on the ground or elsewhere, and no contact with occupants of the object is reported.
- Close encounters of the second kind (CEII). In such cases, the UFO reportedly leaves behind visible evidence of its presence, such as scorched grass at a landing site, or interference with electrical equipment. Close encounters of the second kind may involve (for example) frightened domestic animals or the temporary stoppage of automobile engines in the vicinity of the UFO. These experiences can terrify human observers, even when no direct interaction occurs between the observer and the UFO. An interesting pattern has been observed in close encounters of the second kind: the encounters reportedly often occur in the middle of highways.
- Close encounters of the third kind (CEIII). This is perhaps the most famous category of UFO encounter, partly because of the success of a well-known fantasy motion picture with the same title. Hynek defined this category as that which includes reports of "animated" creatures. (Hynek used the word "animated" to cover the possibility that robots or other non-living, but moving, entities might be involved in such sightings.) This kind of encounter is the most puzzling, in part because of the great variety of "animated" figures reported, and in part because of their often inexplicable attributes and behavior. Beings of many different descriptions have been mentioned in UFO reports in this category. Although some of these entities have been described as nonhumanoid (some having the characteristics of robots, or birds, or other nonhuman beings), many are described as humanoid in appearance. Even within this category, however, there is great variation.

Many close-encounter reports describe humanoids with large heads, spindly limbs and huge, dark eyes. A light or other apparatus on the chest may also be reported. (D. Ritchie)

Some "aliens," such as those mentioned by "contactees" George Adamski and Truman Bethurum in the United States in the 1950s, are said to be virtually identical in appearance to humans, although they may be slightly taller or shorter than the average human. In other cases, however, the putative aliens, while still having a basically humanoid body pattern, may be described as small, gray-skinned and hairless; tall, extremely slender, and bald-headed; long-nosed or noseless; or possessed of many other unusual characteristics. Various kinds of clothing are also reported on the "aliens," including long robes, skintight one-piece coveralls, and garb reminiscent of the traditional diver's suit. Large, hairy, ape-like but still humanoid beings (of the "Bigfoot" variety) have also been reported in connection with UFO sightings. In some instances, two witnesses viewing the same "alien" from almost identical viewpoints will provide different descriptions of the being.

The behavior of alleged aliens in CEIII reports is also extremely varied. Sometimes the "visitors" appear friendly, whereas on other occasions their reported behavior is indifferent to humankind or even hostile. Adamski said his visitors from Venus, for example, expressed benevolent intentions toward the people of Earth. On the other hand, famed UFO investigator Jacques Vallee has investigated reports from South America in which UFOs are said to have attacked and killed humans. There are reports in the CEIII literature of UFO "occupants" stepping outside their craft and paralyzing human onlookers by means of a rodlike device, held in the hand of an "alien," that emits a beam of light. Among the most frightening CEIII cases are those in which humans report being taken aboard UFOs and subjected to humiliating and sometimes painful surgical procedures, such as having artifacts embedded in their bodies. The human sexual organs appear to receive considerable attention in such stories; there are numerous accounts of "aliens" under such circumstances examining and probing the genital areas of men and women.

The element of absurdity, as Vallee has pointed out, is prominent in CEIII reports. Many elements of CEIII reports are simply preposterous. There is, for example, a case in which the alien occupants of a UFO allegedly presented a human observer with several pancakes cooked on board their spacecraft. (The pancakes were analyzed later and said to be of "terrestrial origin.")

The vast potential for hoaxes in CEIII reports means that such stories must be regarded most critically. Factors to be considered in evaluating CEIII reports include the credibility of the witness or witnesses (involving factors such as history of hallucinations, demonstrable motive to fabricate a UFO report, etc.); the internal consistency of the report; its consistency with other reports in the same category; and any corroborative information that may be available from other sources, such as eyewitnesses at other locations, or radar observations or photographic records.

Abduction cases, in which humans allegedly are forced to accompany extraterrestrials into their spacecraft and are subjected in some cases to painful bodily examinations, constitute a fourth major category of close-encounter reports and are sometimes called "close encounters of the fourth kind" (CEIV). Such reported encounters, commonly "remembered" while under hypnosis following the alleged incidents, are extremely controversial and have been interpreted in various ways. One interpretation is that such encounter reports represent fantasies based on the subjects' memories of abuse in childhood. Another interpretation is that the reports from alleged abductees are essentially accurate, and that extraterrestrials actually did abduct and, in effect, torture the human witnesses. There is reason to question the veracity of many abduction reports, because the human mind under hypnosis appears capable of inventing stories similar to widely publicized accounts of UFO abductions. Here again, hoaxes are a strong possibility in many instances, and the CEIV phenomenon must always be viewed with the potential for hoaxes in mind.

Early in the evolution of the modern UFO phenomenon, certain elements in close-encounter cases appeared that would become commonplace in UFO lore over the next several decades:

- UFO sightings commonly are reported in "waves," meaning large numbers of sightings reported in a single nation or region within a period of several days, weeks or months. Some observers believe that the waves generally proceed from east to west and occur at an average interval of about one and a half years. Certain waves have been correlated with astronomical phenomena such as oppositions of the planet Mars, when Mars and Earth are nearest each other and Mars stands out prominently in the night sky.
- The visitors are humanoid, although they may differ from humans in some particular features, such as the shape of eyes or ears.
- They appear repeatedly to a single person in an isolated location, usually at night.
- Material evidence of the visitors' presence on Earth turns out to be either dubious or nonexistent.
- Communication between humans and aliens often is said to involve telepathy, using either words or images.
- Elements commonly reported in messages from alleged aliens include warnings of great dangers and anticipated cataclysms facing humankind, such as the threat of global nuclear warfare; reassurance of the aliens' concern for the welfare of Earth's people; an invitation to trust the aliens' good intentions; and advice to adopt a vaguely defined but evidently syncretic belief system with numerous Hinduistic elements.
- The alleged technology of the visitors, especially the configuration of their "spacecraft," tends to vary markedly from one encounter report to another. Overall, however, technology described in such reports tends to reflect the technological advancement of humankind at the time of the sightings.
- Much of what the visitors say is disinformation or misinformation, or simply ridiculous.
- There is a strong metaphysical component to these stories—dealing with the visitors' relationship to God, in many cases—but the visitors' beliefs are not explained in a coherent fashion. Alternatively, such explanations may seem coherent (up to a point, at least) but conflict strongly with elements of traditional Judeo-Christian faith. The explanations may be delivered by impressive beings such as the "exalted one" who allegedly addressed "contactee" Albert Bender. In one special category of such incidents, apparitions resembling traditional religious imagery, such as "sightings" of the Virgin Mary, may be reported, although messages delivered in such encounters may differ greatly in content from traditional Christian doctrine.
- The "aliens" invite the trust of humans, yet lie to them, then offer no explanation for their mendacity.
- The visitors are averse to being photographed and (in certain cases at least) to being seen in bright light. They also tend to have two-syllable names.
- The visitors say they have no trouble adapting to environmental conditions on Earth, but they offer no clear explanation of how they do so.
- The visitors' activities often seem curiously pointless. The crew of an alleged spacecraft may be seen doing little except strolling outside it or casually examining terrestrial flora.
- The speech, behavior and demeanor of the aliens are filled with inconsistencies. For instance, the visitors express benevolent intentions but apparently do nothing to protect the contactees from bodily injury or from damage to clothing.
- The contactees' stories sound fantastic, but not in the manner one might expect of genuine fantasy. Sometimes detail is lacking where one would expect a human storyteller to provide it in abundance. When contactees do provide detail, it is likely to be contradictory or absurd.
- Strange interference with perceptions may be reported. For example, the witness may claim to have entered a bizarre landscape unlike any ever seen before, or recall later that all noise was suppressed in the vicinity during a close encounter.
- The technology of the alleged alien spacecraft may appear to embody serious inconsistencies. It is an article of faith within the UFO phenomenon that UFOs, if they actually are extraterrestrial spacecraft, must have some means of neutralizing gravitation and inertia in order to perform the feats of flight attributed to them. Yet many UFOs also are said to emit great blasts of flame similar

to the exhaust plumes of rockets, a much less advanced form of propulsion than any anti-gravity system. In certain UFO "crash" reports, such inconsistencies are even greater. It has been argued that rough weather over the southwestern deserts of the United States might have caused the crash of an extraterrestrial spacecraft in the late 1940s. Yet terrestrial aircraft of that time—supposedly much less advanced in technology than any extraterrestrial spacecraft visiting Earth—could withstand a certain degree of stormy weather with ease. Such examples of inconsistencies could be multiplied indefinitely from the literature on UFOS.

- Interference with communications, especially radio messages, is another classic element of UFO encounter stories. The radio in an automobile or truck may make strange sounds or fail completely during an alleged UFO encounter.
- Temperature effects, notably a sensation of cold, are commonly reported.
- Psychological and bodily effects, such as anxiety, nausea and headaches, may be reported in connection with a close encounter. The contactee may come away from the encounter depressed, disoriented or agitated. In some cases the contactee may undergo a marked change of personality or become convinced that he or she has a "mission" to perform on Earth.
- Witnesses may have prior involvement with the occult or with religious cult activities.
- Close-encounter cases may involve a fantasy-prone personality or "encounter-prone personality" who possesses certain traits consistent with a tendency to report encounters with extraterrestrials or other fantastic beings.
- Encounters commonly occur when the subject is entering or emerging from sleep.
- Contactees often express paranoid convictions, such as belief in a postulated "silence group" bent on suppressing the "truth" about the UFO phenomenon. Elaborate conspiracy theories have abounded within the UFO phenomenon for decades.

Later in the evolution of the UFO phenomenon, some of these elements diminished in importance in report of close encounters, whereas other elements became more prominent. Warnings against the danger of nuclear warfare, for example, became less outstanding in UFO lore after the 1950s and were supplanted by warnings about deterioration of the Earth's natural environment and consequent "eco-catastrophe." In the 1970s and 1980s, messages delivered in alleged UFO encounters tended to place strong emphasis on the spiritual state of humankind and to promote specifically a syncretic belief system with an abundance of Hinduistic components. At the same time, the character of many reported UFO encounters changed from one of peaceful contact to that of brutal mistreatment of human subjects, up to and including rape. Alleged extraterrestrials in such accounts appeared to show particular interest in violating abductees in the genital and anal regions. These reports resemble ancient accounts of sexual activity by incubi and succubi, evil spirits said to be capable of having sexual relations with humans

Hoaxes have been part of UFO encounter phenomena since the first "flying saucer" sightings immediately after World War II, and have become more elaborate and sophisticated over the years. Crude early hoaxes involving homebuilt "spacecraft" have evolved into highly detailed encounter stories involving the alleged retrieval of "buried" abduction memories by hypnosis. (This is not to say that all cases involving "memories" retrieved through hypnosis are necessarily hoaxes, but merely to say that the potential for hoaxes in such cases is considerable, and the credibility of many such reports has failed to withstand close examination. Therefore, hoaxes remain a possibility that any student of UFO encounter phenomena must consider at all times when investigating individual cases and the phenomenon as a whole.)

UFO lore is tied closely to mythology, both modern and ancient. UFO sightings in the 20th century contain, and have been used to "explain," various elements of mythology from ancient times. Indeed, it has been said that UFO lore in this century has been involved in the reworking of virtually all of human mythology. The widely publicized "ancient astronauts" phenomenon of the late 1960s and early 1970s, based on the assumption that myths of "gods" and "goddesses" were reports of visitations from extraterrestrial space travelers in ancient times, is a familiar example of such "reworked" lore in the UFO phenomenon.

There is no universal agreement on the purpose behind UFO encounters, nor even that such a purpose exists. Some students of UFO encounters have suggested, however, that such encounters are a mechanism for redirecting human belief systems. Vallee, for one, is a prominent advocate of this interpretation and has described UFOs as a "control system" for human belief. Several elements of the UFO phenomenon have been isolated as possible elements of such a control system, including the warning of impending calamity on Earth; the reassurance of help from friendly "aliens"; and admonitions to trust the aliens' good intentions and advice even when their alleged behavior appears hostile and communications from them are nonsensical. In particular, the absurdity of many reported close-encounter cases has been cited as a possible contributor to a control system for human belief. The human mind is perplexed by such evidence and, in straining to interpret the UFO phenomenon, becomes "malleable" and thus receptive to whatever explanations eventually may be provided.

Who might be responsible for instituting such a control system, and who might benefit from it, are also topics of considerable debate. One view is that no one is responsible for, nor is coordinating, the UFO phenomenon; rather, it represents a largely unrelated set of phenomena that have roots in human imagination and the will to believe. Rejecting this interpretation, some students of the UFO phenomenon envision instead a secular conspiracy to alter human beliefs through staged UFO encounters in an effort to unify the world under a single government, with resultant benefits for a tiny ruling minority. Consistent with this interpretation, but also spiritual and eschatological in character, is the opinion (expressed by the Orthodox Christian theologian Father Seraphim Rose, among others) that UFOs represent a diabolical deception intended to alter human belief systems in ways favorable for the anticipated advent and reign of the Antichrist at the end of this age of human history.

UFO encounter phenomena once were viewed as possible visitations to Earth by intelligent extraterrestrials in material spacecraft. Although this view is still widely held and defended, it is becoming more fashionable to interpret alleged encounters with UFOs as merely one aspect of a much larger spiritual and psychological phenomenon with prominent elements of occultism.

See also ABDUCTIONS; ADAMSKI, GEORGE; ANCIENT ASTRONAUTS; ANIMALS, UFOS AND; AZTEC INCIDENT; BELIEF SYSTEMS; BENDER MYSTERY; BIGFOOT; BODILY EFFECTS; CASH–LANDRUM INCIDENT; CHRIST AND CHRISTIANITY; CLOSE ENCOUNTERS OF THE THIRD KIND; COMMUNICATIONS; CONSPIRACY THEORIES; DEATHS; DECEPTION; ENCOUNTER-PRONE PERSONALITY; EVIDENCE; EXALTED ONES; FANTASY-PRONE PERSONALITY; FOOD AND DRINK; HALLUCINATIONS; HIGH STRANGENESS; HOAXES; HUMANOIDS; HYNEK, J. ALLEN; HYPNOSIS; IMPLANTS; INCUBI AND SUCCUBI; MARIAN APPARITIONS; MARS; MARTIAN OPPOSITIONS; MESSAGES; MYTHOLOGY; OCCULTISM; PARALYSIS; PARANOIA; PERCEPTION; PROPULSION; PSYCHOLOGICAL EFFECTS; RADAR; RADIO; RELIGION, UFOS AND; ROBOTS; ROSE, FATHER SERAPHIM; ROSWELL INCIDENT; SEXUAL ENCOUNTERS; SILENCE GROUP; TECHNOLOGY; TELEPATHY; TEMPERATURE EFFECTS; VALLEE, JACQUES; VON DÄNIKEN, ERICH; WAVES.

encounter-prone personality This expression refers to a certain personality type that is believed to be more than ordinarily likely to report encounters with UFOs. The encounter-prone personality is thought to be characterized by a high degree of "psychological absorption," meaning the ability to concentrate on elements of one's "interior reality" while ignoring what is happening in one's outside environment. Psychological absorption has been linked closely to so-called near-death experiences as well as encounters with UFOs.

See also FANTASY-PRONE PERSONALITY; NEAR-DEATH EXPERIENCE.

energy estimates In some cases, observations of luminous UFOs allow rough estimates to be made of how much energy would be required to produce light effects such as those observed. A case in point is the sighting of a highly luminous UFO at Fort-de-France in Martinique in 1965. The energy output of the object later was estimated at more than two megawatts, or perhaps 2,000 times that of an automobile engine. Such estimates, however, involve only the visible part of the electromagnetic spectrum and therefore may be unduly low. A more accurate estimate probably would be higher if non-visible portions of the spectrum emanating from an alleged UFO could be recorded and incorporated into the estimate.

energy sources The sources of motive power for UFOs are the subject of a vast crackpot literature. Many different (and often poorly defined) sources of energy have been suggested for alleged extraterrestrial spacecraft, from "anti-gravity" technology to anti-matter reactors and bizarre systems of magnetic and gravitational propulsion. Confusing this picture still further are observations that appear to indicate UFOs use old-fashioned chemical rockets in some cases for propulsion.

See also ADAMSKI, GEORGE; ANTI-GRAVITY; ANTI-MATTER; ELEMENT #115; ENERGY ESTIMATES; MAGNETISM; TECHNOLOGY.

environment, UFOs and UFOs have not been alleged to have any proven impact on the natural environment beyond some reported damage to trees and bushes and perhaps a few animal mutilations. The environmental element in the UFO phenomenon is important, however, because messages supposedly delivered from extraterrestrials have emphasized the ecological danger to our world and the need for more careful treatment of the natural world. This emphasis on environmental matters has become more prominent in reported messages from extraterrestrials from the 1960s on, and has paralleled the rise of the environmental movement in the developed countries. Such concern for the environment is a common element of the UFO phenomenon and the New Age movement.

See also MESSAGES; NEW AGE MOVEMENT.

Epsilon Boötis   A star in the constellation Bootes, Epsilon Boötis was considered in the 1970s as a possible home of intelligent extraterrestrial life. This conjecture arose from a study of radio signals, received in Norway in the 1920s, that indicated the possible presence in the Earth–Moon system of a Bracewell probe, an unmanned spacecraft supposedly sent out from another, more advanced civilization to effect contact with humankind. Analysis of signals thought to originate from the probe indicated a possible origin for the probe in Epsilon Boötis, but this interpretation has not been widely accepted.

See also BRACEWELL PROBE.

Erra   The alleged homeworld of the "Pleiadeans," whose representatives reportedly contacted Eduard Meier. According to Meier, Erra was smaller than Earth and had a much smaller population, fewer than 500 million, as compared to the several billion on Earth. The Pleiadeans allegedly modified the planet's environment to support their population, so that Erra looked much like Earth, only more attractive. Industrial facilities were said to be located in remote areas of the planet, far from population centers, whereas mining was conducted on uninhabited planets nearby. Species found on Erra included animals similar to fishes, horses, rabbits and cattle, Meier was told. Most physical labor on Erra was done by robots and androids. The androids were said to resemble humans so closely that the androids had to wear special uniforms that identified them according to the tasks they performed. The people of Erra reached sexual maturity in their teens but waited to marry until they had completed their education, a process that continued to age 70. Erra had no government as humans understood that institution. Instead, the world was allegedly run by spiritual leaders, the highest of which was a "form" called Horralft. This form was somewhere between flesh and spirit, and supposedly governed by "suggestion" rather than by directive.

Besides differing by only one letter from "Terra," another name for Earth, the name "Erra" resembles the two-syllable names reported in many other UFO contact cases, such as UMMO. The sketchy description of life on Erra is also reminiscent of accounts of other "extraterrestrial" homeworlds, which tend to resemble Earth, but without many of the imperfections of terrestrial society. Meier's descriptions of Erra also are similar to the views of "heaven" reported by the Swedish mystic Emanuel Swedenborg, who described having seen in visions a decidedly Earth-like heaven with many institutions of life on Earth preserved there.

See also HOMEWORLDS; MEIER CASE; PLEIADES; SWEDENBORG, EMANUEL; UMMO.

E.T.: The Extraterrestrial   This 1982 fantasy motion picture, directed by Steven Spielberg, concerned the adventures of an extraterrestrial left behind by his colleagues on an expedition to Earth. The alien is befriended by several children and develops an especially close relationship with a young boy. Eventually, the alien is reunited with his comrades. The motion picture was phenomenally popular. The story contains numerous elements of UFO contact cases, including levitation.

See also MOTION PICTURES.

E.T. law   Known officially as Title 14, Section 1211 of the Code of Federal Regulations, the "E.T. Law" was adopted in 1969 before the first manned landing on the Moon by U.S. astronauts and gives NASA and its director authority to quarantine any person who, in the NASA administrator's judgment, has come into contact with "a particular person, property, animal or other form of life or matter whatever [that] is extra-terrestrially exposed." The law provides that "the posted perimeter of a quarantine station shall be secured by armed guard," and that "[a]ny person who enters the limit of any quarantine stations shall be deemed to have consented to the quarantine of his person if it is determined that he is or has become extra-terrestrially exposed." The definition of "extra-terrestrial" exposure is explained as follows in 1211.102 (b):

(b) "Extra-terrestrially exposed" means the state or condition of any person, property, animal or other form of life or matter whatever, who or which has:
(1) Touched directly or come within the atmospheric envelope of any other celestial body; or
(2) Touched directly or been in close proximity to (or been exposed indirectly to) any person, property, animal or other form of life or matter who or which

has been extra-terrestrially exposed by virtue of paragraph (b) of this section.

For example, if person or thing "A" touches the surface of the Moon, and on "A's" return to Earth, "B" touches "A" and, subsequently, "C" touches "B," all of these—"A" through "C" inclusive— would be extra-terrestrially exposed ("A" and "B" directly, "C" indirectly). . . .

This legislation has been cited as a possible effort to discourage contact with "extraterrestrials" by making such contacts punishable by a fine of up to $5,000 and/or imprisonment of up to one year. It has been argued that the law applies to contact with UFOs because the wording of the legislation does not restrict its applicability specifically to NASA missions or other missions originating on Earth. It should be remembered, however, that conditions on the lunar surface were still a matter of speculation before the first manned landing on the Moon, and there was concern that returning astronauts might carry pathogenic lunar microbes that would require the quarantine of astronauts, spacecraft and anyone or anything that might have been "extra-terrestrially exposed" through them. Viewed in the context of its time, therefore, the law appears to provide for coping with microbes rather than intelligent extraterrestrials.

etheric plane Vaguely defined as a dimension or "plane" of existence other than the one we inhabit, this concept has been used as an attempt to explain why conditions on other worlds differ so greatly from descriptions of them supposedly given by alleged extraterrestrials. When conditions on another

"Etheric Plane" is one fanciful explanation of how Venus (shown here in radar image) might be lifeless in our universe but inhabitable in another. (NASA)

world are found to be obviously unsuitable for intelligent organisms to exist there, it is acceptable in some circles of UFO enthusiasts to say that beings do call that world home, but in an "etheric plane" foreign to us. A case in point is George Adamski's reported contact with a visitor from Venus in the southwestern desert of the United States. Adamski said he was given to understand that Venus was a habitable world. Spacecraft that visited Venus later, however, revealed it to be too hot, and its atmospheric pressure far too high, to permit life as we know it to exist there. One way around this inconsistency was to claim that Adamski's visitors and their messages came from Venus as its exists in the "etheric plane." Exactly where the etheric plane exists, and how one might travel to and from it, appear to have gone unexplained. The word "etheric" evidently refers to the now-rejected model of the "ether," a highly rarefied fluid of sorts that once was believed to flow through outer space. The so-called etheric plane bears a strong similarity to the "spirit world" of mediumism.

See also ADAMSKI, GEORGE; HOMEWORLDS; MEDIUMISM; OCCULTISM; PSEUDOSCIENCE; VENUS.

evidence Evidence of UFO sightings and other alleged encounters falls into many categories, each with its particular strengths and shortcomings. Eyewitness testimony is abundant and often detailed but tends to be inaccurate, partly because the human mind tends to invent details and to transpose memories of one event to another. When testimony of alleged UFO encounters (notably abductions) is retrieved under hypnosis, the potential for error appears to increase greatly. Although photography would appear to offer potentially more valuable evidence than eyewitness testimony, and photographs can be subjected to careful analysis, the possibilities for fraud in photography are tremendous, and numerous alleged photos of UFOs have been revealed to be fakes, as have certain widely publicized motion pictures said to show UFOs in flight. Despite the vast number of reported UFO photographs taken since the end of World War II, not one such photograph is accepted as unequivocal evidence for the existence of extraterrestrial spacecraft visiting Earth. Alleged audio recordings of UFOs have produced interesting sound effects, but again provide no proof of extraterrestrial visitations. Certain UFO encounters are said to have left traces on the ground, in the form of damaged vegetation, compacted soil, imprints of landing gear, and so forth; although some of this evidence is impressive, as in the Valensole incident in France, it nonetheless falls short of proving an extraterrestrial origin of UFOs. The same may be said for cases in which witnesses to UFO encounters have reported bodily harm from UFOs, as in the Cash–Landrum incident in the United States, the Falcon Lake incident in Canada and the Dr. X case in France. Evidence of ejecta from UFOs has been intriguing and at least has provided investigators with something to analyze, but no study of alleged UFO ejecta has established the material to be of extraterrestrial origin. It can be stated with reasonable certainty that alleged encounters with UFOs have had dramatic psychological effects on witnesses; emotional distress and domestic upheaval occur often among putative witnesses of UFO sightings. One curious feature of physical "evidence" of UFO encounters is that the evidence often "vanishes" before critical investigators can examine it. These disappearances are said to occur under mysterious circumstances in many cases, as when men who claim to represent some official agency visit a witness and demand that he or she turn over the evidence.

See also ABDUCTIONS; CASH–LANDRUM INCIDENT; CROP CIRCLES; DR. X INCIDENT; FALCON LAKE INCIDENT; HOAXES; HYPNOSIS; MEN IN BLACK; PHOTOGRAPHY; VALENSOLE INCIDENT.

evolution Popular notions of the "evolutionary" development of humankind have played a significant part in the UFO phenomenon by offering one explanation of why the alleged extraterrestrials might visit us: namely, to guide our species into the next step of its "evolution." Speculation on this topic has tended to be uninformed and often ludicrous, but the idea of humankind evolving under the guidance of highly advanced aliens has appealed to a 20th-century audience and now appears to be widely accepted. The ancient astronauts craze of the 1970s, for example, was based in part on the supposition that visiting extraterrestrials had arranged for the rise of humankind by tinkering with the DNA of pre-human apes. Given enough time, humans presumably would evolve into something resembling the big-headed, small-framed humanoids reported in many accounts of UFO abductions. A related theme in the UFO phenomenon is the social evolution of humankind under extraterrestrial guidance. This school of thought maintains that aliens are guiding human society toward some great advancement, although the nature of this change is usually left conveniently undefined. Spiritual evolution is another area in which the alleged extraterrestrials are said to wish to help guide humankind, but the so-called spiritual messages delivered by the aliens

tend to be less than helpful guidance; they may say, for example, that there is only one supreme being, or that this being is merely a set of laws to which all living things must conform. The Orthodox Christian theologian Father Seraphim Rose, in his book *Orthodoxy and the Religion of the Future*, analyzes this view of alien-directed social evolution and finds the future society in such visions to be essentially Hinduistic, with a strong occult element to it. Science fiction authors treating this theme also have tended to envision "advanced" alien societies on the Hinduistic model, with a pronounced caste structure. An example is the society of the "Dawnworlds," as described in the "United Planets" series of stories by the American science fiction author Mack Reynolds.

See also ANCIENT ASTRONAUTS; RELIGION, UFOS AND; ROSE, FATHER SERAPHIM.

exalted ones American "contactee" Albert Bender used this expression to describe the alleged rulers of the extraterrestrials he claimed to have contacted. Describing his meeting with an "exalted one," Bender indicated the being was humanoid and about nine feet tall, with white hair. The being provided a vague description of the cosmos and said that galaxies were created by a vast, central, luminous object that was too hot to approach closely. In response to Bender's queries, the entity reportedly maligned Christ and rejected the foundations of Christian theology, including Christ's divinity and resurrection from the dead. Bender's description of an alien society ruled by "exalted ones" is consistent with the generally Hinduistic character of "extraterrestrial" societies as described by many contactees. The alien society supposedly has a ruling class of beings with tremendous knowledge and intellectual capabilities, and appears in many descriptions to have a caste structure comparable to that in Hindu society on Earth. This model of extraterrestrial society has found a prominent place in modern science fiction, notably the stories of American author Mack Reynolds.

See also BENDER MYSTERY; CHRIST AND CHRISTIANITY; HINDUISM; RELIGION, UFOS AND; REYNOLDS, MACK; SOCIETIES, EXTRATERRESTRIAL.

Exeter, New Hampshire, incidents, United States The widely reported Exeter sightings in 1965 involved luminous objects seen in the night sky. The objects were difficult to explain as aircraft because they behaved in ways atypical of aircraft, such as silent, back-and-forth motion close to the ground. UFO debunker Philip Klass attributed the sightings to misidentifications of phenomena associ-

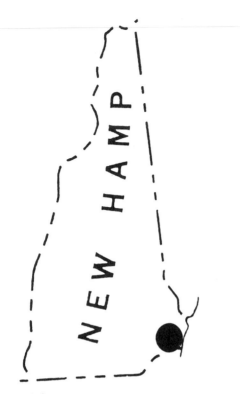

Exeter, N.H., sightings drew nationwide attention. (U.S. Geological Survey)

ated with electrical coronas, or light displays, along high-tension power lines in the area.

See also BALL LIGHTNING; KLASS, PHILIP.

extraterrestrial biological entities (EBEs) This expression refers to hypothetical organisms from other worlds, allegedly visiting Earth in spacecraft. The EBE concept is consistent with some accounts of close encounters with UFO occupants, as when the "extraterrestrials" are reported as being humanoids and have palpable, bodily contact with human witnesses. Perhaps the most colorful expression of the EBE concept is the literature on sexual encounters, in which alleged extraterrestrials are said to have sexual contact with human abductees. Another persistent set of rumors linked with the EBE concept concerns bodies of extraterrestrials supposedly recovered from crashes of spacecraft in various parts of the globe. The EBE concept is difficult to reconcile, however, with many reported elements of UFO encounters, including the high velocities and radical maneuvers executed by UFOs in flight. Such conditions, it is believed, would be impossible for biological entities, or at least humanoids like ourselves, to survive. In any event, there appears to be no unequivocal evidence, in the form of tissue samples or anything else, of the actual existence of EBEs on Earth.

See also AZTEC INCIDENT; CRASHES; EXTRATERRESTRIAL HYPOTHESIS; HUMANOIDS; ROSWELL INCIDENT; SEXUAL ENCOUNTERS.

extraterrestrial hypothesis Known as ETH for short, this hypothesis rests on the presumption that UFOs represent visitations to Earth by "extraterrestrial biological entities" (EBEs) using actual, material spacecraft, in much the same manner as human astronauts who visited the Moon. The ETH has had many supporters since the initial "flying saucer" sighting immediately after World War II, possibly because the hypothesis is easy for modern humans to understand. Belief in ETH requires no subtle understanding of metaphysical concepts or advanced theories of physics, as do some other hypotheses of extraterrestrials' nature and origins. Moreover, the ETH in modern entertainment has been made familiar to a vast audience that now apparently accepts the ETH almost as proven fact.

Solid, material evidence for the ETH is rare to nonexistent. Ancedotal evidence from some "contactees," such as George Adamski, would appear to indicate that alleged extraterrestrials in such encounters have corporeal bodies much like our own. Contactees often describe the tactile sensations of making contact with the bodies of so-called aliens. Such evidence, however, is less than substantial.

Even less substantial as evidence is the body of rumor predicated on the ETH. The literature on UFO "crashes" abounds in descriptions of bodies of extraterrestrials supposedly recovered from crash sites, notably in the southwestern desert of the United States. Such rumors have circulated for decades without ever coming close to substantiation, but have contributed nonetheless to widespread acceptance of the ETH among the general public.

Alleged communications by radio from outer space also have been presented as evidence of extraterrestrial life trying to communicate with humankind. Again, however, this evidence is considered dubious at best, partly because human judgment and imagination play a major part in its interpretation.

In theory, EBEs are a possibility. The well-known Drake equation, used to estimate the potential number of star systems capable of sustaining intelligent beings capable of space travel, has been cited to support the claim that EBEs may exist, and that therefore the ETH should not be dismissed as impossible. Also, laboratory experiments have demonstrated that the essential chemical "building blocks" of life, such as amino acids, are easy to produce from their component chemicals and might be expected to exist in large quantities on other worlds, thus providing at least the foundation for emergence of intelligent life. It is a long step, however, from the Drake equation and the possible existence of certain organic chemicals on distant planets to the appearance of space-traveling EBEs from those planets on Earth. Likewise, tentative evidence from astronomy that certain nearby star systems may have planets is tantalizing but falls far short of proof from the ETH's validity.

Another body of so-called evidence used to back the ETH concerns "hardware" supposedly used in extraterrestrial spacecraft. Numerous objects have been presented as material evidence of alien spacecraft visiting Earth, but none of these objects is universally viewed as genuine, and most, if not all, are clearly terrestrial in origin. These artifacts include pieces of machined metal or samples of solid "ejecta" reportedly retrieved from alleged landing sites and crash sites. In the so-called Roswell incident, for example, a damaged saucer was said to have dropped large amounts of material, including a supposedly undentable metallic foil, over portions of New Mexico. A local rancher reportedly gathered samples of the material, which later (according to widely circulated accounts of the incident) were confiscated by representatives of the United States government. In a systematic pattern of "disappearance," such alleged material evidence of UFO visitations tends to "vanish" in one way or another before critical investigators have an opportunity to examine it. When the alleged ejecta or other material evidence finally has undergone analysis, nothing about it has emerged as unequivocal proof of its extraterrestrial origin. Thus far, no recovered "pieces" from UFOs appear to be beyond the capabilities of manufacturers on Earth. Other alleged material evidence, such as imprints of UFO "landing legs" discovered in the soil at reputed landing sights, tends to be even less persuasive, because similar "evidence" can be fabricated easily with common tools such as shovels.

From literature on abductions comes a large and growing number of reports of scars supposedly left on the bodies of alleged abductees by extraterrestrials who are said to have examined the abductees and, in effect, performed surgery on them during abductions. These marks may appear as linear scars or indentations ("scoop marks") on the skin. These marks may be described, during "retrieval" of "buried" memories by hypnotic regression, as physical evidence of contact with EBEs, and consequently

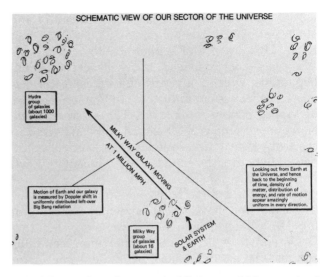

Travel faster than the speed of light would be required to make journeys between galaxies feasible. (NASA)

support for the ETH. This explanation suffers, however, when one considers that an encounter with an extraterrestrial is not necessary to acquire a scar on one's body. Many other, more prosaic experiences can yield such a result.

One of the most potent arguments against the ETH involves the vast distances between stars, and the time that would be required to travel such distances on visits to Earth. According to the theory of relativity, nothing in the known universe can travel faster than the velocity of light, approximately 186,000 miles per second. Even at that velocity, flight between star systems would require years (or, more likely, centuries or millennia) to complete. Organisms with life spans comparable to our own would find such journeys too time-consuming to be practical. Various arguments have been suggested to overcome this obstacle to interstellar travel, specifically the time factor as a function of distance and limited velocity. Exotic concepts of physics such as "wormholes" and "interdimensional gateways" may be presented as means of allowing interstellar travel within a reasonable period; but such concepts are little more than fantasy, and their application to the ETH and space travel is mere speculation. Relativity theory itself has provided a possible way to carry out extended space missions, by accelerating a spacecraft to a velocity very close to that of light. In theory, time would slow down for astronauts on a spacecraft traveling at such velocity, so that a lengthy voyage might be completed within a few decades. Even in this case, however, the existence of such fast interstellar spacecraft is purely speculative and unsupported by any material evidence.

There is, in short, no substantial evidence of any intelligent biological entity on any planet other than Earth. This absence of support for the ETH, however, has not dissuaded many believers in the hypothesis, which forms part of a widespread UFO-related belief system in the United States and other developed nations. From the ETH are derived some of the most famous UFO-related cults and enthusiasms of recent years, including the "ancient astronauts" hypothesis expounded by Swiss author Erich von Däniken.

The ETH is not the only hypothesis put forward to account for the UFO phenomenon. Students of the UFO phenomenon also have suggested that UFOs and their occupants do not represent EBEs and material machines at all, but rather some "spiritual" agency that merely takes the appearance of organisms traveling in spacecraft. This explanation is more consistent with what is known of the UFO phenomenon, and is coming into widespread acceptance. The character and motives of such a spiritual agency are, of course, open to debate.

See also ADAMSKI, GEORGE; ANCIENT ASTRONAUTS; ANGELS; ASTRONOMY; AZTEC INCIDENT; CONTACTEES; CRASHES; COMMUNICATIONS; DEMONOLOGY; ENCOUNTER PHENOMENA; EVIDENCE; EXTRATERRESTRIAL BIOLOGICAL ENTITIES; GRAYS; HUMANOIDS; RELATIVITY THEORY; ROSE, FATHER SERAPHIM; ROSWELL INCIDENT; TECHNOLOGY; VALLEE, JACQUES; VON DÄNIKEN, ERICH.

extraterrestrials, anatomy of

extraterrestrials, anatomy of   Much has been reported and written about the anatomy of alleged extraterrestrials. A bewildering variety of anatomical forms has been attributed to the so-called aliens. Their anatomies may be classified as either humanoid or nonhumanoid, although there appears to be considerable overlap between these two categories.

Humanoids generally are described as bipeds having a torso with human-like upper and lower limbs and a head, although a distinct head is not always reported, and the upper limbs may take the form of wings rather than arms and hands. The head may or may not have a neck. Hands may be described as virtually identical to those of humans, but in many cases nonhuman features such as claws or tiny "suction cups" at the fingertips may be reported. In certain reports, strange implements like tools are seen in place of hands. Legs may be indistinguishable from human legs or held in an unnaturally stiff manner. In certain close-encounter reports, alleged extraterrestrials are said to exhibit numerous "neotenous" traits like those of human infants, such as small stature, a disproportionately large cranium and seemingly weak and spindly limbs.

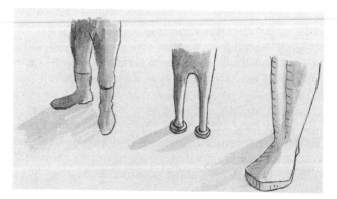

Legs and feet of "extraterrestrials" may look like those of humans (left), but some aliens are said to have cap-like feet (center) or both legs joined and ending in a single foot (right). (D. Ritchie)

Feet are not always described in detail, but descriptions vary greatly, from mere discs to feet that are human-like but completely flat on the bottom. Casts of footprints have been produced as evidence of extraterrestrial visitations, notably in the case of early "contactee" George Adamski, but this evidence is considered dubious at best.

Extremely hairy skin has been reported in certain cases, but encounter stories from the last three decades of the 20th century have tended instead to emphasize the hairlessness of the alleged aliens, another supposedly neotenous trait. Extremely pale or even silvery skin is another alleged trait of certain extraterrestrials. The skin reportedly may be extremely resistant to damage and capable even of deflecting bullets without apparent harm to the entity.

Facial features of reported extraterrestrials tend to resemble those of humans in their general configuration but not always in specific details. The typical extraterrestrial described in a close-encounter report is likely to have two eyes set in the front of the head, as well as a nose (or at least nostrils) and a mouth that is described in many cases as small and lipless. External ears may be seen, or mere orifices where human ears would be. The eyes may be extremely large by human standards and either be completely black or have vertical slit pupils like those of cats. The eyes may glow in darkness and be associated with a paralyzing effect on the observer. A third eye or similar structure in the middle of the forehead has been reported in some instances.

One notable set of reports concerning alleged extraterrestrial anatomy involves a set of autopsies said to have been performed on the bodies of aliens recovered from crashed spacecraft in the southwestern desert of the United States. These reports are unsubstantiated and contradictory in many particulars. According to one report, the so-called extraterrestrials were found to be similar in their internal anatomy to humans. Another story, however, described beings essentially devoid of a digestive system, though humanoid in appearance.

Certain encounter stories also describe "hybrid" beings, allegedly half human and half extraterrestrial, that are said to have been bred through genetic engineering. These reports are widely regarded as mere hoaxes, fantasies or hallucinations. Evidence produced to support them has been exposed as fraudulent.

Nonhuman extraterrestrials may be described as resembling reptiles, amphibians, birds, insects or even robots, although the beings reportedly may walk in bipedal fashion. The anatomy of these alleged aliens is, of course, extremely varied. Their skin allegedly may have a variety of colors and textures, from smooth to scaly. Some observers of the UFO phenomenon have noted that although the alleged nonhuman extraterrestrials described in close-encounter reports are widely believed to be organisms from some other star systems, the anatomy of those beings is essentially the same as that of many terrestrial organisms. The essentially terrestrial character of their anatomy is seen as evidence that the "extraterrestrials" actually have their origins in the human mind and the various influences that affect its operation.

See also ADAMSKI, GEORGE; CRASHES; EXTRATERRESTRIAL HYPOTHESIS; EYES; HALLUCINATIONS; HANDS; HUMANOIDS; INSECTOIDS; NEOTENY; REPTOIDS; ROSWELL INCIDENT; THIRD EYE.

extraterrestrials, behavior of

Alleged extraterrestrials in UFO close-encounter cases are said to have exhibited a great variety of behaviors, from the hostile to the friendly, and often the merely curious. From the beginnings of the "contactee" phenomenon, some aliens were said to be friendly toward humankind, while others were thought to be hostile. The seemingly benevolent space folk whom George Adamski claimed to have encountered, for example, stood in sharp contrast to the sinister, sadistic beings in the account of Albert Bender, who said that his visitors (in effect) tortured him with headaches and threatened to destroy his body if he antagonized them. This strange dichotomy of behavior—benevolent versus hostile—has continued in UFO lore to the present day.

The abduction phenomenon is among the most widely discussed elements of alleged extraterrestrial behavior. In abductions, a human may report being taken against his or her will aboard an "alien" spacecraft and subjected to a quasi-medical examination or other experiences. Abduction experiences in many cases are said to involve indoctrination of some kind, such as instruction in the aliens' view of life, the cosmos and religion.

Perhaps the most lurid aspect of "extraterrestrial" behavior involves so-called sexual encounters, in which a human "abductee" may report being taken aboard an alien spacecraft and being raped or subjected to other forced sexual activity. Much reported activity of extraterrestrials in abduction cases involves the human reproductive and excretory systems in one way or another. Another apparent area of interest to extraterrestrials in such encounters, according to UFO lore, is the nasal region, which figures in many abduction stories as a site for emplacing "implants," artifacts of undetermined purpose that are said to resemble BB shot or small seeds.

In many cases, the reported behavior of extraterrestrials appears curiously pointless, unnecessary or even foolhardy. The so-called aliens may engage in evidently aimless activity such as merely strolling around their spacecraft. They may make a show of collecting samples of soil, plants or animal life (a task that could easily be done by unmanned vehicles), or appear to undertake repairs to their craft in some spot where they can be seen easily and therefore would be vulnerable to attack. Some students of the UFO phenomenon have suggested that in many cases, the behavior of UFOs and their alleged occupants is not what it appears to be, but rather is "staged," so to speak, in order to draw the attention of observers.

Absurdity is another aspect of the behavior of extraterrestrials. The beings reportedly may engage in ridiculous behavior such as printing out (in English, French, Chinese or some other terrestrial language) observations on such decidedly mundane business as the relationships between men and women. The aliens may be reported chasing livestock through fields or cooking pancakes on a stove. Early "contactee" George Adamski was especially notorious for the absurd character of his encounter stories; he tried to persuade readers, for example, that his alleged visitor from Venus had left behind a message in the form of symbols found in the spaceman's footprints. The absurdity of many UFO contact reports has been interpreted as a component of "metalogic," a technique for redirecting human belief systems through absurdity and confusion.

Other patterns also have been observed in the behavior of "aliens" in UFO encounters. Encounters often occur in underpopulated areas such as deserts, forests or mountains. Highways appear to be favorite sites for alleged encounters. Numerous encounters are reported at night, and the alleged aliens in such cases are noted for their aversion to artificial light. According to some reports, the beings also object to being photographed, as did "Captain Aura Rhanes" when alleged contactee Truman Bethurum asked to take a photograph of her.

The reported behavior of the aliens often involves deception. The aliens are said, in many cases, to lie to witnesses and deceive them in other ways as well, such as the generation of realistic illusions. Cruelty is another element of "extraterrestrial" behavior. Aliens in many abduction reports are said to torture their human captives, and more than a few deaths have been attributed to deliberate attacks by UFOs, although these reports may be highly questionable.

See also ABDUCTIONS; ABSURDITY; ADAMSKI, GEORGE; BELIEF SYSTEMS; BENDER MYSTERY; BETHURUM INCIDENT; CAPTAIN AURA RHANES; DEATHS; ENCOUNTER PHENOMENA; IMPLANTS; KELLY–HOPKINSVILLE INCIDENT; METALOGIC; SEXUAL ENCOUNTERS.

eyes   One notable element of UFO close-encounter stories is the eyes of alleged extraterrestrials. The eyes commonly are described as being subtly or grossly dissimilar to human eyes, and supernormal properties are ascribed to the aliens' eyes in some cases. In certain contactee reports, the eyes of extraterrestrials are described as much like our own, only slanted upward slightly at the outer edges. Other

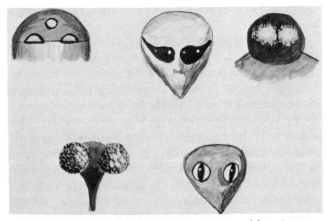

Eyes: Some alleged extraterrestrials are said to have a "third eye" in the middle of the forehead (top left). "Grays" with large, dark eyes figure prominently in many UFO reports (top center). Some extraterrestrials reportedly have glowing eyes (top right). "Insectoids" presumably have large, insect-like eyes (bottom left). Some humanoid "aliens" are said to have vertical, slit pupils (bottom right).

descriptions of extraterrestrials' eyes portray them as large and completely dark, without pupils, whites, or irises, and again slanted upward at the outer edges. Beings with luminous eyes also have been reported, as in the case of early "contactee" Albert Bender and in the Flatwoods, West Virginia, sighting. Two-eyed aliens appear to be the most widely reported, although binocular aliens are by no means the only kind in UFO close-encounter stories. In some instances, extraterrestrials with what appears to be a third eye in their foreheads have been described. This trinocular system resembles the "third eye" mentioned in occult literature and thus supplies a link between the UFO phenomenon and other elements of the occult. Unusual properties sometimes are ascribed to extraterrestrials' eyes in close-encounter reports. Some aliens, for example, reportedly have paralyzed human onlookers merely by gazing at them.

See also BENDER MYSTERY; FLATWOODS INCIDENT; HUMANOIDS; OCCULTISM; PARALYSIS; THIRD EYE; VORONEZH SIGHTINGS.

eyewitness testimony   In many UFO sightings, eyewitness testimony is weak and can be discredited easily, because the human eye and mind do not always perceive a phenomenon as what it really is. "Constructive perception," in which the observer applies a much more elaborate interpretation to an observation than the observation actually deserves, is one problem with eyewitness testimony. In constructive perception, for example, the lights of an ordinary aircraft seen at night may be transformed by the viewer's imagination into a spectacular extraterrestrial spacecraft. Various pathological conditions also may make eyewitness testimony of UFO sightings unreliable. Reports by solitary witnesses also are widely considered unreliable and unacceptable by UFO investigators, because such reports have no corroboration from other sources. The unreliability of single-witness sightings is expressed in a Latin saying quoted often by investigators Jacques Vallee and J. Allen Hynek: "Testis unus, testis nullis." The saying means, "A single witness is equivalent to no witness."

See also CONSTRUCTIVE PERCEPTION; HALLUCINATIONS; HYNEK, J. ALLEN; TEMPORAL LOBE EPILEPSY; VALLEE, JACQUES.

Ezekiel   The Old Testament prophet, who was among the Jews that Nebuchadnezzar exiled to Babylon c. 597 B.C., describes in his book an encounter that has been interpreted by some students of the

UFO phenomenon as a meeting with extraterrestrials. The text of the first chapter of the Book of Ezeiel describes the encounter:

Now it came to pass in the thirtieth year, in the fourth month, in the fifth day of the month, as I was among the captives by the river of Chebar, that the heavens were opened, and I saw visions of God. In the fifth day of the month . . . the word of the LORD came expressly unto Ezekiel the priest, the son of Buzi, in the land of the Chaldeans by the river Chebar; and the hand of the LORD was there upon him.

And I looked, and behold, a whirlwind came out of the north, a great cloud, and a fire infolding itself, and a brightness was about it, and out of the midst thereof as the color of amber, out of the midst of the fire. Also out of the midst thereof came the likeness of four living creatures. And this was their appearance; they had the likeness of a man. And every one had four faces, and every one had four wings. And their feet were straight feet; and the sole of their feet was like the sole of a calf's foot; and they sparkled like the color of burnished brass. And they had the hands of a man under their wings on their four sides; and they four had their faces and their wings.

Their wings were joined one to another; they turned not when they went; they went every one straight forward. As for the likeness of their faces, they four had the face of a man, and the face of a lion, on the right side; and they four had the face of an ox on the left side; they four also had the face of an eagle. Thus were their faces; and their wings were stretched upward; two wings of every one were joined one to another, and two covered their bodies. And they went every one straight forward; whither the spirit was to go, they went; and they turned not when they went.

As for the likeness of the living creatures, their appearance was like burning coals of fire, and like the appearance of lamps; it went up and down among the living creatures; and the fire was bright, and out of the fire went forth lightning. And the living creatures ran and returned as the appearance of a flash of lightning.

Now as I beheld the living creatures, behold one wheel upon the earth by the living creatures, with his four faces. The appearance of the wheels and their work was like unto the color of a beryl; and they four had one likeness; and their appearance and their work was as it were a wheel in the middle of a wheel. When they went, they went upon their four sides; and they turned not when they went. As for the rings, they were so high that they were dreadful; and their rings were full of eyes round about them four. And when the living creatures went, the wheels went by them; and when the living creatures were lifted up from the earth, the wheels were lifted up. Whithersoever the spirit was to go, they went, thither was their spirit to go; and the wheels were lifted up over against them: for the spirit of the living creature was in the wheels. When those went, these went; and when those stood, these stood; and when those were lifted up from the earth, the wheels were lifted up over against them; for the spirit of the living creature was in the wheels.

And the likeness of the firmament upon the heads of the living creature was as the color of the terrible crystal, stretched forth over their heads above. And under the firmament were their wings straight, the one toward the other; every one had two, which covered on this side, and every one had two, which covered on that side, their bodies. And when they went, I heard the noise of their wings, like the noise of great waters, as the voice of the Almighty, the voice of speech, as the noise of an host: when they stood, they let down their wings.

And there was a voice from the firmament that was over their heads, when they stood, and had let down their wings. And above the firmament that was over their heads was the likeness of a throne, as the appearance of a sapphire stone; and upon the likeness of the throne was the likeness as the appearance of a man above upon it. And I saw the color of amber, as the appearance of fire round about within it, from the appearance of his loins even upward, and from the appearance of his loins even downward, I saw as it were the appearance of fire, and it had brightness round about. As the appearance of the bow that is in the cloud in the day of rain, so was the appearance of the brightness round about. This was the appearance of the likeness of the glory of the LORD. And when I saw it, I fell upon my face, and I heard a voice of one that spake. (Ezekiel 1:1–28, King James Version)

Rephrased in modern language, the first chapter of Ezekiel may be summarized roughly as follows. Ezekiel sees something resembling a windstorm approaching from the north. The "storm" consists of a cloud surrounded by bright light and emitting flashes of what appears to be lightning. In the center of this phenomenon, he perceives an object made of luminous metal. Aboard are four creatures with both human and nonhuman features, including wings. These beings apparently are highly luminous themselves and can move very rapidly. The vehicle (or whatever) they accompany has wheels of bright luster and unusual design. It appears that the wheels are omnidirectional: that is, they can move in any direction. Above the creature's heads extends a "firmament," or expanse, made of some material resembling crystal. Atop this firmament sits a "throne," or seat, of some kind, upon which sits a humanoid figure surrounded by a multicolored radiance. Ezekiel is so awed by this spectacle that he falls to the ground, face down. Then he hears a voice addressing him.

This passage from Ezekiel has been the subject of much speculation among UFO enthusiasts, because the phenomenon described by the prophet appears to bear certain similarities to modern UFO close-encounter reports. The cloud, the flashes of "lightning," the luminous flying object, the peculiar beings associated with the object, and the powerful effect of this sight on the observer are all comparable to elements of 20th-century UFO encounters. The wheel within a wheel has been interpreted as a disk-shaped UFO with inner and outer segments, and the loud noise described by Ezekiel has been compared to that of modern aircraft, which make a roaring sound much like that of a waterfall.

Perhaps the most famous piece of UFO-related literature on Ezekiel's vision is *The Spaceships of Ezekiel*, a 1973 popular work by NASA engineer Josef Blumrich, who participated in building the Saturn rocket that carried American astronauts to the Moon. Blumrich used elements of aerospace technology to design a hypothetical craft that appeared to match the description of Ezekiel's vision and, in theory at least, would be capable of powered flight. Blumrich interpreted the four creatures, for example, as landing-gear assemblies, and the beings' wings as rotor blades on helicopter engines used for maneuvering and landing. Blumrich's speculations received widespread publicity during the "ancient astronauts" enthusiasm of the early 1970s.

Famed UFO "debunker" and Harvard University astronomer Donald Menzel offered an alternative explanation of Ezekiel's vision. Menzel suggested that Ezekiel had seen a "parhelion," a meteorological condition in which sunlight refracted by ice crystals in the air produces an image of two concentric circles around the sun.

Seeking purely natural or "UFOlogical" explanations of Ezekiel's vision, however, is to examine the story outside its proper context, namely the Bible. Commentaries on Ezekiel have pointed out that the imagery of Ezekiel's vision is duplicated elsewhere in the Bible, notably in the fourth chapter of the New Testament book of Revelation, where one finds again a mention of four living beings with the features of man, ox, lion and eagle. Moreover, the same chapter of Revelation also describes God's throne as emitting flashes of lightning and being surrounded by a rainbow. When read in the context of scripture, then, the details of Ezekiel's vision are consistent with other examples of biblical imagery and therefore should not be interpreted as descriptions of some extraterrestrial spacecraft, nor as some entirely natural phenomenon such as that invoked by Menzel.

See also ACOUSTICAL EFFECTS; ANCIENT ASTRONAUTS; ATMOSPHERIC PHENOMENA; BIBLE, ALLEGED UFOS IN; ENCOUNTER PHENOMENA; MENZEL, DONALD; RELIGION, UFOS AND; TECHNOLOGY.

F

Face on Mars A geological formation revealed by photos returned to Earth from an American Mariner probe in 1976, the so-called Face on Mars has become a symbol of the belief in extraterrestrial intelligence. Located in the northern hemisphere of Mars, in the Cydonia region, the "face" resembles a stylized human face turned skyward, and is located near a set of symmetrical, pyramidal structures that have been compared to a "city." Through an exercise in imagination, the alleged face and city have been interpreted both in the United States and in the former Soviet Union as possible works of engineering produced by extraterrestrial intelligences. As of this writing, the preponderance of evidence appears to favor a natural origin for the formations of Cydonia.

See also MARS; PHOTOGRAPHY.

fachan A monster from the folklore of the British Isles, the fachan was said to have only one large eye, one hand reaching out of its chest, and a single leg ending in one foot. The fachan bears a certain resemblance to entities reportedly seen in some UFO close-encounter cases.

See also PUCUSANA INCIDENT.

fairies The subject of an extensive folklore, especially in the British Isles, fairies are alleged supernatural beings that resemble in many ways modern accounts of "extraterrestrials" in UFO encounters. According to legend, fairies appear in many different sizes: some tiny, some very large, and some comparable to humans in stature. Fairies are said to practice levitation, inhabit "luminous" homes, exchange food and drink with humans, have sexual intercourse with humans, steal humans' belongings, and on occasion interfere with humans' perceptions. Legend includes tales of humans held captive in the land of the fairies. Women apparently were favored for capture by the fairies, for duty as nursing mothers or as brides, although tales exist of young men being abducted as well. Fairies themselves are said to have been captured by humans, as in the story of the "green children" of England. Time is said to be a different phenomenon among fairies than it is on Earth; there allegedly is no strict correspondence between time as experienced on Earth and in fairyland. Several days' visit among the fairies might translate into hundreds of years by human reckoning. Likewise, "extraterrestrials" in modern UFO reports are said to appear in various forms and sizes; exchange food and drink with human "contactees"; abduct men and women for sexual activity; steal humans' property (such as animals or crops); and alter the perceptions of alleged contactees, so that a person in such an encounter may perceive himself in a strange landscape or other unfamiliar surroundings. Strange discrepancies in time perception, commonly known as "missing time," also are associated with UFO close encounters.

See also ABDUCTIONS; ELIDOR; ENCOUNTER PHENOMENA; FOOD AND DRINK; GREEN CHILDREN; HIGH STRANGENESS; HUMANOIDS; INCUBI AND SUCCUBI; MISSING TIME; SEXUAL ENCOUNTERS.

Falcon Lake incident, Canada The Falcon Lake incident reportedly occurred when one Stephen Michalak encountered a landed UFO near Falcon Lake on the Ontario-Manitoba border on May 20, 1967. As Michalak inspected the UFO at close range, hot air burst suddenly from a grid on the side of the craft, igniting his vest and shirt. He felt intense pain. Michalak tore off his burning clothes. Looking up, he saw the object take off. Physiological effects began as Michalak left the area. He developed a headache and nausea and started vomiting. Eventually, he made his way home, and his son took him to a hospital, where he was treated for first-degree burns and then released. He exhibited a pattern of thermal burns on his chest and abdomen that appeared to match the configuration of the "exhaust" grill from which the hot-air blast had supposedly emanated. Michalak suffered for some time afterward from diarrhea, hives, skin infections and nausea, as well as numbness and swelling of joints. His symptoms later were described as consistent with exposure to a brief but powerful dose of X-rays or gamma radiation, on the order of 100 to 200 roentgens. Later investigation of the landing site turned up no sign of higher-than-normal radioactivity, but two small silver bars, shaped in a W form and about four inches long, turned up at the site a year after Michalak's encounter with the alleged UFO. Analysis of the bars showed signs of radioactivity, bending and heating. Although there was suspicion of a hoax in this case, the Falcon Lake incident is remarkable for providing, in a single case, examples of numerous effects associated with UFO close encounters, including temperature effects, light effects, auditory effects, odor and bodily injury to an observer.

See also BODILY EFFECTS; CANADA, UFOS IN; ENCOUNTER PHENOMENA; ODORS; TEMPERATURE EFFECTS.

falling leaf motion   Also known as "pendulum motion," this pattern of descent is observed in many UFO sightings. The UFO is seen to descend in a gradual, side-to-side motion, in the manner of a falling leaf or a pendulum. No universally accepted explanation has been offered for this phenomenon.

familiar spirits   In the literature of the occult, familiar spirits are evil spirits that form a special attachment with an individual human and become "familiar" with him, hence their name. The lore of familiar spirits resembles in many ways certain stories of close encounters with UFOs and their alleged extraterrestrial occupants. One of the most colorful parallels between UFOs and familiar spirits, for example, involves the "black dog" phenomenon. In some widely publicized UFO encounter cases, black dogs have been associated with extraterrestrials. The black dog is also a prominent element of the lore of the familiar spirits.

See also BLACK DOGS; DEMONOLOGY; OCCULTISM; SORCERY, UFOS AND; WITCHCRAFT.

fantasy-prone personality   Some individuals exhibit normal behavior in most respects but are given to fantasizing and may experience hallucinations easily. They also are given to reporting out-of-body experiences on a frequent basis and may lose part or all of their awareness of time on occasion. Such persons also may perceive strange images either just before falling asleep or immediately before awakening. These images may include frightening humanoids that are interpreted as extraterrestrials. The images may last for minutes and may be either moving or motionless. It has been suggested that fantasy-prone personalities involved in such perceptions may account for "extraterrestrial" entities reported in bedroom encounters.

See also ABDUCTIONS; ALLEN, KIRK; BORDER PHENOMENA; ENCOUNTER PHENOMENA; HALLUCINATIONS; HUMANOIDS; IMAGINAL REALM; OUT-OF-BODY EXPERIENCES; PERCEPTION; SLEEP; SLEEP PARALYSIS.

farfadets   A legendary race of small men, dark and hairy, the farfadets are part of French folklore and resemble descriptions of certain humanoids in modern UFO encounters. In this regard, Jacques Vallee cites an anecdote from the 1850s about the farfadets that contains numerous parallels with 20th-century UFO reports. According to the story, several women were returning home around midnight one evening and had just crossed a bridge when they heard a loud noise and saw a mysterious "chariot" being drawn up a hill at high speed by farfadets. The wheels on the chariot were "whining." Although the women were terrified, one of them had enough presence of mind to make the sign of the cross for protection. At that, the "chariot" flew skyward and disappeared into the night. The women reached home safely and told their husbands what had happened. An investigation after daybreak showed no evidence of the incident.

This story bears numerous similarities to modern UFO encounter reports, including the whining noise associated with the flying "chariot"; the terror induced in the witnesses; the absence of tangible evidence of the encounter upon later investigation; and the chariot's sudden departure when confronted by the sign of the cross. In many 20th-century UFO encounter reports, as in cases from the literature on demonology, UFOs and their alleged occupants display an aversion to the language and symbols of Christianity, especially the name of Christ; likewise, the sign of the cross apparently brought about a strong averse response on the part of the farfadets in this reported incident. The description of the far-fadets as small, dark, hairy humanoids matches accounts of other small humanoids in modern UFO close-encounter stories.

See also ACOUSTICAL EFFECTS; CHRIST AND CHRISTIANITY; DEMONOLOGY; ENCOUNTER PHENOMENA; EVIDENCE; RELIGION, UFOS AND.

Fatima, "miracle" of   The alleged miracle of Fatima, which took place in Portugal in 1917, is often cited in UFO lore for its close resemblance to many reported close encounters with UFOs. A being presumed to be the Virgin Mary reportedly appeared to three children and later to large crowds. The appearance and behavior of the entity, thought by many Roman Catholics to have been the Virgin Mary, were virtually identical in many ways with reports of "extraterrestrial" humanoids in UFO encounters. Such apparitions also resemble certain UFO encounter reports in that both categories of sightings appear designed to redirect or reinforce human belief systems in certain directions.

See also BELIEF SYSTEMS; MARIAN APPARITIONS; METALOGIC.

Fermeneuve incident, Canada   On the night of June 12, 1929, one Levis Brosseau was riding a horse near Fermeneuve when he saw a dark object on the ground nearby. The object had a yellow light on. Brosseau's horse became agitated. Near the object, several small figures could be seen running about and talking in voices like those of children. According to Brosseau, the object took off with a mechanical noise and displaced air. The object was estimated to be about 45 feet in diameter and 15 feet high. The reaction of the horse in this report is interesting, because animals often are said to be highly distressed by UFO encounters.

See also ANIMALS, UFOS AND.

fireballs   These luminous objects, sometimes reported as UFOs, are commonly believed to be meteors, or else some kind of display that occurs around certain electrical facilities. Some fireballs have a green hue.

flaps   A UFO "flap" occurs when the media give extensive coverage to a reported UFO incident, but the incident does not occur as part of an actual "wave," or mass of sightings.

See also WAVES.

The Flatwoods, West Virginia, incident allegedly involved a giant humanoid monster with glowing eyes. (U.S. Geological Survey)

Flatwoods, West Virginia, incident, United States   The widely discussed Flatwoods incident reportedly occurred on September 12, 1952. A party of boys witnessed a "meteor" that appeared to land on a hill. On investigation, they found a spherical object about the size of a house, as well as a giant figure 10-to-15 feet tall, with a red face and luminous eyes. When the apparition moved toward them, the observers fled. The following day, another visit to the site allegedly revealed crushed grass and a peculiar odor near the ground. This case is connected with the so-called Bender Mystery, in which American "contactee" Albert Bender claimed to have seen a vision of a monster similar to that reported in the Flatwoods incident.

See also APPARITIONS; BENDER MYSTERY; ENCOUNTER PHENOMENA; SPHERES.

flying top   The "flying top" sighting near Lavonia, Georgia, on June 29, 1964, bears a strong similarity to the Vins-sur-Camary incident in France seven years earlier. A motorist reported seeing an object of an amber color fly over his vehicle along State Route 59. The object—described as about six feet high and top-shaped, with what appeared to be antennae along its rim—followed the car for two miles, emanated great heat, made a loud hissing noise, had an odor like that of embalming fluid and gave off a yellow light through what looked like openings in the lower portion of the object. The object climbed into the sky and disappeared from sight after the driver stopped his car and turned off the headlights. Another, similar incident reportedly occurred several days later in Tallulah Falls, Georgia, at around 9:00 P.M. In this case, a red, cup-shaped UFO allegedly lit up the surrounding landscape with a brilliant green light from its underside. This UFO, too, reportedly left behind an odor like that of embalming fluid. Interference with television reception reportedly accompanied this UFO's appearance.

See also VINS-SUR-CAMARY INCIDENT.

folklore

Folk tales of the world include many references to phenomena and beings resembling certain elements of modern UFO close-encounter reports. These elements include altered perceptions of time and one's surroundings; encounters with humanoids resembling, but differing in important details from, ordinary humans; abductions; rapid flight over long distances; occasional hostility on the part of the humanoids; bizarre vehicles capable of flight; interdimensional gateways between this world and others; and "alien" interest in humans for reproductive purposes. The numerous close similarities between folklore and UFO lore of modern times would appear to indicate that these two bodies of literature share at least some common origins.

See also CHANGELING; ENCOUNTER PHENOMENA; FAIRIES; GENETIC MANIPULATION; INTERDIMENSIONAL GATEWAYS; MILAREPA; TIME EFFECTS; WANG CHIH INCIDENT.

food and drink

In some close-encounter reports, and notably in abduction cases, alleged extraterrestrials are said to give humans something to eat or drink. (Alternatively, but rarely, the aliens may ask humans for food or drink.) An unidentified liquid may be given to the abductee in a container, or administered by force through a mouthpiece that injects the liquid into the subject's throat. In some cases the beverage is an unusual color, such as bright blue. The drink may be associated with dramatic and unexpected changes in the subject's perceptions. The subject may experience improved vision, for example, or feel ill. Intellectual effects also may be reported, such as a sharpening of one's understanding. In some cases, drowsiness and forgetfulness are associated with the beverages.

Apparently, in such reports, administering drink or food to a human abductee is a means to obtain some kind of control over the person. There is a parallel here with biblical passages in which consuming food is linked to diabolical influence over humans. In chapter three of the book of Genesis, Satan (in the form of a serpent) tempts Eve to eat of the fruit of the tree in the middle of the garden, and the result is a victory for the Devil, namely the fall of hu-

mankind. Also, the gospel of John relates how Satan entered into Judas at the Last Supper after Judas had taken a morsel of food (John 13:27).

See also ABDUCTIONS; DEMONOLOGY.

foo fighters

These curious objects were reportedly seen flying alongside Allied military aircraft over Europe during World War II. The objects were commonly described as red or orange in color and several feet in diameter. They would pace the aircraft for a while, then depart. Foo fighter sightings were not restricted to Europe. The objects were reported seen over Asia as well. Some, if not all, of the sightings may have involved misidentifications of stars or planets, ball lightning or static electricity (St. Elmo's Fire). There are various accounts of how "foo fighters" received their name. According to one story, "foo" comes from the French *feu*, meaning fire. Another explanation is that "foo" was taken from a saying in the then-popular "Smokey Stover" comic strip: "Where there's foo, there's fire."

See also ASTRONOMY.

footprints

Footprints of alleged extraterrestrials occupy a small but interesting niche in UFO lore. Some "contactees" claim to have received messages from aliens through study of the visitors' footprints. George Adamski, for example, claimed to have recovered messages from a visitor from Venus by making plaster casts of the space traveler's footprints. Why beings capable of traveling millions of miles to Earth in highly advanced spacecraft should see fit to communicate through footprints is unfathomable, and such reports are seen as merely one more element of absurdity in the UFO phenomenon. Huge footprints—purportedly those of extraterrestrials—also have been reported in UFO close-encounter cases and bear a strong resemblance to reports of "Bigfoot" tracks in the Pacific Northwest of the United States.

See also ABSURDITY; ADAMSKI, GEORGE; BIGFOOT; DOUGLAS INCIDENT.

Fort, Charles (1874-1932)

An American journalist, Fort spent much of his life collecting information on strange and seemingly inexplicable happenings, which he described in his four books, *The Book of the Damned* (published in 1919), *New Lands* (1923), *Lo!* (1931) and *Wild Talents* (1932). Portions of Fort's work deal with UFOS. Fort suggested that extraterrestrial marauders—"Super Tamerlanes," he called them—had beset our world in ages past, and that humans might be hunted for their brains by predatory aliens. Fort imagined that humans might be "fished for" by mysterious beings, which he described as "super-epicures." Fort even speculated that mysterious falls of colored rain and organic matter from the sky were the results of interplanetary battles and the wrecks of "super-vessels" in outer space. Once, in a passage reminiscent of the traditional Christian view of Satan and Satan's influence on human affairs, Fort imagined that a "super-evil" being with great wings like those of a bat considered Earth his property and was responsible for certain happenings in the skies. Many readers took Fort's work seriously, and his ideas had a strong influence on science fiction in the first half of the 20th century. The noted science fiction author Eric Frank Russell considered Fort a "genius" and based two well-known novels, *Sinister Barrier* (1943) and *Dreadful Sanctuary* (1951) on ideas from Fort. Several journals have been devoted to Fort's ideas, including the British publications *Lo!* and *Fortean Times*, and the American journal *Doubt*. Fort's work has been cited as an example of mildly paranoid thinking, and his career has been analyzed in terms of the "status inconsistency theory," which relates decline in an individual's social status to his or her inclination to report UFO encounters.

See also PARANOID; STATUS INCONSISTENCY THEORY.

Frametown incident, West Virginia, United States

This alleged incident occurred on September 13, 1952, one day after the famous Flatwoods, West Virginia, encounter. According to the Frametown report, Mr. and Mrs. George Snitowski and their young daughter were driving through woods when their automobile stalled. A highly unpleasant odor, like a combination of ether and sulfur, permeated the air. In the woods, Mr. Snitowski allegedly saw a bright light. He walked toward it. As he walked, he felt peculiar prickling sensations all over his body, and soon stopped. On the way back to the car, he lost his balance repeatedly. Arriving at the car, he saw his frightened wife pointing to a giant humanoid figure some 10 feet tall, standing about 30 feet away. The family locked themselves in the car. After inspecting the vehicle, the huge being reportedly glided, rather than walked, into the woods. The light in the woods then rose slowly in a pendulum motion and departed, leaving a glowing trail behind. This report bears numerous similarities to the Flatwoods incident, notably the alleged encounter with a huge, terrifying entity. The sulfurous smell is another likeness between this report and numerous other close-encounter cases, as well as many reports of evil spirits from the literature on demonology.

The pendulum motion of the UFO also is a common feature of UFO reports, as is the stalling of automobiles in the vicinity of UFOs.

See also DEMONOLOGY; FLATWOODS INCIDENT; HUMANOIDS; ODORS; VEHICLE EFFECTS.

France

The site of some of the most famous UFO sightings, France has also been the center for extensive research on the UFO phenomenon. The Valensole incident, in which a farmer reportedly encountered an extraterrestrial craft and two of its occupants in his fields, is a widely known encounter case from French UFO literature. The "Dr. X" case, in which a physician reportedly was marked on his skin with the imprint of a triangle during an encounter with UFOs, is also a familiar case from French UFO files.

Especially notable about alleged UFO encounters in France is that the so-called extraterrestrials appear in many cases to display a character different from the "aliens" reported seen in some other countries. Some extraterrestrials allegedly encountered in France have been compared to tourists out to see the sights of a foreign land, unlike the "UFOnauts" reported elsewhere, who may come across as violent and aggressive. Cases similar to modern UFO encounter reports have been reported in France for centuries.

See also AGOBARD INCIDENT; DR. X INCIDENT; VALENSOLE INCIDENT; VALLEE, JACQUES; VINS-SUR-CAMARY INCIDENT.

frequency

UFO lore often mentions some change in "frequency" that is expected to affect all of human society in the near future and to be linked somehow with alleged extraterrestrial influence. When Earth's "frequency" changes, one is told, society will undergo a dramatic and fundamental change under extraterrestrial guidance. How the word "frequency" applies in this context is not explained clearly. In physics, frequency means the number of cycles per second observed in phenomena such as sound waves, radio waves and light waves. The misapplication of "frequency" is a familiar example of the pseudoscientific aspect of the UFO phenomenon. The expression "vibrations" is also misused in similar fashion in UFO lore.

See also PSEUDOSCIENCE; VIBRATIONS.

Friday demons

These evil spirits are described in the writings of the 16th-century occultist Henricus Cornelius Agrippa von Nettesheim and are comparable to many modern descriptions of "extraterrestrials." The Friday demons are good-looking and of average stature, and a brilliant star precedes their appearances.

See also DEMONOLOGY; HUMANOIDS; OCCULTISM.

frogs   One minor but intriguing element of the UFO phenomenon is the occasional sighting of a frog-like, or at least vaguely amphibious-looking, being with an apparently humanoid stance and gait. The "frog" may be seen on or near a UFO, or by itself. Why such beings should be associated with UFOs has not been explained satisfactorily.

See also JUMINDA INCIDENT.

Fry incident, United States   One of the first "contactee" cases following World War II, the Fry incident reportedly occurred on the night of July 4, 1950. Daniel Fry, a technician employed at White Sands, New Mexico, went for a walk and encountered a football-shaped object, metallic in appearance and about 30 feet wide by 16 feet high, landed in the desert. A voice spoke to him in English and invited him to take a ride in the craft. There he was shown images of the Earth's surface falling away beneath the craft as it rose into the air. He saw pictures of North America passing beneath the craft as it supposedly traveled to New York and back to the desert. The round trip took about half an hour, an interval that would have required a velocity of 8,000 miles per hour for the journey. What exactly Fry saw is open to question, because he indicated the images were displayed by a device resembling a movie projector. He had no face-to-face contact with "alien" visitors. Instead, he heard the voice of a being that identified itself as "Aylan" or "Alan." Fry also indicated he felt no sensation of motion during his apparent journey, except for a feeling of weightlessness at one point.

After this experience, Fry claimed to have received more communications from the visitors, who allegedly originated on Mars, lived now on spaceships and were becoming accustomed to Earth's higher gravitation only gradually, so that they did not expect to adjust to conditions on Earth for several more years. The alleged Martians were supposedly here on Earth to save our world from a frightful war similar to one that, Fry was told, destroyed the Martian civilization some 30,000 years earlier.

Some observers take a skeptical view of the Fry incident and point out that Fry's "experience" could have been accomplished using technology available on Earth at the time. The device that resembled a motion picture projector, for example, perhaps was exactly that.

See also ADAMSKI, GEORGE; AYLAN; ENCOUNTER PHENOMENA.

G

Gallipoli incident, Turkey The alleged disappearance of Britain's First Fourth Norfolk regiment on August 21, 1915, is sometimes cited as a report of a mass abduction. According to the story, the regiment marched into a dense, low-hanging "cloud" near a point known as Hill 60, and was never seen again. The cloud allegedly was shaped like a loaf of bread and was about 800 feet long, 200 feet high and 200 feet wide. After the last members of the regiment entered the cloud, it reportedly arose from the ground and joined several other, similar clouds. The clouds then departed northward as a group. The clouds were described as unchanging in shape and apparently unmoved by wind. According to this report, the Turks did not capture this regiment, nor even make contact with it. The incident is said to have taken place in the last days of the fighting at Gallipoli.

See also ABDUCTIONS; CLOUDS AND VAPORS.

genetic manipulation One element of the UFO phenomenon is a belief that extraterrestrials have manipulated, and perhaps continue to manipulate, the genetics of the human species. Various scenarios have been presented for aliens' tinkering with the human species. One suggestion is that extraterrestrials had sexual intercourse with human women or conceived children by them through artificial insemination. According to another scenario, extraterrestrials induced mutations in humankind by artificial means, thus generating a more intelligent and capable race of hominids on Earth. Although these suggestions have been discredited, the notion behind them—that extraterrestrials may seek to manipulate human genetic material—has re-emerged in the UFO

abduction mythology of more recent years. Various "contactees" have reported that their alleged alien abductors seek human sperm and ova for experimentation and breeding, and that "hybrid" infants, half human and half alien, already have been born. Such reports are questionable at best, yet belief in extraterrestrials conducting genetic research on humans remains a prominent part of UFO lore. Such reports bear a close resemblance to the activity of incubi and succubi, as described in the literature on demonology.

See also DEMONOLOGY; ENCOUNTER PHENOMENA; INCUBI AND SUCCUBI; SEXUAL ENCOUNTERS; VILLAS-BOAS INCIDENT; VON DÄNIKEN, ERICH.

Gentry Part of the "fairy faith" of the British Isles, the Gentry are said to be a tall, noble, supposedly superhuman race similar in many ways to certain alleged UFO occupants described in close-encounter cases from the late 20th century. Powers ascribed to the Gentry include the ability to appear in various forms, including those of small humanoids; to induce paralysis in humans; and to carry away humans to their land in incidents similar to modern UFO abduction reports. The lore of the Gentry also mentions exchanges of food between Gentry and humans. This element of the Gentry mythology has a close parallel in UFO lore, which includes numerous reports of "extraterrestrials" either requesting food from humans or providing food to them.

See also DEMONOLOGY; FAIRIES; FOOD AND DRINK; HUMANOIDS.

geographical distribution of UFO sightings Although UFOs have been sighted in virtually every inhabited area of the globe, even in Antarctica, the geographical distribution of these sightings is far from even. Some areas of the globe have intense concentrations of UFO sightings, whereas other areas show much less activity. These high-activity areas are commonly known as "windows." The geographical distribution of UFO sightings does not appear to be correlated strongly with population density. On the contrary, many notable sightings have occurred in sparsely populated areas rather than in densely settled parts of the world. This distribution—numerous sightings in underpopulated areas—has been interpreted as evidence against the view that UFOs are merely figments of the human imagination. If that were indeed the case, then one probably would expect to find a strong positive correlation between high population density and frequency of UFO sightings.

See also WINDOWS.

Georgian Bay incident, Canada   One of many incidents in which UFO activity is reported in or just above large bodies of water, the Georgian Bay incident reportedly occurred in August 1914 and was observed by witnesses. They allegedly saw a spherical UFO resting on the lake's surface. The UFO's crew reportedly dropped a hose into the water, then

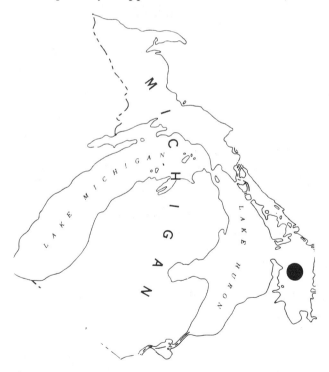

The Georgian Bay incident involved a UFO reportedly seen lowering a hose into the water. (U.S. Geological Survey)

flew away after seeing the witnesses. Two of the crew were described as small men wearing green and purple clothing. Three other crew members were described as wearing brown clothing as well as masks that extended to their shoulders. This report is extremely similar to the Steep Rock Lake incident, also reported in Canada in 1950.

See also AQUATIC OBJECTS; STEEP ROCK LAKE INCIDENT.

ghost aircraft   During the 1930s, numerous reports occurred in Europe and the United States of unidentified aircraft that were seen flying in dangerous weather conditions (in which ordinary aircraft dared not go aloft) and shining bright searchlights onto the ground. In some cases, engine noises were reported, but in other incidents the mysterious craft flew in total silence. The unidentified aircraft were reported over Scandinavia, Britain and the United States. Scandinavia was also the scene of numerous "ghost rocket" sightings immediately after World War II. The ghost aircraft phenomenon is reminiscent of the "airships" reported seen over the United States in the late 19th century and of the unmarked helicopters allegedly sighted and associated with UFOs in the United States in the late 20th century.

See also AIRSHIPS; GHOST ROCKETS; HELICOPTERS.

ghost rockets   In 1946, more than 2,000 "ghost rockets" and other UFOs were sighted in the Scandinavian countries (Denmark, Finland, Norway and Sweden) and later in other countries, including Greece, India, Italy and Portugal. The objects were described as rockets because they left trails of fire. Their velocities varied greatly. Some flew at tremendous speed, whereas others were much slower. The "rockets" also performed maneuvers such as climbing and diving. Occasional crashes were reported. Swedish authorities in particular were alarmed at the incidents and consulted American military experts, including Lieutenant General James Doolittle and General David Sarnoff. It was feared that the ghost rockets represented Soviet tests of a new weapon similar to the V-1 and V-2 military rockets that Nazi Germany had directed against Britain in the latter days of World War II. Later, however, it was pointed out that the Soviets, had they been responsible for the ghost rockets, would have succeeded in more than doubling the range of the German weapons. Such an achievement seemed unlikely for the Soviets. Some of the sightings also were attributed to meteors. Approximately 200 of the UFOs were said to have registered on radar. The ghost rocket sightings followed closely upon reports, from pilots during World War II, of mysterious objects, dubbed "foo fighters," that supposedly accompanied aircraft in flight.

See also FOO FIGHTERS; GHOST AIRCRAFT.

ghosts, UFOs and Often described as manifestations of spirits of the deceased, ghosts occupy, along with many UFO reports and related phenomena, a place among "paranormal" events, meaning those that are difficult or impossible to explain in terms of known physical phenomena. There are numerous similarities between reports of ghostly "hauntings" and close-encounter incidents involving alleged UFO occupants. Ghosts are said to be capable of moving through material objects, making eerie noises and speaking to human witnesses. Messages allegedly delivered through ghosts include prophecies of future events. Ghosts may be seen in various shapes, ranging from humanoid form to spheres of light, and are said to be capable of taking on lifelike human appearance. They have also been described as giants, small humanoids and nonhumans. A feeling of intense cold often is associated with reports of hauntings, as is an unpleasant smell, such as that of sulfur or of rotting meat. Ghosts allegedly may reappear often to the same witness and manipulate objects. Levitation is another capability attributed to ghosts. Domestic animals may exhibit strong averse reactions in the presence of alleged ghosts, and electronic equipment also has been said to malfunction during manifestations of ghosts. Vehicle effects—interference with the operation of a motor vehicle, either by neutralizing its electrical system or by exerting physical force on it—are also part of ghost lore. A certain category of haunting, the "poltergeist" or "noisy ghost," involves loud noises and the translocation of objects in a home; crockery reportedly may fly around the room during a poltergeist event, for example. Ghosts are credited with making a wide variety of sounds, notably powerful explosive sounds like the sonic booms produced by supersonic aircraft. Photographic evidence of ghosts and hauntings has been produced but remains questionable at best, because such evidence may be faked in numerous ways. There is some debate about what kind of phenomenon ghosts and hauntings actually represent. Hoaxes are a strong possibility in many cases and may account for the vast majority of such reports. Hallucinations also may be the source of many tales of hauntings, as may be honest misinterpretation of known physical phenomena such as electrical discharges or the reflection of train lamps or automobile headlights. It is difficult to dismiss all ghost reports as mere fabrications, however, because some such cases apparently do involve events that cannot be explained easily as known physical phenomena. Where spiritual activity is suspected as the cause of alleged hauntings, it is a matter of debate whether these events represent activity by disembodied spirits of deceased humans, or whether other entities, including demons, may be involved.

All these characteristics apply also to numerous accounts of close encounters with UFOs and their occupants. Alleged witnesses of UFO close encounters have described the "extraterrestrials" as humanoids, both large and small, as well as frightening nonhumans with an amphibian, reptilian or insectoid appearance. In some cases, notably those of American "contactees" George Adamski and Truman Bethurum, the alleged aliens have appeared in forms virtually indistinguishable from ordinary humans, though perhaps more handsome and having a few peculiarities of form such as an unusual shape of ears or chin. UFO occupants are said to have delivered messages containing prophecies (many of which turned out to be inaccurate). The "UFOnauts" reportedly are capable of flying and of producing levitation in humans, animals and inanimate objects. Poltergeist activity is commonly reported in homes of witnesses to UFO phenomena. Interference with vehicles and electrical equipment is another widely reported characteristic of close encounters with UFOs. In some cases, alleged extraterrestrials have been seen to pass through solid objects, precisely in the manner of ghosts. Unusual—often unpleasant— odors are associated with UFO close-encounter reports. Temperature effects, notably a fierce chill, reportedly occur as part of UFO phenomena. The aliens may appear repeatedly to the same "contactee." Dogs, cats, cattle and other domestic animals may exhibit intense fear in the presence of "extraterrestrials." Sometimes the same reaction is observed in humans, though a human's response to an "alien" presence may be a deep feeling of peace instead. Peculiar noises are another feature of UFO contact reports, including loud and seemingly inexplicable explosive sounds. Finally, photographic and other evidence of UFOs has been produced and widely published, but no such evidence is accepted universally as proof that UFO encounters actually have occurred, and hoaxes are numerous.

The similarity between ghosts and "extraterrestrials" leads some observers of the UFO phenomenon to conclude that "hauntings" and UFOs represent two different aspects of the same phenomenon—a phenomenon that is more spiritual and psychological than physical in character.

Some students of UFOs have attempted a spiritual explanation of UFOs. Famed "contactee" Albert Bender, for example, tried to explain that his encounters with alleged aliens in terms of traditional Christian theology, and the distinguished Russian Orthodox theologian Father Seraphim Rose argued that UFOs, when not attributable to hoaxes, hallucinations or honest mistakes, represented manifestations of demonic activity. Although many UFO reports bear a strong resemblance to reports of visitations by spirits of the deceased, there is no convincing reason to think that this particular kind of "haunting" is actually responsible for any UFO close-encounter cases.

See also ADAMSKI, GEORGE; BENDER MYSTERY; BETHURUM INCIDENT; DEMONOLOGY; INCUBI AND SUCCUBI; ODORS; ROSE, FATHER SERAPHIM; TEMPERATURE EFFECTS; UFOS, CHARACTERISTICS OF; VEHICLE EFFECTS.

Giant Rock Space Conventions A series of quasi-religious gatherings of UFO enthusiasts starting in 1954, the Giant Rock Space Conventions were organized by George Van Tassel, a prominent "contactee" who claimed to be in communication with a mysterious extraterrestrial "Council of Seven Lights," made up of beings aboard a spaceship circling Earth. The first conference drew more than 5,000 attendees and included an unsuccessful nighttime watch for UFOs. Various other alleged contactees, including George Adamski and Truman Bethurum, attended the conventions. Van Tassel's other projects included the Integratron, a huge, never-completed device that was supposed to reverse or halt the aging process in humans.

See also ADAMSKI, GEORGE; BELIEF SYSTEMS; BETHURUM INCIDENT; COUNCIL OF SEVEN LIGHTS; CULTS; INTEGRATRON; PSEUDOSCIENCE.

Gill incident, New Guinea One of the most widely publicized and discussed incidents in UFO literature, the Gill incident has a unique status among UFO encounter stories, partly because of the lengthy duration of the sighting; the large number of witnesses; the consistency of their observations; and the credibility of the principal witness, a clergyman of the Church of England who was assigned to a mission in New Guinea.

The sighting reportedly occurred on the evening of June 26, 1959, when Reverend William Booth Gill went outside, looked up at the sky and saw a bright, "sparkling" object that descended to an altitude of perhaps 300 feet. He emphasized that he was not looking at the planet Venus, which he could see elsewhere in the sky. The object was perceived to be a disc with a deck on top. Several humanoid figures (Gill described them as "men") emerged from the craft and stood on the deck. They appeared to be manipulating something, perhaps a control mechanism. A column of blue light extended skyward from the center of the disc. The light would appear for one or two seconds, then go off. This activity continued for the remainder of the night. Then the disc climbed to a higher altitude and remained there. Gill said he perceived a structure like the bridge of a ship atop the disc. Under the disc were four legs that pointed downward on a diagonal. Gill admitted that his estimates were poor but said that he figured the craft's diameter at approximately 35 to 40 feet at the base and some 20 feet at the top. The sighting was witnessed by more than 30 people, including a teacher and boys from the local area.

Gill and the teacher tried to make contact with the men on the disc by waving their arms over their heads. The men on deck waved their arms in return. At one point, Gill and his companions tried to signal the craft with a flashlight. As if in response, the craft descended close to the ground but did not land. Gill said his sightings extended over a period of several days. Other sightings were reported in the vicinity at about the same time. Gill said afterward that he had been a skeptic concerning UFO reports before this series of incidents.

See also ENCOUNTER PHENOMENA.

"gods" and "goddesses" The "ancient astronauts" phenomenon of the late 1960s and early 1970s interpreted the "gods" and "goddesses" of antiquity as recollections of visitations by extraterrestrial space travelers who supposedly stopped on Earth millennia ago and impressed our ancestors with their technology. This simplistic interpretation was (and apparently still is) widely believed, although no solid evidence exists to support it. Much of the alleged evidence in favor of this hypothesis has been proven to be erroneous, or a set of outright hoaxes.

According to a more sophisticated interpretation of the connection between UFOs and the "gods" and "goddesses" of antiquity, UFO encounters bear a strong resemblance to the reported activities of "familiar spirits." These are said to be evil spirits that attach themselves, so to speak, to an individual and become "familiar" with that person. In this interpretation, such spirits desire to be worshipped as gods and have encouraged such worship on the part of humans by appearing either in the images of "divinities" in antiquity, or as "extraterrestrials" in our own time.

See also ANCIENT ASTRONAUTS; BELIEF SYSTEMS; DEMONOLOGY; ENCOUNTER PHENOMENA; EVIDENCE; FAMILIAR SPIRITS; HOAXES; MARIAN APPARITIONS; RELIGION, UFOS AND; ROSE, FATHER SERAPHIM.

Goethe incident, Germany The 18th-century German poet Johann Wolfgang von Goethe, author of *Faust*, reported seeing, while traveling by coach between Frankfurt and Leipzig in 1768, a phenomenon much like some reported modern UFO encounters. Goethe reported seeing in a ravine an "amphitheater" filled with numerous brilliant, small lights. Some of the lights were stationary, but others moved with vigor. Goethe investigated the incident and learned that a stone quarry filled with water was located in the vicinity of his sighting. The lights he described could be interpreted as reflections of sunlight off water in the quarry, but Goethe apparently considered the possibility that he had seen "will-of-the-wisps" or other glowing "creatures." This sighting resembles many modern UFO reports in that luminous, moving objects are sighted; a possible natural explanation for the sighting (in this case, reflections of sunlight on water) exists; and the observer admits the possibility of some paranormal phenomenon.

See also ENCOUNTER PHENOMENA.

good and evil The motives of alleged extraterrestrials in UFO abduction reports have been the subject of much discussion among students of the UFO phenomenon. According to one school of thought, reflected in stories of early "contactees" such as George Adamski, the putative aliens are benevolent and seek only to help the human species through an especially perilous phase of its history. Other contactees have reported that the "extraterrestrials" expressed great love for humankind. "Channeled" messages have emphasized the presumed benevolence of the "space people."

Opposed to this image of "good" aliens is a large body of testimony that "aliens" can be highly malevolent and even murderous in their encounters with humans. Reports of mutilation, torture and rape by alleged aliens are commonplace in the lore of UFOs. Even when aliens in such cases are not said to carry out such crimes, numerous threats from "extraterrestrials" have been reported. Albert Bender's account of his meetings with aliens, for example, included descriptions of their alleged ability—and willingness—to cause mass destruction on Earth if humans dared to interfere with their mission. In-

deed, so malignant is the aliens' behavior in many such reports that numerous parallels have been drawn between UFO close-encounter stories and the literature on demonology.

One curious aspect of UFO lore is that even when "extraterrestrials" behavior appears evil, contactees in some cases insist on describing the aliens as "good." This apparent inconsistency has been explained by the Greek theologian Alexander Kalomiros, who points out that Western civilization has a tradition of describing evil things as "good" in hopes of appeasing them. This tradition, continued to the present, may account for the attributed "goodness" of malevolent "alien" entities.

See also ABDUCTIONS; ADAMSKI, GEORGE; AUTOMATIC WRITING; BENDER MYSTERY; BODILY EFFECTS; CHANNELING; COMMUNICATIONS; DEATHS; DEMONOLOGY; INCUBI AND SUCCUBI; SEXUAL ENCOUNTERS; SUICIDES.

Gorman incident, United States One of the early post–World War II reports of encounters between UFOs and aircraft, the Gorman incident involved an alleged set of maneuvers between an F-51 jet fighter, piloted by Second Lieutenant George Gorman of the North Dakota Air National Guard, and a luminous object near Fargo, North Dakota, on the evening of October 1, 1948. Gorman described the unidentified object as round, white and about eight inches in diameter, with fuzzy edges. Gorman allegedly performed a set of maneuvers trying to intercept the object and later to avoid it when the object appeared to be on a collision course with his aircraft. The encounter is said to have lasted almost half an hour and to have been observed by eyewitnesses on the ground. Gorman reported that the object was capable of flying faster than his plane and climbing both faster and more steeply than an Air Force aircraft. The object allegedly did not, however, perform the radical maneuvers often attributed to UFOs, such as instantaneous right-angle turns and immediate acceleration to high velocity from a stationary position. The Air Force investigated the case under Project Sign. The incident was attributed later as a sighting of a balloon, although this explanation has been questioned.

See also AIRCRAFT, UFOS AND; AIR FORCE; SIGN, PROJECT.

grays A category of humanoids described in UFO close-encounter reports, "grays" are said to be perhaps three to four feet tall, with gray skin; oversized, hairless heads; spindly limbs and thin torsos. The eyes are described as large and dark, and slanted upward at the outer corners. There is considerable variation in other details of bodily structure, but the "classic" gray is said to have a small or non-existent nose, as well as a small, lipless mouth and slender fingers. According to some accounts, the fingers may be tipped with claws or small suction cups. Tales of human-gray "hybrids," produced by some kind of genetic engineering, have circulated widely in the popular literature on UFOs and are linked to tales of sexual encounters between humans and alleged extraterrestrials. The mythology of grays is large and detailed. Reports of contact with grays appear to be concentrated largely in the Untied States. Grays apparently figure less prominently in close-encounter reports from other countries.

See also HUMANOIDS; SEXUAL ENCOUNTERS.

Green campaign, United States Founder and president of the Amalgamated Flying Saucer Clubs of America, Inc., Gabriel Green ran for president of the United States in 1960 under the slogan "America Needs a Space Age President." Headquartered in Los Angeles, the Green campaign urged voters to choose Green if they sought the "true Stairway to the Stars," "free energy" and "Utopia now." Green lost the presidential race in 1960. His second presidential campaign, in 1972, was likewise unsuccessful. During a race for the U.S. Senate in California in 1962, however, Green reportedly received more than 170,000 votes.

See also POLITICS AND UFOS.

green children A bit of medieval English folklore, the story of the "green children" bears a strong resemblance to certain elements of UFO lore. The tale concerns two green-skinned children, a boy and a girl, who were discovered near the mouth of a pit in Suffolk. The children spoke some unintelligible language. They were taken to the home of a knight. At first they would eat nothing but beans. The boy died soon, but the girl survived and, after developing a taste for other foods, lost her green color. She entered the service of the knight and reportedly said she and her young friend had wandered into the English countryside through a mysterious cavern but were unable to find their way back. All the inhabitants of her country, she said, had green skin. The country was called "St. Martin's Land," and the girl said its inhabitants were Christians.

Besides its similarity to the 20th-century myth of "little green men" from other planets, the tale of the green children resembles modern UFO encounter stories in that the children allegedly reported on the spiritual life of humanoid aliens. The story also

brings to mind rumors in late 20th-century America of small, humanoid extraterrestrials who were captured and kept alive for a time on terrestrial foods.

See also FOOD AND DRINK; HUMANOIDS; LITTLE GREEN MEN; "STRAWBERRY ICE CREAM SHOW."

Greenhaw incident, United States During a "wave" of UFO sightings in the United States in 1973, Police Chief Jeff Greenhaw of Falkville, Alabama, reportedly encountered a six-foot-tall humanoid in a metallic suit along a road in Morgan County, while investigating a report of an object with flashing lights landing near the town. Greenhaw allegedly took four photographs of the humanoid, then tried to pursue the figure but was unable to keep pace with it, even in a patrol car. Greenhaw indicated that the being ran in long strides and traveled faster than 30-to-40 miles per hour. Greenhaw allegedly experienced a series of unpleasant events following this encounter, including a fire at his home that destroyed the original prints of the photographs.

See also HUMANOIDS.

Greensburg, Pennsylvania, incident, United States The Greensburg incident reportedly occurred in 1973 and involved sightings of large, hairy, ape-like beings in connection with a UFO report. Around 9:00 P.M., one Stephen Pulaski, a farmer, along with more than a dozen other witnesses, including neighbors and relatives, allegedly saw a red ball hovering high above a field. Pulaski and two 10-year-old boys went to investigate, taking along a rifle. While they approached the object, Pulaski (according to the story) noticed that his vehicle's headlights had dimmed. The unidentified object could be seen descending gradually toward the ground. From the crest of a nearby hill, the three could see the object resting on, or suspended just over, the field. The object was now glowing white. Its diameter was estimated at about 100 feet. It was described as "dome-shaped" and making a noise like that of a lawn mower. Then one of the two boys allegedly said he saw something walking near them. Pulaski thought he could see two figures in the darkness. On the presumption that they were bears, he fired over their heads. Then he saw that they were seven to eight feet tall and had hands and long arms. The beings reportedly appeared to be covered with long, dark gray hair and to have yellow-green eyes. One of the beings, slightly shorter than the other, appeared to take lengthy strides, trying to keep pace with its larger companion. The beings made a sound much like that of a crying infant and

The Greensburg, Pennsylvania, incident was a bizarre report involving huge, hairy, ape-like beings. (U.S. Geological Survey)

evidently were communicating with each other. A smell like that of burning rubber was in the air. Allegedly, Pulaski fired a second round over their heads, and saw that the beings were approaching him and the two boys. Then he fired three shots into the larger figure. The being reportedly made a whining noise and raised one hand toward its companion. At this time one of the boys ran away in fear. The light and noise from the unidentified object also ceased. The two tall beings turned and walked away into the woods. A luminous white area remained on the ground where the object had been. Pulaski began having trouble with his vision.

Pulaski reported the incident to police, and a policeman came to Pulaski's farm to investigate. Pulaski and the trooper allegedly went to the site of the encounter and found the luminous area still visible on the ground. One strand of a nearby electric fence was found broken, although Pulaski did not recall it being broken earlier. On their right, about 50 yards away, the two men heard noises as of someone walking through the woods. Evidently some large creature was proceeding toward them, breaking trees noisily as it approached. The sound followed the two men when they moved, and stopped several seconds after they ceased moving. The men debated briefly whether or not to return to the luminous area. The trooper wished to return, but Pulaski was reluctant. The trooper decided it was better to remain with Pulaski than to proceed alone toward the luminous area. As the men started back toward the car, the noise in the woods resumed. When they reached the car, Pulaski said he saw a brown form nearing them and asked the trooper's permission to fire at it. The trooper approved, and Pulaski fired. Then Pulaski shouted that something was moving out of the woods toward them. The men departed in the car and drove about 50 yards. Then they

turned and directed the headlights on high beam into the woods. At this point, Pulaski said, the luminous area vanished. (After the incident, animals reportedly would not enter the formerly luminous zone, which was allegedly about 150 feet in diameter.)

Around 1:30 A.M., a team of investigators from a local UFO study group reportedly visited the scene but found no luminous area, nor any unusual radiation readings on the ground or on Pulaski, who had been checked before the team visited the alleged encounter site. Pulaski and his father visited the site with the investigators. Around 2:00 A.M., a bull in a field nearby allegedly became frightened, as did the Pulaskis' dog, a German shepherd, which began tracking something. The dog stared at a particular spot by the roadside, but the men saw nothing extraordinary at that location. Pulaski started rubbing his head and face and collapsed. Then, according to the report, Pulaski started breathing heavily, growling in animal fashion, and waving his arms around violently. He knocked his father and another man to the ground. The dog approached Pulaski as if preparing to attack him, but retreated when Pulaski defended himself. Another man in the party complained of feeling light-headed, and a third man in the group began having difficulty breathing. Meanwhile, Pulaski continued his growling and the violent motion.

Then Pulaski collapsed and fell forward onto the ground. After a short time, he warned the others to keep their distance, because (he said) "it" was there. A strong smell of sulfur was in the air. As the elder Pulaski and another member of the party helped Stephen Pulaski out of the vicinity, Stephen pointed and warned the group again to stay clear of "it." He is said to have reported seeing a man wearing a black cloak and hat and carrying a sickle. The figure allegedly told him of the existence of a man who could save the world. The dark figure added that "the end" would occur soon, if humankind's behavior did not improve. Pulaski also said he heard his name being called from the woods: "Stephen, Stephen."

During a later psychiatric interview, Pulaski allegedly recalled seeing "fire" behind the dark figure with the scythe. In front of the figure was something Pulaski described as a "force" containing "creatures," who called to him by name and laughed in a manner that made him angry. Pulaski also recalled that behind him was a light, from which some entity urged him to "go ahead" and assured him that he could not be harmed. He had the impression that the dark figure intended for the creatures to kill him.

Pulaski also allegedly perceived intense hatred. Then Pulaski heard a voice say, "He is here." The identity of this individual, however, was not made clear. Pulaski thought someone was presenting him with a puzzle. The date 1976 kept occurring to Pulaski, and Pulaski evidently had the impression that at that date humankind would destroy itself, barring changes in human behavior.

The Greensburg incident contains elements common to many other UFO encounter cases, such as the luminous aerial object that changes color; an encounter with large, hairy humanoids near the UFO; communications from alien beings, evidently through telepathy; and a vague "revelation" of future events. Although a later investigation revealed no evidence that Pulaski had been involved with the occult, certain elements of his story are consistent with evil paranormal activity, including perceptions of hatred and hostility on the part of the alien entities; and strong averse reactions by domestic animals to some presence that was invisible to humans. The sulfurous stench reported in the Greensburg incident is also mentioned in other UFO-related encounter cases, notably that of Albert Bender, who detected a powerful odor of sulfur in his home on several occasions when a mysterious entity appeared there. Such an odor is also linked with alleged demonic manifestations.

See also ANIMALS, UFOS AND; BENDER MYSTERY; DEMONOLOGY; ENCOUNTER PHENOMENA; ODORS; TELEPATHY.

gremlins   Mythical, humanoid beings said to perform sabotage on aircraft, gremlins resemble in many ways the humanoids of UFO lore. Gremlins are said to have been sighted in various shapes and sizes, but usually are described as one foot tall or less. Descriptions of their clothing vary. Some gremlins supposedly wear boots with suction cups on them. Others are said to wear brightly colored jackets and breeches. In some cases, gremlins allegedly are seen as misty, indistinct forms moving around the cabin of an aircraft. Such descriptions resemble strongly certain accounts of UFO occupants or other UFO-related entities. The name "gremlin" apparently was first applied to the imagined beings in 1939 after British bomber crews experienced a run of evident sabotage to their planes.

See also HUMANOIDS.

group abductions   Although many abduction reports involve only a single "abductee," some such cases are said to involve two or more individuals. The celebrated Hill incident falls into this category.

In such cases, the perceptions of the human abductees may differ considerably, even when both allegedly look at the same object or entity. An "extraterrestrial," for example, may appear to one witness to have a long nose, whereas the other witness may recall later seeing no nose at all on the alien. Evidence such as this casts strong doubt upon the presumption that both or all of the human witnesses in similar situations actually look at corporeal, biological extraterrestrials.

Alternative hypotheses are many. For example, both alleged abductees may recall some fictional account of an abduction, altering various details according to their individual memories. Another hypothesis is that an abduction of sorts did occur by nonhuman beings, but the abductees witnessed a series of illusions rather than an appearance by corporeal, "flesh-and-blood" aliens. Such cases bear a strong similarity to certain reports from the literature on demonology.

In some rare cases, large numbers of humans are said to be abducted by UFOs and never returned to Earth. Although such stories fall squarely into the realm of fantasy, as a rule, independent testimony from witnesses in some cases provides at least some verisimilitude to the stories. The alleged disappearances of the First Fourth Norfolk regiment at Gallipoli, for example, reportedly involved the abduction of a large body of troops by a cloud-like UFO. There apparently were enough witnesses to this strange event to create a considerable public controversy at the time.

See also ABDUCTIONS; DEMONOLOGY; GALLIPOLI INCIDENT; HILL INCIDENT; HUMANOIDS; ILLUSION.

Grudge, Project   From 1948 to 1952, the U.S. Air Force investigated UFO sightings under Project Grudge, succeeding Project Sign. Project Grudge became Project Blue Book in 1952.

See also BLUE BOOK, PROJECT; SIGN, PROJECT.

Gulf Breeze incidents, United States   Among the most famous cases in the UFO literature, the Gulf Breeze, Florida, incidents started in November 1987, when one Ed Walters reported seeing and photographing a UFO during an encounter in which he allegedly was paralyzed by a ray of light and raised into the air. Multiple witnesses to the UFO were reported. Walters later produced more pictures of putative UFOs. Other commonplace elements of UFO encounter stories figured in the Gulf Breeze reports, including abductions, missing time and implants. The alleged sightings continued for several

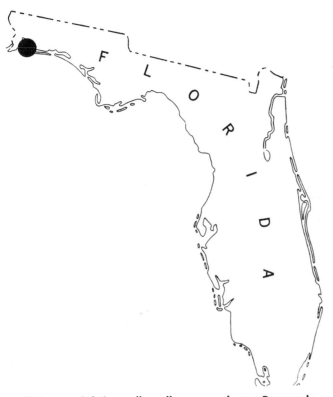

Gulf Breeze sightings allegedly occurred near Pensacola, Florida. (U.S. Geological Survey)

months. Later, considerable doubt was raised about the authenticity of the photographs.

See also ABDUCTIONS; ENCOUNTER PHENOMENA; IMPLANTS: MISSING TIME; PHOTOGRAPHY.

Gut Alt Golssen incident, Germany   The Gut Alt Golssen encounter reportedly occurred near that site in Germany, some 30 miles east of Berlin, in 1944, and is described in a purported FBI file excerpted by UFO investigators Lawrence Fawcett and Larry Greenberg in their book *The UFO Cover-Up*. The unnamed witness is said to have been brought as a prisoner of war from Poland to Gut Alt Golssen in May 1942. Apparently, the witness was part of a work crew traveling with a tractor, when the tractor's engine stopped. The workers could hear a whining noise like that of an electrical generator. The men then met a man described as an S.S. guard, who spoke with the tractor's driver. Several minutes passed before the whining noise ceased. When it stopped, the tractor could be restarted. Several hours later, the witness cited in the document slipped away and, near the spot where the tractor had stalled, caught sight of an enclosure with a wall resembling a tarpaulin. The wall was about 50 feet high, and the enclosure some 100 to 150 yards in diameter. From this enclosure arose a circular object approximately 75 to 100 yards in diameter, with a middle section some three feet wide moving rapidly, so that it was seen as a blur similar to that of a spinning aircraft propeller. A whining noise could be heard again, but this time lower in pitch than on the prior occasion. The tractor engine stalled again. The story reportedly appeared in a memorandum dated November 7, 1957.

H

hallucinations This category of imagined perceptions may play a major role in the UFO phenomenon. When a person imagines seeing an entity or object that in fact is not present, the perception is called hallucination. Other kinds of hallucinations, such as auditory hallucinations involving imagined sounds, are also reported frequently. To illustrate the role that hallucination may play in the UFO phenomenon, note the similarity between UFO "bedroom encounters" and sightings of ghosts. Often, ghosts are reported seen by persons who have just gone to bed and are in a state between sleep and wakefulness. Likewise, many alleged encounters with "extraterrestrials" appear to occur under similar conditions. Hallucinations that occur in this state are called hypnagogic hallucinations. Ghosts also may be sighted after a sleeper has awakened. Such hallucinations are called hypnopompic hallucinations and also have parallels in the UFO phenomenon. Auditory hallucinations may be responsible for certain reports of voices or noises from alleged extraterrestrials in so-called bedroom encounters. The likeness between hallucinations and various UFO encounter reports does not necessarily mean that all such reports are accounts of hallucinations. Visual and auditory hallucinations are well-documented phenomena and at least should be considered as alternatives to extraterrestrial visitation in such cases.

See also ENCOUNTER PHENOMENA; GHOSTS, UFOS AND; PERCEPTION.

haloes One minor but colorful element of the UFO phenomenon is the "halo" sometimes said to surround alleged extraterrestrials and their craft in close-encounter cases. A notable case in point is the Flatwoods, West Virginia, incident, in which a giant humanoid was said to have possessed a halo similar to that seen in certain examples of Japanese religious art. The similarity between such haloes as described in UFO close-encounter reports and in certain examples of Eastern religious art indicates that there may be a common origin to both categories of haloes. In the UFO phenomenon, "haloes" also may refer to optical effects generated by atmospheric conditions, including rings of light around light sources such as the Moon.

See also FLATWOODS INCIDENT.

Ham and Dropa UFO mythology includes a report about the "Ham" and "Dropa" tribes of central Asia, said to be big-headed, yellow-skinned people scarcely more than four feet tall, supposedly de-

Halos: note resemblance between halos around Myo-o Buddhist statue (right) and artist's conception of Flatwoods, West Virginia, "monster" (left). (D. Ritchie) (Buddhist statue after Japan Travel Bureau, *Must See in Kyoto*, 1988.)

96

scended from extraterrestrials whose ship was stranded on Earth more than 12,000 years ago. According to the tale, Chinese scientists in 1938 had discovered, in caves in Central Asia's Bayan-Khara Uula mountains, graves containing unusual skeletons, as well as more than 700 granite discs with inscriptions in an ancient language. The discs allegedly were about an inch thick and resembled modern phonograph records. When deciphered, the discs supposedly told how the alien spacecraft had crashed. Most of the extraterrestrials were slaughtered, but a few survived and left descendants among local tribes. This story came to the attention of Gordon Creighton, a Fellow of Britain's Royal Anthropological Institute and a Fellow of the Royal Geographical Society. Creighton decided to investigate the story, and found it to be groundless. "Ham" turned out to be a confused rendering of the Tibetan word "Kham," the local name for the eastern part of Tibet. "Dropa," or "Drok-Pa," refers to residents of pasture lands in the Tibetan highlands, and may be translated as "solitude." Creighton added, in an article on his research for the journal *Flying Saucer Review*, that the inhabitants of these areas are anything but small. On the contrary, they tend to be large and robust.

Hamilton incident, Kansas, United States　Part of the wave of "airship" sightings reported in the United States in the last few years of the 19th century, the Hamilton incident bears strong similarities to other UFO incidents reported in the latter 19th century. On the night of April 19, 1897, one Alexander Hamilton, a farmer who lived near Yates Center, Kansas, claimed to have sighted an airship that reportedly descended so near to Hamilton's farmhouse that he could see the occupants and hear them talking in some unidentifiable language. Driven by a large "turbine wheel," or propeller, the airship allegedly directed a large, bright spotlight on Hamilton, his son and his hired hand, as the craft ascended. At an altitude of about 300 feet, the airship reportedly lowered a rope tied with a slip-knot, snared a young cow on the ground and hauled the animal aboard. Portions of the cow's body were allegedly found the following day in a neighbor's field. The Hamilton incident includes many parallels with UFO encounter stories of the 20th century, including animal mutilation and a UFO turning a powerful spotlight on observers.

See also AIRSHIPS; ANIMALS, UFOS AND.

hands　In some close-encounter reports, alleged extraterrestrials are said to have hands much like those of humans, only smaller and more delicate. Numerous variations on this pattern have been reported, however, including claws or talons; crab-like pincers; tentacles; and bizarre extremities resembling rolling pins. In one case involving the reported recovery of extraterrestrials' bodies from a saucer crash in the southwestern United States, an alien's hands were described as having long, slender digits with structures resembling multiple suction cups at the tips. In view of such greatly different descriptions, it is difficult to accept any hypothesis that alleged extraterrestrials represent a single species of intelligent organisms visiting Earth.

See also EXTRATERRESTRIALS, ANATOMY OF.

Hangar 18　A famous part of UFO lore is the story of Hangar 18, a structure at Wright-Patterson Air Force Base, Ohio, where the U.S. government is widely believed to keep the bodies of several extraterrestrials, recovered from a crashed saucer or saucers, preserved under cryogenic conditions. Rumors of alien corpses "on ice" at Wright-Patterson appear to have been circulating since just after World War II. Apparently there is no building at Wright-Patterson marked specifically "Hangar 18," although a complex of buildings designated by that number exists (18A, 18B and so forth). A 1980 motion picture titled *Hangar 18* was based upon the rumors of preserved alien corpses at Wright-Patterson.

See also AZTEC INCIDENT; CRASHES; ROSWELL INCIDENT.

hard objects　In one classification system for UFOs, a "hard object" is a UFO that appears to be solid or metallic.

See also SOFT OBJECTS.

Harrison incident, United States　On the night of April 12–13, 1879, one Henry Harrison of Jersey City, New Jersey, reportedly observed a bell-shaped object moving through the skies in an erratic manner. After his report was dismissed as unacceptable by the director of the U.S. Naval Observatory, Harrison took his case to the press. He reported his observation to the *New York Tribune*, and the *Tribune*'s account was later mentioned in *Scientific American*. Harrison did not believe that he had merely sighted a comet, because the object moved at a variable rate. Morris Jessup, an astronomer and 20th-century UFO investigator, analyzed Hamilton's observational data and concluded that the object seen by Hamilton was "organic" and under intelligent control.

See also ASTRONOMY; JESSUP, MORRIS.

Hasselbach incident, Germany On July 7 or 11, 1952 (the date varies from one account to another), one Oscar Linke, a former major in the Wehrmacht, was traveling by motorcycle with his 11-year-old daughter when a flat tire stopped them. In nearby woods, the girl saw what appeared to be a pair of small men in silvery clothing studying something on the ground in a clearing. Near the men stood a pink discoid object about 25 feet in diameter, with a black turret atop it and a row of openings around the disc's circumference. The men boarded the craft, which began vibrating and spinning, then flew away. Though this report has been reprinted widely, the uncertainty about the date of this alleged encounter is reason to think the story may be merely a hoax.

Hav-Musuvs Described in the lore of the Paiute people, the Hav-Musuvs were an advanced civilization that allegedly inhabited California at one time and traveled in silvery flying "canoes," which had wings and made a whirring sound. Their weapons included a small, hand-held tube that would induce paralysis. The aerial "canoes" are, of course, similar to modern descriptions of flying saucers, and the "tube" with the power to cause paralysis also is a widely known element of modern UFO lore. A virtually identical device was described in the famous Valensole encounter case in France.

See also PARALYSIS; VALENSOLE INCIDENT.

healing and illness Disease and its healing are notable elements of the UFO phenomenon as well as of supernatural lore. Although illness has been associated with certain reported close encounters with UFOs, healing has been alleged in some such instances too. Healing attributed to UFOs may involve, for example, the disappearance of wounds following an encounter with a UFO. Incidences of illness attributed to contact with UFOs, however, appear to outnumber by far alleged cases of healing. Healing of illness by extraterrestrials is a parallel element of the fairy lore of Europe.

See also BODILY EFFECTS; CASH–LANDRUM INCIDENT; FAIRIES; FALCON LAKE INCIDENT; ILLNESS AND INJURY.

helicopters Unmarked helicopters are a curious feature of many UFO reports. The helicopters may be reported flying alongside a UFO, as in the widely publicized Cash–Landrum incident. In many cases, unmarked helicopters are said to appear frequently near investigators of UFO sightings, as if conducting surveillance. Sometimes the helicopters are said to land, and personnel in military or paramilitary uniforms, in some cases with weapons in hand, allegedly disembark from the craft. Helicopter sightings have been associated with numerous animal mutilations, especially in the United States. Peculiar flight characteristics sometimes are reported. In certain cases, for example, helicopters have been sighted flying so close together that their rotors appeared to intermesh. Much speculation surrounds the possible origins of the "mystery helicopters," but no universally accepted explanation has been devised.

See also ANIMALS, UFOS AND; CASH–LANDRUM INCIDENT.

Hessdalen Valley, Norway Known as a UFO "window," this portion of central Norway became famous in 1981 and 1982 for a wave of UFO sightings involving lights of various colors in the skies. Other reports have involved a curious, striped ovoid allegedly seen above the valley, and a mysterious red light said to move about on the ground. The Hessdalen Valley UFOs received intensive investigation, but nothing was discovered to prove that beings from outer space actually were visiting Norway.

See also WINDOWS.

Higdon incident, Wyoming, United States An alleged abduction case from 1974, the Higdon incident involved one Carl Higdon, who, while hunting elk in Medicine Bow National Forest, reportedly encountered a mysterious man who offered him some pills. Higdon allegedly took the pills without hesitating, although he usually was reluctant to take any kind of medication. According to the story, Higdon found himself afterward aboard a UFO, following a "blackout."

Several elements of the Higdon case are of interest. For example, Higdon reportedly fired a bullet at a group of elk, but the bullet fell to the ground after traveling only about 50 feet. Higdon also allegedly surrendered his own will to some extent in this encounter with the stranger, and did as the man advised, in a state of naive trust. The element of the pills offered to Higdon is comparable to reports of food and drink offered to humans in many alleged encounters with extraterrestrials.

See also FOOD AND DRINK.

high strangeness This quality of certain reports in the UFO phenomenon refers partly to differences between the familiar world of human experience and the environments perceived by UFO "contactees."

In an experience of high strangeness, a person may report visiting an alien land where scenery differs greatly from landscapes known to that individual; yet the alien territory appears to occupy the same physical location as a familiar, "everyday" locale. How the two environments are connected is not made clear. In other situations of high strangeness, an individual may find himself or herself apparently transported over great distances instantaneously to some familiar location, but many miles away from the point of departure. The subject may recall being at home one moment, and the next moment translocated somehow to a far distant city through "extraterrestrial" or other alleged supernormal intervention. Cases of high strangeness are not confined to the UFO phenomenon, but are numerous in the literature on the paranormal as a whole, and are seen as links between UFO encounter cases and various other occult phenomena. Hoaxes, hallucinations and misinterpretations are also possibilities in individual cases of high strangeness.

See also BENDER MYSTERY; DR. X INCIDENT; ELIDOR; OCCULTISM; TELEPORTATION; TENGU.

highways

Alleged close encounters along highways play a major part in the UFO phenomenon. In a typical case, a witness driving a car along a highway sees a bright light in the sky and is paced by the light for some minutes. In other accounts, the light may land alongside the highway or even in the middle of the road directly in front of the witness. Vehicle interference—the stalling of the car's engine—may be reported. Sometimes the UFO is reported seen by large numbers of motorists in a single sighting, as in the Hudson Valley sightings in the United States.

Various non-extraterrestrial explanations for such sightings are possible. Private aircraft following the routes of highways are one possibility, and the Hudson Valley sightings are suspected of being nothing more than reports of light aircraft flying in formation at night with their lights on. A single bright light "pacing" or following an automobile along a highway may be nothing more than a planet or bright star hanging low in the sky, transformed by the viewer's imagination into a UFO traveling along with, and at the same speed as, the car.

When a UFO allegedly lands in the middle of a highway, traces of its subsequent takeoff may be reported in the form of scorch marks on the pavement. Such "evidence" is easily faked, however, and should be viewed with skepticism.

See also ENCOUNTER PHENOMENA; HUDSON VALLEY SIGHTINGS; ILLUSION; MARS; VEHICLE EFFECTS; VENUS.

Hilarion, Christian monk and abbot, 4th century A.D.

A resident of Palestine, Hilarion is known for experiences that resemble aspects of modern UFO encounters, specifically strange noises and spectacular, violent images. He would hear mysterious and doleful sounds, such as the crying of women and infants, the lowing of cattle and the roar of lions, as well as noises like those of armies in combat. On one occasion he watched what appeared to be a battle of gladiators, in which one of the contestants fell dead. He interpreted these experiences as manifestations of demonic activity.

See also ACOUSTICAL EFFECTS; DEMONOLOGY; ENCOUNTER PHENOMENA.

Hildegard of Bingen, 12th century A.D.

The visionary Hildegard described in her work *Scivias* a vision similar to some modern UFO reports. She reported seeing a "splendid" star, accompanied by a great host of "sparks," which turned into dark coals and fell into the "abyss." Hildegard thought this vision symbolized the fall of the angels.

Hill incident, New Hampshire, United States

The case of Barney and Betty Hill is one of the most famous in UFO literature and includes elements that later would become commonplace in abduction reports. The incident allegedly occurred on the night of September 19, 1961, as Barney Hill and his wife were driving home to Portsmouth, New Hampshire, after a vacation in Canada. They were on U.S. Route 3 when they saw a bright object traveling across the sky to the southwest. They stopped the car and examined the object through binoculars. At first, they judged it to be a small aircraft. Then the object approached them and hovered near the highway, some 80 to 100 feet above the ground. Through binoculars, Barney HIll could see that the object was shaped like a saucer and appeared to have illuminated portholes, through which could be seen several humanoid beings apparently wearing billed caps and dark uniforms. The couple fled the scene in their car. Later Barney Hill began having nightmares about an encounter with a UFO. He also reportedly was unable to account for some two hours of time on the night of the UFO encounter along Route 3. The Hills sought medical advice and were referred to a psychiatrist in Boston. Under hypnotic regression, Barney recalled being taken aboard an extraterrestrial spacecraft and subjected to something like a medical examination by big-eyed aliens. Betty Hill reported a similar experience and said her examination involved inserting a needle through her navel. She also said she had seen a "star map." The "map" was crude, but later analysis appeared to indicate it placed the aliens' origins in Zeta Reticuli, a star system about 30 light-years from Earth.

The Hill case has been discussed widely and has been criticized strongly, notably by UFO investigator Jacques Vallee, who interpreted the "star map" as an absurdity. Serious doubts also have been expressed about the accuracy of the Hills' testimony delivered under hypnosis. Regressive hypnosis is known as a notoriously fallible way of retrieving allegedly suppressed "memories."

Several elements of the Hill case became prominent in later abduction reports, notably the quasi-medical examination involving insertion of a needle into the abductee's body; the period of "missing time" involved in the case; and the use of regressive hypnosis to "reconstruct" portions of the alleged UFO encounter. The Hill incident was described in John Fuller's 1966 book *The Interrupted Journey* and later became the basis for a 1975 NBC television movie, *The UFO Incident.*

See also ABDUCTIONS; ENCOUNTER PHENOMENA; HUMANOIDS; MISSING TIME; REGRESSIVE HYPNOSIS; VALLEE, JACQUES; ZETA RETICULI.

Hinduism   Elements of Hinduism are prominent in the UFO phenomenon. The notion of spiritual "evolution," as expressed by modern UFO "contactees," is derived in large part from Hinduism. Alleged extraterrestrial societies, as described by contactees, also appear to be essentially Hinduistic in character, with individuals tending to lose their identities as they become incorporated into some larger, collective identity. (It may be worth noting here that individual "extraterrestrials" described in close-encounter cases often appear devoid of personality and might be described almost as automata operating under the control of some greater "overmind.") The Hinduistic model of society also figures prominently in science fiction; a notable example is the "United Planets" series of stories by American author Mack Reynolds, who portrayed an advanced alien society ruled by "Brahmins" having telepathic powers. Hinduistic belief in reincarnation has become an element of the UFO phenomenon in recent years, so that it has become almost commonplace to hear UFO "believers" speak of their imagined previous incarnations on other worlds. In some cases, the Hinduistic element in the lore of UFOs and alleged extraterrestrials is extremely subtle. In the celebrated case of "Kirk Allen," for example, there is a reference to an imaginary world called "Seraneb," a backward spelling of Benares, a so-called holy city of Hinduism.

See also ALLEN, KIRK; CONTACTEES; REINCARNATION; REYNOLDS, MACK.

hoaxes   The history of the modern UFO phenomenon is, in large measure, a history of hoaxes, either proven or alleged. A hoax may be defined as a deliberate attempt to persuade investigators and/or the public at large that an alleged UFO encounter really occurred, when in fact no such event happened. In other words, the hoaxer knows the story is untrue, although he or she tries to persuade others to accept it as truthful. The word "hoax" should not be applied to cases in which a person believes sincerely that a particular experience represents an actual UFO encounter, even if the incident was actually no such thing.

A hoax may involve fabricated material "evidence," such as faked photographs of a UFO; untruthful testimony, devised in imitation of other such reports; or falsified documents. Other elements of hoaxes may include lights arranged to resemble luminous UFOs; falsified readings on instruments arranged to detect magnetic fields or other anticipated evidence of a UFO's passing; or aircraft flying in formation, and illuminated so as to resemble classic UFOs. Hoaxes may even involve "extraterrestrial" biological specimens, which on examination turn out to be terrestrial organisms, in some cases altered to make them look otherworldly. (The author recalls seeing one "alien" organism that bore a striking resemblance to an ordinary fetal pig.)

Physical evidence of an alleged UFO landing may be fabricated easily, using a shovel to produce purported impressions made by a spacecraft's landing legs, or setting fires to create a scorched area of ground that may be attributed to a spaceship's exhaust. Apparently, in some rare cases, a hoaxer may go so far as to mutilate his body, through self-inflicted burns or other wounds, in hopes of providing persuasive "evidence" of a UFO encounter.

Although hoaxes involving UFO reports tend to be crude, some are relatively sophisticated and involve careful planning and execution. In many cases, it is possible to identify a UFO report as a hoax after only cursory study of the alleged evidence. A photograph that shows clear signs of being a mere double exposure, for example, is good reason to presume that a report is a hoax. Also, if a UFO encounter story shows numerous close parallels with other such stories already circulating in popular literature and entertainment, then one should at least consider the possibility of a hoax.

The consistency of a report may help to determine whether the individual involved is sincere or merely trying to carry out a hoax. A story free from contradictions, and reasonably specific in its particulars, may indicate that the person is sincere, even if he or she has misinterpreted the experience as a UFO encounter when it actually was some other phenomenon. An inconsistent and/or extremely vague story, on the other hand, is strongly indicative of a hoax.

The reputation and the behavior of the person reporting a UFO encounter are two additional factors to be considered in deciding whether or not a given report is a hoax. If the individual has a prior record of untruthful behavior, or is reluctant to produce alleged physical evidence of the reported UFO encounter, or stands to gain financially from the telling of the story, then the person's sincerity should be questioned.

Several factors combine to make hoaxes attractive both to would-be perpetrators and to the public in general. One factor is popular fascination with outlandish stories. People simply enjoy tales, whether truthful or not, of encounters with beings from other worlds. Thus, a hoaxer is virtually guaranteed an appreciative audience for any reasonably well-crafted UFO report.

Media coverage of UFOs also may help to engender hoaxes. The mass media both encourage and satisfy popular taste for UFO tales. The tabloid press in particular has made a staple of bizarre UFO reports. A hoaxer who understands the public's enthusiasm for UFO tales, and the media's role in supporting that enthusiasm, may be able to fabricate a highly successful and profitable encounter report. One should not underestimate the lure of monetary gain in such cases. A persuasive UFO contact story, if properly written and promoted, can make the storyteller both wealthy and famous.

Another factor working in a hoaxer's favor is the uncritical attitude of some UFO investigators. Certain investigators have pronounced faked "evidence" of alleged UFO encounters as genuine, although a reasonably close investigation of the so-called evidence would have revealed its inadmissibility.

The list of hoaxes in the literature on UFOs is extensive. Famous cases that are widely considered to be hoaxes involve George Adamski, an early "contactee" who claimed to have met a visitor from Venus in the California desert; and Richard Shaver, whose story of an underground realm inhabited by malignant aliens became a colorful part of UFO lore.

One interesting category of hoaxes is the historical UFO hoax, in which the hoaxer produces an alleged historical text describing a UFO encounter or related incident from decades, centuries or even millennia ago. Disproving such hoaxes may require extensive research. Examples include the Byland Abbey incident in Britain and the case of the so-called Piri Reis map.

For about the last 50 years, technology has placed certain limitations on the UFO hoaxer's art. A hoaxer with an ordinary camera, for example, was limited in what he might contrive in the way of alleged UFO photographs. The result often was a photo that exhibited clear signs of fakery. Recent advances in imaging technology, however, have made much more sophisticated hoaxes possible. Now, someone with a computer, suitable software and certain peripherals can produce a high-quality "photograph" of a UFO encounter, including an image of an extraterrestrial greeting humans (or vice versa), within minutes. Although such capabilities do not mean that hoaxes will become undetectable, the public may soon find itself presented with more, and seemingly more persuasive, UFO "encounter" pictures than ever before. Debunkers may find their work more difficult.

See also ADAMSKI, GEORGE; BODILY EFFECTS; BYLAND ABBEY INCIDENT; DEBUNKERS; DECEPTION; ENCOUNTER PHENOMENA; EVIDENCE; MEDIA, UFOS IN THE; PHOTOGRAPHY; PIRI REIS MAP; SHAVER MYSTERY.

"Hodomur, Man of Infinity" A science fiction story by Ege Tilms, published in 1934, "Hodomur" concerns a Belgian man named Belans who has a close encounter with extraterrestrials. Belans meets the aliens in a wheat field where unusual patterns of crushed plants had been reported. Belans meets a man dressed in black waiting under a tree and decides to see what the man is waiting for. Next Belans feels a strange fatigue, as if it were imposed on him by some external agency. Then he hears an odd buzzing noise, followed by a brilliant light and the landing of an extraterrestrial spacecraft. A door opens in the ship, and the man in black enters. Belans follows, seemingly under some kind of compulsion, and finds himself inside the vehicle, in a room that is illuminated without an evident light source. He feels a slight vibration as the craft takes off. A tall figure joins Belans in the room. Belans has the impression that this man can read his mind. Addressing Belans in French, the alien claims to have come from a distant star. When Belans asks why the aliens do not reveal their presence openly, the tall man replies that the extraterrestrials wish to avoid accelerating the evolution of "elements" foreign to their own civilization. Eventually, the aliens return Belans to Earth. He finds himself suffering from a period of amnesia. Many elements of UFO "contactee" and abduction cases from later decades are found in "Hodomur," including crushed vegetation, which came to be known as "crop circles"; a man dressed in black; bodily effects on the human subject, in this case profound and inexplicable fatigue; the spacecraft appearing in a blaze of light; the lighted room with no apparent light source inside the spacecraft; an alien who appears to have mind-reading ability and addresses Belans in Belans's own language; a strange explanation of why the extraterrestrials decline to reveal themselves openly; and Belans's amnesia, which later would become a significant element of the UFO phenomenon known as "missing time."

Bertrand Meheust, a French sociologist, located "Hodomur" among a body of fantastic literature published between 1880 and 1940. This literature, Meheust found, contains references to many phenomena that would become elements of the UFO phenomenon after World War II, including interference with vehicles and abductions.

See also BODILY EFFECTS; CROP CIRCLES; ENCOUNTER PHENOMENA; MEN IN BLACK; MISSING TIME; PRECEDENTS; TELEPATHY.

Hoganas—Helsingborg incident, Sweden

On December 20, 1958, two young men driving along a highway between Hoganas and Helsingborg reportedly saw a peculiar light among the trees alongside the road and stopped to investigate. They allegedly discovered a diffuse glow hanging just above the ground and surrounding an object that they could not perceive clearly. From the glow emerged several luminous objects, described later as "blobs," about three feet in diameter. According to the story, the "blobs" tried to overpower the men and force them into the glowing area mentioned earlier. The blobs felt like jelly. The men allegedly perceived a powerful, unpleasant smell like that of burning flesh. A loud whistling noise seemed to emanate from the blobs. The entities appeared to concentrate their attention on one of the men, who resisted them by hanging on to a fence post, even as his body was lifted off the ground. The other man tried to drive away the blobs by sounding the horn of the automobile. The noise of the horn appeared to discourage the blobs, for they backed away and retreated to the glow from which they had emerged. The glow then rose and departed, accompanied by a loud whine. The men fled the area. They continued to perceive the unpleasant smell even after the incident was over. After visiting a doctor, the men reportedly were interrogated by police, psychiatrists and representatives of Sweden's defense forces. Further investigation reportedly revealed the presence of in-

dentations, like those of landing gear, in the soil at the site of the incident. The case was allegedly classified as unexplained. This case combines, in a single incident, several UFO-related phenomena also associated with reports of demonic apparitions, including levitation and a foul smell.

See also ACOUSTICAL EFFECTS; DEMONOLOGY; LEVITATION; ODORS.

hollow Earth hypothesis

In an effort to resolve the question of where UFOs originate, the hollow Earth hypothesis, a staple of pseudoscientific thinking and occultism, was applied to the problem in the 1950s and 1960s. The hypothesis rests on the assumption that the Earth is a hollow sphere, and that access to the planet's interior may be obtained through great portals at the North and South Poles. Various fantasists and occultists have developed an elaborate model of a hollow Earth with a vast internal chamber some 6,000 miles in diameter, illuminated by a miniature "sun" at the center of the planet and inhabited by a highly developed civilization descended from ancient Atlantis and Lemuria. Although the idea of a hollow Earth had been popular for many years before the flying saucer phenomenon arose (science fiction author Jules Verne, for example, used the concept of a hollow Earth as the basis for his famous adventure novel *Journey to the Center of the Earth*, published in 1864), the hollow Earth hypothesis in the 20th century provided a convenient—though scientifically worthless—explanation for the origin of postulated spacecraft visiting our world. Because it was hard to imagine how extraterrestrials from other planetary systems might make the lengthy, time-consuming journey to our planet, it was tempting to look elsewhere for a postulated origin of alien spacecraft, which UFOs were (and still are) widely supposed to be. If the "saucers" were presumed to originate from within the Earth and commute to and from the surface through huge openings in the polar regions, the distance problem involved in the extraterrestrial model of UFOs' origins could be dismissed along with the extraterrestrial hypothesis itself. Instead of ranges in the millions or hundreds of millions of miles, the imagined craft would need to be able to fly only a few thousand miles if they were based somewhere inside a hollow world. Among the proponents of this hypothesis was author Raymond Bernard, who drew on earlier work by one O.C. Huguenin to bolster the view that UFOs originated from inside the Earth. The civilization within our globe supposedly was disturbed when humankind started testing nuclear bombs and dispatched saucers to the surface to keep track of developments there. Bernard also was familiar with the work of Ray Palmer, the American editor and science fiction writer who played an important role in popularizing the UFO cult, to establish a link between UFOs and the hollow Earth hypothesis. Bernard cited an article by Palmer in the December 1959 issue of Palmer's magazine *Flying Saucers,* which stated flatly that flying saucers "come from this earth." Bernard dubbed the imagined subterranean civilization "Agartha" and wove a brief but wide-ranging explanation of how he believed flying saucers and their passengers played a role in human mythology. (Here Bernard's work parallels that of Swiss author Erich von Däniken, who argued that the "gods" of antiquity might have been extraterrestrial astronauts visiting our planet.) Bernard also cited various classical authors, including Cicero and Livy, whom Bernard imagined had made references to UFOs in their writings. The link between the UFO phenomenon and occultism is made clear at many points in Bernard's work, and his descriptions of the imagined super-civilization within the Earth resemble the visions that various occultists such as Emanuel Swedenborg claim to have had of otherworldly realms. UFO debunker Martin Gardner claims that "Bernard" actually was one Walter Siegmeister, a writer on occultism and proprietor of a health-food store in New York City.

See also ATLANTIS; LEMURIA; PALMER, RAYMOND; PSEUDOSCIENCE; SWEDENBORG, EMANUEL; VON DÄNIKEN, ERICH.

homeworlds This expression, borrowed from science fiction, may be used to refer to the planets from which alleged extraterrestrials in UFO encounter cases are said to have come. "Contactees" have reported hearing about, and seeing, a wide variety of homeworlds. Their descriptions contain a strong element of the absurd. A case in point is "Clarion," the mythical homeworld of the aliens in Truman Bethurum's contact story. Clarion was described as a beautiful world whose inhabitants enjoyed dancing polkas. As a rule, homeworlds described in such cases resemble a sanitized version of Earth. (In this regard, it is instructive to compare alleged homeworlds in UFO encounter cases with the visions of "heaven" reported by the Swedish mystic Emanuel Swedenborg, who described a realm much like Earth, with similar institutions including schools and churches.) Specific descriptions of homeworlds in UFO encounter cases, however, are rare. When details of life on an extraterrestrial's homeworld are given, they are likely to be either unverifiable or demonstrably false, such as an inhabited planet Mars.

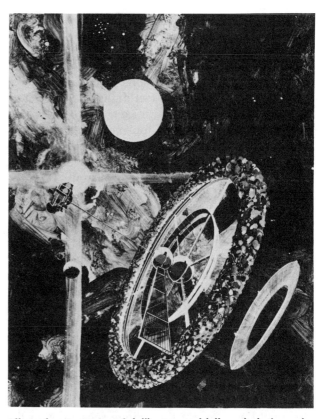

Alleged extraterrestrial "homeworlds" and their societies tend to resemble modern plans for space colonies in that they resemble life on Earth, but are much more orderly and attractive. (NASA)

See also ASTRONOMY; BETHURUM INCIDENT; ENCOUNTER PHENOMENA; SWEDENBORG, EMANUEL.

Hook incident, United Kingdom A case of vehicle interference associated with a UFO sighting, the Hook incident is significant because of the presumed credibility of the witness (the director of a transport company in Sussex) and because of the great detail of his recollections. He was driving a bus along the A.32 highway near Hook in Hampshire at around 4:30 P.M. on October 26, 1967, when the whole electrical system of his vehicle failed suddenly. He checked the battery but found everything in order. (While outside the bus, he noticed a dark object hanging in the air above the roadway ahead of him, but paid little attention to it.) Then he tried twice to start the vehicle and succeeded on the second attempt. After he had traveled several hundred yards, the vehicle stopped again. As he got out of the bus to investigate, he perceived an odd change of pressure in his ears and noticed a strong odor that reminded him of heated insulation or the arcing of an electric motor. He satisfied himself again that the engine was in order and that the odor did not originate from under the hood of his bus. Again, he saw the object above the road ahead, but did not associate it with the engine trouble. His recollections later allowed the object's dimensions to be estimated at about 60 feet wide and 30 feet high. The object had the approximate shape of an ice-cream cone with a flange where the rounded top met the conical bottom. No details of the object could be seen. It appeared to have a dull luster. After several minutes, the object moved horizontally out of sight. Then the driver found that the bus would start, and he continued his journey. He reported afterward that he experienced a throbbing sensation in his fingertips, and that a toothache that had troubled him before the encounter ceased to bother him thereafter.

A doctor who interviewed the driver after the incident said the man mentioned a sense of "oppression" associated with the encounter, as well as problems in coordinating the motions of his feet and hands. This lack of coordination made driving difficult for him. The doctor suggested that something about the incident had caused temporary interference with peripheral nerves and their links to the spinal cord. The doctor thought such interference also might account for the strange sensations in the man's fingertips. The doctor speculated that the driver had been affected by some kind of "force-field" associated with the UFO.

The driver told his story to *Flying Saucer Review*, which printed an account of the incident. The pseudonym of "Mr. Colley" was applied to the driver in *Flying Saucer Review*'s coverage of the incident, but a television program later revealed that "Colley's" actual name was Collett.

See also BODILY EFFECTS; VEHICLE EFFECTS.

Hooton incident, Arkansas, United States

A curious incident in the string of "airship" sightings reported in the United States, the Hooton incident allegedly occurred around 6:00 P.M. on April 20, 1897, when one James Hooton encountered an airship and its occupants while hunting near Homan, Arkansas. The craft allegedly made a hissing noise and had the configuration of a cylinder with pointed ends. The airship's occupants looked like ordinary men. One of them informed Hooton that this was indeed "the airship." Hooton also was told that the vessel was propelled by compressed air. As Hooton watched, the craft took flight and flew rapidly out of sight. The Hooton incident is of interest because the technology described in this account is essentially the same as American technology of the late 19th century. A similar parallel would be noted in many later UFO reports between the technology of alleged UFOs and the technological development of the society where the reports were made.

See also AIRSHIPS; TECHNOLOGY.

Hopkins, Budd

One of the most prominent investigators of abduction reports, American artist Budd Hopkins became famous for his study of the case of "Kathie Davis," a woman who allegedly had a close encounter with extraterrestrials in Copley Woods, near Indianapolis, Indiana, in 1983, when she was 24 years old. Hopkins found similarities between the Davis case and those of other alleged abductees. Those similarities included scars or marks on the bodies of alleged abductees, as well as the appearance in dreams of small humanoids with pale skin and very dark eyes. Hopkins said his studies showed that none of the alleged abductees appeared to be schizophrenic, but they did display a certain lack of self-esteem and seemed more reluctant to trust other people than the average person would be. Hopkins has popularized the concept of "missing time," or intervals of time of which an alleged abductee recalls nothing.

See also ABDUCTIONS; MISSING TIME.

Horseshoe Lagoon incident, Australia

The Queensland Flying Saucer Research Bureau in 1968 installed a system for taking pictures automatically of UFOs, at Horseshoe Lagoon along the Queensland coast. Over the previous two years, there had been reports of UFO activity in the areas, and "saucer nests," flattened, circular areas of reeds (similar to "crop circles"), had been reported found as well. After a news report of March 2, 1968, said that an airliner in flight between Cairns and North Range had been accompanied briefly by a UFO, the monitoring system at Horseshoe Lagoon was checked, and one camera was found operating, having run through one side of its film. The film was turned over, and the camera was reset to cover a broader area. Following another UFO report on March 4, the camera was found to have been set off again, although only several frames were exposed. The film reportedly was sent by mail to Melbourne for developing but vanished somewhere along the way, although the container for the film was returned, empty. Attempts to locate and recover the film failed. This incident exemplifies the widely observed pattern in UFO cases of evidence, or even potential evidence, disappearing under mysterious circumstances.

See also AUSTRALIA, UFOS IN; CROP CIRCLES; EVIDENCE.

Hudson Valley sightings occurred along the border between New York state and Connecticut. (U.S. Geological Survey)

Hudson Valley sightings, United States

In 1983 and 1984, the Hudson Valley of New York state was the site of numerous UFO sightings supposedly involving huge, triangular or boomerang-shaped craft studded with lights. Other sightings in this group have been reported from nearby Connecticut and New Jersey. The UFOs were said to move slowly along the routes of highways and, in one spectacular case, to have hovered above a nuclear power station. The sightings were examined by UFO investigators, including the esteemed Dr. J. Allen Hynek, and have been the subject of at least two books. Debunkers have dismissed the sightings as a hoax perpetrated by pilots of aircraft based at an airfield in Stormville, New York. According to this explanation, the pilots would fly in formations that resembled the "boomerang" UFO configuration. The pilots would fly at first with their lights out. Simultaneously, on signal, they then would turn on their lights and appear to be a huge, boomerang-shaped, lighted UFO that had materialized somehow out of thin air. By turning their lights on and off in unison, the pilots also reportedly created the illusion of large UFOs shifting abruptly from one position in the sky to another. Believers in the "extraterrestrial" nature of the Hudson Valley sightings were unconvinced by this explanation.

See also AIRCRAFT, UFOS AND; BELGIAN INCIDENTS; BOOMERANGS; HIGHWAYS; HOAXES; HYNEK, J. ALLEN; TESLA GLOBE.

humanoids

"Extraterrestrials" reported in close-encounter cases are described, in many cases, as humanoids, meaning they appear to follow the same basic bodily plan that humans have: a cylindrical trunk surmounted by a head, with two arms and two legs attached respectively at the shoulders and hips, and hands (or something roughly equivalent to hands) at the ends of the arms. Many minor variations on this pattern have been reported, but even some highly exotic-looking "aliens" still may be described as humanoid. In some contact reports, notably those of George Adamski, the alleged extraterrestrials are all but indistinguishable from ordinary humans.

Certain extraterrestrials are said to be extremely handsome and similar in appearance to the so-called Nordic ideal, with blond hair, attractive facial features and impressive physiques. Others reportedly have swarthy complexions and are compared to stereotypical Italians or gypsies, as in the case of "contactee" Truman Bethurum. Humanoids also may appear in the form of extremely beautiful women.

Humanoid "aliens" may vary greatly in size, from giants approximately 10 feet tall to tiny beings only several inches high. Some humanoids in UFO close-encounter stories appear clothed in coverall-like garments with a metallic luster. Others are described as wearing robes or some kind of armor. In certain cases, a humanoid's upper limbs may consist of tentacles rather than jointed limbs like those of humans. Extremely long arms are reported in some instances. The number of eyes may differ from one account to another, but many humanoids mentioned in UFO close encounters reportedly have two eyes, often described as dark and slanted upward at the outer corners. Alternatively, some humanoids are said to have luminous eyes, as in the celebrated encounters of American "contactee" Albert Bender. A wide range of facial and cranial features has been reported. Humanoids may be described as eared or earless, or even having antennae where a human's ears would be; noseless, or possessing sharp, prominent noses; mouthless, or having small, narrow mouths without lips. Although legs are said to be present in some cases, they are not necessarily used for locomotion, for some alleged extraterrestrials are said to be capable of flight. In some reports, the humanoids have feet like those of humans, whereas in other cases (notably the Kelly–Hopkinsville incident) the aliens are said to have disk-like structures in place of actual feet. Wings have been reported seen, though not often, on extraterrestrials in some close-encounter incidents.

Humanoids reported seen in UFO encounters tend to be apparently male or androgynous, although there are notable exceptions to this rule, such as "Captain Aura Rhanes," the beautiful female extraterrestrial who figured in the adventures

Small, hairy humanoids sometimes are reportedly seen in UFO encounters. (D. Ritchie)

of alleged contactee Truman Bethurum. In some reports, the UFO humanoids appear capable of eating terrestrial food. Small, furry humanoids have been reported on occasion, and large, hairy humanoids—sometimes classified under the name "Bigfoot"—also are associated with UFO sightings.

UFO lore contains detailed descriptions of humanoid "extraterrestrial" physiology and anatomy. According to rumors of autopsies conducted on bodies of aliens recovered from alleged UFO crashes in the southwestern deserts of the United States, certain "aliens" have hands and fingers much like our own, but with tiny structures resembling suction cups at their fingertips. Other alien autopsy rumors include reports of teeth in good condition, and an absence of any digestive system. Such reports tend to contradict one another and to contain highly dubious information.

Descriptions of UFO humanoids may vary significantly from one country to another. American UFO contact reports, for example, are characterized by numerous alleged encounters with "grays," small gray-skinned humanoids with large dark eyes. The grays reportedly wear tight-fitting clothing and exhibit neotenous characteristics that give them a close resemblance to a human fetus. Reports from other countries, by contrast, may feature giant humanoids resembling robots, as in the Voronezh incidents in Russia, or goblin-like creatures, as were reported in the case of Torakichi's encounters with tengu in 19th-century Japan.

An interesting category of UFO humanoid reports involves the "men in black," sinister masculine figures who appear after UFO encounters to harrass witnesses. These humanoids are described as resembling ordinary men dressed in dark suits. The "men in black" are said to be distinguishable from ordinary men, however, by their awkward movements, stilted language and sometimes extraordinarily pale complexions. The men in black reportedly are often encountered in groups of two or three and are said to threaten witnesses of UFO encounters with harm. One of the most vivid accounts of meetings with men in black is that of "contactee" Albert Bender, who claimed that several such individuals had visited him at home in connection with his interest in UFOs.

Communications from humanoids in UFO encounter incidents may take many forms. They may occur by spoken words or by written messages, but in many cases communication appears to be by some kind of telepathy, or direct mind-to-mind contact. The messages delivered tend to be nonsensical, incoherent or highly untruthful.

Humanoids in 20th-century close-encounter stories exhibit, in many cases, an inordinate interest in the reproductive and excretory systems of humans, and reportedly subject human captives to painful examinations and surgical procedures involving these systems. The humanoids allegedly leave "implants," usually described as small metallic or ceramic spheres, in the nasal passages or elsewhere in the bodies of human abductees.

Humanoids in UFO close-encounter incidents bear a close resemblance to apparitions described in reports of ghosts and demonic activity. Descriptions of UFO humanoids often include mention of an intense sensation of cold; foul odors; deception; and an ability to change shape and to appear as luminous figures or as celebrities. These are all traits commonly attributed to ghosts and to demons, and help to place UFO close encounters in the realm of the paranormal.

See also ABDUCTIONS; ADAMSKI, GEORGE; BETHURUM INCIDENT; BENDER MYSTERY; COMMUNICATIONS; DECEPTION; DEMONOLOGY; ENCOUNTER PHENOMENA; GRAYS; GHOSTS, UFOS AND; IMPLANTS; MEN IN BLACK; MOTHMAN; ODORS; TELEPATHY; TEMPERATURE EFFECTS; TENGU; VORONEZH SIGHTINGS.

Hyades   A star cluster in the constellation Taurus, the Hyades cluster has been recognized since ancient times and figures in the case of alleged Swiss UFO contactee Eduard Meier, as one of the homes of his extraterrestrial visitors. Supposedly, the aliens settled in the Hyades, in the Pleiades and around the star Vega after their homeworld was destroyed. The Hyades cluster is close to Earth, only about 150 light-years away, and is known for its "convergent point," a point in the sky upon which the stars in the cluster appear to be converging. The convergent point may be merely a trick of perspective.

See also MEIER CASE; PLEIADES.

hybrids   The literature on UFO encounters contains numerous reports of "hybrid" entities, half human and half "extraterrestrial," produced by impregnation of female abductees or by some kind of genetic manipulation involving ova extracted from women. Some women have claimed to have been given a chance to see and hold babies produced in this manner; these alleged encounters are known as "wise baby dreams," because the woman may claim to have perceived that the child was extremely intelligent. In the absence of any solid evidence for such hybrids, however, reports of their existence are widely considered to be mere dreams, fantasies or hoaxes.

See also ABDUCTIONS; GENETIC MANIPULATION; SEXUAL ENCOUNTERS; WISE BABY DREAMS; WOMEN, UFOS AND.

Hynek, J. Allen (1910–1986)   American astronomer J. Allen Hynek was one of the most prominent UFO investigators and devised the famous three-category classification scheme for UFO close encounters. He served as professor of astronomy at Northwestern University. Hynek became involved in UFO studies in 1948, when he began performing investigations for the U.S. Air Force. He served as consultant to Project Blue Book, Project Grudge and Project Sign. At first Hynek was a debunker of UFO reports, but later he changed his mind about the UFO phenomenon and came to believe that it could not be explained merely as a collection of hoaxes, hallucinations and misidentifications of familiar phenomena. He also was critical of the so-called extraterrestrial hypothesis and more "esoteric" explanations of UFO activity. He made a cameo appearance in the motion picture *Close Encounters of the Third Kind*, which took its title from one of Hynek's categories of UFO encounters and depicted a meeting with humans and humanoid extraterrestrials.

See also BLUE BOOK, PROJECT; DEBUNKERS; ENCOUNTER PHENOMENA; GRUDGE, PROJECT; HALLUCINATIONS; HOAXES; SIGN, PROJECT.

hypnosis   The practice of placing a subject into a trance state, hypnosis has been used to "retrieve" memories of alleged UFO abductions. Much controversy surrounds this application of hypnosis, although its use has yielded numerous detailed and colorful (but questionable) accounts of abductions.

See also REGRESSIVE HYPNOSIS.

I

identification The identification of UFOs, thus transforming them from unidentified into identified flying objects, can be a complicated process. Before a UFO sighting can be accepted as truly unidentified, a long list of natural phenomena and manmade flying objects must be eliminated as possibilities. These include aircraft, artificial satellites, aurora, balloons, birds, clouds, contrails ("vapor trails"), coronal discharges, explosions, flares, kites, meteors, methane ("marsh gas"), parachutes, planets, searchlight beams, stars, streetlights, "sundogs," vehicle headlights, and "space junk" (pieces of booster rockets and other hardware in orbit) re-entering the atmosphere and burning up. Psychological and behavioral phenomena that must be eliminated include hallucinations, hoaxes and honest mistakes in identifying familiar objects. Although the identification process can be highly subjective and fallible, most UFO reports can be identified as some kind of terrestrial, natural or manmade phenomenon or object.

ikals Dark, hairy humanoids in Mexican folklore from the Tzeltal people, ikals are said to be about three feet tall and to be associated with a luminous flying object. Ikals reportedly have been sighted since ancient times. In modern times, they have been said to perform abductions and to be capable of paralyzing humans. All these attributes are common to ikals and to humanoid "extraterrestrials" in modern UFO encounter reports.

See also ABDUCTIONS; HUMANOIDS; PARALYSIS.

illness and injury Although most UFO encounter cases reportedly involve no harm to witnesses, a substantial minority of reports does mention injury to observers during the encounter or illness developing after the encounter. Early "contactee" George Adamski, for example, reported injury to an arm after allegedly straying too close to the rim of a "saucer." Another contactee, Albert Bender, claimed that his encounters with extraterrestrials gave him headaches. In the widely publicized Cash–Landrum incident, an encounter with an alleged UFO reportedly led to illness serious enough to require hospitalization. Similar reports involve the Falcon Lake incident in Canada, where a man allegedly was burned and made ill by a landed UFO, and the Dr. X case in France, in which a physician and his young son both were said to have suffered burns from a UFO encounter at their home. Alleged abductees may report receiving scars or marks on their bodies during quasi-medical examinations aboard UFOs. Although there appears to be no clinical proof that anyone ever has been injured or made ill by an encounter with a UFO, such reports sometimes are interpreted as evidence of the physical reality of UFOs.

See also ADAMSKI, GEORGE; BENDER MYSTERY; BODILY EFFECTS; CASH–LANDRUM INCIDENT; DEATHS; DR. X INCIDENT; FALCON LAKE INCIDENT; RADIATION EFFECTS.

illusion Defined in a broad sense as a mistaken perception, illusion is a major element of the UFO phenomenon. Illusions reportedly involved in UFO encounter cases may be visual (such as large, luminous objects perceived at close range), auditory (humming or buzzing sounds) and even olfactory (unpleasant odors associated with UFOs). Visual illusions are perhaps the most common in UFO reports. A luminous UFO following and keeping pace with an automobile on a highway at night, for example, has been attributed to an illusion of motion on the part of a planet, such as Venus or Mars. The illusion of such a "UFO" moving in front of the vehicle and hovering above the highway may be explained, in similar fashion, by a curve in the highway bringing the "UFO" into a different position relative to the car. In daylight sightings, distance and perspective may give a blimp the appearance of a hovering, silvery sphere or disc. Illusions may mislead even experienced observers into mistaking a familiar airborne object or terrestrial phenomenon for a UFO. Illusions are distinct from hallucinations, which are pathological conditions involving visual perception.

See HALLUCINATION.

imaginal realm   This expression refers to another, "alternate" reality that sometimes is thought to be experienced by humans through "border phenomena," which occur when humans find themselves on the "border" between ordinary reality and the aforementioned "alternate" reality. The imaginal realm supposedly may be experienced when the subject is in an altered state of consciousness. The concept of an imaginal realm has been applied to UFO encounter reports, in which the witness may seem to experience some reality different from ordinary reality.

See also BORDER PHENOMENA; ENCOUNTER PHENOMENA; HALLUCINATIONS; HIGH STRANGENESS; HYPNOSIS; PERCEPTION; REALITY.

implants   Alleged abductees sometimes report having had small devices implanted in various parts of their bodies. According to many such reports, the implant is a small metal object about the size of a BB shot, emplaced in the nasal passages, but implants in other parts of the body also have been reported. Material evidence of implants is scarce to nonexistent. It has been suggested that implants are equivalent to the tracking devices sometimes placed on "tagged" animals in the wild on Earth and are intended to help alleged extraterrestrials keep track of abductees. According to another suggestion, implants have something to do with intensifying psychic ability in the recipient. To date, these suggestions remain mere speculation, and the UFO implant phenomenon remains a mass of unproven claims.

See also ABDUCTIONS; STRIEBER, WHITLEY; TECHNOLOGY.

incubi and succubi   Familiar figures in the lore of demonology, incubi and succubi bear a close resemblance to "extraterrestrials" reported in many abduction cases. An incubus is an evil spirit that can take the form of a man and have sexual intercourse with a woman, whereas a succubus can appear as a woman and have sexual relations with a man. Such beings, both male and female, are mentioned in the literature on sexual encounters involving UFOs. An incubus commonly is said to approach a woman in bed, at night, while her husband sleeps through the encounter. The incubus may take the form of a small man and communicate with the woman in a strange, unearthly voice. He may strip the woman naked during their encounter and cause poltergeist activity to occur in the home where he appears. Physical abuse may be involved, such as blows to the face or body.

The parallels between certain alleged UFO encounters and reports of incubi and succubi are virtually exact. The extraterrestrials often are said to appear in the woman's bedroom, at night, as small humanoids. Her husband may sleep through the whole encounter. The alien may address the woman in an unusual voice (or by telepathy) and remove her clothing before subjecting her to some kind of quasi-medical procedure involving the sex organs, such as retrieval of ova. Later, the woman may find a scar on her body and attribute it to the extraterrestrials. Strange noises and other activity similar to poltergeist activity may be reported in the home about this time. When the abductee is male, a supposedly female extraterrestrial may entice him to have sex with her or merely display a strong interest in his genitalia while a machine performs some kind of operation in the man's anal or genital area. Some UFO abduction reports mention collection of semen by special apparatus placed on the genitals. Beyond these characteristics, alleged encounters with extraterrestrials bear other similarities to reports of incubi and succubi. For example, one incubus reported from Latin America, "El Duende," is described as a small humanoid dressed in red and black. This description resembles closely that of "Captain Aura Rhanes," whom "contactee" Truman Bethurum described as wearing a red-and-black outfit.

See also BETHURUM INCIDENT; DEMONOLOGY; ENCOUNTER PHENOMENA; GENETIC MANIPULATION; SEXUAL ENCOUNTERS; SINISTRARI, LODOVICO MARIA; STRIEBER, WHITLEY; VILLAS-BOAS INCIDENT.

Indonesia   The UFO phenomenon appears to have been a matter of particular concern for the Indonesian government, which reportedly has admitted that UFOs presented a "problem" for the nation's air defenses. The Indonesian air defenses

Indonesian air defenses reportedly have had to contend with UFOs on occasion. (U.S. Geological Survey)

reportedly have fired upon UFOs on occasion. UFO activity appears to have been especially intense in Indonesia in the early 1950s and between 1964 and 1965.

Indrid Cold   This was the name of a mysterious figure who reportedly met with one Woodrow Derenberger alongside Interstate Route 77 in West Virginia, after a black craft resembling a huge kerosene lamp landed on the highway in front of Derenberger's truck. "Cold" was described as being about five feet, 10 inches tall and having a swarthy complexion and long black hair. He had his arms folded and his hands tucked under his armpits, and wore a black topcoat over some kind of green outfit. The being reportedly communicated with Derenberger by telepathy while the strange vehicle hovered some 50 feet in the air and was seen by passing motorists. Later, Derenberger allegedly received other telepathic communications from Cold, to the effect that Cold hailed from a planet named Lanulos—a beautiful world where war, hunger and poverty were unknown—in the "galaxy" of Ganymede. Lanulos bears a certain resemblance to the planet Clarion as described by "contactee" Truman Bethurum. Also, it should be noted that Ganymede is a moon of Jupiter, not a galaxy.

See also ABSURDITY; BETHURUM INCIDENT; CLARION; HUMANOIDS; TELEPATHY.

inertia   An intrinsic property of all matter, inertia is an object's tendency to remain stationary, or in motion, unless some force is applied to it. As Sir Isaac Newton put it in his laws of motion, objects at rest tend to remain at rest, and objects in motion tend to remain in motion. The more massive an object, the greater inertia it has, and the more energy is required to put it in motion when stationary, or bring it to a halt when in motion. This means that an object subject to inertia cannot make instantaneous changes from zero velocity to high velocity; a period

of acceleration is required. Although that period may be very brief by everyday standards (as when a bullet is fired from a gun, for example), the object still requires time to accelerate from a standing stop to whatever velocity it finally attains. In similar fashion, a material object in motion cannot execute an instantaneous turn in flight, as some UFOs have been seen to do. For example, a material UFO could not execute an immediate, 90-degree turn. The object's inertia means that some time would have to be allowed for a more gradual turn, because of the object's tendency to keep going on its initial course.

Although UFOs are widely thought to be material spacecraft visiting Earth from some other planet, many UFO sightings indicate that the UFOs behave as if they were free from inertia—an impossibility for any material objects according to the laws of physics. The UFOs in such cases accelerate to great velocities from zero velocity and perform radical changes of direction in mid-flight, seemingly unencumbered by the limitations of inertia. This characteristic has led some observers to speculate that certain UFOs are not material objects, but rather some non-material phenomenon that is not subject to Newtonian laws of motion. On the other hand, certain UFOs reportedly have left physical traces of their activities, in the form of indentations on the ground (during landings); scorched or flattened vegetation; and even damage to vehicles and other manmade structures during close encounters. It is difficult to explain by the conventional laws of physics, how a non-material object could achieve such effects on material objects such as automobiles and plants.

See also UFOS, CHARACTERISTICS OF.

Insectograms   This category of crop glyphs, a phenomenon sometimes associated with UFOs, consists of segmented glyphs with protrusions like the antennae of insects. Insectograms started appearing in Britain in 1991.

See also CROP CIRCLES.

insectoids   Extraterrestrials reported seen in some close-encounter cases are described as resembling insects, with long, spindly limbs. Some students of the UFO phenomenon have suggested that insect-like aliens might be better suited than mammals such as ourselves to withstand extreme gravitational stresses imposed by violent maneuvering of the kind often observed in UFO encounter cases; this speculation, however, has never been widely accepted. "Insectoids" evidently are not reported often in UFO incidents, but they occupy a prominent place in the literature of science fiction. Insectoids featured in the

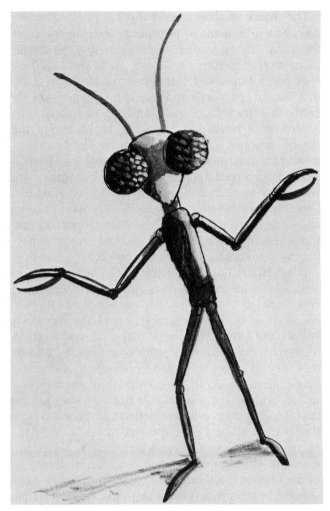

Insectoids are alleged extraterrestrials resembling insects. (D. Ritchie)

1968 British motion picture *Quatermass and the Pit* (released in the United States as *Five Million Years to Earth*), in which a Martian spacecraft with the bodies of its insect-like crew still aboard is discovered during a subway excavation in London. Numerous elements of UFO lore were reflected in the story, such as development of paranormal abilities, including poltergeist phenomena, by people near the spacecraft. At the climax of the film, the Martians are equated in some sense with the Devil.

See also DEMONOLOGY; MOTION PICTURES; POLTERGEIST.

Integratron   This bizarre project was the work of American "contactee" George Van Tassel. In 1954, Van Tassel began building the Integratron, a device some four stories tall and incorporating an electrostatic armature more than 50 feet wide, to "rejuvenate" the elderly and prevent the young from aging.

Van Tassel claimed to have received plans for the Integratron from extraterrestrials. Never completed, the Integratron is one of the most spectacular examples of pseudoscience in the UFO phenomenon. One of the early "contactees" in the years immediately after World War II, Van Tassel was an airport manager by profession. He became a celebrity among UFO enthusiasts and claimed to have had numerous contacts with extraterrestrials.

See also ASHTAR; COUNCIL OF SEVEN LIGHTS; PSEUDOSCIENCE.

interactivity   In some cases, witnesses to UFO sightings report what appears to be interactive behavior between the observer and the UFO. For example, the witness may think, "I wish the UFO would come closer," and the UFO allegedly does just that. UFO literature contains many reports of UFOs that come when called, so to speak. Numerous interpretations may be put upon such reports. One view is that the report is merely a hoax, hallucination or misinterpretation of some phenomenon such as an aircraft in flight. According to another interpretation, however, certain UFOs are thought to be under intelligent direction and to be capable of reading and responding to the thoughts of observers.

interdimensional gateways   This vaguely defined concept may be used to explain certain mysterious features of UFO reports, such as the apparent ability of flying saucers to appear and disappear instantaneously. In principle, if the saucers represent visitations by beings from some other dimension, given access to our universe by some "gateway," then their appearances and disappearances may be understood as a simple translation from one dimension or set of dimensions to another.

Although it is unclear how this "gateway" concept might be applied in practice, similar phenomena have been elements of science fiction for more than

Interdimensional gateways: in this artist's conception, a vintage 1960 flying saucer "fades into" our universe from some other postulated universe, using an "interdimensional gateway." (D. Ritchie)

a century. British author Edwin Abbott, in his 1884 fantasy *Flatland: A Romance of Many Dimensions*, imagined polygonal life forms existing in a universe consisting of a plane. When visited by a spherical being from the universe of three dimensions, the inhabitants of Flatland perceive the visitor as a circle of varying diameter that appears in, then disappears from, their perception. What they perceive of the sphere is its cross section, as the sphere intersects with the Flatlanders' planar universe. In similar fashion, visitors from other dimensions, entering our familiar universe, might give the impression of materializing suddenly and then vanishing with equal abruptness, as their set of dimensionalities intersects with our own. The "multidimensional gateway" concept thus far, however, has been mainly an exercise in speculation.

intermarriage   The theme of intermarriage between humans and extraterrestrials is prominent in UFO lore. Apocryphal texts have been interpreted as referring to angels (fallen or otherwise) having sexual relations with human women and producing extraordinarily large, strong offspring. In modern accounts, such intermarriage may be expressed as alleged production of "hybrid" babies—half human, half "alien"—by artificial insemination and/or "genetic engineering." Such stories, essentially occultist in character, are commonplace in modern abduction reports, and resemble stories of incubi and succubi.

See also ABDUCTIONS; ANGELS; DEMONOLOGY; GENETIC MANIPULATION; HYBRIDS; INCUBI AND SUCCUBI; SEXUAL ENCOUNTERS.

intervention   According to this element of UFO lore, alleged extraterrestrials either have been intervening in the history of human society for many years, or stand ready to do so at some unspecified time in the future. Opinions have differed on the character of this intervention and the possible motives behind it. According to some beliefs, the so-called aliens are benevolent and are prepared to land on Earth and save humankind if and when our civilization should bring itself to the point of self-destruction. Another widely held belief is that the alleged extraterrestrials are intervening now in our "evolutionary" development to guide humankind toward some imagined quantum advancement in our biological and/or spiritual evolution. Some students of UFO lore have claimed to perceive acts of intervention by extraterrestrials on numerous occasions in human history, from earliest times to the present. This particular school of thought provided the basis for the "ancient astronauts" phenomenon of the 1960s and 1970s.

The theme of alien intervention in human history has been prominent in popular entertainment since the initial "flying saucer" sighting in 1947. In the famous motion picture *The Day the Earth Stood Still*, for example, a humanoid extraterrestrial lands on Earth in a discoid spacecraft and warns the planet's inhabitants that they face total annihilation unless they control their warlike inclinations. The aliens in the classic Japanese science fiction movie *The Mysterians* try to hide their nefarious motive—to abduct human women for breeding purposes—but eventually are shown to be inimical to humankind as a whole. Later motion pictures, such as *2001: A Space Odyssey* and *Close Encounters of the Third Kind*, appear to portray aliens not as openly hostile, but rather as having mysterious motives of their own.

In science fiction and in the UFO phenomenon itself, aliens are perceived as hostile to humankind and prepared to invade Earth and subjugate its people, as in H.G. Wells's famous novel *The War of the Worlds* and other "invasion" tales derived from it. Modern UFO abduction stories, in which "abductees" report being subjected (in effect) to torture on board alien spacecraft, also commonly are interpreted as evidence of less than benign motives on the part of imagined extraterrestrials. In recent years, however, popular belief appears to favor an image of benevolent extraterrestrials trying to help humankind through an especially difficult period in human history, although the character of this intervention often is described only in the vaguest terms.

See also ABDUCTIONS; ANCIENT ASTRONAUTS; BELIEF SYSTEMS; CLOSE ENCOUNTERS OF THE THIRD KIND; DAY THE EARTH STOOD STILL, THE; EVOLUTION; INVASION; MOTION PICTURES; MYSTERIANS, THE; 2001: A SPACE ODYSSEY; WAR OF THE WORLDS, THE.

Invaders, The   American television series, ABC-TV, 1967–1968. Starring Roy Thinnes, "The Invaders" concerned a man's efforts to thwart an extraterrestrial invasion of Earth. The aliens look like humans but can be identified by the rigidity of their little fingers. When killed, the aliens disintegrate, so that evidence of their activity is difficult to produce. This problem reflected the scarcity of physical evidence for UFO activity in actual close-encounter cases. The aliens' spacecraft were depicted as saucers reminiscent of those in photographs by George Adamski.

invasion   UFOs often have been depicted, especially in motion pictures, as vehicles for an invasion of Earth by extraterrestrials. The motives for such invasion have varied from one story to another. In some cases the invasion is benevolent, and the aliens wish only to save humankind from self-destruction. In other stories, the extraterrestrials' motives are more like those of the European colonial powers of the 19th century, and the aliens seek to conquer the planet and exploit it for their own gain. The planet Mars has been a favorite point of origin for extraterrestrial invaders in fiction, possibly under the influence of H.G. Wells, whose novel *The War of the Worlds* described a fictional Martian invasion of Earth, and perhaps also because of Mars's identification in mythology with warfare and destruction.

See also MARS; MOTION PICTURES.

invisibility Certain UFOs and their alleged occupants are said to be capable of making themselves invisible at will. Considerable thought has gone into explaining this capability. According to one speculation, UFOs and "extraterrestrials" are visitors from another time—either in the future or in the past—and can appear or disappear by altering their coordinates in time. This ability to appear and disappear is attributed to many other paranormal phenomena besides UFOs, and helps to establish UFOs as such a phenomenon. The invisible visitor who can appear in humanoid form is a major element of the literature on occultism and demonology.

See also DEMONOLOGY; OCCULTISM; SINISTRARI, LODOVICO MARIA.

Invisibles A collection of spirits who reportedly were contacted through Ouija-board use and automatic writing in the early 20th century, the Invisibles resemble "extraterrestrials" in present-day encounter stories. The Invisibles became known through the work of the American occultist Stewart Edward White and his wife Betty. The Whites were using a Ouija board on March 17, 1919, when they first made contact with the Invisibles. The Invisibles communicated with the Whites first through automatic writing and later through Betty's own speech. Messages delivered by the Invisibles sound much like those attributed to extraterrestrials in the UFO phenomenon. The Invisibles said their goal was to encourage the spiritual growth of humankind. Puzzling statements about God also were delivered.

See also COMMUNICATIONS; ENCOUNTER PHENOMENA; MESSAGES; OCCULTISM; OUIJA BOARD; RELIGION, UFOS AND.

Iran A number of widely publicized UFO reports have come out of Iran, notably the Mehrabad incident of July 18, 1978, when a luminous UFO was sighted over Teheran. Another alleged UFO encounter in Teheran, in 1954, involved the sighting of a small humanoid.

See also TEHERAN INCIDENT.

Irwin incident, Utah, United States The story of Private First Class Gerry Irwin does not involve encounters with humanoids or other "extraterrestrial" entities but is remarkable for its account of altered mental states in an alleged witness to a UFO sighting. Irwin reportedly was driving from Idaho to Texas on February 28, 1959, when he saw a luminous object fly across the sky near Cedar City, Utah. Thinking he might be witnessing a plane crash, he stopped his car and went to investigate. An hour and a half later, he was found unconscious and taken to a hospital, where he could not be awakened. When he eventually did wake up, he said he felt well but thought it strange that his jacket was missing. The search party had not found the jacket, nor any evidence of a plane crash. He was flown to his base at Fort Bliss, Texas, and kept under observation at a hospital there for several days, then went back to duty. He had an incident of fainting some days later but recovered. Then another spell of fainting occurred, and he was taken to a hospital again, this time in the same condition he had experienced in Utah. When he awakened, he asked if there had been any "survivors." This time he was placed under observation by psychiatrists and remained hospitalized for more than a month. Tests reportedly indicated there was nothing wrong with him, so he was discharged. The following day, he took a bus from El Paso to Cedar City and returned to the site of his encounter with the UFO, where he discovered his missing jacket on a bush. In a buttonhole he found a pencil with a paper wound about it. He burned the paper, then appeared to emerge from some altered state of consciousness. He had no idea why he had come to that location. After reporting to the local sheriff, Irwin was told the story of his initial incident in Cedar City. Irwin returned to Fort Bliss and underwent yet another examination. On August 1, he did not report for duty and was listed as a deserter one month later. Reportedly, that was the last anyone heard or saw of Private Irwin. The case apparently has never been resolved.

See also PSYCHOLOGICAL EFFECTS.

Israel Israel has had its share of UFO reports in the 20th century but also occupies a special place in UFO lore because of alleged references to UFOs in the Bible, notably the vision of the prophet Ezekiel. The prophet's encounter with an astonishing wheeled apparatus that evidently descended from the sky has been interpreted as an early UFO encounter, although this interpretation is fanciful and cannot be supported when Ezekiel's account of the vision is read in the context of the Bible as a whole. Other, similar efforts to interpret mysterious biblical passages as evidence of "extraterrestrial" visitations in ancient Israel have proven equally unsuccessful.

See also ANCIENT ASTRONAUTS; BIBLE, ALLEGED UFOS IN; VON DÄNIKEN, ERICH.

Istrana incident, Italy   In an incident in November 1973, security guards at a military base at Istrana, near Venice, reportedly saw an unfamiliar object on the ground with two small humanoids wearing white coveralls beside it. The humanoids allegedly climbed aboard the object and flew away in it when sighted by the guards. Traces of a landing reportedly were discovered on the ground where the object was seen. The Istrana incident is one of a number of notable UFO reports from Italy in the 1970s.

See also AVIANO INCIDENT; ITALY; PORDENONE.

it   This pronoun refers to a tale from Shetland folklore about a bizarre creature that appeared as something different to everyone who saw it. One observer saw it as something like a jellyfish, while another perceived it as resembling a legless beast or a headless humanoid. Although it was noiseless, the being somehow could make itself understood without speaking. Each year, the being vexed a particular house at Christmas. One night, a man sat in that house reading a Bible by candlelight when the strange being intruded with a noise that resembled a mass of dead meat being thrown on the floor. Ax in hand, the man pursued the creature and eventually caught up with it. He threw his ax, which lodged in the creature's body just as it was about to dive over a cliff into the ocean. The man returned home and asked friends to return with him to the site. There they found the creature with the ax stuck in it; but again, the beast looked different to the eyes of each man, and they could not determine whether it was dead or alive. They buried the being on the spot and surrounded its grave with a deep ditch, so that no one could get close to it. When a man did approach the creature's grave, he witnessed a bright light and a strange mist around him, and something arose from the being's grave and fell into the sea.

The unidentified creature in this story bears certain similarities to alleged extraterrestrials in modern UFO close-encounter reports. Specifically, it looks different to each witness, as "aliens" may look different to observers in close-encounter reports. The unnamed being also appears capable of communicating by telepathy and taking on humanoid form, two characteristics of extraterrestrials in 20th-century encounter cases. Even the minor details of the case—the bright light and mist observed at the thing's grave, and its final disappearance into the sea—resemble elements of modern UFO reports, in which a brilliant UFO descends into a body of water or is surrounded at its landing site by a peculiar mist.

See also CLOUDS AND VAPORS; ENCOUNTER PHENOMENA; MYTHOLOGY; POLYMORPHY.

"Italians"   Alleged UFO contactees, especially Americans, sometimes describe humanoids seen in close encounters as resembling Italians. The beings, usually slightly smaller than an average American male in stature, are described as having black hair and olive or swarthy skin. Beings matching this description were reported, for example, in the encounters of Truman Bethurum and Joe Simonton. Why the entities should resemble stereotypical Italians in such cases is not known. Other ethnic stereotypes also are represented in UFO close-encounter reports. Some UFO humanoids are said to resemble East Asians or stereotypical blond Nordics.

See also BETHURUM INCIDENT; HUMANOIDS; "NORDICS"; SIMONTON INCIDENT.

Italy   The Italian peninsula and its adjacent islands have been the sites of so many notable UFO sightings that Italy is widely considered to be a UFO "window." Outstanding sightings include those over Rome in 1954, in which large numbers of UFOs were sighted maneuvering over the city; the Aviano incident in 1977, where a UFO sighting was linked to a power failure at a military base; and the widely publicized Arezzo incident, in which a close encounter reportedly involved two small humanoids.

See also ARREZO INCIDENT; AVIANO INCIDENT; MOUNT ETNA INCIDENT; ROME INCIDENTS.

J

Janos An alleged planet mentioned in an abduction story from Gloucestershire in the United Kingdom. On June 19, 1978, a family returning home by car from a visit to Berkshire reportedly encountered a UFO manned by pale-skinned, blue-eyed humanoids wearing silvery clothing. One of the aliens allegedly indicated his people came from a planet called Janos, which suffered a great calamity when a meteorite struck a nuclear power facility. Survivors of the catastrophe on Janos, the alien said, were looking for a place to live and found Earth attractive.

Japan The Japanese have been especially active in UFO studies in the late 20th century, and Japan itself is widely recognized as a UFO "window" because of the numerous sightings reported there. These sightings are said to be especially frequent on the northern island of Hokkaido. Japan's history of UFO sightings includes one celebrated incident witnessed by a general at his camp in 1235. The Japanese armed forces are believed to have conducted official studies of the UFO phenomenon.

See also NAKAMURA INCIDENT; NICHIREN INCIDENT; SAITAMA INCIDENT; TERAUCHI INCIDENT; TOMAKOMAI INCIDENT; YORITSUME INCIDENT.

Jersey devil, the A mythical monster said to haunt the Pine Barrens of southern New Jersey, the Jersey devil bears some likeness to "extraterrestrials" allegedly seen in UFO close encounters.

The Jersey devil is said to have been sighted on occasion over more than 200 years. In 1909, the beast reportedly was seen flying over a river and was described as having a head like a ram's, with curled horns. Its legs were short, and its wings long and thin. Its call was described as "mournful" and unpleasant, like a combination of a whistle and a squawk. The Jersey devil is thought to leave behind a noisome smell like that of rotting potatoes or dead fish.

The Jersey devil is said to have caused mass panic in the Pine Barrens in the years immediately prior to World War I. Thousands of residents of the area reportedly fled their homes before the rumored approach of the monster. The being's footprints allegedly were found on the ground in the Pine Barrens, sometimes ending abruptly, as if the creature had taken flight at that spot. Animal mutilations—specifically of dogs—were attributed to the Jersey devil.

Between World War I and 1950, little was heard of the Jersey devil in the Barrens. Reports of the monster's appearances resumed in the 1950s, however, soon after the modern "flying saucer" phenomenon originated following pilot Kenneth Arnold's alleged sighting of silvery UFOs in flight near Mount Rainier in Washington state. Sightings of the Jersey devil during the 1950s included an alleged encounter between the beast and two boys who claimed to have seen the Jersey devil looking at them through a window, in the manner of the small humanoids reported in the Kelly–Hopkinsville, Kentucky, incident.

In 1979, according to another (unsubstantiated) report, several children skating on a pond detected a foul smell and, in tracing the source of the odor, found themselves confronted by a monster seven feet tall, glaring at them with terrifying eyes. This particular report resembles the Flatwoods, West Virginia, incident, in which several witnesses reportedly encountered a huge being with frightening eyes in the woods. The case of Spring-Heeled Jack, in which a tall being with frightening eyes allegedly terrorized portions of Britain in the 19th and early 20th centuries, also bears notable similarities with reports of the Jersey devil.

Parallels between the Jersey devil myth and the UFO phenomenon are numerous and include sightings of a bizarre, nonhuman creature capable of flying and of making unusual noises; animal mutilations; encounters in remote places between humans and a tall being with frightening eyes; a highly unpleasant odor attributed to the entity; widespread public fear associated with the alleged being; and footprints of the creature, reportedly found in puzzling patterns. The coincidence between the resumption of "devil" sightings in the 1950s and the rise of the "flying saucer" phenomenon also may be significant.

This body of evidence, taken altogether, indicates that the modern UFO phenomenon and the myth of the Jersey devil may have common origins.

See also ANIMALS, UFOS AND; ARNOLD INCIDENT; DEVIL'S FOOTPRINTS; FLATWOODS INCIDENT; FOOTPRINTS; KELLY–HOPKINSVILLE INCIDENT; ODORS; SPRING-HEELED JACK; UFOS, CHARACTERISTICS OF.

Jessup, Morris, American astronomer, (1900–1959)

Jessup, author of the widely read 1955 book *The Case for the UFO,* argued that UFOs originated from a point within our solar system, some 170,000 miles from Earth. He considered the great numbers and variety of UFOs to be almost "a priori proof" that UFOs originated from some point near Earth rather than on another planet. Jessup argued that UFOs had a propulsion system far in advance of anything in our technology, and he suggested that UFOs seen in terrestrial skies were exploratory craft of "solid" and "nebulous" character. He expressed the hope, in the mid-1950s, that UFOs might provide the means to advance research greatly into space flight and make space travel possible within 10 years (from 1955) at much lower cost than rocket technology. Jessup also speculated that the Soviet Union might have captured a UFO and started investigating its technology.

Jessup was involved in the mysterious "Allende letters" episode, in which he received several letters from a man who signed himself "Carl Allen" or "Carlos Allende," describing an alleged experiment in which a Navy ship was rendered invisible. Another element of the "Allende letters" episode concerned a copy of Jessup's book *The Case for the UFO,* which was mailed to the Office of Naval Research in Washington, D.C., bearing written notes that indi-

cated the annotators were intimately familiar with UFO technology. Jessup appears to have committed suicide.

See also ALLENDE LETTERS; SUICIDES.

Julian of Norwich, English anchoress, late 14th to early 15th century

Although little is known about the life of the English mystic Lady Julian of Norwich, she left a detailed account of a set of visions that she allegedly received on May 8–9, 1373. These visions are described in her book *Showings or Revelations of Divine Love.* The document includes what Julian describes as encounters with the Devil. These alleged incidents bear a strong similarity to certain UFO close-encounter cases reported in the 20th century. In the first such incident, Julian writes, the Devil assaulted her during sleep, after she had suffered illness for some time. The Devil wished to strangle Julian but was unable to do so. Julian describes him as having a horrible stench. The evil spirit, she said, had a long, lean face, red in color with black spots. His hair was rust-red and hung in sidelocks at his temples. The Devil also had deformed hands and great white teeth, Julian reported. She felt great heat at the time of this encounter, and smoke entered her room at the doorway. Later Julian asked if anyone else had noticed this apparition, and she was told they had not. Later, evil spirits allegedly returned to trouble Julian again. Once more, she reported a foul smell and intense heat. She also claimed to hear multiple voices in her ears, as if two individuals were talking at the same time; the voices were low and indistinct and appeared to be carrying on a "confused" conversation. This experience lasted through the night and into the morning and ceased soon after daybreak. The stench lingered for a short while afterward.

Julian's visions of evil spirits resemble modern UFO "contactee" stories in several important respects. They occurred at night. Temperature effects and a foul odor were reported, and the Devil reportedly tried to subject Julian to bodily harm. The "voices" she reported also resemble descriptions of "telepathic" messages delivered by alleged extraterrestrials in our own time. Finally, the "smoke" that Julian mentions has a parallel in the mist or vapor sometimes reported at UFO landing sites in certain modern close-encounter cases.

See also DEMONOLOGY; ENCOUNTER PHENOMENA; ODORS; TEMPERATURE EFFECTS.

Juminda incident, Estonia

In either 1938 or 1939, two witnesses reportedly saw a strange "man" resembling a frog, about three feet tall, at Juminda on the coast of Estonia. The being was described as having a round head without a neck; a lengthy, straight slit for a mouth; and smaller slits for eyes. The skin was greenish-brown, and the creature had a curious gait. The being fled when pursued, then disappeared. Though the date is uncertain, this case is interesting because frog-like entities are reported in numerous UFO close-encounter incidents.

See also FROGS; HUMANOIDS.

Jung, Carl Gustav, (1875–1961)   A Swiss psychiatrist and one-time colleague of Sigmund Freud, Jung analyzed the UFO phenomenon and interpreted the circular forms of UFOs as a manifestation of modern society's desire for wholeness and unity, as symbolized by the circle. Among his patients was a woman, identified as "S.W.," who claimed to have encountered an extraterrestrial seated next to her on a train. In view of the link between occultism and the UFO phenomenon, it may be significant that Jung was deeply interested in the occult. He was especially interested in mandalas, circular emblems with occult significance, which he related to the circular forms of UFOs.

See also MANDALA; OCCULTISM; S.W. INCIDENT.

Jupiter   The fifth planet from the Sun, Jupiter once was considered a possible home for intelligent extraterrestrial life, but studies of the planet by unmanned probes indicate that conditions on the planet probably are unsuitable for intelligent life as known on Earth. The astrological lore of Jupiter occupies a small but interesting place in the UFO phenomenon. In astrology, Jupiter is identified by a sign resembling the numeral 4. This sign occurs in the recollections of some alleged UFO abductees. In the Tujunga Canyon abduction story, for example, one of two women reportedly abducted by a UFO was said to have been marked on her back with a glyph resembling the astrological sign for Jupiter. The woman allegedly claimed the mark had been applied to her in some earlier lifetime so that extraterrestrials could identify and monitor her in successive "incarnations."

See also ASTROLOGY; REINCARNATION; TUJUNGA CANYON CASE.

K

Kandahar incident, Afghanistan On November 8, 1959, a large glowing object was reported moving very rapidly over Kandahar, Afghanistan. The object moved in a northwesterly direction and is said to have caused minor earth tremors when it crashed and exploded in the Shurad Mountains. The U.S. Army reported this sighting to the U.S. Defense Intelligence Agency (DIA), says British UFO investigator Timothy Good in his book *Above Top Secret*. He adds that DIA's main interest in UFO reports concerned possible Russian missile tests, and that a Soviet missile test near the Afghan border appears to be the most likely explanation for this particular incident. Another UFO was reported seen on November 29; a third UFO report from Afghanistan occurred on December 2. This time a circular object was sighted flying southwest over Ghazni.

See also MISSILES, UFOS AND.

Kelly–Hopkinsville incident, Kentucky, United States One of the most violent reports in the literature on UFO close encounters, the Kelly–Hopkinsville incident allegedly occurred on the night of August 25, 1955, on a family's farm. A teenage boy in the family had left the farmhouse to get water from the well when he noticed a circular, luminous object overhead. He reported the sighting to his father, who presumed the boy had seen part of the annual Perseid meteor shower. An hour later, dogs outside began barking loudly. The father and one of his sons investigated and found a humanoid being less than four feet tall crouching some 50 feet away from the farmhouse. The being was luminous and appeared to be wearing a suit of reflective material. The head had two large eyes and appeared to be dis-

proportionately large for the body. The arms were long and ended in hands with webbing between the fingers, and what looked like claws or talons. The entity moved with a gait resembling that of a monkey. When the being was about 20 feet away, the father of the family fired at it with a shotgun. The being was knocked down but then sprang to its feet and ran away. Other, similar entities also appeared. Time and again, the humans fired at the intruders. The shots appeared to do the strange beings no harm, although the humans reported hearing a metallic sound when a shot struck one of the entities. At one point, one of the intruders was seen looking into the house through the living room window, which was destroyed by a shot that dislodged the creature.

According to one account of the incident, the unearthly beings approached from the darkest side of the house and maintained a considerable distance from outdoor lights. During a pause in the confrontation, the family got into their truck and drove to a

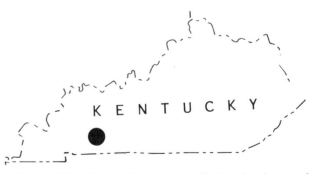

Kelly–Hopkinsville incident reportedly involved a rural Kentucky family's encounter with dwarfish "extraterrestrials." (U.S. Geological Survey)

police station several miles away. A law enforcement officer visited the farmhouse later and saw the evidence of the family's resistance, including the broken window. The Kelly–Hopkinsville incident contains many elements of classic UFO close encounters, including humanoid "aliens," an isolated setting and vigorous response on the part of domestic animals to the intruders' presence.

See also ENCOUNTER PHENOMENA; HUMANOIDS.

Keyhoe, Major Donald (1897–1988)

An officer in the U.S. Marine Corps, Keyhoe served also as director of the National Investigations Committee on Aerial Phenomena (NICAP), one of the world's most prominent UFO investigatory groups. Keyhoe favored the view that UFOs probably represented visits to Earth by extraterrestrials. During a television interview in 1958, Keyhoe's remarks were interrupted on the air, as he tried to say that UFOs could be proven to be actual machines under intelligent control. This incident of "censorship" has been interpreted as an attempt to protect "national security." Keyhoe served as NICAP's director until 1969.

Kiev incident

Reported several months before the Voronezh sightings in 1989, the Kiev incident involved the report of an attempted abduction by a UFO at a park along the Dnieper River. Two women and a six-year-old girl, the daughter of one of the women, allegedly were walking in the park when they encountered three beings with large eyes and blond hair, wearing silver clothing resembling nightgowns. The beings said that they came from another planet and intended to take one (or possibly more) of the women back to their planet. One of the women reported that she felt overpowered somehow by the presence of the aliens and had a sensation like needles on her skin when the beings looked at her. The aliens conducted the women and child to a silver craft like a giant barrel surmounted by a circular antenna. When the women protested and the girl began crying, the aliens reportedly said they had decided not to carry out the abduction after all. The aliens then entered the craft and departed in it.

See also ABDUCTIONS; RUSSIA; VORONEZH SIGHTINGS.

Kingman incident, Arizona, United States

Rumors have circulated about an incident that supposedly occurred near Kingman, Arizona, in 1953 and involved an engineer who reportedly was driven to a saucer crash site and saw the body of an "extraterrestrial" about four feet tall. The engineer allegedly was driven to the site in a bus that had its windows blacked out. This report has many parallels with the so-called Roswell incident.

See also CRASHES; ROSWELL INCIDENT; RUMORS.

Kinross incident, United States

The Kinross incident reportedly occurred on the evening of November 23, 1953, over Lake Superior. U.S. Air Force radar detected a UFO over Soo Locks, in restricted airspace, and an F-89 was sent up from Kinross Field to investigate. The jet chased the UFO for several minutes and eventually caught up with it. The two returns on the radar screen appeared to merge into one return, which then disappeared. Attempts to contact the jet by radio were unsuccessful, and no trace of the aircraft or its occupants was reported found later, despite a search. One interpretation of the incident was that the F-89 plunged directly into the lake, leaving no wreckage or oil slick behind. Another view was that the jet had been captured or destroyed somehow by the UFO. The Kinross incident bears a certain similarity to the Mantell incident, in which a U.S. military aircraft was reportedly lost in pursuit of a UFO, and to the disappearance of pilot Frederick Valentich and his aircraft over the Bass Strait between Australia and Tasmania.

See also AIR FORCE; MANTELL INCIDENT; VALENTICH CASE.

Klass, Philip (1919–)

A former editor at *Aviation Week and Space Technology* magazine, and one of the most influential debunkers of the UFO phenomenon, Klass has publicized what he considers hoaxes in the UFO field. He also has pointed out inconsistencies in evidence and arguments presented by defenders of the hypothesis that UFOs represent visitations by extraterrestrials in material spacecraft.

Klass has suggested that most UFO sightings are merely mistaken identifications of mundane phenomena such as aircraft, and the remainder of reports may be dismissed as hoaxes and self-deception. Klass also has emphasized that even a highly intelligent observer may be susceptible to error in identifying phenomena seen in the skies. To show the problems involved in studying UFO reports, even those related by intelligent and sincere witnesses, Klass emphasizes the difficulty in estimating the size, distance and altitude of an object seen in the skies, because observers cannot make such estimates with accuracy unless the object being observed is near to some well-known object of an established altitude or size.

Some UFO reports, Klass has written, turn out to be practical jokes. He tells of an unnamed military pilot, for example, who would generate a mistaken

UFO report by flying close to a civilian jetliner with his aircraft's external lights turned off. The military pilot then would aim his emergency cockpit flashlight at the jetliner, flash the light on and off until he noticed reactions from passengers in the cabin, then move to the other side of the civilian plane and make further signals with his flashlight. Finally, the pilot would fly beneath the jetliner, turn on his afterburner (which produces augmented thrust and a long tail of fire) and move quickly ahead of the civilian aircraft. The result was a report of a UFO with a flashing light and the characteristics of a rocket.

In his criticism of abduction reports and the dubious "evidence" associated with them, Klass wrote in 1983 that not one person claiming to have been abducted by UFOs has reported such an incident to the Federal Bureau of Investigation (FBI), which has the responsibility to investigate kidnappings. Neither, he pointed out, has any "UFOlogist" reported such an abduction to the FBI. The result of such a report would be an FBI investigation, and reporting a "spurious abduction" to the FBI carries a penalty of five years' imprisonment and/or a $10,000 fine, Klass pointed out.

The use of hypnosis to retrieve "memories" of abductions from alleged abductees has also come under criticism from Klass. He argues that in cases where individuals who never claimed to have undergone "abduction" by UFOs were put under hypnosis and asked to imagine such an encounter, the resulting accounts were substantially the same as reports made under hypnosis by persons who claimed to have undergone UFO abductions.

Klass has faulted the American news media for what he considers misleading and one-sided coverage of the UFO phenomenon. He argues that the public has been "brainwashed" by inaccurate media coverage into accepting exotic explanations of UFO sightings and "abductions."

Klass has rejected the allegation that the United States government is concealing physical evidence of UFO visitations and is using technology derived from UFOs to produce new generations of sophisticated aircraft and spacecraft. He points out that almost half a century after the first reported recovery of UFO debris in the so-called Roswell incident, space technology still depends upon chemical-fueled rocket boosters for launches. Had advanced "alien" technology become available through the crash and subsequent recovery of an extraterrestrial spacecraft, it seems highly unlikely that chemical rockets would still be in such widespread use.

Part of Klass's work is a set of "UFOlogical principles" which he applies to the UFO phenomenon. One principle is that even an intelligent, honest person may provide a highly inaccurate description of an unexpected event of short duration. Also, it may be difficult, if not impossible, to tell the difference between accurate and inaccurate portions of an observer's account of a UFO. Some of Klass's other principles state that news media tend to give UFO reports more publicity than any "prosaic" explanation that may be offered later for a sighting; and that once news coverage persuades the public that UFOs are nearby, many phenomena may be interpreted as UFOs by wishful observers, whose reports of UFOs add to general excitement, which in turn leads to still more observations of UFOs. The resulting "flap" lasts until media coverage of the UFO sightings ceases, at which point the flap diminishes. Another of Klass's principles is that numerous UFO sightings appear baffling and inexplicable merely because investigators have not done an adequate job of investigating.

See also ABDUCTIONS; DEBUNKERS; FLAPS; HOAXES; TECHNOLOGY.

Knock incident, Ireland   A case of an alleged apparition of the Virgin Mary, the Knock incident reportedly occurred on August 21, 1879, at Knock, a village in western Ireland. A woman passing the village church reported seeing several unusual figures and what appeared to be an illuminated "altar" in a field nearby. When she returned later in the company of a friend, she saw the forms of three people standing in a meadow, surrounded by brilliant light.

The witnesses identified one of the figures as the Virgin Mary, another as Saint Joseph, and the third as St. John the Evangelist. Other witnesses of the incident also were reported. A church commission convened to investigate the sighting studied testimony from more than a dozen witnesses to the event. According to testimony before the commission, the area surrounding the apparition was illuminated by a brilliant golden light that sometimes became whiter. The light reportedly fluctuated in intensity. The figure identified as Mary was said to wear a white robe and a crown adorned with crosses. She reportedly was barefooted and held her hands apart. The figure identified as St. John was said to hold an open book in one hand. A witness said he had approached closely enough to see writing in the book. Besides the three radiant figures, the apparition allegedly included an altar with a cross on it, and before the cross stood a lamb.

During the several hours that the vision was reported seen, one woman allegedly tried to embrace the figure of "Mary." The figure was insubstantial, however, and the woman found herself trying to grasp thin air. Also, though rain had been falling for some time before the incident, this same witness reported that the ground felt dry to her touch.

Further investigation determined no known means of staging, by trickery, such an apparition. Tests utilizing a lantern to project photographic images on a wall failed to produce results comparable to the witnesses' observations. Seemingly miraculous healings were reported afterward at the site of the apparition.

The Knock incident contains numerous parallels with UFO encounter phenomena of the latter half of the 20th century. The luminous but insubstantial humanoids; the brilliant though fluctuating light; and the reported "miraculous" cures are all elements of UFO encounter reports from our own time.

See also ENCOUNTER PHENOMENA; FATIMA, "MIRACLE" OF; HUMANOIDS; MARIAN APPARITIONS.

kundalini A vaguely defined "energy" that occultists believe to reside in the human body, kundalini is associated with numerous experiences reported by witnesses in UFO close-encounter cases, including perceptions of bright light, strange bodily sensations and assorted psychic phenomena. Kundalini energy is said to be concentrated at the base of the spine.

See also KUNDALINI GUN.

kundalini gun A postulated device, the kundalini gun is a hand-held instrument that supposedly immobilizes witnesses during close encounters with UFOs. The kundalini gun allegedly is pointed at the witness, who then becomes paralyzed temporarily. It has also been suggested that this hypothetical device may be used to induce a "pseudomystical" state of mind in abductees so as to manipulate their beliefs. The kundalini gun is named for an occultist theory of bodily "energy" that allegedly produces effects similar to those reported in many close-encounter cases.

See also BELIEF SYSTEMS; KUNDALINI; OCCULTISM.

L

Lago Argentina incident, Argentina Early in the evening on March 18, 1950, a rancher named Wilfredo Arevalo is said to have encountered two UFOs. One of them landed, and he approached to within about 450 feet of it. The craft reportedly appeared to be made of aluminum. It allegedly gave off a blue-green vapor and an odor like that of benzene. In the transparent cabin of the craft, the witness could see several tall men, wearing garments resembling cellophane and attending to certain instruments. When the figures saw him, they directed a light at him. At the same time, the vehicle was illuminated with blue light. The vapor output of the UFO increased, and flames of red and green hues emanated from the underside of the craft as it rose from the ground with a humming noise. This craft and the other then flew toward Chile.

See also ACOUSTICAL EFFECTS; ARGENTINA; ENCOUNTER PHENOMENA; HUMANOIDS; ODORS.

Laigle incident, Normandy, France This incident reportedly occurred near Laigle in Normandy on the afternoon of April 26, 1812. A brilliant globe of fire was seen moving rapidly through the air. A strong explosion followed the globe's appearance and allegedly was heard for some 90 miles in every direction. Three or four noises like cannon discharges were reported, followed by noise resembling musket fire, and then a commotion like the beating of a drum. The noise reportedly came from a small, rectangular cloud that hung motionless in the sky while the noises continued. The cloud gave off vapor, apparently in connection with the explosions. The cloud must have been at high altitude, for witnesses in two communities three miles apart thought it was directly overhead. Numerous meteorites fell, accompanied by a hissing noise. The sky was clear at the time, except for a few clouds. UFO investigator Morris Jessup drew attention to the peculiar shape of the cloud in this incident and cites it as evidence of "artificiality."

See also ACOUSTICAL EFFECTS; ATMOSPHERIC PHENOMENA; CLOUD CIGARS; JESSUP, MORRIS.

Lamy, New Mexico, incident, United States On the evening of March 26, 1880, several men walking near Galisteo Junction reported seeing a curious, balloon-like object fly low over them and emit what sounded like voices. The object allegedly was fish-shaped and had a fan-like apparatus at one end. Several figures were seen aboard the vehicle, but their speech was unintelligible. After flying over Galisteo Junction at low altitude, the UFO departed toward the east. This incident bears a strong similarity to the "airship" sightings reported in the United States in the 1890s.

See also AIRSHIPS.

language A complex element of the UFO phenomenon, language involves communications between humans and alleged extraterrestrials, and among the so-called aliens themselves. In some close encounters, the extraterrestrials reportedly speak with their human contacts in the humans' native languages: English, Russian, or whatever. The visitors' level of fluency may vary greatly. Some seem highly articulate, while others barely speak at all. In other instances, communication takes place by "telepathy," or the direct transmission of words from one mind to another. Written communications also have been reported. In certain close-encounter reports, alleged extraterrestrials are said to speak with one another in languages that tend to resemble, but remain substantially different from, terrestrial languages such as Chinese.

Sometimes, the extraterrestrials are said to bypass written or spoken language altogether and communicate through telepathically transmitted images. These images sometimes are terrifying and depict global devastation through warfare or some other calamity.

The Sanskrit language is a minor but significant element in the UFO phenomenon. Ancient manuscripts in Sanskrit are said to refer to the building and operation of aerial craft in centuries past; inscriptions in some language resembling Sanskrit were reportedly found in a crashed "saucer" in the southwestern desert of the United States in 1947; and one classification system for UFOs uses Sanskrit terminology to identify their various classes.

Specimens of extraterrestrial "languages" relayed by alleged contactees have proven to be unconvincing, as in the UMMO hoax. One curious aspect of "extraterrestrial" languages is the recurrence of childish, two-syllable proper nouns, such as names of entities and planets: Hoova, Affa, Masar and the like.

See also AUTOMATIC WRITING; AZTEC INCIDENT; COMMUNICATIONS; CRASHES; SANSKRIT; TELEPATHY; UMMO; VIDYA; VIMANA; VULYA; VUNU.

Laputa   The fictional flying island described in *Gulliver's Travels* by Jonathan Swift, Laputa bears many similarities to UFOs described in modern close-encounter reports. Swift's descriptions of Laputa were intended as satire, however, rather than a factual narrative of a UFO encounter.

See also LITERATURE, UFOS AND.

Larch incident, United States   The Larch incident (the name is spelled Lerch in some accounts) reportedly occurred on Christmas Eve of 1889 and may be seen as an early example of what would become the UFO abduction stories of the late 20th century. According to the story, 11-year-old Oliver Larch went outside at night, carrying two buckets to fetch water during a holiday celebration at his family's farmhouse near South Bend, Indiana, and was abducted by an entity or entities unknown. The family heard Oliver scream that "they" or "it" had him, and cry for help. The boy's screams brought his father outside to see what had happened. The screams continued for several minutes and seemed to emanate from overhead rather than ground level. The

cries grew fainter, as if something or someone were lifting Oliver away into the sky. Oliver's father reportedly found that the boy's footprints simply stopped some 225 feet from the house, about halfway between the house and the well. Nearby lay one of the water buckets Oliver had been carrying. The other bucket was not found. A search for Oliver was organized immediately but was unsuccessful. Then the voice was heard one last time, calling from the skies for help. Astronomer and UFO investigator Morris Jessup cited a possible explanation: a passing balloon snagged Oliver with a grappling hook and carried him away. This explanation seems unlikely, however, on the ground that weather conditions prevented balloons from taking flight that evening. A less exotic explanation, namely murder by a rival for a young lady's attentions at the party, has been advanced to account for Oliver Larch's disappearance. Had a murderer grabbed one of the buckets and crushed Oliver's skull with it, then concealed the murder weapon along with the body, this would account for Oliver's disappearance, his initial screams, and the absence of the second bucket at the scene. The evidence in the case, however, does not appear to support this interpretation. Only one set of tracks (Oliver's) was reported found in the snow, and those tracks simply ended, short of the well; Oliver's body was not reported found, despite an extensive search; and the witnesses clearly heard screams coming from overhead after Oliver's apparent abduction. If this incident has been reported accurately, then it may belong in the literature on UFO abductions.

See also ABDUCTIONS.

lasers   The word laser is short for "light amplification by stimulation of radiation." A laser emits a narrow beam of intense, highly coherent light. This technology was developed around 1960. About the same time, eyewitnesses to alleged UFOs began describing the UFOs as emitting bright lights similar to laser beams. In similar fashion, reports of "airships" from the late 19th century described the alleged aircraft in the imagery of then available technology, such as compressed-air machinery. Such technological elements of UFO encounter stories are widely viewed as examples of how the technology of a given land and time affects popular perception and interpretation of the UFO phenomenon.

See also AIRSHIPS; CULTURAL TRACKING; TECHNOLOGY.

Lawson experiment   In 1977, two students of the UFO phenomenon, Dr. Alvin Lawson of California

State University at Long Beach and technical writer John De Herrera, decided to carry out experiments to see if a person without prior UFO "encounter" experience could tell a persuasive story of abduction while under hypnosis. The two men collaborated with Dr. William McCall, a physician with experience in clinical hypnosis, to conduct the experiment. Using 20 volunteer subjects who were interviewed beforehand to eliminate any who might have sighted UFOs or become informed about the subject, Dr. McCall placed the subjects under hypnosis individually and told each subject to imagine that he or she had seen a UFO, had been taken aboard an alien spacecraft and had undergone a physical examination there. Next, the subject was asked to describe the imagined experience. Lawson and De Herrera expected that prompting would be required to make the subjects imagine specific details. Instead, the subjects produced such details easily, without prompting. McCall, when asking a subject to describe the inside of the flying saucer, needed to offer no more prompting than to ask, now and then, what was happening. A later analysis of the subjects' accounts showed no significant difference between their imagined experiences and the accounts of persons who claimed to have been abducted.

See also ABDUCTIONS; HYPNOSIS.

Lemuria   A mythical "lost continent" that was said to have extended from the island of Madagascar (today's Malagasy Republic) to Ceylon (Sri Lanka) in the Indian Ocean, Lemuria featured in the so-called Shaver mystery, which American editor Ray Palmer used to promote a hypothesis of UFOs originating from within a hollow Earth. The occult literature on Lemuria includes the speculations of the famed occultist Madame Helena Blavatsky, who imagined Lemuria was populated by four-armed telepathic creatures 15 feet tall, bearing some resemblance to certain "extraterrestrials" reported seen in UFO close-encounter cases. The myth of Lemuria resembles in many ways that of Atlantis.

See also ATLANTIS; BLAVATSKY, HELENA PETROVNA; HOLLOW EARTH HYPOTHESIS; HUMANOIDS; OCCULTISM; PALMER, RAYMOND; SHAVER MYSTERY; TELEPATHY.

Levelland, Texas, incident, United States   On the night of November 2–3, 1957, numerous eyewitnesses in the vicinity of Levelland, Texas, reported sighting a large, luminous UFO. Several vehicle stoppages were associated with the sightings. The object was said to be about 200 feet long, and shaped either like an egg or like a torpedo. The Levelland incident is noteworthy in that the reports appeared to be made and reported independently. Also, the sky reportedly was overcast that night, so that misidentifications of celestial objects—a common source of UFO reports—would appear unlikely in this case.

levitation   The raising of a person, animal or other object from the ground with no visible mechanism of support, levitation has been reported often in UFO close-encounter cases, especially those involving abduction reports. Individuals have reported being lifted from the ground and carried considerable distances through the air. The phenomenon may be described as lifting something "as if by unseen hands." Reports of levitation are also commonplace in the literature on occult phenomena (such as "hauntings") and on the exorcism of evil spirits. Fraud has been exposed in certain cases of alleged levitation. Whether real or fraudulent, levitation provides a link between the UFO phenomenon and other branches of occultism. Levitation is akin to "anti-gravity," a quixotic quest to neutralize gravitation. Anti-gravity has occupied the minds of some prominent "UFOlogists," without apparent success.

See also ANTI-GRAVITY; DEMONOLOGY; REICH, WILHELM.

ley lines   An occult element of the UFO phenomenon, ley lines are said to be straight lines linking ancient sites of mystical importance, such as megaliths and stone circles. Although ley lines have been a subject of popular interest since the 1920s, enthusiasm for their study has increased in recent years with the rise of the New Age movement, and ley lines have been suggested as means of explaining concentrations of UFO sightings at certain areas. According to one hypothesis, ley lines are used as navigational aids by UFOs. It remains unclear, however, what exactly constitutes a ley line, and what kind of "energy" it might involve. Discussions of ley lines in the UFO phenomenon illustrate the close links between it and occultism.

See also OCCULTISM.

light-bending   A few cases from the literature on UFO encounters mention a peculiar phenomenon known as "light-bending." Through some process, beams of light such as those from automobile headlamps are allegedly bent or deflected upward. A famous case of this kind is the Pudasjarvi abduction report from Finland.

See also PUDASJARVI INCIDENT.

Linn Grove, Iowa, incident, United States   On the morning of April 15, 1897, five men near Linn

Grove reportedly found a strange craft on the ground and approached to within about half a mile of it. The craft then allegedly spread out four huge wings and flew away northward. Two long-haired beings on board the vehicle reportedly were seen, but not clearly, because they tried to conceal themselves. This sighting occurred at the time of the airship "wave" in the United States and bears certain similarities to UFO close-encounter reports from the 20th century, including the long-haired occupants.

See also AIRSHIPS.

literature, UFOs and   Even when one excludes the voluminous writings on UFOs in modern science fiction, references to UFOs and extraterrestrials are abundant in literature. One of the earliest treatments of extraterrestrials in Western literature is that of the second-century Syrian-Greek satirist Lucian of Samosata, whose fictional *True History* (apparently a parody of fantastic travel stories that were popular in his day) deals in part with an extraterrestrial war. German astronomer Johannes Kepler described the fictional inhabitants of the Moon in his 1634 story *Somnium*. Kepler's contemporary, the French fantasist Cyrano de Bergerac, described travels through outer space, as did English bishop Francis Godwin in his 1638 fantasy *The Man in the Moone*. (Godwin's character Domingo Gonsales, a space traveler who uses a flying machine drawn by birds, appears also in Cyrano's stories.) Voltaire's 1750 fantasy *Micromegas* describes a visit to Earth by a gigantic inhabitant of the star Sirius and his companion, a native of Saturn. Jonathan Swift, in his 1726 novel *Gulliver's Travels*, relates the story of the flying island of Laputa, with its population of mad scientists. Fictional extraterrestrials have provided authors with a convenient and politically safe perspective for looking at the follies of humankind.

"little blue man" incident, United Kingdom
A literally colorful incident from British UFO lore involves the "little blue man" who reportedly appeared to several schoolboys in England on January 28, 1967, following a stroke of lightning during a rainstorm. The small figure was surrounded by a blue glow and wore a hat some two feet tall. When the boys approached him, the little man vanished in a cloud of yellow-blue mist. Later he reappeared, then vanished again in similar fashion when the boys tried to approach him a second time. The little man appeared a third time, accompanied by what sounded like a deep voice babbling in an incomprehensible tongue. This time the boys did not approach the little man, and he was still visible to them

"Little green men" became figures of fun in the 1950s. (D. Ritchie)

when they had to leave the site and go to school. The boys reported the encounter to their teacher, who had them write down their accounts of the incident individually. The "little blue man" resembles small humanoids reported in UFO close-encounter cases.

See also DEMONOLOGY; HUMANOIDS.

little green men   This expression—widely used to refer to alleged extraterrestrials—is thought to have originated in a series of science fiction stories published in the American science fiction magazine *Amazing Stories* in the late 1940s. The stories, "The Green Man" and "The Green Man Returns," were by Harold Sherman and involved an extraterrestrial with psychic ability. Also, reports of small humanoids having green skin or wearing green clothing may be found in the literature on UFOs. Such stories bear a strong resemblance to the account of the "green children" from English folklore, and the British case of the "little blue man."

See also GREEN CHILDREN; HUMANOIDS; "LITTLE BLUE MAN" INCIDENT, UNITED KINGDOM.

Loch Raven Dam incident, Maryland, United States   One of the most famous sightings in the United States, the Loch Raven Dam incident reportedly occurred around 10:30 P.M., Eastern time, on October 26, 1958. Two men riding in a car toward a

Chesapeake Bay region has been the site of many famous UFO sightings, including the Washington, D.C. sightings and the Loch Raven Dam incident near Baltimore. (NASA)

metal bridge near the Loch Raven Dam near Baltimore reported seeing a luminous, unidentified object hovering above the bridge. The car engine stopped and could not be restarted. Because there was no shelter along the road in which to hide, the men got out, hid behind their car and observed the object from there. They estimated the object's "height" (presumably its altitude) at 75 to 150 feet, and its length at approximately 100 feet, or one-third the length of the bridge. About one minute later, the object departed after emanating a "blinding" light and intense heat, and giving off a very loud noise comparable to a clap of thunder or an aircraft's sonic boom. The men experienced minor burns on their faces. Other witnesses in the vicinity reported, about the time of the incident, seeing a luminous white object in flight and hearing a "boom." The following night, two other men reported seeing a luminous object hovering above a field along nearby Loch Raven Road. Two additional witnesses made a similar report the same evening. The Loch Raven Dam incident resembles in many ways the Pont-la-Dame incident, reported only two days later in France.

See also PONT-LA-DAME INCIDENT; VEHICLE EFFECTS.

London–Kent sighting, United Kingdom One widely publicized UFO sighting in Britain reportedly occurred on the afternoon of December 15, 1980, along the boundary between Kent and southeast London. The object was described as resembling an elongated triangle and was multicolored. The nose reportedly was reddish-orange in color, the midsection silvery, and the tail blue. The object halted briefly at several moments during its flight, and allegedly emitted puffs of smoke or vapor. The UFO reportedly was seen by 40 or more witnesses before splitting into two separate objects that departed in a vertical direction. This case illustrates the "splitting" phenomenon, in which a UFO is said to divide into two or more distinct segments, which then may rejoin after performing independent maneuvers. The London–Kent incident bears a strong similarity to another sighting reported in Beijing in 1981.

See also BEIJING INCIDENT; SPLITTING.

Loosley incident, United Kingdom This incident involves one "William Robert Loosley," an undertaker who allegedly encountered a spacecraft from another star system in Britain on October 4, 1871. According to the story, Loosley took a walk in his garden that night and saw a light move across the sky, followed by a noise like thunder. The brilliant object he saw ceased moving and descended into woods nearby. The following morning, Loosley walked to what he presumed was the landing site. He found a metal object, about 18 inches high, that emitted a bright purple beam of light and then followed Loosley as he tried to leave. At one point, the mysterious object collected the body of a dead rat and stored it inside the machine. The object also stole Loosley's walking stick. Although widely reported as fact, the Loosley story now is considered to have been a hoax devised by a British science fiction writer.

See also HOAXES.

Lothian, Scotland, United Kingdom A famous UFO "window," the Lothian country around Edinburgh has been the site of many notable UFO reports. The Livingston incident, in which a partly transparent UFO reportedly was seen on the ground in the Dechmont woods north of Livingston, allegedly took place on November 9, 1979. This incident reportedly involved an "attack" by two "spheres" upon a witness. Another widely publicized UFO report from Livingston originated on November 17, 1978, when a discoid UFO was reported to have risen from a forest and then dropped back among the trees. Other local communities, including Tranent and Broxburn, also have been the sites of significant UFO reports.

See also UNITED KINGDOM, UFOS IN; WINDOWS.

Lovecraft, Howard Phillips (1890–1937)

An American fantasy author best known for his tales of horror and the supernatural, Lovecraft incorporated into his work themes that would become important elements of the UFO phenomenon in the middle and late 20th century. Lovecraft's story "The Shadow Out of Time," for example, concerns a "Great Race" of extraterrestrials who took over Earth millions of years ago and can invade and possess the bodies of humans. The story involves an academic who is driven from his own body and finds his consciousness transferred to an alien's body in the age of dinosaurs. When the man is returned to his own body, he experiences amnesia but, through recollections in dreams, is able to determine what happened while he was displaced from his original body. In Lovecraft's work, parallels with elements of the modern UFO phenomenon—notably amnesia and "missing time"—are close and numerous.

See also LITERATURE, UFOS AND; MISSING TIME.

Lubbock Lights, Texas, United States

On August 31, 1951, a mysterious, V-shaped formation of lights appeared in the skies above Lubbock, Texas. Eventually, controversy over the nature of the "Lubbock Lights" was resolved. Investigation showed that the formations appeared to be flocks of birds reflecting light from streetlamps below. The Lubbock Lights bear a strong resemblance to the "boomerangs," or V-shaped UFOs, reported seen in the Hudson Valley of New York state and Connecticut years later.

See also BIRDS; BOOMERANGS; HUDSON VALLEY SIGHTINGS.

Luce Bay, Scotland, United Kingdom

This isolated area of the United Kingdom has generated some notable UFO reports, such as the West Freugh incident of 1957. Another widely reported incident dates from October of 1955, when a saucer-shaped UFO emitting a buzzing noise allegedly was seen flying over a van on a highway. This incident was associated with vehicle interference, namely the stopping of the van's engine when the UFO approached close to the vehicle. A cigar-shaped UFO was reported seen in the same vicinity in a series of sightings on January 23–24, 1979. The object was described as gray, with portholes emitting light of various colors. Waves of UFO sightings also were reported around Luce Bay in 1981 and 1982.

See also UNITED KINGDOM, UFOS IN; VEHICLE EFFECTS; WEST FREUGH INCIDENT; WINDOWS.

Lyra

The constellation Lyra, particularly its star Vega, has drawn attention as a potential location of planetary systems and extraterrestrial life. Long-wave radiation from Vega—the kind of radiation commonly associated with cool objects such as planets—indicates to astronomers that dense matter surrounding Vega is intercepting some of the star's radiation. This information does not establish, however, that intelligent life exists in a planetary system surrounding Vega.

"Lyra" was also the name of an alleged alien in the case of "contactee" Orfeo Angelucci.

See also ANGELUCCI CASE; ASTRONOMY.

M

Madison Square, New York City, incident, United States An early 20th century UFO incident was reported in New York City on the night of August 30, 1910, when a dark object allegedly passed low over Madison Square in sight of hundreds of witnesses. A newspaper report said the object looked like a biplane. It made a sound like that of an airplane engine and carried green and red lights. The object circled the park once that night and departed, then returned the next night and was seen again by numerous witnesses. Although the object indeed may have been a biplane, there were few pilots in the United States in 1910, and a night flight into New York City might have been extremely dangerous for aircraft of that day.

See also AIRCRAFT, UFOS AND.

magnetism One of the great subjects of pseudoscientific literature, magnetism occupies an important place in the alleged technology of UFOs. Numerous suggestions have been made for using magnetism to lift and propel a flying saucer. Early "contactee" George Adamski, for example, suggested that two-way "rivers" of magnetism, made up of "pulses" moving alternately in opposite directions, flow between planets. Adamski imagined that extraterrestrial "liners" moved in a particular direction along these "rivers" by using only half of a given two-way pulse moving in a particular direction. "Inward" pulses supposedly moved a spacecraft toward a planet, whereas "outward" pulses shoved the ship outward into space. He also explained some visual and radar sightings of saucers by arguing that a flying saucer would open a "magnetic window" now and then in its surrounding "force field," allowing the craft to be seen and detected on radar.

Magnetism has also been a favorite topic of occultists, who have tried to work it into crackpot theories of human nervous function. Among the most famous occultists who specialized in magnetism was Franz Anton Mesmer, the 18th-century hypnotist and impostor whose notions of "animal magnetism" were based on an analogy between the human body and a magnet. Mesmer thought a hypothetical magnetic "fluid," if controlled, could cure nervous ailments. Mesmer left behind many disciples in Europe, and his ideas on magnetism remained popular, in various forms, into the early 20th century. Pseudoscientific views of magnetism are among the many correspondences between occultism and the UFO phenomenon.

See also ADAMSKI, GEORGE; ANTI-GRAVITY; OCCULTISM; PSEUDOSCIENCE; TECHNOLOGY.

Magonia A legendary land where ships were made to fly among the clouds, Magonia figured in the famed Agobard incident in France in the 9th century and has come to symbolize, in a general way, the purported origins of UFOs.

See also AGOBARD INCIDENT.

MAJESTIC 12 A secret investigative group codenamed MAJESTIC 12 was reportedly set up by the U.S. government after the alleged saucer crash at Roswell, New Mexico, in 1947. As is the case with many other aspects of the UFO phenomenon, mystery surrounds MAJESTIC 12. The very existence of the group is open to question. Although documents purporting to prove its existence have been made

Malaysia has been the site of noteworthy UFO reports. (U.S. Geological Survey)

public, the same documents have been dismissed as forgeries, and the story of MAJESTIC 12 is widely considered to be a hoax. Whether or not MAJESTIC 12 actually existed, it is said to have included some of the most prominent scientists and military men of the time, including Dr. Vannevar Bush of the Massachusetts Institute of Technology; Vice Admiral Roscoe Hillenkoetter, a former director of the Central Intelligence Agency; James Forrestal, former secretary of defense; and Dr. Donald Menzel, a noted astronomer who wrote books highly critical of reported UFO sightings. The group and its activities were portrayed in fictional form by author Whitley Strieber in his 1989 novel *Majestic.* Strieber also wrote the 1987 bestseller *Communion,* about his alleged encounters with extraterrestrials.

See also CRASHES; ROSWELL INCIDENT; STRIEBER, WHITLEY.

Malaysia Malaysia occupies a special place in UFO lore because of numerous reported sightings of extremely small humanoids, only a few inches tall. A wave of such sightings was reported in August 1970. In one sighting, a tiny "extraterrestrial" wearing a one-piece suit was reported, along with a correspondingly small UFO. There is reason to think the reports were hoaxes, because many of the witnesses were young children. The island of Pinang and the mountains of the Malay peninsula are said to be foci for UFO sightings.

See also HUMANOIDS.

mandala A circular design widely used in religion, especially in Buddhism and Hinduism, the mandala resembles the reported configuration of many UFOs. Psychiatrist Dr. Carl Jung saw in this similarity of form a connection between modern fas-

cination with circular UFOs and human longing for completeness or perfection, as symbolized by the figure of the circle. It may be significant that the mandala became most highly developed in Tibet, whose intellectual and religious heritage has played a small but important part in the modern UFO phenomenon.

See also JUNG, CARL GUSTAV; TIBET.

Mantell incident, United States One of the best-known accounts of an aircraft and its pilot coming to grief in pursuit of a UFO, the Mantell incident occurred on January 7, 1948, in the vicinity of Godman Air Force Base, Kentucky. On that date, observers in communities in Kentucky reported sighting a shining UFO that moved slowly and noiselessly across the sky. A police department trying to cope with a heavy load of calls concerning the sightings contacted the base to see if any information about the object was available there. Reportedly, the UFO was detected on radar (at an altitude of 13,000 feet) several minutes after the police department called the base, and the UFO itself was detected visually at the base ten minutes after the radar contact was reported. The UFO was described later as circular and shining and was estimated to be about 500 feet wide. After hanging for a time just below the cloud base (which was at 14,000 feet), the object ascended into the clouds and remained visible there as a red glow. At 2:30 P.M., about an hour after the radar contact was made, Captain Thomas Mantell, leader of a flight of five P-51 Mustang fighter aircraft approaching the base, was contacted by radio from the base and asked to investigate the unidentified object. Mantell complied and climbed to an altitude of 14,000 feet, although his aircraft was not equipped with oxygen apparatus, which was required for flights above that level. Mantell reached 23,000 feet while other aircraft in his flight followed the pursuit from a lower altitude. Mantell allegedly reported seeing a "huge" metallic object directly above him, with a diameter of 500 to 1,000 feet, moving at a speed of about 200 knots. Next, he was credited with saying the object was giving off heat. Then his radio transmissions ceased, and his plane crashed on a farm near Franklin, Kentucky. His body was recovered from the wreckage.

What Mantell pursued has not been determined with any certainty. It was suggested that he was trying to chase the planet Venus, which he presumed to be the UFO. This explanation, however, does not seem consistent with the reported appearance and behavior of the UFO. There is reason to think Mantell was trying to intercept a high-altitude balloon when he blacked out from lack of oxygen, and subsequently crashed.

The story of Mantell's pursuit appears to have been embellished in the telling and retelling. Evidently, for example, he did not actually report intense heat emanating from the UFO. This detail apparently was supplied in press accounts of the incident. Other dubious elements of the story include reports of finding wreckage from the aircraft damaged by intense heat, as if seared somehow by the UFO.

See also AIRCRAFT, UFOS AND; DEATHS.

Maralinga incident, Australia.
A UFO of blue-silver color, with a metallic appearance, was reported seen hovering over a former British atomic test site at Maralinga in South Australia in 1957, following nuclear tests there in September and October of that year. The object was described as having portholes or windows and showing signs of "plating" on its hull. The UFO reportedly departed silently and rapidly after some 15 minutes at the site.

See also AUSTRALIA, UFOS IN.

Marduk
The hypothetical planet Marduk (also known as Nibiru) features in the writings of Zecharia Sitchin, who proposes that the human species originated through genetic manipulation of terrestrial animals by extraterrestrials called "Nefilim," from Marduk. Marduk supposedly circles the Sun in a highly elliptical orbit with a period of more than 3,000 years.

Marduk is also the name of the principal god of Babylonian mythology.

See also NEFILIM; RELIGION, UFOS AND.

Marfa lights, United States
Yellowish lights with some characteristics of UFOs, including a reported tendency to display "intelligent" behavior such as following automobiles, are said to appear above the Chinati Mountains in Texas and to have become a tourist attraction. The lights are named after the community of Marfa, Texas. See also EARTH LIGHTS.

Marian apparitions
These phenomena are said to involve apparitions of the Virgin Mary and, in some cases, bear close resemblances to UFO sightings. The alleged miracle of Fatima, which occurred in Portugal in May 1917, is perhaps the most famous case in point. Several appearances of an entity said to be Mary were involved at Fatima, and elements of the apparitions included such UFO-like events as the appearance of glowing spheres; the revelation of the entity to three children; spectacular displays of light described as the "dancing" of the Sun; the sighting of a flying disc; lights descending from the sky in the "falling leaf" motion often described in UFO sightings; temperature effects, including heat so intense as to dry wet ground and clothing; and an alleged fall of substances resembling the "angel hair" reported in many UFO close-encounter reports. In a possibly significant parallel with the UFO phenomenon, "channelers" have become involved in investigations of Fatima, similar to their efforts to contact alleged extraterrestrials in the UFO phenomenon. Other alleged appearances of Mary have been reported at Knock, Ireland, and at Medjugorje in former Yugoslavia.

Although many Roman Catholics appear convinced that the alleged apparitions at Fatima and elsewhere represent genuine miracles and appearances of Mary, Protestants and Orthodox Christians tend to be skeptical of such claims. Students of the UFO phenomenon also point out that apparently female entities have been reported in UFO sightings without a specifically Christian identification, and that these sightings bear a certain similarity to the reported Marian apparitions at Fatima and else-

UFO-like "Marfa lights" have been reported in western Texas. (U.S. Geological Survey)

where. One interesting aspect of Marian apparition reports is that believing Roman Catholics appear to see Mary distinctly, whereas non-Catholics' perceptions of the entity are less distinct.

See also BELIEF SYSTEMS; CHANNELING; CHILDREN, UFOS AND; CHRIST AND CHRISTIANITY; COMMUNICATIONS; DISCS; ENCOUNTER PHENOMENA; FALLING LEAF MOTION; FATIMA, "MIRACLE" OF; HUMANOIDS; MESSAGES; OCCULTISM; SPHERES; TEMPERATURE EFFECTS.

marine phosphorescent wheels Thus far unexplained, this phenomenon is part of UFO lore and involves wheel-like displays of light with straight or curved "spokes" seen rotating in the ocean and sometimes in the air just above the ocean. The wheels may be only a few feet in diameter, or as much as several miles wide. The light appears to emanate from the surface or just below the surface in most cases, but sometimes has been reported as a glowing mist above the water. The light tends to be white or green in color. On occasion, more than one wheel has been sighted turning in a particular vicinity. Marine phosphorescent wheels have been sighted often in the Indian Ocean, the China Sea and the Persian Gulf. Similar phenomena are thought to occur in other seas, but these are reportedly stationary and less impressive. Marine phosphorescent wheels resemble certain displays of aurora, and electromagnetic effects have been suggested as a possible explanation for the wheels. Seismic activity also has been suggested as a possible source of the wheels. Marine phosphorescent wheels are difficult to interpret in terms of bioluminescence, because of their clearly defined structure and systematic motion. Also, it is difficult to explain how luminescent marine organisms could account for the wheels seen above the waters. The wheel-like geometry of marine phosphorescent wheels resembles that of many UFOs, and aerial phosphorescent wheels may be interpreted as UFOs.

Two reports of marine phosphorescent wheels in recent years involve ships traveling through the Gulf of Siam in 1976 and the Arabian Sea in 1980. In the Gulf of Siam incident, on March 27, 1976, a set of advancing parallel bands of light was seen to assume the form of a wheel, which rotated rapidly in a clockwise direction. At one point, its spokes (each about 70 feet wide, with approximately 70 feet between spokes) passed the ship at a rate of two spokes per second. The light grew more intense as the wheel rotated faster. After several minutes, the wheel turned into a set of parallel, advancing bands of light, then reorganized itself as a wheel again, this time rotating in the opposite direction. This second wheel vanished after several minutes. From start to finish, the display lasted perhaps 17 minutes.

The Arabian Sea incident on March 6, 1980, reportedly occurred when white lights took forms compared to whirlpools and cartwheels and reached to the horizon. The "cartwheels" were most luminous at the center, and the spokes were estimated to be six to eight feet wide. The "whirlpools" appeared to be about four to six feet wide and up to approximately 45 feet long. The displays were seen for more than half an hour.

See also AQUATIC OBJECTS.

Mars The red planet has been associated in the public mind with UFOs and tales of extraterrestrial visitations for a long time. Indeed, the expression "men from Mars" became synonymous with extraterrestrials by the mid-20th century. The notion that Mars might harbor intelligent life arose much earlier than that. The Swedish mystic Emanuel Swedenborg imagined he had visited Mars in one of his bizarre visions, as did other dabblers in the occult. The dream of a native Martian civilization owed much to 19th-century astronomer Giovanni Schiaparelli, who reported in 1877 that he had observed a network of canali, or "channels," on the Martian surface. The Italian word *canali* was translated inaccurately into English as "canals," thus conveying quite a different meaning from the original Italian. The word "canals" implied channels built by design and by intelligent beings, as canals are built on Earth. The existence of such canals would indicate the presence of some kind of technological civilization. Thus a

Mars was long thought to be a possible home of extraterrestrial life. This photo shows "layered" terrain on Mars. (NASA)

popular image of great Martian cities, served by great canals bringing water to them from the polar caps, arose among fantasy writers and was perpetuated in the press.

The writings of 19th-century New England astronomer Percival Lowell also contributed to this vision of Mars as an inhabited, or at least habitable, world. In his 1896 book *Mars,* Lowell envisioned the planet as a world that could support life. He imagined Mars had, in addition to vast red deserts, areas of arable land. Science fiction authors of the late 19th and early 20th centuries had a field day with the idea of life on Mars. Perhaps the most famous work in this subgenre of science fiction is H.G. Wells's 1898 novel *The War of the Worlds,* in which Martians invade Earth and overwhelm its military defenses but are then brought down by terrestrial microbes, against which they have no defenses. Wells's fantasy provided the model for many later tales of invasion from other worlds, and was dramatized in a particularly terrifying manner by Orson Welles and his Mercury Theater for a Halloween radio broadcast in 1938. Edgar Rice Burroughs, creator of Tarzan, produced a series of fantasy novels set on Mars and contributed further to the popular dream that a civilization might exist there.

Wells and Burroughs together exerted a tremendous influence on thinking about the possibility of life on Mars. (A less powerful, but interesting, influence in this respect was novelist and Christian apologist C.S. Lewis, who in his 1938 novel *Out of the Silent Planet* depicted a fictional Martian civilization based on Christian principles.)

Science fiction author Ray Bradbury expanded on the theme of an inhabited Mars in his 1950 book *The Martian Chronicles,* in which the first human visitors to the red planet confront a living, indigenous Martian culture as well as mysterious images of their own lives on Earth.

Before exploration of Mars by unmanned probes in the 1970s showed the planet to be apparently lifeless, Mars was a favorite choice for UFO enthusiasts speculating about the possible origins of flying saucers. There were, at the time, good reasons for suspecting that extraterrestrial spacecraft might come from Mars. With Venus, Mars is one of the two planets closest to Earth. Also, Mars is an Earth-like world in many respects, although much smaller and cooler and possessed of a thinner atmosphere. Mars was thought to have large amounts of water locked up in its polar caps, and so it seemed possible that liquid water—one of the necessities for life as known on Earth—might exist on Mars in substantial quantities. From time to time, certain areas of the Martian surface appeared to change color and brightness. These changes encouraged speculation that they might be the results of intelligently directed activity. From the slender evidence at hand to visions of space-traveling Martians visiting Earth was a gigantic step, but certain dreamers took it easily, and by the early 1950s UFO "contactees" such as Truman Bethurum were reinforcing the popular vision of Mars as an inhabited world by relaying descriptions—allegedly given by spacefaring aliens visiting Earth—of the impressive civilization to be found on Mars.

Although pictures returned by American spacecraft destroyed forever the classical image of Mars as a presently inhabited world (and therefore a potential base for alien spacecraft visiting Earth), photos of one small area of the planet have revived speculation that intelligent life once may have existed on Mars. The photographs show a peculiar formation known as the "face on Mars," in the northern hemisphere at approximately 41 degrees north latitude and 9.5 degrees west longitude. The "face" does indeed resemble a gigantic sculpture of a human face, although there is disagreement as to whether this resemblance reflects the actual configuration of the formation, or merely a pattern of light and shadow. Several miles southwest of the "face," NASA photographs also show a cluster of structures known as the "pyramids of Mars." These are roughly pyramidal structures, some with four sides and some with five. The "face" and "pyramids" have been presented as evidence of intelligent life having existed on Mars in some much earlier age.

Richard Hoagland, in his 1987 book *The Monuments of Mars* (updated 1992), attempts to establish a connection, on the basis of design, between the Martian "face" and "pyramids" and various ancient constructions on Earth, including Stonehenge in Britain and the Sphinx and pyramids in Egypt. Hoagland expresses disdain for the "ancient astronauts" hypothesis, as popularized by authors such as Erich von Däniken, but suggests that an extraterrestrial influence—as expressed in the alleged constructions on Mars—might account for the sudden rise of the early civilizations of Earth's history.

See ANCIENT ASTRONAUTS; BETHURUM INCIDENT; FACE ON MARS; SWEDENBORG, EMANUEL; VON DÄNIKEN, ERICH.

Martian oppositions   A 1962 study by UFO investigators Jacques and Janine Vallee found a well-verified coincidence, for the years 1949–1957, between large numbers of UFO sightings and oppositions of Mars, the periods when Mars is closest to

Earth. Peaks of UFO sightings coincided with Martian oppositions in 1950, 1952, 1954 and 1956, but the coincidence failed beyond that point.

See also MARS; VALLEE, JACQUES; WAVES.

Martin of Tours, Saint, 4th century A.D.

An anecdote from the life of Saint Martin of Tours, as related by Sulpicius Severus, resembles certain incidents from the UFO literature on "contactees." Because of false humility, a young monk named Anatolius experienced deception by evil spirits and thought he had contact with angels (that is, angels who had not fallen from heaven by joining in Satan's rebellion against God). To convince others of the monk's imagined holiness, the demons arranged to give him a robe from "heaven," though the garment was in fact merely an illusion created by the evil spirits. One night, a sound as of dancing feet and many voices was heard from Anatolius's cell, and a brilliant light filled the room. Then the light and sound ceased. Anatolius emerged from the room holding the robe, which was bright red and very soft. No one could tell, however, what kind of material it was made of. The next morning, one of Anatolius's superiors, suspicious of the circumstances under which the "heavenly" robe had arrived, started to take the young monk to Saint Martin to see if the robe was really some illusion of the Devil. The deceived monk became frightened and resisted, but was dragged along against his will. Then the garment vanished. The narrator, who may have witnessed this incident personally, supposed that the robe disappeared because the Devil knew he could not maintain his illusion before the keen discernment of Saint Martin, who had the ability to recognize the Devil in any form the evil spirit might assume.

Anatolius's experience resembles modern UFO "contactee" cases in many important respects. He is approached at night, in his bedroom, which is flooded with brilliant light; and he receives a remarkable piece of evidence that disappears soon afterward. Moreover, the contact involves evil spirits, which many observers in our own time have linked with various UFO-related phenomena.

See also DEMONOLOGY; ENCOUNTER PHENOMENA; EVIDENCE.

Mary Celeste incident

The two-masted brig *Mary Celeste* was found deserted in the North Atlantic Ocean between Portugal and the Azores on December 5, 1872. The ship carried a cargo of crude alcohol. The lifeboat was missing, there was some damage to the sails, and the cargo hatches had been torn off. The last entry in the logbook was dated November 25. That meant the ship had sailed, abandoned, for nine days before being discovered. Evidently the ship had been abandoned in a hurry, because the seamen's belongings were still in their quarters.

The *Mary Celeste* incident made its way into the literature on UFOs by a long and circuitous route. Arthur Conan Doyle, creator of the fictional detective Sherlock Holmes, wrote a celebrated story based on the facts of the case, but introduced many errors through his account, notably by misidentifying the ship as the *Marie Celeste* and by reporting that the aforementioned lifeboat was still in place when the ship was found. That latter error—the matter of the lifeboat—led future students of the case astray and brought about all manner of bizarre speculation as to how the captain, crew and passengers could abandon the ship without taking to the lifeboat. At one point, abduction by UFOs was invoked to account for the abandonment of the *Mary Celeste*. A less exotic scenario is that something on board alarmed the captain, who ordered everyone into the lifeboat for safety. In the rush to leave, the captain neglected to tie the lifeboat to the ship with a cable. Before the crew and passengers could return to the *Mary Celeste*, the wind blew up, and the ship sailed away, leaving the lifeboat behind. There is, then, no need to invoke UFOs in trying to "solve" the *Mary Celeste* mystery, when a more likely explanation involves fright, haste, carelessness and a change in weather.

mass hysteria

This expression refers to situations in which large numbers of individuals, responding to suggestion, report seeing something that actually is not there. Mass hysteria has been suggested as a possible explanation for numerous UFO sightings.

See also COLLECTIVE DELUSION.

Matles–Barbosa incident, Brazil

This incident, which allegedly occurred on January 21, 1976, incorporates many prominent elements of UFO encounter lore. Two witnesses named Herminio and Bianca Reis reportedly were stopped along a road in the vicinity of Matles–Barbosa, Brazil, when they and their automobile were taken aboard an extraterrestrial spacecraft by levitation. Inside the craft, they allegedly met two tall "aliens" and communicated with them through some kind of headsets connected with what appeared to be a computer. The abductees were given a green liquid to drink. More entities then appeared, including a dark-haired, tall woman. The beings claimed to be conducting medical research and said they had overcome death and aging. The elements of levitation, "medical" research, abduction along a highway, and the strange beverage given the abductees to drink are all well-known elements of modern UFO lore.

See also ABDUCTIONS; BRAZIL; FOOD AND DRINK; LEVITATION.

Maury Island incident, Washington State, United States

One of the most famous cases in the American literature on UFOs, the Maury Island incident now is widely regarded as a hoax. The case supposedly occurred on June 21, 1947 (although the date is uncertain), and involved one Harold Dahl and his teenage son, as well as two other crewmen on a boat in Puget Sound near Maury Island, in the vicinity of Tacoma, Washington.

Dahl reported sighting six toroidal, or doughnut-shaped, UFOs at an estimated altitude of about 2,000 feet. The objects were said to be about 100 feet in diameter, with an opening about 25 feet wide in their centers. They had a metallic luster, and what looked like portholes. One of the objects appeared to be having difficulty staying aloft.

The witnesses said an explosion occurred, and the apparently malfunctioning UFO discharged flakes of metal, followed by hot lumps of slag. These lumps allegedly injured the younger Dahl and killed his dog, who had accompanied the expedition. The UFOs then departed.

Only three days after the June 21 sighting, Kenneth Arnold reported seeing several UFOs in flight near Mount Rainier, in the sighting that gave rise to the expression "flying saucers." At the request of science fiction magazine editor Ray Palmer, Arnold investigated the Maury Island incident with the assistance of two military intelligence specialists. Arnold met with Dahl, who said he had been contacted by one of the "men in black," mysterious and intimidating presences who were said to shadow and harass UFO witnesses in the early days of the UFO phenomenon in the United States. Dahl reportedly showed Arnold a chunk of the Maury Island UFO's ejecta, which resembled volcanic rock.

The military intelligence specialists seemed unimpressed by Dahl's story and his alleged evidence, but they took away the material anyway and loaded it on a military plane for transport. The two intelligence specialists then took off on the same plane but were killed when the aircraft exploded several minutes after leaving the ground.

See also ARNOLD INCIDENT; EJECTA; MEN IN BLACK.

McChord Air Force Base incident, United States

The reported crash on April 1, 1959, of a four-engine C-118 cargo plane belonging to the U.S. Air Force's 1705th Air Transport Wing has been associated with UFO activity, although there is no proof that UFOs had any direct role in the destruction of the aircraft. Allegedly, the aircraft, with a four-man crew aboard, took off from McChord Air Force Base near Tacoma in western Washington state at 6:30 P.M. and made a distress call at 7:45 P.M., saying that the plane had hit something, or something had hit it. The aircraft crashed into a mountain in the Cascade range near Mount Rainier, and the crash site reportedly was placed under armed guard. After the crash, a report began circulating that radar at the Air Force base had detected several objects accompanying the cargo plane immediately before the aircraft was lost. Also, around 7:00 P.M., residents of the area reportedly heard several loud noises like explosions and saw several luminous objects traveling across the sky. Another report said that the aircraft, with all four engines stopped and a portion of its tail assembly missing, had passed over the community of Orting in the company of three shiny discs that appeared to be darting close to the plane. A minute after the C-118 passed from view, two bright bursts of light reportedly lit up the sky to the northeast of the observers at Orting. The flashes of light coincided with the cessation of radio messages from the aircraft. A report of the investigation at the crash site indicated that the wreckage consisted of a great number of small, charred fragments scattered over a wide area, and that the bodies of only three of the four men aboard the aircraft were located. The tail assembly reportedly was found north of Mount Rainier, miles away from the rest of the wreckage.

See also AIRCRAFT, UFOS AND.

Maury Island incident allegedly occurred near Tacoma, Washington. (U.S. Geological Survey)

McGuire Air Force Base incident, New Jersey, United States

One colorful UFO rumor involved

an incident that allegedly occurred on January 18, 1978, at McGuire Air Force Base, New Jersey. UFOs were sighted over Fort Dix, nearby, and an "extraterrestrial" reportedly was seen in an outlying section of the air base, and was shot and killed.

See also RUMORS.

media, UFOs in the   Media coverage of UFOs is a vast topic with many aspects, but in general appears to have evolved toward increasingly tolerant and even sympathetic treatment of the UFO phenomenon since the initial "flying saucer" sighting in 1947.

UFO enthusiasts in the 1950s were viewed as eccentrics and crackpots by all but a few elements of the mass media. "Little green men" in flying saucers were treated as figures of fun. By the late 1960s and 1970s, however, much of the early scorn and skepticism had been replaced by a more credulous attitude toward UFOs. For example, the success of the "ancient astronauts" phenomenon in promulgating the concept of extraterrestrials as "gods" illustrates how much more friendly media coverage of UFOs, and specifically the extraterrestrial hypothesis, had become by the early 1970s. Although prominent skeptics remain active in covering the UFO phenomenon, the prevailing trend in media coverage of UFOs appears to be one of uncritical acceptance of many sightings. The tabloid press has proven especially eager to print lurid reports of UFO sightings and face-to-face "contacts" with extraterrestrials, including abductions.

Critical or not, the mass media made popular, and capitalized on the popularity of, the UFO phenomenon. Numerous specialty publications emerged to provide more detailed coverage of the phenomenon than the mainstream media could supply. UFOs became the particular province of occult journals such as *Fate*. (This connection between the UFO phenomenon and occultism in the media reflects a similar link between numerous UFO contact reports and elements of the occult, including automatic writing and precognition.) As the "occult revival" of the 1980s and 1990s progressed, mainstream media and a vast collection of "New Age" publications began promoting, in most cases favorably, the occult aspect of the UFO phenomenon.

Media coverage of UFOs apparently helped to shape U.S. government policy toward UFOs in the years immediately after World War II. To ensure that sensational UFO reports did not undermine public confidence in the government and its ability to defend the nation, the federal government allegedly began a campaign of "debunking" UFO reports by attributing them to misidentifications of familiar phenomena such as clouds and aircraft.

The entertainment media have promoted the extraterrestrial hypothesis of UFO origins for decades. Motion pictures such as *The Day the Earth Stood Still, The War of the Worlds, This Island Earth, The Mysterians, Close Encounters of the Third Kind* and numerous others have depicted UFOs as material spacecraft from other planets, and their occupants as biological entities. Television entertainment generally has treated the UFO phenomenon in the same manner as motion pictures, with emphasis on the extraterrestrial hypothesis.

Coverage of the UFO phenomenon often has been pseudoscientific in character and has contained a marked element of paranoia. The paranoid element of UFO lore as reported in the media may take the form of elaborate and unlikely conspiracy theories alleging collaboration between the government and extraterrestrials, or efforts on the government's part to suppress the "truth" about UFOs. (The "truth," in such cases, often is alleged to be "proof" of the extraterrestrial hypothesis, such as actual spacecraft and dead aliens supposedly recovered from UFO crash sites.) In many such stories, the U.S. Central Intelligence Agency (CIA) is cast in the villain's role and is accused of masterminding "cover-ups" of UFO "secrets" while conducting alleged investigations of its own into the UFO phenomenon. Popular though such CIA tales may be, there is no proof that the CIA is, or ever has been, engaged deeply in such investigations. CIA materials on UFOs, declassified and studied by UFO debunker Philip Klass, indicate that the CIA actually has generated only a few pages of UFO-related classified documents per year since the end of World War II. Such a small output is not consistent with media accounts of reputedly huge official studies and "cover-ups."

The impact of media coverage on public perception of the UFO phenomenon is difficult to gauge exactly. Moreover, it is hard to determine how much media treatment of UFOs shapes public opinion of the phenomenon, and how much the media's coverage of UFOs merely reflects attitudes that the public already holds. It appears well established, however, that there is a huge audience, both in the United States and abroad, for tales of UFOs, and that the media profit from satisfying the public hunger for such stories, regardless of whether the reports are factual or fictional.

See also ABDUCTIONS; ANCIENT ASTRONAUTS; CENTRAL INTELLIGENCE AGENCY; CONSPIRACY THEORIES; DEBUNKERS; EXTRATERRESTRIAL BIOLOGICAL ENTITIES; EXTRATERRESTRIAL HYPOTHESIS; KLASS, PHILIP; LITTLE GREEN MEN; MOTION PICTURES; OCCULTISM; PARA-

NOIA; PENTACLE; PSEUDOSCIENCE; PUBLIC OPINION; ROBERTSON PANEL; RUMORS; SILENCE GROUP.

medical research　This justification sometimes is given for the quasi-medical examinations that alleged UFO abductees are said to have received during their encounters with "extraterrestrials." The abductee may report being placed on a table in a room similar in some respects to an operating room or a medical examination room, and subjected to study with various instruments that may surround or be applied directly to the body. What appear to be surgical techniques may be applied to certain parts of the body, notably the cranium. In many reports, however, the "research" tends to resemble various occultic practices and initiation rituals more than what medical science would recognize as research. For example, the "research" reportedly may involve sexual violation of the human subject and/or implantation of small objects in the body, in the manner of certain shamanic practices.

See also ABDUCTIONS; IMPLANTS; OCCULTISM; SEXUAL ENCOUNTERS; SHAMANISM.

mediumism　The practice of trying to contact non-incarnate beings by inviting them to enter one's body and communicate through it, mediumism has played a small but significant role in the UFO phenomenon. Early UFO "contactee" George Hunt Williamson, for example, apparently tried to establish mediumistic communications with extraterrestrials in 1952. In the process, Williamson and his associates appear to have re-invented the Ouija board, a widely used tool for contacting the "spirit world." In 1953, alleged contactee Albert Bender also attempted a mediumistic contact with extraterrestrials as part of "World Contact Day," an international experiment in communication with aliens. The reported results of these experiments bear many similarities to contacts reported between mediums and demons in the literature of occultism. Today, efforts at mediumistic communication with extraterrestrials are made under the name of "channeling." Although accounts of such communications are entertaining, there is no conclusive evidence that mediumism actually has brought anyone into contact with inhabitants of other planets. In some cases, descriptions of conditions on other worlds, provided through such communications, have turned out to be grossly incorrect when unmanned space probes returned data from those planets.

See also BENDER MYSTERY; CHANNELING; COMMUNICATIONS; OCCULTISM; OUIJA BOARD; TELEPATHY; WORLD CONTACT DAY.

Meier case, Switzerland　One of the most famous and controversial cases in the literature on UFOs, the Meier case involves one Eduard "Billy" Meier, a Swiss farmer and pensioner who claimed to have made contact in 1975 with extraterrestrials from the Pleiades. To support his claims, Meier produced films and still photographs of the alleged aliens' saucer-like spacecraft (described as "beamships"), as well as what were supposed to be audio recordings of the craft. The recordings reproduced a high-pitched, unpleasant noise. The photographs were of high quality and showed the alleged spaceships hovering above the Swiss countryside. Meier also produced crystals that he said came from other solar systems, as well as samples of metal from which the "beamships" were said to be built. On analysis, the crystalline material turned out to be ordinary amethyst, a mineral found widely on Earth. The metal contained elements abundant on Earth, including aluminum, silver and copper. Other evidence in the case included circular areas of crushed grass similar to the "crop circles" that came to widespread notice in Britain around 1990. Controversy arose over the authenticity of Meier's photographs, partly because he said his original negatives were stolen and partly because rumors began circulating about models being used in making the photos. Also, the photographs were taken with a camera pointing toward the sun, a situation in which bright sunlight might mask wires or other structures supporting a model. There is also debate, however, about whether or not Meier himself had the capabilities to perpetrate such a sophisticated hoax, if hoax it was. Meier has only one arm and is said to have only a sixth-grade education: hardly the optimum qualifications for carrying out a UFO hoax of this complexity and magnitude.

Meier claimed to have had face-to-face meetings with two of the extraterrestrials, an attractive young woman named Semjase, and a venerable man named Sfath. He also allegedly made contact with a female being named Asket, who served as his guide when Meier was engaged in many different kinds of employment. Meier also delivered descriptions of the aliens' homeworld, called Erra. As in many other such cases, the descriptions of Erra resembled a sanitized image of earth.

See also ASKET; ENCOUNTER PHENOMENA; ERRA; PHOTOGRAPHY; PLEIADES; SEMJASE; SFATH.

Mendoza incident, Argentina　One of the most colorful UFO encounter cases from Argentina involves two men, employees of a casino in Mendoza, near the Chilean border, who allegedly had a close encounter with several humanoids near a UFO on September 1, 1968. According to the report, the men were driving home around 3:42 A.M. when their car's engine stopped. They then found themselves confronted by three humanoids who had hairless heads and were slightly shorter than a typical human. Nearby hovered a UFO, which the men estimated at about four meters (approximately 13 feet) in diameter, and described as circular or oval in shape. The beings allegedly wore uniforms similar to those of attendants at gasoline stations. The entities told the men not to be afraid, and then delivered a peculiar message to the effect that mathematics was the "universal language." The men also reportedly received, on a television-like screen suspended in the air near the hovering UFO, a series of images that included a waterfall and a mushroom cloud like that of a nuclear explosion. After pricking the men's fingers several times, the entities departed in their vehicle.

The Mendoza incident illustrates the elements of absurdity and "metalogic" in UFO close-encounter reports: in this case, the baffling message about mathematics and the seemingly unrelated images presented on the screen.

See also ABSURDITY; ARGENTINA; HUMANOIDS; METALOGIC.

Menger case, United States   An early "contactee" in the years immediately following World War II, New Jersey sign painter Howard Menger became a celebrity in 1957 when he appeared on television, on Steve Allen's "Tonight" show, to describe an alleged trip to Venus aboard a flying saucer. Menger's account resembled in many ways the claims of an earlier contactee, George Adamski, who claimed to have encountered a visitor from Venus in the southwestern desert. Menger said he had seen images of a city on Venus and found it similar to cities on Earth, although quieter and more attractive. Menger also claimed to have visited the Moon and had no difficulty breathing there. Most of the aliens who had supposedly contacted him had been from Venus, but he had encountered others from Saturn and Mars. Some extraterrestrials, Menger added, were stationed on Earth. Menger cut a commercial recording titled "The Song from Saturn," which was said to be real music from another world. On another occasion, Menger reportedly said that scientific analysis was being conducted on vegetables returned from the Moon.

Menger supplied no proof of his adventures. His claims were typical of many "contactee" cases in that he offered no proof; he described an alien world that looked very much like Earth, only more pleasant; and his report of conditions on other worlds, specifically the Moon and Venus, turned out to be demonstrably false.

See also ADAMSKI, GEORGE; PRECEDENTS; VENUS.

men in black   Witnesses and students of UFO encounter phenomena have reported being visited by curious figures commonly known as "men in black." The men in black may appear individually but have been reported more often in groups of three. They inquire about the subject's experiences and, in many cases, caution him or her to avoid speaking with anyone else about UFOs. The men in black are said to be distinguished by their black suits (sometimes badly wrinkled, but on other occasions well-pressed) and black ties, as well as their curious manner of speaking. Their voices may be heavily accented, and the men in black reportedly have used either very formal, precise language or slang reminiscent of gangsters and other villains in American motion pictures. Other peculiar behavior may include an intense interest in everyday objects, such as pens or tableware. Men in black have allegedly threatened some witnesses with bodily harm, although there appears to be no evidence that the strange visitors actually have harmed anyone. One extensive account of a meeting with men in black is that of Albert K. Bender, in his book *Flying Saucers and the Three Men*. He describes them as threatening beings who could cause him pain merely by looking at him. Variations on the "men in black" phenomenon have been reported, such as a black automobile that follows investigators of UFO cases.

See also BENDER MYSTERY; BLACK DOGS; CONSPIRACY THEORIES; EVIDENCE; "HODOMUR, MAN OF INFINITY"; HUMANOIDS; MAURY ISLAND INCIDENT.

Menzel, Donald (1901–1976)   American astronomer Donald Menzel of Harvard University was one of the most prominent "debunkers" of UFO lore and argued that UFOs represented misidentifications of less exotic phenomena, such as aircraft lights and reflections of sunlight. Moreover, Menzel argued that actual extraterrestrial visitors to Earth might be expected to have landed and presented themselves to civil authorities and the scientific community. Menzel criticized UFO "believers" for being too eager to make a judgment on the character of the UFO phenomenon, and for using "innuendo" to discredit anyone who disagreed with their views. There has been speculation that Menzel was a member of the MAJESTIC 12 group that reportedly was assembled to study UFOs, but this claim is dubious, because of

Menzel's reputation as a debunker and because of doubts concerning the authenticity of documents relating to MAJESTIC 12.

See also DEBUNKERS; MAJESTIC 12; NATURAL PHENOMENA.

merging In the UFO phenomenon, different reports sometimes are merged, either deliberately or by mistake, to create "composite" stories much different from whatever evidence may have existed initially. A UFO sighting at location A, for example, may be merged in the retelling with an airplane crash several days later at location B, to produce a report of an aircraft being knocked out of the sky by a UFO. Investigators must beware of such merging when studying UFO reports. A familiar example of merging, cited by investigator Jacques Vallee, is the so-called Roswell incident, in which alleged incidents at two different locations were merged to produce an account of a single UFO "crash" involving the recovery of an alien spacecraft and the bodies of extraterrestrials.

See also ROSWELL INCIDENT; VALLEE, JACQUES.

messages Alleged extraterrestrials have delivered many messages in reported UFO encounters, often in the form of warnings of calamities to come; pledges of assistance in time of trouble; and advice on how to improve one's secular or spiritual life. A pattern of messages has emerged from UFO encounters and includes several particular themes.

A repeated message of UFO contacts, from George Adamski's day to ours, is that some worldwide cataclysm is near, and that benevolent extraterrestrials are stationed on or near our world and intend to save our civilization if and when humankind reaches the point of self-destruction. The extraterrestrials have been presented as sources of tremendous, ancient wisdom, despite the banal and absurd nature of their alleged communications. The true meaning of the messages, we are assured, will be revealed eventually.

Admonitions to trust the aliens are also a part of such communications. Even when the aliens reportedly exhibit hostile behavior, we are expected to believe that they have our best interests at heart and can be trusted to look after our well-being.

Syncretic faith, meaning belief assembled from many different sources, is another part of the messages in certain alleged UFO encounters. The so-called space people appear to encourage humankind to adopt a syncretic belief system that incorporates elements of Hinduism, Buddhism, shamanism and the occult.

Belief in Earth's approaching "transformation" is yet another element of UFO-related messages. Many UFO devotees believe that a great transformation of human thought, belief and society in general is imminent, and that UFOs will play a part in the change. The nature of that transformation, however, is left unspecified.

Some students of the UFO phenomenon see this collection of messages as an apparent "control system" for human beliefs, designed to persuade humans that extraterrestrials someday will intervene in human history, with benevolent intent. There is, of course, no proof that such faith is justified.

See also BELIEF SYSTEMS; COMMUNICATIONS; METALOGIC.

metalogic UFO analyst Jacques Vallee uses the expression "metalogic" to describe certain puzzling aspects of close-encounter cases in which human witnesses are presented with absurd or contradictory information without adequate explanation, and are left to interpret that information for themselves. The widely publicized Simonton incident is an example of metalogic at work. A man reportedly encountered a landed UFO whose humanoid occupants asked him to fill a jug with water for them, and left him with several items of food described as cookies or pancakes. The absurdity of such an encounter is plain. There is no apparent reason why extraterrestrial visitors to Earth should require water from humans, nor why the visitors should leave curious items of food with a human contactee. The incident is so bizarre that it simply makes no sense; it goes beyond the familiar bounds of common sense and logic. Vallee refers to the information content of such strange incidents as "metalogic" because it requires the observer to abandon established, logical patterns of thought and seek some new, unfamiliar explanation. Vallee also has suggested that such encounters constitute a "control system" for human belief, aimed at modifying our belief systems.

See also ABSURDITY; BELIEF SYSTEMS; ENCOUNTER PHENOMENON; FOOD AND DRINK; SIMONTON INCIDENT; VALLEE, JACQUES.

meteors Luminous trails left by meteoroids falling through the atmosphere, meteors can be very bright and probably account for many UFO sightings. Observers' imaginations may supply "details" such as glowing portholes and exhaust flames, and thus transform a meteor into a "spacecraft." Even experienced observers may err greatly in estimating the size and distance of a meteor, and interpret it erroneously as a UFO. One famous UFO sighting over the

Midwestern states of the United States on June 5, 1969, for example, was reported as a group of UFOs about to collide with an airliner, when the alleged UFOs appear to have been actually a meteor passing some 125 miles away.

See also NATURAL PHENOMENA, UFOS AND.

methane A hydrocarbon that is commonly produced by decomposition of organic material in swamps and marshes, methane, also known as "swamp gas" or "marsh gas," may be responsible for certain UFO sightings. Methane burns with a blue flame. Accumulations of methane burning just above the ground may have been seen and reported as UFO sightings. Burning methane also is suspected of causing certain other phenomena such as "earthquake light," a glow seen in the sky during some earthquakes.

See also EARTHQUAKE LIGHTS; SWAMP GAS INCIDENT.

Milarepa (c. 1052–1135) A famed Tibetan yogi, Milarepa is said to have possessed certain characteristics and abilities widely attributed today to extraterrestrials in UFO encounters. Milarepa allegedly had greenish hair and skin (supposedly acquired by living on nothing but broth of green nettles), could fly, and experienced out-of-body travels to other lands on Earth and to other worlds, where he is said to have met "masters" of the spiritual realm. Early in his career, Milarepa allegedly practiced black magic, could kill from a considerable distance and could conjure up storms to destroy crops. Later he renounced black magic. In addition to his unusual color, Milarepa's story contains numerous parallels with modern UFO lore, including his alleged flying ability, his reported meetings with spiritual "masters" in some non–Earthly environment, and his ability to cause bodily harm to others from a distance. Moreover, Milarepa's involvement with the occult is another similarity between his story and personal histories of modern UFO "contactees"; and his Tibetan origins are reminiscent of the Tibetan element in the UFO phenomenon.

See also BODILY EFFECTS; DEATHS; EXALTED ONES; LITTLE GREEN MEN; OCCULTISM; TIBET.

mirages Well-known phenomena in desert lands, mirages may occur almost anywhere and may be responsible for some UFO sightings. Layers of hot and cold air may make an object on the ground appear to be hovering just above the ground, as in many alleged UFO encounters.

missiles, UFOs and The development of various kinds of missiles in the United States and the Soviet Union in the latter half of the 20th century has been accompanied by reports of UFOs interacting with those missiles. A UFO reportedly destroyed an American Atlas liquid-fuel missile in a test in 1962, and another UFO over Russia allegedly caused interceptor missiles to explode far short of their target during an incident near Moscow in 1961. Missile tests themselves probably have been responsible for some reports of luminous UFOs, as the bright exhaust of a rocket was mistaken for a UFO. Some UFO sightings from Afghanistan in 1959, for example, are thought to have been misidentifications of Russian missile tests. Some UFO reports from the former Soviet Union itself also are thought to have been related to tests of weapons delivery systems. Rumors of UFOs in the Soviet Union may have been encouraged by the authorities there to help divert public attention from tests of such systems.

See also ATLAS INCIDENT; KANDAHAR INCIDENT; RYBINSK INCIDENT.

missing persons and aircraft Although incidents of persons and aircraft vanishing, never to be seen again, during alleged UFO encounters are rare, such cases have been reported. Perhaps the most famous encounter of this kind is that of pilot Frederick Valentich, who is said to have disappeared, along with the private plane he was flying, during an encounter with a UFO over Bass Strait between Australia and Tasmania in 1978. Another incident in this category is the San Germán incident in Puerto Rico in November 1988, in which two jet fighters allegedly were "swallowed" by a huge UFO. The San Germán incident is very similar to another reported UFO sighting at Cabo Rojo, Puerto Rico, in December 1988, in which two aircraft also were said to have "disappeared" from sight during an encounter with a triangular UFO.

See also AIRCRAFT, UFOS AND; CABO ROJO INCIDENT; SAN GERMÁN INCIDENT; VALENTICH CASE.

missing time Commonly presumed by UFO "believers" to indicate that an abduction has occurred, "missing time" is a period of time of which the alleged abductee inexplicably has no memory. After a UFO sighting, if a witness takes an hour or two longer than usual to return home and has no recollection of that extra time, some believers in UFO abductions might suspect the witness had undergone an abduction and had the memory of it erased or supplanted with a misleading, or "cover," memory. The alleged phenomenon of missing time provided the title for a 1981 book by UFO analyst Budd Hopkins, who has investigated alleged cases of missing time and has retrieved stories of encounters with extraterrestrials from his subjects. It should be pointed out that other, less exotic phenomena than UFO abductions can account for missing time. UFO debunker Philip Klass has described accounts of missing time, retrieved under hypnosis, as "fantasy."

See also ABDUCTIONS; HOPKINS, BUDD; HYPNOSIS; KLASS, PHILIP; PSYCHOLOGICAL EFFECTS.

Mohican incident In 1908 off the Delaware coast, the British ship *Mohican* reportedly encountered a strange, luminous cloud that enveloped the vessel and appeared to magnetize everything on it. The compass swung erratically, and chains allegedly were "frozen" to the metal deck. The cloud then lifted abruptly. Clouds and vapors are an important element of many UFO sightings, as are curious eletromagnetic effects.

See also CLOUDS AND VAPORS.

Mojave incident, California, United States In the late evening of November 2, 1951, two witnesses driving in a canyon about 30 miles north of the Mojave reportedly saw a discoid UFO estimated to be approximately 30 feet in diameter and 10 feet thick. The object was well-defined and had a blue-green color with a similarly colored glow surrounding it. The observers stopped and signaled to the UFO, which appeared to respond as if under intelligent direction. It approached to within several meters, then flew away. At last, the UFO vanished in the manner of a conjuror's trick. The southwestern portion of the United States is noted as a focal point for such alleged close encounters with UFOs. Reports of such encounters were especially numerous and well-publicized during the 1950s.

See also BENDER MYSTERY; FRY INCIDENT.

Moon The nearest major celestial object to Earth, the Moon once was suspected of being a base for extraterrestrials visiting Earth. Some UFO enthusiasts imagined large communities of extraterrestrials on the Moon, complete with lush vegetation. Exploration of the Moon by manned and unmanned spacecraft, however, showed it to be both uninhabited and incapable of supporting life as we know it. Likewise, Mars and Venus, our nearest planetary neighbors, have been virtually ruled out as homeworlds for space travelers.

See also HOMEWORLDS; MARS; VENUS.

Morro de Vintem incident, Brazil The Morro de Vintem ("Hill of the Penny Coin") incident occurred in the Niterói suburb of Rio de Janeiro, Brazil, in 1966. The bodies of two men, dressed in suits and raincoats, were found side by side on the hill by a boy who was looking for a kite. Beside the bodies were crudely devised metal masks. Also present were pieces of paper filled with notes, including what UFO investigator Jacques Vallee describes as electrical formulae. One of the notes appeared to be a set of instructions, telling the men to meet at a specified location at 4:30 P.M., swallow capsules at 6:30 P.M., and shield their faces with the metal masks after some unspecified "effect" was produced. Then they were to await a prearranged signal. Also discovered at the site were a piece of aluminized paper and some cellophane. A police investigation found no blood nor any signs of violence where the bodies were discovered. Decomposition of the bodies was advanced by the time they were discovered. The date of death was established at between Tuesday, August 16, and Saturday, August 20. The cause of death was given as natural causes, specifically cardiac arrest. No poison was detected. The victims were identified as electronics technicians Manuel Pereira de Cruz, age 32, and Miguel Jose Viana, age 34. They were last seen alive around 5:00 P.M. on August 17, on their way to the Morro de Vintem. Robbery was considered as a possible motive for killing the two men, because they reportedly had a large sum of money with them on the way to the Morro de Vintem, but only a small sum was found on their bodies after death. The absence of signs of violence at the site, however, indicated foul play probably was not involved. Other hypotheses were considered and rejected. A prisoner claimed to have been hired to kill the two men and had participated in their murder, but this confession was viewed as questionable, partly because the prisoner, in his statements, allegedly misidentified the site where the bodies were found. Later the police received a telephone call from a woman who claimed to have seen an orange, ovoid UFO emitting rays of light over the Morro de Vintem on Wednesday, August 17. Other calls to police reported sighting a similar object in the vicinity of the Morro de Vintem around the time the two men were believed to have died.

Further investigation revealed evidence that the two deceased men had been involved in spiritualism and were members of an occult society. It was suggested later that the men had been taking part in a spiritualist exercise of some kind at the time of their deaths. Vallee, investigating the case in 1980, observed that no vegetation was growing, 14 years after the event, at the location where the bodies were discovered. Vallee also was told that the bodies neither stank nor had been attacked by predators. Vallee also reports that a Brazilian physician provided him in 1967 with personal reports on a luminous, elliptical object that reportedly was seen in the Niterói area on March 16, 1966, two months before the deaths of Miguel Jose Viana and Manuel Pereira de Cruz. The Morro de Vintem case bears similarities with numerous other UFO reports, notably the apparent involvement of the victims with the occult and the reported avoidance of the bodies by predatory animals.

See also ANIMALS, UFOS AND; BRAZIL; DEATHS; OCCULTISM; VALLEE, JACQUES.

mother ships Hypothetical, large spacecraft supposedly used to carry smaller, discoid "scout craft" on missions to Earth, mother ships figure prominently in some discussions of UFOs as possible extraterrestrial spacecraft. According to one school of thought, the mother ships include huge, cigar-shaped vessels called "vunus" (in one classification system based on the Sanskrit language) that approach close to Earth and release their saucers (or "vimanas") for trips to the surface, in much the same manner as a naval vessel dispatching a helicopter on a mission to shore. Mother ships also are a commonly used device in science fiction, from which much of the modern UFO phenomenon appears to be derived.

See also CIGARS; SANSKRIT; VIMANA; VUNU.

Mothman A humanoid or quasi-humanoid entity reported seen in West Virginia on numerous occasions in the 1960s, Mothman was said to have no head, but to possess huge wings, as well as glowing "eyes" where an ordinary human's shoulders should be. The sightings appear to have been restricted to West Virginia. Mothman has become part of UFO lore, although the connection between the alleged being and UFOs appears unclear. If Mothman actually existed outside the human imagination, then the creature apparently did no harm beyond frightening eyewitnesses. Mothman resembles certain other winged humanoids reported seen in various countries, from Vietnam to the British Isles.

See also HUMANOIDS; WINGED BEINGS.

motion pictures Soon after the initial "flying saucer" sighting in 1947, saucers became a favorite subject for motion pictures and have remained so ever since. Filmmakers have tended to portray extraterrestrials as menacing beings intent on taking over Earth and exploiting it for their own purposes, in much the same manner as European colonial powers in Africa and Asia in the 19th century. This image of extraterrestrials as ruthless conquerors probably owes much to H.G. Wells's images of invading Martians in his fantasy *The War of the Worlds.* Motion pictures have presented many different views of extraterrestrials and their motives, however, ranging from evil nonhumans to benevolent humanoids. In some cases, elements of motion-picture treatments of the UFO phenomenon have prefigured popular interest in those elements many years later. Waves of UFO sightings also have been linked with the prior release of motion pictures depicting such incidents.

See also CLOSE ENCOUNTERS OF THE THIRD KIND; DAY THE EARTH STOOD STILL, THE; EARTH VERSUS THE FLYING SAUCERS; E.T., THE EXTRATERRESTRIAL; MYSTERIANS, THE; PRECEDENTS; THIS ISLAND EARTH; WAR OF THE WORLDS, THE.

motives of extraterrestrials Much speculation surrounds the motives behind the alleged activities of supposed extraterrestrials on Earth. According to one school of thought, the aliens take a benevolent interest in humankind and are prepared to intervene dramatically in our history if and when our society reaches the point of self-destruction through war or pollution. An opposed point of view is that the aliens are not benevolent, but rather hostile toward humankind, and have no inhibitions about abducting and torturing humans.

Some observers of the UFO phenomenon have gone so far as to equate UFOs and their occupants with angels. Other students of "UFOlogy" have plainly identified the alleged extraterrestrials as demons and can cite numerous incidents from the spiritual literature of Christianity to support their case. Among the most articulate exponents of the UFOs-are-demonic school of thought was the Russian Orthodox theologian Father Seraphim Rose, who saw the UFO phenomenon as a diabolic campaign of disinformation designed to prepare the world for the arrival of the Antichrist.

Just as there is no universal agreement on the strategy behind the activities of alleged aliens on Earth, there is no consensus on what exactly the aliens might be doing here on a short-term basis. Numerous individual projects have been attributed to aliens, from extracting some mysterious but valuable substance from sea water to robbing women of their ova for use in experiments on genetic manipulation.

The New Age movement, with which the UFO phenomenon has numerous close ties, has promoted an essentially "Aquarian" interpretation of the so-called aliens' motives. According to New Age thinking, the extraterrestrials are on Earth to help guide humankind into a new era of harmony with itself and with nature. The specifics of this harmony are vaguely defined, however, and this image of benevolence is difficult to reconcile with the numerous accounts from UFO lore of extraterrestrials abducting, assaulting, raping and torturing humans.

See also ABDUCTIONS; ANGELS; ANTICHRIST; BELIEF SYSTEMS; CHRIST AND CHRISTIANITY; DEMONOLOGY; NEW AGE MOVEMENT; ROSE, FATHER SERAPHIM.

Motovilov incident, Russia   Shortly after the death of St. Seraphim of Sarov in 1833, his friend and servant Nicholas Motovilov, while on a trip to Kursk to gather information about the saint's life, had an experience similar to that of many modern UFO "contactees." Motovilov found himself surrounded by a very cold and evidently foul-smelling "cloud" that left him paralyzed and unable to move his arm to make the sign of the cross. Motovilov attributed this experience to the Devil's assault. The same experience occurred again and again over some 30 years.

See also DEMONOLOGY; ENCOUNTER PHENOMENA; ODORS; PARALYSIS; TEMPERATURE EFFECTS.

mountain-top glows   These electrical phenomena are thought to resemble certain UFO reports. Mountain-top glows reportedly occur in various forms, including rays of light, steady glows and bright flashes along the crests of mountains. The light usually is yellow-white but also has been described as orange or green. Such discharges have been reported in the Alps, the Andes Mountains and other parts of the world. Mountain-top glows occur on a very large scale and may be visible for hundreds of miles. In some cases, the light is believed to occur on a periodic basis. The phenomenon is said to become more intense during earthquakes and is thought to be related to earthquake light, a glow sometimes seen in the sky at the time of major earthquakes. Likewise, UFO sightings have been associated tentatively with earthquake activity.

See also EARTHQUAKE LIGHTS.

Mount Etna incident, Sicily   On July 4, 1978, three off-duty Italian military officers and a civilian companion reportedly sighted a triangular formation of three red lights, one of which removed itself from the formation and appeared to land. On investigating, the witnesses allegedly saw a saucer-shaped UFO approximately 40 feet in diameter. The craft had an illuminated dome, bright yellow in hue. Standing beside the object were several tall, humanoid entities with handsome features and blond hair, wearing closely fitting black suits resembling overalls. Two of the entities began climbing toward the witnesses, who found themselves unable to move. The two beings approached within several feet of the witnesses, smiled at them and returned to the object. The witnesses reported that the object then began glowing with tiny, multicolored points of luminosity, but ceased this light display momentarily as an automobile passed on the road. The witnesses found themselves able to move again and left the area without waiting to see the craft depart. They reportedly felt exhausted following the encounter. This case is notable for the number of witnesses involved; for the richness of detail in the report; and for the apparent credibility of the witnesses—military officers who would appear to have nothing to gain and much to lose by reporting such a story.

See also HUMANOIDS; ITALY; "NORDICS".

Mourieras incident, France   This incident is said to have occurred only about two hours before the famous Quaroble incident in France, on September 10, 1954. Around 10:30 P.M., a farmer named Mazaud allegedly was walking home when he encountered a helmeted entity of average human height who gestured to him in a friendly manner and then climbed aboard a cigar-shaped craft some 12 feet long. The craft then flew away in the direction of Limoges, where witnesses some minutes later reportedly saw a discoid, red UFO that left a blue trail behind it.

See also HUMANOIDS; QUAROBLE INCIDENT.

mowing devil incident, England   Some three centuries before crop circles became a widely known element of the UFO phenomenon, a similar case was reported from Hartfordshire in England on August 22, 1678. According to the story, a farmer negotiated with a crop mower to cut down an acre and a half of oats. The mower's price was too high, and the farmer vowed that the Devil would mow the oats before the mower got the job. That evening, a glow like that of fire was seen above the oats, and in the morning they were found mowed more neatly than a human mower could have accomplished. The mown area was evidently circular (like the crop circles reported in England in the late 20th century),

Landing Gear: the three-ball arrangement of the Adamski saucer (left); four landing legs ending in pads (center); and the "mushroom" with its central column. (D. Ritchie)

and the deed was attributed to the Devil or to some other "infernal" being.

See also CROP CIRCLES; DEMONOLOGY.

multiple abductions See SEQUENTIAL ABDUCTIONS.

mushrooms This category of UFO sightings involves a discoid UFO with a central column extending downward from it. The column apparently serves as a landing support or transport mechanism, or both.

See also DISCS.

music A minor but colorful element of UFO lore is music that is said to accompany some close encounters with UFOs and their occupants. The "extraterrestrials" in such cases allegedly may communicate through music, or in a spoken language described as musical. In the 1977 motion picture *Close Encounters of the Third Kind*, the fictional aliens communicate with contactees on Earth through a five-note musical theme. The climax of the film depicts a musical "concert" of sorts between humans and a huge extraterrestrial spacecraft at Devil's Tower, Wyoming. Fragments of song were reported heard coming from the "airships" allegedly seen over wide areas of the United States in the 19th century. The music associated with UFO reports is reminiscent of the concept of "music of the spheres," music based on the mathematical and geometrical relationships in the Platonic solids once believed to form the "machinery" of the cosmos. In at least one piece of Native American folklore, the story of the Algonquin flying bas-

ket, music apparently serves to propel a "spacecraft" into the skies.

See also AIRSHIPS; ALGONQUIN FLYING BASKET.

Mysterians, The A 1957 Japanese science fiction film, *The Mysterians* concerns the invasion of Earth by extraterrestrials who wish to use the planet's women for purposes of breeding. The movie incorporates notable elements of the UFO phenomenon. For example, the aliens establish an underground base on Earth; seek assistance from humans in perpetuating their race; and are resolved to take by force what humans will not surrender voluntarily. Eventually, the aliens are defeated by a joint U.S.–Japanese military effort and forced to abandon their base. The aliens in the film are humanoids who travel in luminous spacecraft like the classic flying saucer, and their craft arrive and depart from their base through the waters of a lake, in scenes reminiscent of alleged UFO encounters in which UFOs reportedly dive into or arise from bodies of water. An abduction scene in the movie also resembles abduction reports that would become widely known some 25 to 30 years later. A Toho/MGM release, *The Mysterians* was directed by Inoshiro Honda and starred Kenji Sahara and Yumi Shirakawa. Special effects were by Eiji Tsuburaya.

See also AQUATIC OBJECTS; BASES; MOTION PICTURES.

mythology The connections between mythology and the UFO phenomenon are numerous and complex. Psychiatrist C.G. Jung considered "flying saucers" to be a modern myth and noted a connection between the circular shape of many reported UFOs and the "mandala," a circular occult symbol signifying wholeness. Accounts of flying vehicles similar to modern UFO reports are found in the mythology of many countries, from Japan to Native American civilization, although no proof exists that the myths in such cases actually describe extraterrestrial spacecraft and their occupants. The figure of Proteus, the shape-shifting god of Greek mythology, has been identified especially with the UFO phenomenon because of the many forms UFOs and their alleged occupants are said to assume.

The modern mythology of UFOs is vast and complicated and is associated with myths of rumored ancient civilizations such as Atlantis and Lemuria. The mythology of UFOs also is tied closely to the lore of Tibet, which has been identified (though again, with little or no evidence to support this claim) as a possible base for UFOs operating on Earth either today or in the distant past.

Among the most colorful elements of UFO mythology is the "hollow Earth hypothesis," according to which UFOs are spacecraft visiting the surface of the Earth from bases in the allegedly hollow interior of the planet. Although this hypothesis has been disproven in every way, it continues to exert a certain fascination on believers in UFOs and formed the basis of the so-called Shaver mystery in America during the 1940s.

The links between mythology and the UFO phenomenon became clear to the public as a whole during the "ancient astronauts" phenomenon of the late 1960s and early 1970s, when postulated extraterrestrial visitors to Earth in ancient times were identified as the "gods" of antiquity.

See also ALGONQUIN FLYING BASKET; ANCIENT ASTRONAUTS; ATLANTIS; BLAVATSKY, HELENA PETROVNA; DEMONOLOGY; DZYAN; HOAXES; HOLLOW EARTH HYPOTHESIS; LEMURIA; OCCULTISM; PROTEAN-PSYCHOID PHENOMENA; PROTEUS; RELIGION, UFOS AND; SHAVER MYSTERY; TENGU; VON DÄNIKEN, ERICH.

N

Nakamura incident, Japan One Lieutenant Colonel Toshio Nakamura reportedly was killed in an encounter with a UFO on June 9, 1974. According to the report, Nakamura and Major Shiro Kubota were sent up in an F-4 Phantom to investigate a bright light that was reported by numerous observers and sighted on radar. The object was described as discoid and red-orange in color, and approximately 30 feet in diameter. As Nakamura armed the plane's cannon and approached the UFO, the object reportedly reversed course and started making high-speed passes at the aircraft, missing it by very narrow margins. On one pass, the UFO allegedly struck the jet, and both men ejected. Kubota reached the ground safely by parachute, but Nakamura's parachute caught fire, and he was killed. There appears to have been no official statement about this incident from the Japanese military, except to say that the jet indeed did crash after colliding with some aircraft or unidentified object, and Nakamura was killed.

See also AIRCRAFT, UFOS AND; DEATHS; JAPAN.

names One curious aspect of the UFO phenomenon is the large number of childish, two-syllable names among the "extraterrestrial" entities reportedly contacted. Aylan, UMMO, Hoova, Masar and Saras are examples of names given to so-called extraterrestrials and their homeworlds. No universally accepted explanation of this pattern is available.

See also AYLAN; COMMUNICATIONS; LANGUAGE; UMMO.

Nash–Fortenberry incident Shortly after 8:00 P.M. on July 14, 1952, Captain William Nash and William Fortenberry, pilot and co-pilot respectively of a Pan American DC-4 aircraft flying between New York and Miami at an altitude of 8,000 feet, reportedly spotted a red, luminous UFO in the vicinity of Norfolk, Virginia. The UFO allegedly was perceived as six bright red objects, each about 100 feet in diameter, flying in echelon formation some 2,000 feet above Chesapeake Bay. Nash described the objects as "well-defined," with clear rather than fuzzy edges. Two additional objects reportedly joined the initial six objects in flight. While maneuvering, the objects turned on edge and appeared to be disk-shaped, with a thickness estimated at approximately 15 feet. The Air Force's Project Blue Book investigated the incident but eventually classified it as

The Nash–Fortenberry sighting allegedly occurred over Hampton Roads, Virginia. (U.S. Geological Survey)

145

unexplained. Various other explanations for the sighting were put forward, including a distortion of lights on the ground by atmospheric conditions. The Nash–Fortenberry incident preceded by only four days the first of a series of widely publicized UFO reports from the nation's capital.

See also AIRCRAFT, UFOS AND; BLUE BOOK, PROJECT; WASHINGTON, D.C., SIGHTINGS.

National Aeronautics and Space Administration (NASA)

As America's civilian space agency, NASA has been in the public eye since 1960 and has been drawn into UFO-related controversies on numerous occasions. Sensational rumors have circulated about NASA's alleged role in covering up encounters between "extraterrestrials" and American manned space missions, but these rumors remain unsubstantiated. One such story, for example, concerns the rumored meeting in 1969 between *Apollo 11*, the first manned mission to land on the Moon, and extraterrestrial spacecraft shortly after Apollo's landing. Similar rumors have accumulated around the Soviet manned spaceflight program.

See also APOLLO 11; ASTRONAUTS, UFO REPORTS ATTRIBUTED TO; RUMORS.

National Security Agency (NSA)

America's mysterious high-tech intelligence agency is thought to have conducted extensive investigations of the UFO phenomenon, although security restrictions make a thorough investigation of such claims difficult. The NSA is believed to have prepared an article in 1968 reviewing the various hypotheses concerning the nature and origins of UFOs, including the extraterrestrial hypothesis, although the document's author or authors reportedly did not conclude whether or not UFOs represented visitations to Earth by intelligences from other planets.

See also EXTRATERRESTRIAL HYPOTHESIS.

natural phenomena, UFOs and

Many natural phenomena may be misidentified as UFOs. Atmospheric phenomena such as unusually shaped clouds or "sundogs" may be mistaken for UFOs. Birds in flight at night, their breast feathers reflecting lights from the ground, also may give the appearance of a formation of luminous flying objects. "Marsh gas," or methane, arising from the ground and burning with a faint glow, has been implicated in at least one widely publicized UFO sighting. Meteors, especially if large and bright, may be mistaken for UFOs. "Ball lightning," a poorly understood phenomenon of meteorology, may account for some sightings of luminous, spherical UFOs.

See also BALL LIGHTNING; BIRDS; CLOUDS AND VAPORS; METEORS; METHANE.

Nazca lines, Peru

During the "ancient astronauts" enthusiasm of the 1970s, it became fashionable to interpret the "Nazca lines," a mysterious set of lines on Peru's Nazca Plain, as a landing site for extraterrestrials who supposedly visited Earth in ancient times. The lines, which were formed by removing stones from the surface and exposing the lighter soil below, are clearly visible only from the air and appear in the forms of geometric figures as well as diagrams of animals, including fish, birds, lizards, a monkey and a spider. The lines are thought to have been made between 400 A.D. and 900 A.D.

The interpretation of the Nazca lines as some kind of landing site for spacecraft had been put forward before the 1970s by various authors, but Erich von Däniken took the idea and made it widely acceptable through his best-selling writings, in which he argued that the "gods" of prehistory actually had been extraterrestrial astronauts visiting Earth. Von Däniken dismissed the idea that the Nazca lines might have been intended for use as roads, and pointed out their similarity to a modern airfield. Von Däniken's suggestion that spacecraft might have used the Nazca lines as a landing area has been refuted effectively. Extraterrestrial spacecraft would hardly need lengthy horizontal strips for landing and takeoff if the vehicles were capable of vertical takeoff and landing, as flying saucers are widely supposed to be. Also, some of the lines run directly into ridges and hills, and thus would be unsuitable as airfield facilities. The soil of the Nazca plain is sandy and soft, instead of the firm material needed to support a heavier-than-air craft when it rests on the ground. Finally, the Nazca lines can be seen from the air only during daylight hours, and this limitation would have made night landings difficult.

Another interpretation of the Nazca lines is that they were part of an astronomical facility. A Nazca bird figure dubbed the Condor resembles the ancient constellation of Pavo, the Peacock, visible in the southern hemisphere. In this interpretation, the Nazca figures representing constellations might have been intended to make "gods" in the heavens notice the presence and activities of humans on Earth.

How the Earthbound Peruvians of ancient times managed to execute such geometrically precise markings on the Nazca plain has been a matter of debate. One suggestion is that the Nazcans developed an early hot-air balloon that allowed a passenger to rise to an altitude of several hundred feet. From there, it would have been possible to direct work on the ground below. A drawing on a piece of Nazcan pottery, resembling a hot-air balloon, has been found, and the native peoples of South America in pre–Columbian times appear to have had textiles suitable for constructing such a balloon. A successful test of a hot-air balloon was conducted on the Nazca plain in 1975 using materials the earlier inhabitants are thought to have possessed. The balloon was made of fabric similar to textiles discovered at Nazca, and the gondola was made of reeds from Lake Titicaca. Coals in an earthenware pot provided hot air for the ascent.

See also ANCIENT ASTRONAUTS; PSEUDOSCIENCE; VON DÄNIKEN, ERICH.

near-death experience This phenomenon, in which a person who has experienced temporary clinical death (or at least approached such a condition) may report meeting a "being of light" at a gateway to "the other world," has been linked at least tentatively with UFO encounter reports, which also may involve meetings with brilliantly luminous beings and messages concerning conditions on other worlds. There is no unanimous agreement on the origins of the so-called near-death experience, nor exactly what connection it may have to UFO encounter experiences.

See also ENCOUNTER-PRONE PERSONALITY; FANTASY-PRONE PERSONALITY; ROSE, FATHER SERAPHIM.

near misses In these cases, a UFO in flight reportedly passes very close to an aircraft, narrowly avoiding a collision. Numerous incidents of this kind have been reported and often involve luminous UFOs encountered at night. Various explanations for these reports are possible. A meteor, for example, may resemble a cigar-shaped UFO and may appear to be much closer than it really is. An example of a reported near miss involving a UFO is the Chipping Warden incident in 1988.

See also CHIPPING WARDEN INCIDENT.

Neff–Spaur incident, Ohio–Pennsylvania, United States Among the most famous sightings of the 1960s in America, the Neff–Spaur incident involved two policemen, Dale Spaur and Wilbur Neff, who reportedly chased a luminous UFO from eastern Ohio into Pennsylvania early on the morning of April 17, 1966. Spaur described the UFO as approximately 50 feet wide, with a dome or some other superstructure barely visible on top. Spaur also described a beam of light emanating from the underside of the UFO. The UFO reportedly traveled at more than 80 miles per hour, at an estimated altitude of about 900 feet. The chase extended for about 85 miles. Airport radar contact with the UFO was reported but later denied. The incident was investigated by Project Blue Book, which said the policemen had been chasing an artificial satellite and subsequently the planet Venus.

See also BLUE BOOK, PROJECT; SATELLITES; VENUS.

Nefilim A hypothetical race of extraterrestrials, the Nefilim feature in the writings of Zecharia Sitchin, who suggests that humans were created to serve as slaves for the Nefilim when the aliens supposedly came to Earth to mine gold and other valuable metals. According to Sitchin's hypothesis, the Nefilim came from Marduk, a planet in the far outer reaches of our solar system. Sitchin suggests that the Nefilim became the deities of human mythology. Sitchin's speculations about the Nefilim resemble the tenets of the "ancient astronauts" phenomenon.

See also ANCIENT ASTRONAUTS; MARDUK; MYTHOLOGY; NEPHILIM; RELIGION, UFOS AND.

neoteny Defined generally as the retention of juvenile traits in an adult, this concept of anatomy has been applied to the UFO phenomenon in an effort to explain the similarities between the human fetus and certain "extraterrestrials." The alleged aliens in such cases are described as having extraordinarily large heads, big eyes and small bodies. These are also traits of the human fetus and of new-born babies. The doctrine of biological evolution has been cited in an attempt to account for these similarities between human infants and alleged extraterrestrials. Just as humans exhibit certain neotenous traits, such as large heads and relatively hairless skins, not found in other species, the postulated evolution of "higher" forms of life on other worlds would supposedly give those beings neotenous traits even more pronounced than those seen in humans, including abnormally large heads and bodies devoid of hair. In other words, the more babylike the "alien" looks, the more advanced it is presumed to be. This interpretation of "neotenous" traits in extraterrestrials is, of course, mere speculation. Moreover, it does not explain why certain alleged extraterrestrials in UFO encounter reports are said to be exceptionally large or hairy.

See also EVOLUTION; HUMANOIDS.

Nephilim The Nephilim are the subject of an obscure reference in the Old Testament that has been cited in connection with imagined breeding activities involving humans and extraterrestrials in ancient times. In Genesis 6:4, the Nephilim are described as powerful men or giants who lived on Earth when the "sons of God" had children by human females. There are various interpretations of this passage. One interpretation is that it refers merely to very large, strong men. According to another interpretation, the passage refers to the godly descendants of Seth, third son of Adam, taking wives from among the ungodly descendants of Cain. A third interpretation is that the Nephilim were fallen angels (that is, demons) who had intercourse with women on Earth and produced a monstrous race that was destroyed in the biblical flood. In any event, it is a long step of the imagination from Genesis 6:4 to the genetic manipulation attributed to extraterrestrials in modern UFO mythology.

See also ANCIENT ASTRONAUTS; GENETIC MANIPULATION; NEFILIM.

neutercane A meteorological phenomenon described as an isolated, violent storm that covers a small area, appearing and disappearing rapidly, the neutercane is said to be only a few miles in diameter, and to cause great swells in the ocean and generate numerous tornadoes and waterspouts. Although meteorologists apparently disagree on whether or not neutercanes actually occur, pilots report unpleasant encounters with them. Such storms might be responsible for certain incidents, sometimes attributed to UFO activity, in which aircraft and vessels at sea simply "disappear" without a trace.

See also ATMOSPHERIC PHENOMENA.

New Age movement A collection of numerous occultist activities and social concerns, the New Age movement has incorporated many elements of the UFO phenomenon, such as a belief in intelligent beings on other worlds, and attempts to contact those beings through mediumistic techniques, known as "channeling." Numerous aspects of the New Age movement, including belief in reincarnation and the veneration of crystals, are reflected in various modern UFO reports. In recent years, it has become almost fashionable to refer to one's imagined previous incarnations on other planets, and modern reports of UFO encounters may include descriptions of extraterrestrials gathered around a huge crystal and performing what appears to be an act of worship. The convergence of New Age belief with public enthusiasm for UFOs has persuaded some observers that both phenomena are merely different aspects of the same popular fascination with the occult.

See also CHANNELING; MEDIUMISM; OCCULTISM.

New Haven specter ship, Connecticut, United States A story from 17th-century New England about a spectral ship seen in the air bears a close likeness to certain modern UFO reports. Puritan religious leader Cotton Mather recorded the case of a new but unseaworthy ship that had departed from Rhode Island for England in 1646 but apparently foundered at sea. The ship did not reach its destination, nor did any news of the vessel reach New England via ships returning from England. A pastor in New Haven wrote to Mather that some months after the ship set sail (and presumably was lost at sea), an "apparition" of an airborne ship appeared above New Haven harbor, following a thunderstorm. The aerial phantom ship appeared about an hour before sunset and was said to resemble the lost ship. The spectral ship at first appeared to have its sails filled with a strong wind, on a northward course, and was observed for half an hour by numerous witnesses. The ship approached within a stone's throw of the shore. Then witnesses apparently saw the ship's main-top blown away; then the mizzen-top, and finally all the masts. The phantom ship then appeared to careen and overturn, and finally disappeared into a "smoky" cloud, which dissipated and left only clear air behind. Witnesses allegedly could distinguish the colors of the ship's components. The incident was interpreted as a sign from God, showing the people of New Haven what had happened to the ship. This case resembles many modern UFO sightings in the aerial character of the phenomenon; the level of detail observed; and the cloud or vapor reportedly involved. Various interpretations of this sighting are possible. One interpretation is that methane, or "marsh gas," arising from water collected near the surface, was ignited (possibly by electricity associated with the passing thunderstorm) and burned with a flame that was transformed by active imaginations into the image of a ship. New England is seismically active, and some geologists believe that methane commonly escapes from the Earth's interior to the surface in such areas.

See also METHANE.

Nichiren incident, Japan Just before a priest named Nichiren was scheduled to be beheaded at Tatsunokuchi, Kamakura, Japan, on September 12, 1271, a shiny object resembling a full Moon reportedly appeared in the sky, scaring officials so badly that they did not conduct the execution.

See also JAPAN.

noctilucent clouds These high-altitude clouds may catch the rays of the setting sun long after sunset has occurred at ground level. The clouds thus resemble glowing, airborne objects that may be mistaken for UFOs but are easy to identify because they are stationary or move very slowly.

See also CLOUDS AND VAPORS; NATURAL PHENOMENA, UFOS AND.

"Nordics" Some humanoids reported in UFO close encounters are described as handsome blonds, or "Nordics," with superb physiques. These Nordics resemble the model of the stereotypical "Aryan" of Nazi racial theories. The Nordics commonly are said to have long hair and little sense of humor. Other ethnic stereotypes represented in the literature on humanoids and close encounters include "Italians," humanoids about five feet tall with allegedly Mediterranean features and coloring, and East Asians. Why these alleged entities should resemble ethnic stereotypes known to humans has not been determined.

See also HUMANOIDS; "ITALIANS."

Nostradamus, French occultist (1503–1566) A leading European astrologer of the 16th century was Michel de Notredame, alias Nostradamus. He became court physician to King Henri II of France in 1556. Toward the end of his life, Nostradamus attempted prophecy and compiled a book of verses called *Centuries*, written in more than 1,000 stanzas of four lines each. These impenetrable verses were supposed to reveal, when properly deciphered, the history of the world for hundreds of years to come. The vagueness of the alleged prophecies, however, made numerous interpretations possible.

So many different interpretations of Nostradamus's writings are possible that they cannot qualify as prophecies at all. Nonetheless, Nostradamus still has a large following. In the United States, numerous book-length "interpretations" of his writings are available.

Nostradamus's work has been applied, with less than enlightening results, to the modern UFO phenomenon. One quatrain, for example, alleges that a great king will descend from the skies in the year 1999, during a time of horrible warfare. According to one interpretation, this quatrain refers to invasion by extraterrestrials. In view of the opaque and obscure character of Nostradamus's work, however, this interpretation is dubious at best.

See also OCCULTISM; PROPHECIES.

Nouatre incident, France On September 30, 1954, the leader of a group of construction workers wandered away from the other men and began to feel drowsy. He then allegedly encountered, on a hillside, a humanoid wearing what appeared to be gray coveralls, with an opaque helmet having a visor that extended to the chest. The figure held in one hand an object that might have been either a pistol or a "rod" of metal. He stood in front of a large, shiny "dome" that hovered above the ground. Atop the object was a set of rotating blades. The entity disappeared suddenly; the witness emphasized that the figure did not walk out of sight, but simply disappeared on the spot. With a loud whistling sound, the object then moved upward in a series of "jerks" before disappearing in a bluish haze. The witness found himself unable to move during the incident. His co-workers experienced a similar paralysis. Several members of the group confirmed all the particulars of the sighting. This incident allegedly took place at the beginning of a major "wave" of UFO sightings. Elements of this sighting are found in many other UFO contact reports, including the mysterious hand-held device and the temporary paralysis of witnesses.

See also PARALYSIS.

O

occultism A collection of pseudosciences and "paranormal" practices ranging from astrology to mediumism, occultism is a major element of the UFO phenomenon. Many famous "contactees" in the early history of the modern UFO phenomenon had backgrounds in occultism, and in some cases their descriptions of "extraterrestrials" resemble manifestations of demons, as described in the spiritual literature of Christianity. Automatic writing, an attempt to relay messages from the "spirit world," is a prominent element of UFO lore, as is "channeling," a modern mediumistic practice in which a human receiver claims to make contact with "extraterrestrial" entities. Messages supposedly relayed through such contacts tend to be either trite or incoherent, and suspicion is widespread that the alleged communications in many cases are invented by the human "channeler." The coherent portions of such communications deal in many instances with the alleged (and vaguely defined) spiritual evolution of humankind. The symbolism of astrology also has played a small but interesting part in the UFO phenomenon.

See also ADAMSKI, GEORGE; ASTROLOGY; AUTOMATIC WRITING; BENDER MYSTERY; BLAVATSKY, HELENA PETROVNA; COMMUNICATIONS; DEMONOLOGY; MARIAN APPARITIONS; ROSE, FATHER SERAPHIM.

odors Various odors, many of them unpleasant, have been associated with UFOs. Smells reported in connection with UFOs include sulfur, embalming fluid, pepper, nitrobenzine and decaying meat. In some cases, the foul odor may be perceived at exactly the same time each day for several consecutive days. Domestic animals also may be affected in some way, as if responding to an invisible assailant or threat. Such cases resemble certain reports of other paranormal phenomena, notably demonic activity, in which foul smells are believed to signify the presence of evil spirits, and animals (especially dogs) exhibit strong reactions to some invisible influence.

See also ANIMALS, UFOS AND; DEMONOLOGY.

Ogden, Utah, United States A report of a mysterious facility at the U.S. Army's Dugway Proving Grounds in Utah is typical of lore surrounding the UFO phenomenon with respect to possible military possession of "alien" artifacts. From the 1950s through the early 1970s, an aircraft hangar at Dugway reportedly was kept under unusual security. According to the story, a convoy arrived at Dugway one night in June 1950. The convoy included a flatbed truck that made its way into the hangar. The truck's cargo, covered by a tarpaulin, was said to be circular or oval in shape and approximately 30 feet wide. Five men were on the truck. They remained at the hangar until dawn, when engineering and security personnel relieved them. The engineers reportedly affixed metal plating to the hangar and painted over the windows. Three concentric fences were built around the hangar. Restricted airspace was established above it, and a security team guarded it.

There were several possible explanations of the need for such high security at the hangar. One explanation was that the hangar contained an SLR-1 portable nuclear reactor. Another rumor was that the hangar contained some secret military device stolen from the Soviet Union. A third story was that the hangar housed the wreckage of a crashed UFO. That hypothesis seemed consistent with the alleged size and configuration of the object on the truck and with the time of the convoy's arrival, shortly after the first reports of U.S. military personnel recovering crashed saucers and the bodies of the saucers' occupants.

Another aspect of the Dugway story was the alleged untimely death of the five men who handled the truck and its cargo on arrival at Dugway. All five were said to have died within a year of delivering the mysterious cargo to the hangar. Two were killed in a single airplane crash between Chicago and Denver; the third died in an auto wreck when his car fell off a cliff in northern California, presumably because of brake failure; the fourth committed suicide by hanging himself with a necktie, for no apparent reason; and the fifth man simply was reported missing one day after leaving home for work.

Professor Gene Snyder, who taught a course in the literature of the occult at a community college in New Jersey, investigated the Ogden story and found little or no confirmation of it. He did learn, however, that such an isolated structure was shown on maps of Dugway, and that the airspace over it was indeed restricted. Later Snyder wrote a novel based on his investigation, called *The Ogden Enigma*. The Ogden mystery resembles many other such stories from the literature on UFOs, in its description of a mysterious object being kept under heavy security at a military installation; in the reports of mysterious deaths of persons associated with the facility; and in the unverifiable character of the story's details. It is possible that the story is merely disinformation spread with the aim of confusing and distracting researchers into the UFO phenomenon. Who might be responsible for such a disinformation effort, however, is uncertain.

See also ALLENDE LETTERS; AZTEC INCIDENT; CRASHES; DECEPTION; HANGAR 18; ROSWELL INCIDENT; RUMORS.

Orlon

An alleged extraterrestrial who supposedly communicated with a human contactee named Aleutia Francesca in Oregon in the 1950s, Orlon was said to warn humankind of some sweeping change that was about to affect Earth. Orlon also indicated that he and his people had a mission to rescue humankind from its troubles and bring "enlightenment" to the world. He added that Earth faced great and imminent changes in its "frequency" and "density." Orlon's messages were characterized by a peculiar use of capitalized words for emphasis, in the manner of quasi-literate extremists writing letters to newspapers. Orlon's alleged warnings are typical of such communications in UFO lore, specifically in their warning of vast changes ahead for Earth; a promise of deliverance and "enlightenment"; and vague, pseudoscientific use of expressions such as "frequency" and "density." Even Orlon's simple, two-syllable name matches a pattern seen widely in such alleged communications from "extraterrestrials."

See also CHANNELING; COMMUNICATIONS; NAMES; PSEUDOSCIENCE.

Orthon

This being was one of early "contactee" George Adamski's alleged visitors from Venus. Orthon supposedly used sign language and telepathy to communicate to Adamski the extraterrestrials' concern over the testing of nuclear weapons on Earth. Orthon's name matches the widely observed pattern of simple, two-syllable names among alleged extraterrestrials. The name Orthon also is very similar to "Orlon," the name of the alleged extraterrestrial supposedly channeled by an Oregon woman in the 1950s. Whatever connection may exist between these two names and "alien" entities, however, is uncertain.

See also ADAMSKI, GEORGE; CHANNELING; NAMES; ORLON.

orthoteny

This approach to UFO study was first formulated by French "UFOlogist" Aimé Michel, who plotted UFO sightings on a map of France and found that the sightings appeared to be located along straight lines. The "straight-line mystery," as orthoteny also was called, has been discredited, because straight lines may be imposed on a selection of sightings on a map without the lines necessarily reflecting any existing pattern in the data.

Otto incident

A case involving attempted radio contact with UFOs, the Otto incident was partly the work of John Otto, a UFO investigator active in the 1950s. With the help of an announcer in Chicago, Otto arranged to use a radio station to broadcast an invitation to extraterrestrials (the "Space Visitors," as Otto called them) to make contact by radio. On Sunday, November 28, 1954, Otto reported, station WGN in Chicago carried the announcer's appeal to the extraterrestrials to communicate with the people of Earth through the station's transmitter. At 11:25 A.M., Chicago time, the station maintained silence for 15 seconds. Listeners were invited to monitor their radio sets at home and contact the station if they heard anything. Some listeners reported hearing a sound like that of sleigh bells. One listener recorded the sound and played it back for Otto. He thought it sounded not like sleigh bells, but rather a coded message. Later investigation revealed that the signal lasted 19 seconds and had blocked several of the announcer's words. When Otto submitted recordings of the signals to a laboratory for analysis, he was told first that the message could be decoded easily. Then he was informed that the message was government-related and of high security, and that the laboratory was not allowed to decode it. Otto identified the signal as a transmission on 10.8 megacycles (MC), a band used for teletype. This, Otto pointed out, was not a band used for high-security government transmissions, but rather for ordinary news wire service messages. He added that it was impossible for a standard AM radio receiver, on WGN's frequency, to pick up signals on 10.8 MC, although the signal may be received on FM sets. For approximately two weeks after the message was reported to have been received, Otto wrote later, signal strength increased greatly on 10.8 MC, to such an extent that the signal interfered with FM reception in the Midwest. Otto suggested that the "Powers-That-Be," as he called them, had increased signal strength on that band to persuade the public that such a signal was what had been heard on WGN on November 28, instead of a message from extraterrestrials. Otto attributed this action, and the confusion over decoding the recorded transmission, to the machinations of the "Silence Group," a shadowy organization that figures in UFO lore.

See also COMMUNICATIONS; RADIO; SILENCE GROUP.

Ouija board A well-known piece of occult paraphernalia, the Ouija board consists of a wooden board inscribed with the letters of the alphabet, the numerals 0 through 9, and the words "yes" and "no." A pointer is used to indicate individual items on the board. The Ouija board is commonly used at seances to contact spirits. The name Ouija is derived from the French and German words for "yes" ("oui" and "ja," respectively). Although such equipment has been used for many centuries to contact spirits, the modern Ouija board originated with the American inventor Elijah Bond in 1892 and achieved great popularity in the United States during and after the first World War.

Ouija board use has been involved in numerous cases of channeling, a phenomenon linked to alleged communications from extraterrestrials in recent decades. Early in the 20th century, a session with a Ouija board started the reported communications between humans and the "Invisibles," a group of spirits whose messages bear a strong similarity to communications from alleged aliens in the UFO phenomenon. The American UFO "contactee" George

Hunt Williamson claimed to have made contact with beings from the planet "Masar" (Mars) in 1952, using a device that appears to have been a re-invention of the Ouija board. Williamson's claims provide an important link between the modern UFO phenomenon and occultism. Because highly unpleasant and dangerous spiritual phenomena, up to and including demonic possession, have been associated with the use of Ouija boards, their use has been discouraged.

See also AUTOMATIC WRITING; CHANNELING; COMMUNICATIONS; DEMONOLOGY; INVISIBLES; OCCULTISM.

out-of-body experience The out-of-body experience (OBE) is an occult experience with connections to the UFO phenomenon. An OBE involves a perception that one's consciousness, or "soul," has left the body and is moving independently of the body. If the OBE occurs at a time of medical crisis, when the survival of the body is in question, the OBE may be termed a near-death experience (NDE). In an OBE, the subject may travel to distant places and witness scenes that appear to be of other worlds. The "body" that does this traveling is not the physical body (which remains behind) but rather a noncorporeal, "astral" body that may resemble the physical body but can pass unimpeded through solid objects. In some cases, the subject later reports having had no discernible form at all, or having existed as a mere point of light, during the OBE. During an OBE, the subject may encounter a wide variety of "beings," some terrifying and others apparently benign. The OBE may involve an encounter with a luminous being that expresses great love for the subject and for humankind in general. Some kind of message may be delivered to the subject, for transmittal to others once the OBE is completed and the subject returns to his or her corporeal body. The subject may witness a rapid "replay" of events in his or her life on Earth. Visions also may involve beautiful landscapes or, alternatively, frightening visions such as that of an ocean of fire. OBEs may occur during a state of consciousness, during sleep, or in moments of illness or trauma. If the subject has undergone illness or violent mishap just before the OBE, he or she may report afterwards feeling no pain during the OBE. The OBE may begin with a perception of vibrations or a buzzing noise, followed by the separation of the corporeal and "astral" bodies. The subject may perceive the two bodies to be connected by a thread or cord, and understand that actual death will occur if the cord is severed. One prominent exponent of OBEs is Robert Monroe, a cable television company executive. In 1958, he started having spontaneous OBEs during his sleep.

During later experiments and investigations into OBEs, he had many different experiences while in the out-of-body state, including apparent attacks from demonic beings, and an encounter with a tremendously impressive being who, Monroe speculated, might have been God. His experiences resemble those reported by certain UFO contactees.

Controversy surrounds the issue of the actual nature of OBEs, partly because many different kinds of events may be reported in a particular OBE. Various interpretations of the OBE have been put forward. One interpretation is that a non-physical "double" of the subject actually travels in the physical universe. According to another interpretation, the travel occurs within one's own mind. A more traditional interpretation is provided by theologians such as the Eastern Orthodox Christian author Father Seraphim Rose, who argued that OBEs consisted largely of illusions generated by demons seeking to deceive and/or possess the human subjects.

A number of efforts have been made to link OBEs and NDEs with the UFO phenomenon. OBE expert Guy Spataford, who claims to have had more than 80 OBEs since 1987, claims that OBEs resemble reports of UFO abduction experiences in many respects. For example, the setting of OBEs and abductions tends to be the same: both kinds of experiences occur at night when the subject is in bed. "Vibrations" are another common feature of OBEs and abduction stories. Early in an OBE, electrical impulses seem to move through the body. This experience in a UFO "abduction" may be interpreted as the work of some extraterrestrial device. Paralysis is also a common feature of both OBEs and abduction reports. Telepathy occurs in both kinds of experiences, as information is passed between the subject and other entities without using spoken words. The subject in an OBE may meet "guides" who provide instruction or convey the subject to a certain location; likewise, UFO abduction cases commonly involve such guides, who may deliver a seemingly profound message to the subject or accompany the subject on a journey to some distant location. Descriptions of the guides in such cases differ from one culture to another; in one incident in Japan, a boy reported traveling to faraway lands in the company of a tengu, or long-nosed mountain goblin. Gravitation and the Newtonian laws of motion appear to have no importance during OBEs, because subjects report floating "weightlessly" in the air, traveling at tremendous velocities and executing maneuvers that would be impossible for physical objects, such as abrupt 90-degree turns. These traits are also attributed to UFOs, which are seen hovering in the air with no apparent mechanism of support; going from immobility to high velocity with little or no period of acceleration; and carrying out seemingly impossible maneuvers. Absurdity and strangeness are also characteristics of OBEs and UFO abductions alike— so much so, in fact, that the subject may be unwilling to discuss the experience afterward for fear of disbelief and ridicule. "Post-traumatic stress" is another aspect of OBEs and UFO abductions, Spataford adds. The experience may be so frightening that the subject afterward fears that he or she is going mad.

See also OCCULTISM; PSYCHOLOGICAL EFFECTS; ROSE, FATHER SERAPHIM; TENGU.

Oz factor This term, named after the celebrated dream sequence that composes most of the movie *The Wizard of Oz*, is used by British UFO researcher Jenny Randles to describe a collection of symptoms often reported by witnesses to alleged abductions. The Oz factor involves a dream-like state in which the incident is perceived. This condition may be described in terms of "timelessness" or "disassociation," or a trance. The subject has the impression that the experience is taking place outside the familiar framework of time and space, and in some other environment where different, seemingly magical conditions apply. There may be an impression that time has slowed down or even stopped altogether. The Oz factor also may involve a peculiar silence or condition of motionlessness that appears to affect the area just around the encounter site. Randles interprets the Oz factor as an induced state of sensory deprivation that appears to influence the subject's state of consciousness. Medical conditions such as epilepsy and narcolepsy may be responsible for the Oz factor in certain cases. The Oz factor also has been interpreted tentatively as the effect of hypothetical "transients," natural, short-lived radiation phenomena in the atmosphere. Conditions like those reported in the Oz factor resemble those perceived in various other paranormal phenomena.

See also ENCOUNTER PHENOMENA.

P

Pachomius, Christian monk, 4th century A.D. Known for his skill in organizing and administrating monastic communities, Pachomius reportedly had an experience that brings to mind certain elements of 20th-century UFO encounters. Once Pachomius saw very small demons tie a rope to a leaf and then pretend to struggle to move it. In similar fashion, certain modern UFO encounter cases involve tiny beings engaged in seemingly pointless or ridiculous activity.

See also ANDREASSON CASE; ANTHONY, SAINT; DEMONOLOGY; ENCOUNTER PHENOMENA; HILARION.

Palatine light The 18th- and early 19th-century legend of the Palatine light, from New England, resembles certain UFO contact stories of our own time. The story involves a ship, evidently named the *Palatine*, that allegedly set sail from Germany to America and was wrecked somehow near Block Island. There were two different accounts of the wreck. According to one story, the ship's captain and crew ran the ship aground deliberately, so as to plunder it. In another version of the story, the islanders used lights on shore to lure the ship to destruction, likewise with plunder in mind; then the ship allegedly was burned with the crew and passengers still aboard, to eliminate witnesses to the crime. In either case, according to the legend, the image of the ship could be seen sometimes thereafter at night, glowing as if in flames, and hovering near the island. One elderly man on the island who supposedly participated in the looting and destruction of the ship was said to go mad each year around the time the ship was wrecked. The man would speak madly about seeing a ship on fire, and sometimes would profess to see the ghosts of two women whose hands he cut off or slashed as they tried to grasp the gunwale of the last boat to leave the ship.

The tale of the Palatine light resembles modern UFO lore in several particulars, namely the glowing object seen above the waters; the profound psychological effects upon the aforementioned elderly man; the humanoid "ghosts" he supposedly saw; and the recurrence of these events. The legend of the Palatine light also bears a close resemblance to that of the New Haven specter ship, which in turn contains prominent parallels with UFO reports. Such legends help to demonstrate the kinship that UFO lore has with ghost stories and other accounts of paranormal activity.

See also NEW HAVEN SPECTER SHIP.

Palenque carving, Mexico This carving, cited in the writings of Erich von Däniken as a depiction of a space traveler, is located on a Mayan tomb at Palenque, Chiapas, Mexico. The tomb has been dated at 683 B.C. and is thought to have contained the remains of Pacal, a king who died at age 80. Von Däniken argued that the alleged astronaut depicted in the carving is shown seated inside a rocket, manipulating controls, wearing something resembling a helmet with antennae, and watching some device in front of his face. The "vehicle" in this case, von Däniken wrote, is pointed at the nose and has flames emerging from its rear. Numerous flaws have been identified in this interpretation. For example, the "flame" at the base of the so-called spacecraft probably stands for the roots of a corn stalk, which also is represented in the carving. A likely interpretation of the symbolism in the carving is that the picture is a collection of Mayan religious symbols depicting Pacal either at the moment of death or suspended between this world and the next.

See also ANCIENT ASTRONAUTS; VON DÄNIKEN, ERICH.

Palmer, Raymond (1910–1977), American magazine editor,

Born in Milwaukee, Wisconsin, Palmer played an important role in the growth of the UFO phenomenon in the 1940s and afterward, partly through his publicizing the "Shaver mystery" in *Amazing Stories* magazine, which Palmer edited for several years. He also played a minor role in the Maury Island incident, which brought him into contact with Kenneth Arnold, who reported the initial "flying saucer" sighting in 1947. In 1948, Palmer started *Fate* magazine, a journal devoted to various occult and pseudoscientific subjects. The first issue of *Fate* contained a cover story about the "flying discs," as certain UFOs were called at that time. Palmer also wrote some science fiction.

See also ARNOLD INCIDENT; HOLLOW EARTH HYPOTHESIS; MAURY ISLAND INCIDENT; PSEUDOSCIENCE; SHAVER MYSTERY.

Paracelsus, European physician, occultist and alchemist (1491?–1541)

Paracelsus wrote about spiritual beings that resemble descriptions of modern "extraterrestrials" in UFO contact cases. Paracelsus believed that these beings could manifest themselves under many different appearances, tall or short, beautiful or ugly, and that it was hazardous to associate with them, because they were dangerous when angered, and could kill. Paracelsus's descriptions of "elemental beings" resemble UFO operators in modern reports. Paracelsus's links with the occult also are comparable with those of some modern UFO enthusiasts and "contactees." He presented himself as a sorcerer and boasted that he commanded legions of spirits. He also claimed to have maintained a correspondence with the ancient Greek physician Galen in hell, and to have summoned the philosopher and physician Avicenna from hell to dispute with him. Paracelsus evidently exhibited many of the personality traits associated with pseudoscientists, who have been prominent in the modern UFO phenomenon. He held a grandiose view of himself and claimed to possess special wisdom surpassing anyone else's on Earth. Likewise, one can cite modern UFO cultists who claim to overflow with special wisdom, which they imagine the rest of the world will have to acknowledge someday.

See also PARANOIA; PSEUDOSCIENCE; REICH, WILHELM.

paralysis In many UFO close-encounter reports, a witness is paralyzed temporarily by the UFO or its occupants. The paralysis may be general, encompassing the entire body, or partial, affecting only one portion of the body. As a rule, the paralysis is brief. The individual may feel as if he or she has been overpowered and is being held down, as in the Broadlands incident in the United Kingdom, where a bricklayer watching a UFO hovering near the ground allegedly was knocked down and felt as if he were being pinned there. In certain cases, occupants of a UFO, seen outside the craft, may point a "wand" or other object in the direction of a witness and subject him or her to paralysis through that means. Such a device has been dubbed a "kundalini gun," named after an occultist theory of energy. Alleged abductees may undergo paralysis when taken aboard UFOs and subjected to examinations. Paralysis is one example of ways in which "extraterrestrials" in UFO encounter cases are said to be capable of controlling the movements of a human subject's body.

Various interpretations may be placed on such reports. One is that the events actually occurred as described. According to another interpretation, the "encounters" were merely dreams, and the paralysis reflects the dreamer's feeling of helplessness. Paralysis also is reported often in various phenomena of the occult. This similarity between UFO encounters and occult phenomena helps to establish the UFO phenomenon as a manifestation of the "paranormal."

See also BODILY EFFECTS; BROADLANDS INCIDENT; DEMONOLOGY; ENCOUNTER PHENOMENA; KUNDALINI GUN; MOTOVILOV INCIDENT; OCCULTISM; SLEEP PARALYSIS; WITCHCRAFT.

paranoia The paranoid mentality has appeared frequently in the UFO phenomenon. Individuals engaged in studying UFOs may develop feelings of persecution and worry that they are being watched or followed by hostile strangers who are part of some great but vaguely defined conspiracy. UFO historian Martin Kottmeyer traces the evolution of paranoid thinking in individuals through a succession of stages, starting with some precipitating incident, such as a minor humiliation, and ending in a grandiose belief that the individual is the universe or even God. Some of the intermediate steps include withdrawal from society; conspiracy thinking, or a view of events as elements in some kind of conspiracy; "projection," or a belief that one's illness is caused by some external influence; and a conviction that one has been chosen for some great mission.

Kottmeyer finds a close correspondence between this progression in paranoid thinking and the history of the UFO phenomenon. For example, he traces the origins of "UFOlogy" to social setbacks in the lives of believers in UFOs. Kottmeyer cites here the "status inconsistency theory," according to which belief in UFOs may be the result of tumbles from a higher to a lower status in society. One study cited by Kottmeyer indicates that well-educated men trapped in positions lower than their education would justify are many times more likely to report UFO sightings that other men who are more successful.

Kottmeyer examines the life of a prominent figure in the history of the UFO phenomenon, author Charles Fort, in light of the status inconsistency theory. Kottmeyer points out that after making a promising start in his literary career, Fort spent some years in relative failure and obscurity. Fort became an angry and bitter man. He began writing bizarre novels with paranoid elements in them. One of these novels, titled simply *X*, concerned the notion that Mars regulated life on Earth by means of some kind of rays. Another novel, *Y*, apparently dealt with Kaspar Hauser, an enigmatic young man who appeared in Nuremberg in 1828. Fort's tale allegedly suggested that Hauser had originated in a land at the South Pole and was murdered to keep him from disclosing news about that polar country. Neither novel was published. Fort evidently discarded or destroyed the manuscripts. Kottmeyer writes that he considers "paranoid" too strong a word for Fort himself, but Kottmeyer finds considerable evidence of paranoid thinking in Fort's later works. Kottmeyer asserts that "UFOlogy" has roots in the paranoid thinking of Fort.

The history of the UFO phenomenon follows much the same pattern as the evolution of paranoia in the individual, Kottmeyer suggests. Early in the phenomenon, many "UFOlogists" withdrew from the community of investigators of the phenomenon and pursued their so-called research in secret. Later, it was widely believed that some external agency was affecting the minds of persons who perceived UFOs. And of course, numerous conspiracy theories have been put forward to account for the scarcity of solid evidence of extraterrestrial visitations: for ex-

ample, the suggestion that the U.S. government is hiding the bodies of extraterrestrials killed in UFO crashes.

See also CONSPIRACY THEORIES; FORT, CHARLES; STATUS INCONSISTENCY THEORY.

Pascagoula incident, Mississippi, United States

One of the most widely publicized of all encounter phenomena in the UFO literature, the Pascagoula incident reportedly took place on October 11, 1973, when two fishermen, Charles Hickson and Calvin Parker, claimed to have been abducted by occupants of a UFO. The alleged extraterrestrials were said to be humanoid, small in stature, and equipped with claws in place of hands. Another reported incident, this one involving a curious metallic object in the water, occurred at the mouth of the Pascagoula River less than one month later, on November 6, 1973. Fishermen allegedly saw a metallic object, about three feet long and three to four inches wide, and bearing an amber light. The fishermen and representatives of the Coast Guard are said to have tried beating on the object with boathooks and oars, but it moved away from them and was lost from sight after some 40 minutes. These incidents oc-

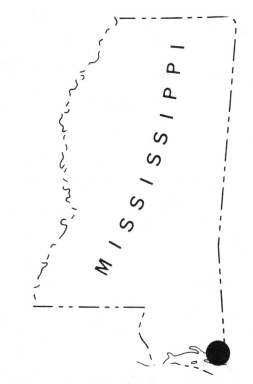

The Pascagoula incident, Mississippi, allegedly involved two fishermen and a close encounter with humanoid "aliens." (U.S. Geological Survey)

curred at the time of a widespread wave of UFO sightings that also coincided with public fascination over the "ancient astronauts" hypothesis.

See also ANCIENT ASTRONAUTS; AQUATIC OBJECTS; ENCOUNTER PHENOMENA.

pendulum   A weight suspended on a string, thread or wire from some stable, unmoving structure, the pendulum has been used to investigate the UFO phenomenon. Ordinarily, a pendulum set in motion will continue swinging in gradually diminishing arcs until it comes to rest. Unusual pendulum motions have been reported, however, in areas where UFOs are thought to have landed, such as "crop circles" in Britain. Interpretations differ on the possible meanings of any such unusual pendulum effects, and there is reason to question whether any such effects have occurred at all. Experiments of this kind with pendulums are widely viewed as occult practices, in which considerable danger to the practitioner may be involved.

See also BIOLOCATION; CROP CIRCLES; OCCULTISM.

Pennines, United Kingdom   The Pennine Hills of England, on the border between Yorkshire and Lancashire, are known as a UFO "window" and have been the location of many sightings. Jenny Randles, in her 1992 book *UFOs and How To See Them*, mentions that sightings of unusual lights have been linked with demonic activity and witchcraft. At one location, known as the Devil's Elbow, a peculiar light has been reported seen for hundreds of years. A particular concentration of sightings has been reported in the Rossendale Valley.

See also UNITED KINGDOM, UFOS IN WINDOWS.

Pentacle   This name was given by UFO investigator Jacques Vallee to an unnamed man who, in 1953, allegedly sent a secret communication to Wright-Patterson Air Force Base about how to deal with the UFO controversy, on the basis of prior extensive experience in analyzing UFO reports. Vallee says the memorandum, discovered in the files of Dr. J. Allen Hynek, indicates that large-scale analysis of UFO reports was already under way before the Robertson Panel was established in 1953 to study the UFO phenomenon. The memo allegedly recommended that the Robertson Panel's meetings be canceled or postponed until complete results of an analysis could be obtained. Vallee interpreted the Pentacle memorandum as evidence that the scientific community had been led astray in its investigation of UFOs, starting with the Robertson Panel. Although the memo indi-

Perception of UFO-related events may be faulty. Here, an observer sees two adjacent lights blinking on and off in sequence and imagines them to be a single light moving from one place to another.

cates that analysts already had studied UFOs extensively and had even formulated scientific hypotheses about the UFO phenomenon, the Robertson Panel evidently was not made aware of this activity and information. Vallee cites the memo as an indication of manipulation of the Robertson Panel and of the intelligence community's "betrayal" of science. The memo also referred to a mysterious "Project Stork."

See also HYNEK, J. ALLEN; ROBERTSON PANEL; VALLEE, JACQUES.

perception   Errors in perception are commonplace in UFO reports and can transform an ordinary phenomenon into a mysterious, unidentified object. For example, when a luminous object appears in the sky, with no other objects of known size and distance for purposes of comparison, the glowing object may be perceived as much larger and nearer than it really is. In one well-publicized case from 1969, a meteor passing over the Midwestern United States apparently was perceived mistakenly as a group of UFOs about to collide with an airliner. In similar fashion, an aircraft seen from an unfamiliar angle may be misperceived as a formation of unidentified lights. Not all UFO sightings can be attributed safely to misperception, of course, but all possible errors of perception involving familiar objects and phenomena should be eliminated before trying to assign an extraterrestrial or supernatural explanation to a UFO.

See also AIRCRAFT; AUTOKINETIC EFFECT; BALL LIGHTNING; DEDUCTIVE-PSYCHOLOGICAL EFFECT; IDENTIFICATION; METEORS.

Peropava River incident, Brazil   The Peropava River incident reportedly took place on October 31, 1963, in the Sao Paulo province of Brazil. According to one account of the incident, several children were playing along the banks of the river when a roaring sound startled them. The children looked up and saw a shiny metallic disc moving in their direction at treetop height. The disc struck the trunk of a tree, then appeared to go out of control and land in the river. Bubbles rose to the surface, along with debris and mud, where the disc entered the water. Eyewitnesses included several fishermen, who reported that the disc had been about 15 to 20 feet wide and three feet thick. The noise was allegedly loud enough to be heard by other persons who did not see the object itself. The collision between the object and the tree reportedly left a large gash in the tree trunk. Divers are said to have explored the river bottom at the alleged crash site but found no trace of the disc. The Peropava River incident fits the pattern of many UFO sightings in that it is witnessed by a number of individuals, contains vivid elements (such as the loud noise and the crash in the river), and is supported by little or no physical evidence.

See also BRAZIL.

photography Numerous photographs purportedly of UFOs have been produced, but many of these clearly have been hoaxes, and questions surround the authenticity of the rest. Skeptics have pointed out that it is easy to produce a photograph resembling the popular image of a "flying saucer." In the early days of the UFO phenomenon, it was possible to fabricate a reasonably convincing UFO photograph using little more than a lens cap suspended by a thread, or a garbage can lid tossed into the air and photographed in flight. With the advent of sophisticated techniques of photo analysis, hoaxes have become harder to perpetrate. Computer enhancement of a photograph, for example, may reveal the telltale trace of a strand of fishing line supporting a model hung between two trees.

Although some hoaxers display considerable sophistication, the crudeness of some other photographic UFO hoaxes is outstanding. It is not unheard of for a charlatan to draw an airplane's image with an ordinary pen on a photograph of some strong outdoor light source, such as the sun, and try to pass off the result as the record of an encounter between a UFO and an aircraft in flight. Close-ups of ordinary objects can be transformed by the imagination into pictures of alien spacecraft. Multiple exposures of an overhead light may fool some credulous viewers into thinking the lights represent luminous spacecraft. An ordinary streetlight photographed at night, or a lenticular cloud formation, can become a "UFO."

See also HOAXES.

physics and UFOs Physicists have tended to take a skeptical view of the UFO phenomenon, because so many elements of it are at gross variance with the science of physics as understood today. For example, many UFOs in flight have been said to perform maneuvers that would be impossible for any material object. Also, visits to Earth by extraterrestrial organisms in material spacecraft would appear to be impossible, because of the vast distances to be covered between Earth and other star systems, and because relativity theory imposes a velocity limit on such travel, namely the velocity of light. These limitations would make travel even between neighboring star systems so time-consuming as to make numerous extraterrestrial visits to Earth, as described in the literature on UFOs, effectively impossible. Pseudoscientists have tried to invoke exotic principles of physics to circumvent the relativistic limitations on interstellar travel, but without persuasive results. The crank literature on physics in the UFO phenomenon is huge and includes treatises on such chimeras as anti-gravity, perpetual motion and "free energy."

See also ANTI-GRAVITY; INERTIA; PSEUDOSCIENCE; REICH, WILHELM; TIME BARRIER; TIME TRAVEL.

Piri Reis map The "ancient astronauts" phenomenon of the 1970s included speculation about the so-called Piri Reis map, a 16th-century document attributed to Piri Reis, a Turkish pirate turned naval officer. A portion of the map allegedly represents the coast of Antarctica as it would appear if free from its ice cover and viewed from orbit. It was suggested that the Piri Reis map was the work of ancient astronauts. Numerous errors, however, on the Piri Reis map—including great inaccuracies in its depiction of Cuba and the western Mediterranean, and the fact that several hundred miles of the South American coast are simply missing from the map—indicate that the map was not produced by an orbital survey. The map is sometimes described as being 5,000 years old but is actually a product of the 16th century A.D.

See also ANCIENT ASTRONAUTS; PSEUDOSCIENCE; VON DÄNIKEN, ERICH.

plasma vortex This phenomenon has been suggested as a possible explanation for the mysterious crop circles—flattened areas of grain sometimes attributed to UFO activity—that have appeared in various parts of the world. According to this hypothesis, the crop circles are produced when a rotating, ionized mass of air similar to ball lightning affects air flow in its immediate vicinity—just above the ground. Plasma vortices also are suspected of generating UFO reports not linked specifically with crop circles, because the plasma vortex bears a strong resemblance to the classic, luminous, spherical or ovoid UFO.

See also BALL LIGHTNING; CROP CIRCLES.

Pleiades A cluster of stars in the constellation Taurus, the Pleiades figure in UFO lore as the home of certain alleged extraterrestrials, notably Semjase in the case of Swiss "contactee" Eduard Meier. The Pleiades may be seen with the unaided eye on clear nights. Seven stars in the cluster are most easily seen with the unaided eye, although some sharp-eyed observers may be able to spot more than a dozen. The Pleiades are thought to be youthful stars and to generate a radiation environment unfavorable to life as we know it, although this objection evidently has done nothing to stem reports of visits from "Pleiadeans."

See also MEIER CASE; SEMJASE.

Plesetsk A huge rocket launching facility in the northwestern part of the former Soviet Union, Plesetsk is thought to have been the cause of some notable UFO reports resulting from rocket launches or the re-entry of payloads and rocket debris launched from the base.

politics and UFOs Despite rumors of massive government cover-ups of the "truth" about UFOs, the UFO phenomenon appears to have played only a minor part in domestic American politics. During his campaign for president in 1976, for example, Jimmy Carter is said to have pledged to make public the information from government files on UFOs, but no major release of such information occurred after Carter was elected president.

If one extends the definition of politics to include domestic policy regarding national defense, public interest in flying saucers apparently did move the United States government to try diminishing public fear of UFOs during the 1950s, in the interest of avoiding potential threats to America's air defenses against Soviet attack.

Analysis of formerly classified government documents on UFOs, obtained under the Freedom of Information Act, apparently has revealed little official interest in UFOs, as demonstrated by the very small amount of released material, which amounted to only several dozen pages of material generated annually on that subject. Nonetheless, America's ru-

mor mill, aided by the tabloid press and popular entertainment, continues to propagate stories of "space aliens" controlling the United States government. Various fringe parties and candidates also have tried to make a political issue of UFOs, with limited success.

See also CHADWELL MEMORANDUM; GREEN CAMPAIGN; RUMORS.

poltergeist A poltergeist is defined in occult lore as a spirit that makes noises, relocates objects and harasses humans and animals. The name comes from the German words *poltern*, "to knock," and *geist*, "spirit" or "ghost." Poltergeist activity has been associated with UFOs, specifically in cases of abductions, and appears to provide a link between UFO activity and certain other paranormal phenomena. Many phenomena associated with poltergeists—including unearthly lights, loud noises, "ghostly" apparitions and inexplicably displaced objects—are also reported in close-encounter cases involving UFOs. Also significant are reports of poltergeists interfering with the operation of electrical equipment. The electrical systems of automobiles, for example, have reportedly been affected by the presence of UFOs nearby.

There are numerous other parallels between poltergeist activity and the UFO phenomenon. Poltergeists are said to conduct sexual attacks upon humans, in much the same manner as the sometimes brutal sexual encounters reported in UFO abduction cases. Also, just as UFO abductions allegedly occur repeatedly in some cases over a period of months or years, poltergeist activity may be prolonged and frequent. Poltergeist activity is thought to occur most often at night; in similar fashion, night appears to be the prime time for sightings of UFOs and reports of related phenomena.

See also DEMONOLOGY; ENCOUNTER PHENOMENA; SEXUAL ENCOUNTERS; VEHICLE EFFECTS.

polygraphy Commonly known as a lie detector test, polygraphy has been used to investigate certain UFO contact reports. In various cases of UFO sightings and abductions, subjects have "passed" a lie detector test, and this result has been interpreted as verification that the subject actually underwent an encounter with extraterrestrial beings and/or their technology. Such an interpretation appears to be unjustified, however, because polygraphy has been found to be unreliable in significant tests.

The polygraph consists of a machine that monitors and records the heart rate, rate of respiration and electrical conductivity of the subject's skin. By studying the record of these variables, a polygraph operator, in principle, can determine when a subject reacts to a question with increased anxiety, as if fearing to be discovered telling a lie. In many cases, the telling of a deliberate lie indeed can be correlated with physiological responses as detected and recorded by a polygraph. This is not true in every case, however, and so there are instances when a subject can tell a conscious untruth without the polygraph operator recognizing that a lie has been told. Consequently, it is fallacious to accept results of polygraph tests of UFO "contactees" as verifying that contact between the subjects and "extraterrestrials" actually occurred.

See also EVIDENCE; HOAXES.

polymorphy   The condition of having more than one particular shape or configuration, polymorphy is said to have been observed both in UFOs and in their alleged occupants. UFOs have been reported in many different shapes, including spheres, discs, cigars and cones. Extraterrestrials also are said to occur in a great variety of shapes and sizes, from giant, robot-like entities to diminutive humanoids. Polymorphy in the UFO phenomenon is seen as evidence against the extraterrestrial hypothesis, in which UFOs are presumed to be material spacecraft visiting Earth from other worlds, and extraterrestrials are supposed to be intelligent organisms with a biology comparable to our own. If the extraterrestrial hypothesis were valid, then one would expect to see more consistency in descriptions of UFOs and their so-called passengers, rather than the polymorphous objects and entities described in UFO literature.

See also EXTRATERRESTRIAL HYPOTHESIS.

Pont-la-Dame incident, France   Similar in many ways to the Loch Raven Dam incident, which occurred only two days earlier in the United States, the Pont-la-Dame incident took place just before 8:00 P.M. on October 28, 1958, when a motorist saw a luminous disc hanging stationary in the air over the Pont-la-Dame bridge across the Grand Buech river. The motorist stopped his car and got out to observe the disc, which he described as having the classic "saucer" shape of two plates joined together. The object was approximately 900 feet above the ground and 300 to 360 feet in diameter, and consisted of two concentric circles, from the smaller of which emanated red sparks. The motorist observed the disc for several minutes, until it gave off a stream of brilliant sparks and disappeared instantaneously. As the object vanished, a strong gust of air shook the motorist's car. Five other witnesses also reportedly saw the object.

See also LOCH RAVEN DAM INCIDENT; VEHICLE EFFECTS.

Pordenone, Italy   The Pordenone region near Venice in northeastern Italy has been the site of numerous widely publicized UFO reports, notably the Aviano incident, in which UFO activity was associated with the blackout of a military base, and the Istrana incident, which resembled in some ways the mysterious Bentwaters incident in Britain.

See also AVIANO INCIDENT; BENTWATERS INCIDENT; ISTRANA INCIDENT; ITALY; POWER FAILURES, UFOS AND.

power failures, UFOs and   Although there is no solid evidence linking UFO activity to massive power failures (that is, failures of electricity grids) in the United States and elsewhere, there is some evidence that UFO sightings have coincided with such failures on a number of occasions. Several such blackouts in the United States in 1965 reportedly were accompanied by UFO sightings, notably the great Northeast blackout on November 9, 1965, in which some 80,000 square miles of the northeastern United States, over a six-state area, along with portions of Canada, lost electrical power. The blackout affected the entire New York City metropolitan area. One report says objects like fireballs were sighted just before the blackout, above a substation that directed electrical power from Niagara Falls to New York City. Similar, though less spectacular, blackouts were reported in November and December of 1965 in Minnesota, Texas and New Mexico, allegedly following UFO sightings. On September 23, 1965, numerous witnesses in Cuernavaca, Mexico, reportedly saw a luminous, discoid object approach the town, and lights and electrical equipment began to fail throughout Cuernavaca. Power allegedly was restored when the disc departed. An earlier blackout, in Tamaroa, Illinois, on November 14, 1957, reportedly was accompanied by UFO sightings. Reports of blackouts linked with UFO activity also include a power failure that affected the Chinese cities of Xuginglong and Huaihua in September of 1979.

See also AVIANO INCIDENT.

precedents   This concept applies to close-encounter cases where the person recounting a meeting with "aliens" may be drawing upon memories of similar, fictional incidents in novels or short stories; popular accounts of actual close-encounter reports;

or radio, television or motion picture treatments of UFO-related themes. There are numerous cases in which the "extraterrestrials" described by an "abductee" or other witness to a close encounter resemble certain characters in fantasies that have been published or broadcast earlier. A close resemblance has been noted between some of "abductee" Barney Hill's recollections and details of an episode of the television series "The Outer Limits," broadcast in 1964.

Precedents from science fiction literature may be involved in the American "airship" sightings around the beginning of the 20th century. Certain airship reports resemble the story of Jules Verne's novel *Robur the Conqueror*, published years before the American airship wave occurred. The story concerned a mysterious inventor and his amazing airship.

Although it may be impossible to prove that many elements of modern UFO abduction cases have their origins in popular entertainment, that possibility must be considered.

See also AIRSHIPS; HILL INCIDENT; "HODOMUR, MAN OF INFINITY."

precognition   Defined as the apparent ability to perceive events before they actually occur, precognition, or something like it, figures in some UFO encounter cases. A "contactee" may have a vision of some event that is soon to take place. This phenomenon often turns out to have no basis in actual events.

prophecies   Images and verbal accounts of alleged events to come are an important element of the UFO phenomenon. Many "contactees" have reported receiving prophetic communications from extraterrestrials in such encounters, although these so-called prophecies often have turned out to be questionable at best, partly because they were less than specific. In many cases, the prophecies have concerned nuclear warfare. According to one interpretation, the alleged prophecies of the 16th-century French occultist Nostradamus describe some kind of extraterrestrial invasion to occur in the year 1999, but Nostradamus's reputation is such that this interpretation has been discounted.

Biblical prophecies have been interpreted in light of the modern UFO phenomenon, especially a reference in the gospel of Luke to "fearful sights and great signs" that are expected to precede the return of Christ.

See also COMMUNICATIONS; MESSAGES; NOSTRADAMUS; OCCULTISM; "SIGNS AND WONDERS."

propulsion   Much speculation has centered on the propulsion systems of alleged UFOs, based on the presumption that UFOs represent material spacecraft visiting Earth from other star systems. If eyewitness accounts of UFOs are to be believed, the alleged spacecraft utilize a curious mixture of advanced and comparatively archaic propulsion systems, from "anti-gravity" to chemical rockets, sometimes on the same vehicle. The crank literature on such topics, especially anti-gravity, is tremendous and includes many ill-informed speculations about magnetism and its role in spacecraft propulsion. In recent years, students of the UFO phenomenon, keenly aware of the problems in applying current knowledge of physics to the needs of imagined interstellar spacecraft, have tended to adopt the view that UFOs do not represent material objects, but rather some kind of metaphysical, non-material phenomenon to which the laws of physics (as understood on Earth) do not apply. This conception of the nature of UFOs, however, is seen by some observers as more of a rhetorical tactic than anything else.

See also ANTI-GRAVITY; PSEUDOSCIENCE; REICH, WILHELM.

protean-psychoid phenomena   This expression refers to a variety of phenomena including UFOs. "Protean" here refers to the changing nature of the phenomenon, reflecting belief of a given time. "Psychoid" means that the phenomena are paraphysical and are linked to the observer's psychological state. Protean-psychoid phenomena include mythological characteristics and resemble dreams.

See also ENCOUNTER PHENOMENA; PROTEUS.

Proteus   A figure from Greek mythology, and mentioned in Homer's *Odyssey*, Proteus was said to be an ancient being who inhabited the sea, herded seals, had vast knowledge and was capable of appearing in different forms as he wished. According to one legend, the actual Proteus was a king of Egypt. Proteus bears many similarities to "extraterrestrials" and their technology reported in alleged UFO encounters, including his tremendous knowledge and shape-changing capabilities.

See also MYTHOLOGY; PROTEAN-PSYCHOID PHENOMENA.

pseudoscience   Much of the UFO phenomenon falls into the category of pseudoscience, which is distinguished from genuine science by its approach to evidence and conclusions. In the genuine scientific method, one observes a phenomenon and draws tentative conclusions, or hypotheses, about it on the basis of those observations. These hypotheses then are tested in light of further observations. If the hypotheses hold up, they advance to the status of theories. The pseudoscientific method reverses this procedure, starting first with an arbitrarily selected premise and then seeking data to support it. Numerous examples of pseudoscientific thinking may be found in the literature on UFO studies. Perhaps the most common example might be called the "spaceman" syndrome. This widely held collection of beliefs is based on the premise that UFOs represent appearances by material, "nuts-and-bolts" spacecraft from some other planet and are manned by living, intelligent, corporeal creatures much like ourselves (although supposedly at a much more advanced stage of "evolution"). Many adherents of the spaceman syndrome appear to embrace it merely because it appeals to their desires and fantasies, and not from any objective appraisal of evidence. Having settled on that premise, they then defend it vigorously, despite any and all evidence against it, or lack of evidence for it.

Because formal training in the scientific method is rare, even in many technologically sophisticated countries, pseudoscience has a certain advantage over true science in competing for the hearts and minds of the public, especially where the complex, confusing and emotionally charged issue of UFOs and their nature is involved. This advantage was dramatized in the early 1970s, when the "ancient astronauts" myth, a now-classic example of pseudoscience, became popular in the United States and Europe. The allure and power of pseudoscience account for much of the popularity of the UFO cult.

One curious feature of certain pseudoscientists dealing with the UFO phenomenon is their interest, almost to the point of obsession, in electromagnetism. That these pseudoscientists seldom understand the physics and capabilities of electromagnetism does not stop them from trying to apply its principles to the operation of imagined alien spacecraft, sometimes with amusing results.

See also ANCIENT ASTRONAUTS; ANTI-GRAVITY.

psychic phenomena   Various psychic phenomena, including precognition, telepathy and levitation, are associated closely with the UFO phenomenon, especially with abduction reports. Persons who experience UFO close encounters may report that their "psychic powers" have been enhanced thereby. Some reports may be purely imaginary, but the association between UFO encounters and psychic phenomena resembles the link between such alleged powers and involvement with the occult. That psychic phenomena should be associated with both occultism and the UFO phenomenon is not surprising to many observers, since the UFO phenomenon appears to be basically occultist in character and incorporates many occultist practices, from astrology to automatic writing.

See also ASTROLOGY; AUTOMATIC WRITING; LEVITATION; OCCULTISM; TELEPATHY.

psychological effects   A perceived close encounter with a UFO may have dramatic effects on the psychology of the witness. The effect depends partly on the nature of the alleged encounter. If the experience is highly unpleasant, as in many abduction reports, then the subject may come away with fears of certain objects, persons or situations. A pleasant experience, on the other hand, may leave the person disposed to look favorably on UFOs and their perceived occupants. Confusion is one effect noticed after many reported UFO encounters, because the witness may report having been given puzzling information or subjected to a seemingly pointless ritual or procedure. Amnesia, in the form of "missing time," also may be reported. Grandiose delusions may occur following an encounter, as in the case of Valens the monk, whose experience with an entity much like those in modern UFO encounter reports encouraged him to believe, incorrectly, that he was specially favored by God. The witness may believe he or she has some special mission to perform on Earth, such as spreading a particular message or setting up an organization as directed by the alleged extraterrestrials. During an abduction or some other perceived encounter with UFO occupants, the human subject may report altered states of awareness, such as drowsiness or a heightened awareness of one's surroundings. These changes in awareness often are attributed to some unidentified beverage given to the subject to drink. In numerous cases, a UFO encounter may accompany an exalted state of emotion in the witness, followed by depression and a descent into substance abuse. The witness's family life may suffer from his or her changes of mood following such an experience, as well as from the witness's newfound obsession with UFO's—another effect observed in many witnesses to UFO encounters. The witness may experience a longing to see UFOs again and accompany the imagined space travelers on their voyages.

See also ABDUCTIONS; ABSURDITY; BELIEF SYSTEMS; ENCOUNTER PHENOMENA; FOOD AND DRINK; MISSING TIME; SEXUAL ENCOUNTERS; VALENS INCIDENT; VALLEE, JACQUES.

public opinion The public's perception of the UFO phenomenon has changed greatly since the first "flying saucer" incident immediately after World War II. During the late 1940s and the 1950s, UFOs commonly were perceived as a potential threat to humankind. This fear, fed by memories of the recent global war and the military threat posed by the Soviet Union, was expressed in motion pictures of the time, such as *The War of the Worlds* and numerous other films depicting invasion of Earth by extraterrestrials. Many events that later would become prominent elements of the UFO phenomenon, such as abductions, were incorporated into motion pictures during these years.

Public fear of UFOs appears to have been a factor in determining official United States government policy toward the UFO phenomenon. Washington evidently perceived public anxieties over UFOs as a threat to national security and recommended a policy of "debunking" UFO sightings.

In the 1960s and 1970s, public fear of UFOs diminished and was replaced by interest in the religious and mythological aspects of the phenomenon. For example, the "ancient astronauts" fad of the late 1960s and early 1970s made popular the notion that "extraterrestrials" had visited Earth thousands of years ago, had impressed humankind with their advanced technology, and were described in mythology and religion as accounts of visits by "gods" and "goddesses." At the same time, the public apparently began to see UFOs less as possible material spacecraft than as something metaphysical—nonmaterial constructs or entities that could make themselves perceptible as machines or corporeal beings.

An "interventionist" interpretation of the UFO phenomenon also became popular in the 1960s and 1970s. According to this interpretation, UFOs represented visitations by an alien race who either had been intervening in human history and culture or stood ready to do so if circumstances appeared to justify such action. (Such a view of the UFO phenomenon had circulated in the writings of various UFO cultists and "contactees" in earlier decades but took years to influence public opinion on a major scale.) Opinions differed on the motives for such postulated alien intervention. Although some speculation attributed benevolence to alleged extraterrestrials, public fear of the UFO phenomenon had not yet died, and UFOs continued to be viewed by some "UFOlogists" as potentially hostile.

From the 1970s to the present, some students of the UFO phenomenon, notably investigator Jacques Vallee, have speculated that the UFO phenomenon represents a "control system" designed to redirect human belief. There is no general agreement on how such a control system might attempt to alter the belief systems of humankind, but some observers have claimed to notice a pattern of themes in alleged messages from extraterrestrials in UFO contact cases. This pattern includes admonitions to trust the alleged extraterrestrials; believe in their alleged wisdom (despite the obscurity and absurdity of many reported messages); anticipate their benevolent intervention in human history in the not-too-distant future; and adopt a syncretic belief system in which virtually anything is acceptable as a creed. Vallee has pointed out that the UFO phenomenon apparently utilizes absurdity and deception to confuse witnesses. Such confusion makes human minds more receptive to whatever explanation eventually is provided for sightings, abductions and other alleged UFO-related events.

Since the 1960s, efforts of "debunkers" to explain UFOs as familiar phemomena (such as misidentifications of stars and planets, aircraft, clouds and so forth) have generally been unsuccessful. Although many skeptics maintain, with good reason, that there is no evidence of extraterrestrial visitations to our world in material, "nuts-and-bolts" spacecraft, widespread public faith in an extraterrestrial origin of UFOs endures.

Religious interpretations of the UFO phenomenon have won some adherents. According to one school of thought, UFOs represent heavenly, "angelic" visitations to Earth. An opposing interpretation has it that demonic activity is involved in UFO activity, notably abductions. Supporters of this latter interpretation cite many close parallels between the modern UFO phenomenon and elements of demonic manifestations from the literature on demonology and exorcism. These similarities include deception; a perception of intense coldness in the presence of "aliens" and demons alike; and the reported ability of "extraterrestrials," as well as evil spirits, to appear in many different shapes and sizes. These particular interpretations do not appear to have won large numbers of converts, but they represent the view of small, articulate minorities.

Conspiracy theories have played a colorful part in the UFO phenomenon and apparently have done much to influence public opinion about UFOs. According to many conspiracy theories, the U.S. government supposedly is engaged in a vast, well-organized conspiracy to suppress "the truth" about UFOs. There are various opinions about what this "truth" may be. One widely circulated set of conspiracy theories is based on a rumor that the government has recovered crashed saucers from the southwestern desert of the United States, along with bodies of the spacecraft's alien occupants, and is trying to keep this information from the public. Another conspiracy theory concerns alleged "deals" between the government and extraterrestrials to allow abductions in return for access to advanced alien technology. If conspiracies do indeed exist to suppress such information, then one can only say they appear to have been unsuccessful. Conspirators sometimes are described as a shadowy and vaguely defined "Silence Group" bent on keeping the public ignorant of genuine information on UFOs.

Although a large percentage of the population appears to "believe in" UFOs, it is uncertain what form this belief may take. That the UFO phenomenon exists is undeniable, but the limitations of opinion surveys have made it difficult to ascertain, in many cases, exactly how the phenomenon is interpreted.

Public opinion of the UFO phenomenon is becoming more complex, and therefore less amenable to analysis, as it becomes incorporated into the so-called New Age movement, the vast collection of occult and quasi-occult practices that has become well-established in the 1980s and 1990s. Belief in the extrarerrestrial origin of UFOs now has been compounded with practices such as mediumism (also known as "channeling"), in which occult symbolism and beliefs merge with faith in "extraterrestrials" to produce new, syncretic belief systems that are just beginning to be studied.

See also ABDUCTIONS; ALLENDE LETTERS; ANCIENT ASTRONAUTS; ANGELS; ARNOLD INCIDENT; BELIEF SYSTEMS; CENTRAL INTELLIGENCE AGENCY; CHANNELING; COMMUNICATIONS; CONSPIRACY THEORIES; CONTACTEES; CRASHES; DEALS; DEBUNKERS; DECEPTION; DEMONOLOGY; ENCOUNTER PHENOMENA; INVASION; MESSAGES; MOTION PICTURES; NEW AGE MOVEMENT; OCCULTISM; PARANOIA; POLYMORPHY; RELIGION, UFOS AND; ROSE, FATHER SERAPHIM; ROSWELL INCIDENT; SILENCE GROUP; VALLEE, JACQUES; VON DÄNIKEN, ERICH; WAR OF THE WORLDS, THE.

Pucusana incident, Peru

Late one afternoon in February 1949, a 30-year-old man employed by an oil company allegedly encountered a shiny, discoid UFO on or near the ground while he was driving to Lima. The man approached the disc on foot. When he was about 60 feet from the object, three strange entities reportedly emerged from the craft. They resembled mummies, had joined legs with a single foot, and traveled along the ground with a sliding motion. The beings' skin was said to resemble the cloth used in towels. They asked the man where they were, spoke with him at length and reportedly took him for a ride in their vehicle. Elements of this report are found in certain other UFO encounter stories, such as the aliens' request to know where they were. The one-footed aliens in this story bear a certain resemblance to the "fachan," a figure from the folklore of the British Isles.

See also FACHAN.

Pudasjarvi incident, Finland

This incident allegedly occurred on April 2, 1980, and involved a female motorist who was driving over a bridge when a peculiar fog surrounded her and something deflected her automobile headlights upward. She then reportedly was taken aboard a UFO, placed on a table and examined by three entities that presumably were humanoids, because they were described as "men." The beings gave her a message opposing war and then returned her to her car. She drove home surrounded by the aforementioned fog and suffered from great fatigue for about a week afterward. This case is interesting for its element of "light-bending," an optical effect reported also in certain other UFO encounter stories.

See also LIGHT-BENDING.

Putney Hill globes, New Hampshire, United States

The folklore of New England includes the story of the Putney Hill globes, which bear a strong resemblance to certain modern UFO reports. A forested area on the northern side of Putney Hill, near Hopkinton, New Hampshire, was reportedly the site of numerous luminous "balls" or globes seen floating in the air, usually in the evening, between 1750 and 1800. The globes were said to drift slowly through the air and to display apparently intelligent behavior. According to at least one report, the glowing globes would follow a traveler, halt when he stopped to look at them, and then resume following him as soon as he continued on his way. The globes allegedly kept at least 50 feet distance from whomever they were following. The luminous character, spherical shape and seemingly intelligent behavior of the globes is virtually identical to numerous 20th-century accounts of UFOs and their behavior.

See also ENCOUNTER PHENOMENA; FOO FIGHTERS; SPHERES; UFOS, CHARACTERISTICS OF.

pyramids

Pyramidal structures and formations on Earth and Mars play a part in UFO lore. The "ancient astronauts" phenomenon of the 1960s and 1970s incorporated a suggestion that the pyramids of Egypt were works of a highly advanced extraterrestrial race who visited Earth in prehistory. Archaeological evidence indicates, however, that the technology needed to build the Egyptian pyramids was indeed available to the ancient Egyptians, and that the marks of stone tools have been found at quarries from which limestone blocks for the pyramids were taken. The discovery of a closely spaced set of pyramid-like formations on Mars, as revealed by photographs taken by an American Mariner space probe, has led to speculation that these pyramid formations might be artificial, the works of an ancient race of space travelers that settled on Mars. According to one fanciful and widely published scenario, extraterrestrials landed on Mars ages ago and remained there after finding that Earth's gravitation was too strong to allow them to settle on our world. The pyramids, according to this scenario, may represent huge "arcologies," or pyramidal homes similar to those designed by the Italian architect Paolo Soleri. These arcologies would be far larger than any structures ever built on Earth. The Martian pyramids have attracted considerable attention both in the United States and in the former Soviet Union.

See also ANCIENT ASTRONAUTS; CYDONIA; FACE ON MARS; MARS.

Q

Quaroble incident, France Marius Dewilde, a metalworker, reportedly encountered two small humanoids and a landed UFO on the night of September 1, 1954, around 10:30 P.M. Attracted by the barking of a dog, Dewilde allegedly found himself confronted by a pair of small, heavy-set humanoids wearing what appeared to be diving suits and walking toward a dark craft resting on railroad tracks. Dewilde tried to intercept the humanoids but was paralyzed by a bright orange light that was turned upon him. He could see neither faces nor arms on the entities. An investigation by police and the French Air Force allegedly revealed traces of a very heavy weight, estimated at 30 tons, having rested on the railway ballast. This incident reportedly occurred only two hours after another widely publicized incident at Mourieras, France.

A second incident involving Dewilde at Quaroble allegedly occurred on October 10, 1954. A disc estimated at about 18 feet in diameter allegedly landed on railroad tracks. Several small humanoids got out of the craft and spoke in an unfamiliar language. Then the vehicle disappeared, with no noise or smoke reported. The case allegedly was witnessed by Dewilde and his young son.

See also MOURIERAS INCIDENT.

R

radar Developed during World War II, radar (short for "radio detection and ranging") keeps track of objects in flight by aiming electromagnetic waves at them and analyzing the reflected "echoes" to determine the distance, direction and velocity of the objects. Radar has played an important part in some UFO sightings, notably the Washington, D.C., sightings of 1952, in which sets of UFOs were reportedly detected on radar over the nation's capital on two occasions during the summer. Although radar contacts may have been interpreted in some cases as solid evidence of extraterrestrial spacecraft visiting Earth, radar contacts in such cases are in fact much more ambiguous. Numerous familiar phenomena, both manmade and natural, may create unidentified images on radar screens, and such phenomena should be eliminated as possibilities before any more exotic explanations are considered.

See also ATMOSPHERIC PHENOMENA; TEMPERATURE EFFECTS; WASHINGTON, D.C., SIGHTINGS.

radiation In general terms, radiation is defined as the phenomenon in which an object emits energy as light or heat, or as particles from the disintegration of atomic nuclei. Radiation is also known as "radiant energy" and may take many forms, from radio waves to infrared (heat) radiation. Visible light is a form of radiant energy, although the visible spectrum is only a small segment of the total spectrum of radiant energy. Radiation may occur as particles or as waves, depending on how it is measured. Radioactive materials may give off radiation in the form of alpha or beta particles (relatively low-energy radiation) or gamma rays—high-energy radiation that can be harmful if absorbed in large amounts by the human body. Various forms of radiation—thermal and visual radiation as well as radioactivity—are associated with UFO reports. An example of a UFO phenomenon involving strong visual radiation is the "nocturnal light," a commonly observed category of UFO. Thermal radiation is also reported in some close-encounter incidents, and in some cases allegedly has been strong enough to require medical treatment. Radioactivity appears to be reported infrequently, partly because it requires special equipment to be detected.

See also RADIATION EFFECTS; RADIOACTIVITY.

radiation effects Depending on how one defines "radiation," the radiation effects associated with UFOs are numerous. Radiation in the visual spectrum is, of course, reported in many cases of UFO sightings, such as "nocturnal lights." In some cases, the output of visible radiation from UFOs has made possible an estimate of the energy required to produce such an effect. For example, the energy output in the visual spectrum of a luminous UFO sighted in 1965 in the Caribbean was estimated at 2.3 million watts (or megawatts, MW), approximately the same energy output as from a very powerful automobile engine. The actual total, however, may be far greater than the light output alone would indicate.

Other radiation effects include apparent cases of thermal radiation and of X rays or gamma radiation. There are reports of individuals being burned during close approaches to UFOs. Among the most famous cases in this category is the Falcon Lake, Canada, incident, in which a man allegedly experienced burns on his skin in a pattern matching the configuration of an exhaust outlet on a landed UFO, as well as other bodily symptoms evidently consistent with exposure to a large dose of X rays or gamma radiation over the whole body. Radiation effects, or symptoms indicating such effects, were also reported in the Cash–Landrum incident.

See also CASH–LANDRUM INCIDENT; DR. X INCIDENT; ENCOUNTER PHENOMENA; FALCON LAKE INCIDENT; RADIATION.

radio   Alleged radio contact with "extraterrestrials" has been reported on occasion. One of the most famous reports in this category is that of the so-called Otto incident, in which radio communications allegedly occurred with extraterrestrials. One rumor—unsubstantiated—circulating in Washington, D.C., is that the U.S. government has catalogued more than 100 received transmissions thought to be of extraterrestrial origin. UFOs in close-encounter reports are said to interfere somehow with radio reception in automobiles, although numerous other, less exotic explanations are possible for such effects. Mysterious radio signals from space once were interpreted as evidence that an unmanned space probe from the Epsilon Bootis star system was orbiting Earth and signaling both its presence and its point of origin, but this interpretation of the signals has been rejected.

See also BRACEWELL PROBE; COMMUNICATIONS; EPSILON BOOTIS; OTTO INCIDENT; RUMORS.

radioactivity   Radioactivity—the release of particulate radiation from the disintegration of the nuclei of atoms—has been reported in connection with UFO landings. One case in this category reportedly occurred in December of 1964 near Staunton, Virginia. A motorist allegedly encountered a landed UFO that resembled an upside-down, rotating top approximately 125 feet in diameter. Alpha radiation from the object was reportedly measured at 60,000 counts—or particles detected—per minute. A high radiation reading also is said to have been registered the following month in the area where the object allegedly was sighted.

See also RADIATION; RADIATION EFFECTS.

Raelian movement   A "contactee" cult, the Raelian movement originated in France and has become a prominent feature of the UFO subculture. The goal of the Raelian movement is to set up an embassy on Earth through which extraterrestrials may be contacted. The movement is named for "Rael," also known as Claude Vorilhon, a journalist who reportedly had a close encounter with a UFO and its occu-

pants in a park in France on December 13, 1973. Vorilhon allegedly was told, during a series of such encounters, that the human species was created by extraterrestrials. Vorilhon's instruction supposedly included a visit to the extraterrestrials' planet and encounters there with various eminent "prophets" from human history. The symbol of the Raelian movement, said to represent infinity, is a swastika inside a Star of David. The Raelian movement has many elements in common with the "ancient astronauts" phenomenon, which was popular at the time the Raelian movement arose. For example, the Raelian explanation of the origin of humankind presents aliens advanced in scientific knowledge as both the creators and the divinities of early humans. The myth of Prometheus, who stole fire from the gods for the benefit of humankind, also is reflected in Raelian doctrine, which claims that a renegade group of aliens gave early humans knowledge that was forbidden by the other extraterrestrials.

See also ANCIENT ASTRONAUTS; MYTHOLOGY; TEESDALE INHERITANCE; VON DÄNIKEN, ERICH.

Rainbow, Project   A rumored effort by the U.S. military during World War II to render a ship invisible, Project Rainbow is better known in connection with the "Philadelphia experiment," in which the U.S. Navy allegedly tried to "teleport" a warship from Philadelphia to Norfolk, Virginia. According to other elements of UFO lore, Project Rainbow later became involved with postwar U.S. experiments, in collaboration with German scientists, to study and test-fly extraterrestrial vehicles. Such reports of Project Rainbow must be considered, at best, wild rumor.

Rainbow City   A legendary settlement supposedly built beneath the ice cap of Antarctica by extraterrestrials. The extraterrestrials allegedly left examples of their technology behind at the Antarctic installation. The Rainbow City legend is part of a peculiar literature on extraterrestrials and underground facilities. "Contactee" Albert Bender described a visit to an underground base in Antarctica, where he said he boarded a alien spacecraft, encountered a frightening being, and saw some mysterious process involving liquids being conducted. Subterranean bases also figure in the writings of Ellen Crystall, who in her coverage of the Hudson Valley sightings in the United States suggests that extraterrestrials are constructing subterranean bases on Earth. Underground installations are also an element of the hollow Earth hypothesis, according to which UFOs originate from inside the Earth and travel between the planet's surface and interior through openings at the poles.

See also BENDER MYSTERY; HOLLOW EARTH HYPOTHESIS; HUDSON VALLEY SIGHTINGS; TESLA GLOBES; UNDERGROUND INSTALLATIONS.

Ramayana   The Indian mythological epic *Ramayana* describes an incident, similar to modern UFO abduction reports, in which a young woman named Sita is carried away in some kind of celestial vehicle. The craft is described as radiant and fast moving. Some imagination is required to identify this account as an encounter between a human and an extraterrestrial spacecraft, although such an interpretation appears to be widely accepted among UFO enthusiasts.

See also ABDUCTIONS.

ratchet effect   UFO investigator Jacques Vallee describes this effect as the refusal to surrender certain beliefs about UFOs even after those beliefs have been shown to be unfounded or demonstrably untrue. These beliefs have been "ratcheted" upward, in the manner of a ratchet mechanism, and could not be surrendered, just as a ratchet prevents a mechanism from sliding backward. As an example of the ratchet effect, Vallee cites the belief that extraterrestrial humanoids are being held at an underground base in the United States. This belief actually is held by some UFO researchers. When Vallee tracked down the individual who originated these rumors, Vallee learned that the man actually never had seen the humanoids in question. Nonetheless, believers in the story did not discount it. They began searching instead for evidence that would support their already accepted belief in the aliens at the underground base. Their belief had become too valuable to them to be examined critically, despite the knowledge that their belief was wrong.

See also RUMORS; VALLEE, JACQUES.

Raveo incident, Italy   On August 14, 1947, a witness named R.L. Johannis allegedly saw a discoid UFO on the ground with two small humanoids, about three feet tall or less, beside it. The humanoids reportedly wore blue coveralls with red belts and collars and had large heads with big dark eyes. The eyes were said to lack eyebrows and eyelashes and to be surrounded by what appeared to be a ring of muscle. The beings were said to wear headgear like crash helmets and to have green hands with eight fingers resembling claws. From their belts issued a "vapor" that induced a suffocating feeling in the witness, who also reported feeling an electrical shock. This report is similar in many details to other close-encounter stories from the late 20th century, such as the small, large-eyed humanoids and the incapacitating vapor released by them.

See also HUMANOIDS.

reality   The concept of reality, whether the "ordinary" reality that most people experience most of the time, or altered or "imaginal" reality where UFO abductions and other "border phenomena" are said to occur, has been discussed frequently in the literature on UFOs. Numerous alleged witnesses to close encounters with UFOs and their occupants report afterward that reality seemed altered somehow during such experiences. Time may seem to slow down, for example. Various interpretations are possible of these "alternate" realities, as described in UFO encounter reports. One possibility is that the "imaginal" realities are generated somehow entirely within the witness's own mind. Another possibility is that the "alternate" realities are imposed upon, or somehow revealed to, the human witness by nonhuman entities capable of manipulating human thought and perception. So-called alternate realities in the UFO phenomenon are difficult to study on a quantitative basis, and numerous factors can introduce error into such studies. Much of the evidence for alternate realities in this case is highly anecdotal and, while colorful and thought-provoking, should be viewed with skepticism. For many practical purposes, however, it may not matter whether an individual who claims to have undergone an experience in alternate reality had a purely imaginary experience or not; as long as the person believes that he or she visited some alternate reality that has some kind of objective existence, then the person is likely to behave as if that reality did have objective existence. In other words, if a person truly believes that he or she was abducted by extraterrestrials and taken on a visit to another planet, then the person will believe and behave as if such an incident actually happened, regardless of whether the incident was purely imaginary or had an existence as objective and "real" as a visit with neighbors.

See also ABDUCTIONS; BORDER PHENOMENA; COMMUNICATIONS; ENCOUNTER PHENOMENA; HALLUCINATIONS; HIGH STRANGENESS; HYPNOSIS; IMAGINAL REALM; PERCEPTION; TIME EFFECTS.

real time   In physics, "real time" means time as perceived by a person under ordinary circumstances:

60 seconds to a minute, 60 minutes to an hour, and so forth. In some close-encounter reports, however, witnesses have said that real time did not appear to apply to their experiences. In such an experience, a person may think that he or she has spent only an hour or two in the presence of alleged extraterrestrials, then find, when the visitation ends, that a much longer period has elapsed. The same effect is sometimes reported in spirit lore.

See also MISSING TIME; TENGU.

regressive hypnosis This controversial technique involves hypnotizing a subject and asking him or her, under hypnosis, to recall details of an alleged encounter with UFO occupants. Although a subject may tell colorful stories while under hypnosis, and these stories may carry the ring of conviction, there is reason to doubt their accuracy. Many "recollections" gathered using this technique are believed to be mere products of the subject's imagination, rather than recollections of actual events. When encouraged, under hypnosis, to reach back into memory and recall what the "saucer people" did to him or her, the subject may simply invent a "memory" of an event that never occurred. Reports of UFO "abductions," as related under hypnosis, therefore must be viewed with a certain degree of skepticism, if they are considered as evidence at all.

See also ENCOUNTER PHENOMENA; HYPNOSIS.

Reich, Wilhelm, Austrian-born American psychoanalyst (1897–1957) Known for his devotion to pseudoscience, Wilhelm Reich is viewed by some as a martyr of the UFO movement. He claimed to have made contact with extraterrestrial "machines" in 1954, using a device of his own invention. He believed these spacecraft were propelled by a kind of energy that he dubbed "orgone." This, Reich apparently believed, was the primordial energy that makes life possible. He died in prison after successful prosecution by the U.S. government.

Reich was born in Austria in 1897, served in the Austrian army from 1915 to 1918, and obtained a medical degree in 1922. He appears to have investigated the mysterious "orgone" energy while at the University of Oslo in Norway from 1934 to 1939. Reich moved his activities to the United States in 1939 and continued his work on "orgone" energy there. He reportedly invented a device called the "orgone energy accumulator" in 1940. In 1942, Reich founded the "Orgone Institute" and set up its headquarters at an estate near Rangeley, Maine. Reich's workshop came to be known as Oranur. Reich's work on "orgone" continued over the next several years and led to the "Oranur experiment" in 1950. In this so-called experiment, Reich appears to have been exploring ways in which his imagined orgone energy might be used to counteract the effects of nuclear weapons. The work allegedly involved placing radioactive material in contact with "orgone." What happened in the "experiment" seems unclear, but several individuals at Oranur reportedly fell ill from its effects.

Reich postulated the existence of "deadly orgone energy," or DOR, which traveled in clouds and supposedly resulted in epidemics, drought and desertification. (Reich considered the spread of deserts a threat to human existence on Earth.) Reich's plan to clear DOR clouds from the sky over Orgonon brought about the development of what he called a "cloud buster," a device for generating and halting rainfall. Such a device was said to have been used in Reich's alleged contact with extraterrestrial spacecraft. Reich claimed to have made contact with aerial "luminous objects" on the night of May 12, 1954. In this alleged encounter, two stars in the western sky faded when energy was drained from them, Reich said. Reich reported that he did not repeat this procedure until October 10, 1954, because he feared setting off an interplanetary war. Reich added that the orgone energy utilized by the "spacemen" could not be described according to traditional scientific models.

In 1954, the Food and Drug Administration (FDA) issued an injunction claiming that Reich's orgone energy was nonexistent, and that Reich's work amounted to "misbranding." The FDA won the case against Reich. He was sentenced to jail and died after eight months in prison.

See also PSEUDOSCIENCE.

reincarnation An occult belief that a human soul may be incarnated in a series of bodies over successive "lifetimes" on Earth, reincarnation is a minor element of the UFO phenomenon and demonstrates the occult associations of that phenomenon. In recent years, it has become almost fashionable in the United States to speak of one's imagined previous incarnations on distant planets. Reincarnation also exemplifies the strong Hinduistic influence on the belief systems underlying the UFO phenomenon.

Reincarnation figured in the alleged Tujunga Canyon abduction case in California, in which a young woman claimed to have been marked on her back with a glyph resembling the astrological symbol for the planet Jupiter. The mark, she indicated, was the extraterrestrials' way of identifying her in successive incarnations. (How such a mark would do so is difficult to imagine, because the person's body would decay and become unidentifiable soon after death. The individual then would have to be tracked down and marked again.)

See also ABDUCTIONS; ASTROLOGY; HINDUISM; OCCULTISM; PSEUDOSCIENCE; TUJUNGA CANYON CASE.

relativity theory Albert Einstein's theory of relativity is applicable to the UFO controversy because the theory rests on the assumption that no physical object in the known universe can exceed the velocity of light, approximately 186,000 miles per second. Experimental evidence has substantiated this assumption. This "light barrier" imposes a "time barrier" on interstellar travel. Because distances between stars are so vast, many years—probably much longer than a human lifetime—would be required for a journey even to the nearest star. This set of limitations indicates that any space-traveling extraterrestrials, if forced to obey such constraints, would be unable to complete a voyage to Earth within their lifetimes, unless they happened to be extremely long-lived by our standards.

Attempts have been made to overcome this obstacle to interstellar travel. One suggestion, based on a provision of relativity theory, is that extraterrestrials in a spacecraft traveling close to the velocity of light would experience "slowed-down" time. For the space travelers, time would pass more slowly than on Earth or on their home planet, so that the voyagers might complete a mission requiring centuries in, by their reckoning aboard the spacecraft, a relatively brief period. This "loophole" in relativity theory has been invoked to support the extraterrestrial hypothesis (ETH), according to which UFOs represent actual visitations to Earth by "extraterrestrial biological entities" (EBEs) in material spacecraft. Supposedly, a sufficiently advanced civilization of EBEs would have found by now a way to travel close to the velocity of light, and thus make the ETH a plausible explanation of the UFO phenomenon. Such speculations are virtually unsupported by any acceptable evidence, however, and as a rule are not taken seriously outside the community of ETH and EBE enthusiasts.

See also EXTRATERRESTRIAL BIOLOGICAL ENTITIES; EXTRATERRESTRIAL HYPOTHESIS.

religion, UFOs and Especially in the last three decades of the 20th century, there has been an intensive effort to interpret the UFO phenomenon in a religious context. Some students of the phenomenon have seen it as an attempt to replace traditional Judeo–Christian belief with a new belief system that substitutes a pseudoscientific view of extraterrestrial visitations for biblical accounts of God's relationship to humankind and the activities of angels. This new belief system, exemplified by the "ancient astronauts" phenomenon of the 1960s and 1970s, has been incorporated to some extent into the New Age movement.

The Old Testament story of Ezekiel's vision has been interpreted as a highly symbolic account of a UFO encounter. This interpretation, however, has been discredited, because it does not appear sustainable when the story of Ezekiel's vision is read in the context of the Old and New Testaments.

Some traditionalists in the Christian religious community have interpreted UFOs as a demonic campaign to undermine faith in Christ and to prepare the way for the arrival of the Antichrist. These traditionalists cite numerous parallels between reports of "extraterrestrials" and the behavior of evil spirits as reported in the centuries-old Christian literature on demonology.

Even among "contactees," there has been a tendency to interpret encounters with so-called extraterrestrials in terms of traditional Christian faith. Albert Bender, for example, interpreted a communication from an "exalted one" during his UFO encounters as an account of God's relationship to the rest of the universe.

Numerous alleged communications from "aliens" mention God or an unnamed, supreme Creator, although it is not clear from many of these messages exactly what the "extraterrestrials" believe about God. Christ is mentioned in some reported communications from extraterrestrials, but often in a manner that denies or de-emphasizes Christ's divinity.

Some observers of the UFO phenomenon find it significant that the "ancient astronauts" phenomenon, in which the "gods" of antiquity are viewed as space travelers who supposedly visited Earth in ancient times, arose at a time when traditional Christian faith was declining in the West. Similar observations have been made concerning the rise of the New Age movement, with its close connections to the UFO phenomenon. There is a strong element of Hinduistic belief in the UFO phenomenon. Occultist influence also is prominent in the UFO phenomenon, and occult practices such as channeling and automatic writing are commonly used in alleged contacts with extraterrestrials.

The religious element of the UFO phenomenon has included the rise of numerous quasi-religious cults based on faith in the existence of "extraterrestrials." These cults tend to emphasize the anticipated arrival, in force, of extraterrestrials on Earth at

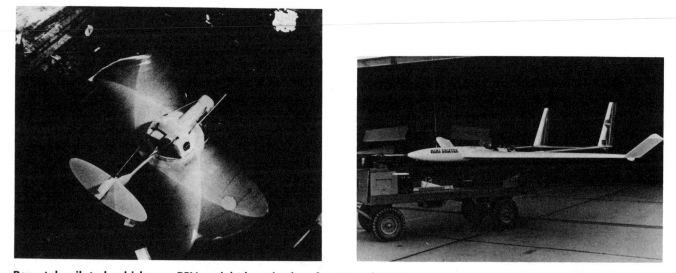

Remotely piloted vehicles, or RPVs, might be mistaken for UFOs. (NASA)

some time in the not-too-distant future. The activities and true purposes of these cults often are mysterious.

See also AETHERIUS SOCIETY; ANCIENT ASTRONAUTS; ANTICHRIST; BELIEF SYSTEMS; BENDER MYSTERY; CHANNELING; CHRIST AND CHRISTIANITY; COMMUNICATIONS; CULTS; DEMONOLOGY; ENCOUNTER PHENOMENA; EXALTED ONES; EZEKIEL; HINDUISM; INCUBI AND SUCCUBI; MESSAGES; NEW AGE MOVEMENT; OCCULTISM; OUIJA BOARD; RAELIAN MOVEMENT; ROSE, FATHER SERAPHIM; TEILHARD DE CHARDIN, PIERRE; TIBET; UNARIUS FOUNDATION; VON DÄNIKEN, ERICH.

remotely piloted vehicles   Also known as RPVs, these are small, unmanned, remotely guided aircraft that are built in many different configurations and may account for certain UFO sightings. RPVs are widely used for military reconnaissance and may exhibit many commonly reported characteristics of UFOs, including rapid acceleration and the ability to hang stationary in the sky. Because an RPV can carry out maneuvers that are difficult or impossible for larger, manned aircraft, an observer at a distance might easily mistake an RPV for an extraterrestrial spacecraft.

See also AIRCRAFT, UFOS AND.

remote viewing   An occult practice, remote viewing allegedly involves seeing objects at a considerable distance through the use of one's "inner eye." Remote viewing is a small but colorful element of UFO lore. Various "contactees" have reported seeing vistas of distant planets, although these visions have tended to be proven incorrect when information was available from independent sources

such as space probes. Swedish visionary Emanuel Swedenborg reportedly used remote viewing to observe inhabitants of other planets, which turned out to be uninhabited when visited by spacecraft in the 20th century. Though no more than rumors, reports have circulated in recent years that the United States military has conducted experiments in remote viewing and detected at least one UFO by this method. Remote viewing generally is considered to be either fraudulent or, at best, a chimera of pseudoscience.

See also ASTRONOMY; BENDER MYSTERY; HOMEWORLDS; OCCULTISM; PSEUDOSCIENCE; SWEDENBORG, EMANUEL.

repairs   One curious element of close-encounter reports involving UFOs is the apparent need to repair such craft on a frequent basis during their visits to our world. Many close-encounter stories describe UFO occupants emerging from their craft to conduct repairs. These alleged repairs often are made within sight of homes or highways or other points from which human witnesses could observe the operation easily. Unless one is prepared to dismiss all such reports as mere fantasies, it is difficult to imagine why repairs would have to be conducted so often on such highly advanced vehicles, and why the repairs would be conducted in places that would leave the UFO occupants so highly visible and vulnerable to attack. Some students of the UFO phenomenon have suggested that incidents such as these may not be actual repair operations at all, but rather staged events intended to give humans an opportunity to view the craft and their occupants, and to spread the UFO mythology further. There is no universal agreement on who or what might benefit from such staged encounters.

See also ABBIATE GUAZZONE INCIDENT; AIRSHIPS; ENCOUNTER PHENOMENA.

Report from Iron Mountain

A study by one "John Doe" (said to be economist John Kenneth Galbraith), *Report from Iron Mountain on the Possibility and Desirability of Peace* was published in 1967. The study considered the possibility that belief in UFOs might be used to improve prospects for peace and redirect humankind toward a unified social order. In theory, the report pointed out, a perceived threat from extraterrestrial beings might provide an incentive for human civilization to abandon its internal strife and present a unified front against the alleged menace from alien beings. A threat from "extraterrestrials" was one of several suggested means for helping to unify human society and discourage warfare on Earth. The report presented other possible scenarios including the threat of ecological catastrophe. The study also suggested that some flying saucer reports were actually experiments in manipulating public belief, with the aim of reshaping society by encouraging belief in hostile extraterrestrial powers menacing Earth. The report ultimately dismissed the threat-from-aliens scenario, however, as "unpromising" and encouraged investigation of other ways to manufacture "fictitious . . . enemies" that might serve to unify humankind. *Report from Iron Mountain* treats the UFO phenomenon from a viewpoint complementary to that of prominent UFO investigator Jacques Vallee, who has argued that UFOs may constitute a system to control human belief.

See also BELIEF SYSTEMS; METALOGIC; VALLEE, JACQUES.

reptoids

A reported category of extraterrestrial beings, "reptoids" are said to be humanoids with the skin of reptiles. Their behavior is reportedly characterized by cruelty toward, and even sexual abuse of, human abductees. Reptoids allegedly show a strong aversion to the name of Christ. The characteristics of reptoids are similar to those of the Devil as described in the New Testament, which characterizes Satan as a serpent or dragon. In that context, the reptoids' alleged aversion to Christ's name may be significant.

See also DEMONOLOGY; HUMANOIDS.

Reynolds, Mack (1917–)

In the 1960s, American science fiction writer Mack Reynolds (real name Dallas McCord Reynolds) wrote a series of stories involving a fictional alien society—the "Dawnworlds"—arranged along Hinduistic lines and resembling the basically Hinduistic social order of alleged extraterrestrial societies described by some modern UFO "contactees." The alien society in Reynolds' stories had its "Brahmins," tremendously advanced intellects capable of communicating with humans by mental telepathy, as well as lower castes of extremely handsome but unintelligent humanoids. Reynolds's aliens have a policy of destroying all life on the homeworlds of any intelligent species that commits criminal acts, such as stealing technology, against the Dawnworlds. This is another point of similarity between Reynolds's extraterrestrials and the beings mentioned in certain UFO contact reports, who are said to be capable of murder and unwilling to part with any samples of their technology.

See also HINDUISM; TELEPATHY.

Robertson panel, United States

Established in 1953 as an official scientific advisory panel to review UFO cases, the Robertson panel was headed by physicist Dr. H.P. Robertson of the California Institute of Technology. The Robertson panel examined photographs and motion picture film of alleged UFOs and studied reports supplied by the Air Technical Intelligence Center.

The panel concluded that UFOs represented no "direct physical threat" to America's national security, and that there was no evidence for an extraterrestrial origin of UFOs. The panelists added, "we firmly believe that there is no residuum of cases which indicates phenomena which are attributable to foreign objects capable of hostile acts, and there is no evidence that the phenomena indicate a need for the revision of current scientific concepts."

The panel did perceive potential danger, however, in widespread public attention to the UFO phenomenon. "[The] continued emphasis on the reporting of these phenomena does . . . result in a threat to the orderly functioning of the protective organs of the body politic." The group continued: "We cite as examples the clogging of channels of communication by irrelevant reports, the danger of being led by continued false alarms to ignore real indications of hostile action, and the cultivation of a morbid national psychology in which skillful hostile propaganda could induce hysterical behavior and harmful distrust of duly constituted authority."

To neutralize such perceived dangers, the Robertson panel recommended that America's national security agencies "take immediate steps to strip the Unidentified Flying Objects of the special status they have been given and the aura of mystery they have unfortunately acquired; [and] . . . institute policies on intelligence training and public education designed to prepare the material defenses and the morale of the country to recognize most promptly and to react most effectively to true indications of hostile intent or action."

The panel recommended "an integrated program designed to reassure the public of the total lack of inimical forces behind the [UFO] phenomena, to train personnel to reject false indications quickly and effectively, and to strengthen regular channels for the evaluation of and prompt reaction to true indications of hostile measures."

A censored version of the originally secret report—minus the references to UFO reports blocking communication channels, interfering with America's air defenses, inducing hysteria and undermining trust in public authorities—was made public in 1958. This censorship has been interpreted as a government effort to conceal "secret" information that public authorities supposedly knew in the early 1950s about UFOs. Such an interpretation is consistent with various hypotheses alleging a high-level conspiracy to suppress supposedly dangerous knowledge in the government's possession about UFOs.

UFO debunker Philip Klass examined the declassified text of the Robertson report, however, and pointed out that the panel's concerns over UFO reports undermining national defense seemed legitimate when the report was written in the early 1950s. The Soviets might have used their own version of "UFOs," such as large numbers of weather balloons equipped with flashing lights, released from ships offshore, to "saturate" and overwhelm U.S. air defenses. Such concerns were a good reason for the Robertson panel's conclusions to be "sanitized" before release to the public, Klass added.

The Robertson panel also has been criticized for conducting only a cursory review of the materials on UFOs, and then only examining information provided by the government itself.

See also CENTRAL INTELLIGENCE AGENCY; CHADWELL MEMORANDUM; CONSPIRACY THEORIES.

robots   Beings described as "robots" are mentioned in many UFO close-encounter reports. The so-called robots are said to vary greatly in form and behavior. Some allegedly have humanoid form. The robots are said to perform many different operations, from dismembering animal corpses to emitting clouds of apparently soporific gas.

See also HUMANOIDS; TECHNOLOGY.

Robozer incident, Russia   On August 15, 1663, witnesses in the vicinity of a monastery near Mos-

cow reported seeing great flames arise from an area about 450 feet wide on Lake Robozer, a lake slightly more than a mile across. Blue smoke accompanied the flames, and two luminous objects appeared as well. The flames vanished for about an hour, then reappeared several hundred yards from their initial location. After 10 minutes, these flames subsided again, and then reappeared one last time. The flames emitted great heat and were accompanied by a loud noise. Witnesses who approached the flames in a boat received minor burns. Fish were reported killed. Red material resembling rust was allegedly seen on the water after the fiery phenomena ended. The Robozer incident bears some similarity to later reports of UFOs arising from bodies of water.

See also AQUATIC OBJECTS; RUSSIA.

rockets   Many UFO sightings have been attributed to misidentifications of rocket launches. A rocket launch at night may illuminate the sky and produce light effects like those of a classic UFO, such as a luminous object rising in the sky. If seen from a distance of some miles, the rocket may be silent and create the impression of a classic UFO, noiseless and luminous. Such launches from the Soviet military complex at Plesetsk in the northwestern U.S.S.R. are thought to have generated some UFO reports from northern Europe before the breakup of the Soviet Union. Rocket stages re-entering the atmosphere after launch also may produce reports of UFOs, as in the Zond 4 incident. In certain UFO sightings, alleged extraterrestrial spacecraft are described as us-

Robots figure in some UFO reports. (D. Ritchie)

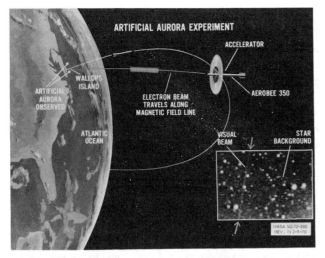

Rockets and experiments borne on them may be interpreted as UFOs. (NASA)

ing rockets or similar propulsion systems on launch and in flight. The use of relatively primitive chemical rockets in such cases is difficult to reconcile with the supposedly advanced propulsion technologies (magnetic drives, anti-matter reactors and the like) widely attributed to "alien" craft in UFO lore.

See also PLESETSK; ZOND 4 INCIDENT.

rockets, UFOs and   The development of large liquid- and solid-fueled rockets has accompanied the origin and development of the modern UFO phenomenon, and in many cases rockets are thought to have given rise to reports of UFOs. The light from the launch of a large rocket at night, for example, may be misinterpreted as a UFO. The lore of UFOs contains accounts of UFOs intercepting rockets and missiles in flight, but these reports are less than fully substantiated. A curious element of some UFO reports is a rocket-like flame that is said to emanate from certain UFOs. If UFOs truly were extraterrestrial spacecraft utilizing technology much advanced over our own (anti-gravity, for example), then it is difficult to understand why such craft would require the relatively primitive technology of rocket propulsion. Reports of rocket-propelled "alien" UFOs may be viewed as cultural elements of the UFO phenomenon, in that such reports reflect the technology of the observer's age and culture.

See also ATLAS INCIDENT; TECHNOLOGY.

Rockland, Texas, incident, United States   One of the "airship" sightings from the United States in the late 1890s, this incident allegedly occurred near Rockland, Texas, one night in 1897. One John Barclay had gone to bed when he heard his dog barking

and arose to investigate. He also heard a peculiar whining sound.

Hovering about 15 feet above his yard was an oblong flying machine with "brilliant" lights. Barclay thought he recognized it as one of the mysterious airships he had read about. The craft allegedly circled the property several times, then landed in a pasture near Barclay's home.

Armed with a rifle, Barclay went out to investigate and met an ordinary looking man whom he presumed to be an occupant of the ship. The visitor asked for the use of some equipment including lubricating oil and cold chisels. He handed Barclay a $10 bill to pay for the hardware.

Barclay complied with the man's request and asked for a closer look at the craft. The visitor refused to let him examine the ship closely. He then thanked Barclay and prepared to depart. Barclay asked where the craft was from, and was told, "From anywhere, but we will be in Greece day after tomorrow." The visitor boarded the craft, which departed quickly with a "whirling" noise.

This account bears numerous similarities to UFO encounter cases reported in the 20th century, including the witness's previous acquaintance with the phenomenon; the visitor's humanoid appearance and absurd remarks; the bright aerial lights; the remarkable maneuvers of the vehicle; and the alleged unrest of the dog in the UFO's presence.

See also ABSURDITY; AIRSHIPS; ANIMALS, UFOS AND; ENCOUNTER PHENOMENA; TECHNOLOGY.

Rogo hypothesis   D. Scott Rogo, an editor of *Fate* magazine, formulated the following hypothesis for testing in UFO abduction cases: Whenever an abduction experience is revealed, psychological investigation of the witness's life would show that the person was experiencing a crisis at the time or was recovering from psychological "trauma." Rogo proposed paying more attention, through psychological and physical investigations, to the abductees themselves, rather than to the alleged events they relate.

See also ABDUCTIONS; PSYCHOLOGICAL EFFECTS.

Rome incidents, Italy   The city of Rome allegedly witnessed a spectacular aerial display in October and November of 1954, as an entire fleet of supposed UFOs maneuvered overhead. The Rome incidents were part of a wave of UFO sightings occurring in Italy and appear to have begun with a sighting, on October 30, of two unidentified white objects above the Church of Santa Maria Maggiore. On November 6, several dozen white UFOs appeared above the city, moving at speeds of up to approximately 840 miles per hour. The objects were described as "white dots" and in some cases left a trail behind. The objects sometimes appeared in formations including V shapes and diamonds. Around noontime, two formations of such objects met in the sky above Vatican City, formed a "St. Andrew's Cross" (similar to the pattern of bars on the American Confederate flag used during the Civil War), then altered formation to assume more of a conventional X shape before dividing into two curved formations and moving apart. A few minutes later, the objects returned in various formations, though this time they were not over the Vatican. A shiny, filamentous material later dubbed "angel hair" reportedly fell from the sky on this occasion, but evaporated within a few hours. Similar events, including another fall of "angel hair," allegedly occurred the following day. The UFOs returned on November 12. Two UFOs reportedly flew over the Vatican Observatory at Castel Gandolfo near Rome, noiselessly and at high speed.

See also ANGEL HAIR.

Room 801   Located in an Air Ministry building in London, Room 801 was allegedly a central "clearinghouse" for collection and study of UFO reports in Britain. The existence of Room 801 was reported in 1957. Only authorized personnel were allowed to enter. The room reportedly included a large map of Britain with thousands of colored pins on it, representing UFO sightings over the British Isles. There was said to be an especially heavy concentration of sightings around Norwich in East Anglia.

Rose, Father Seraphim (Eugene) (1934–1982)
An Eastern Orthodox Christian theologian, Hieromonk Father Seraphim Rose was also a prolific author and co-founder of the St. Herman of Alaska Brotherhood, a monastic community in Platina, California.

Before adopting a monastic way of life, Rose graduated from Pomona College and the University of California at Berkeley. Trained in linguistics, philosophy and many other fields in addition to theology, Rose studied UFO phenomena in light of the teachings of the Orthodox church and concluded that many such phenomena were manifestations of demonic activity. Reporting on the upsurge of public interest in UFOs during the 1970s, he noted the connection between experiences of UFO close encounters and occultism. Rose placed UFOs in the category of "signs" that are expected, according to traditional Christian teaching, to precede the coming of the Antichrist and, following the Antichrist's brief reign over all the Earth, the second coming of Christ. Citing the suggestion that UFOs constitute a "control system" for influencing human beliefs, Rose wrote that UFOs might serve to draw humankind away from traditional Christian faith and persuade the public instead to worship as divine a diabolical presence that announced its advent with spectacular and mysterious light shows in the skies. Rose noted numerous and close similarities between UFO close-encounter phenomena and manifestations of demonic activity as described in the experiences of Eastern Orthodox saints. Other modern observers of the UFO phenomenon have reached essentially the same conclusions as Rose did.

See also CYPRIAN, SAINT, THE FORMER SORCERER; DEMONOLOGY; ENCOUNTER PHENOMENA; OCCULTISM; SINISTRARI, LODOVICO MARIA; VALENS INCIDENT; VALLEE, JACQUES.

Rosicrucians   Many elements of the UFO phenomenon have parallels in the history of the Rosicrucians, an ancient occult society. The Rosicrucian society supposedly was founded by one Christian Rosenkreutz ("Rose-Cross"), a German philosopher who traveled in the Holy Land in the late 1300s and received instruction there from learned Arabs, then returned to Europe in 1401 to share his newly acquired knowledge with his friends. There is disagreement as to whether or not such a person as Christian Rosenkreutz actually existed. In any event, the society had acquired a notorious reputation by the early 17th century in Europe. Early in March of 1623, Parisians found mysterious placards posted all over the city, with the following message: "We, the Deputies of the principal College of the brethren of the Rose-cross, have taken up our abode, visible and invisible, in this city, by the grace of the Most High, towards whom are turned the hearts of the just. We shew and teach without books or signs, and speak all sorts of languages in the countries where we dwell, to draw mankind, our fellows, from error and from death."

Some weeks later, two sensational books appeared about the Rosicrucians. One was titled *The frightful Compacts entered into between the Devil and the pretended "Invisibles"; with their damnable Instruction, the deplorable Ruin of their Disciples, and their miserable end.* The other book was called *Examination of the new unknown Cabala of the Rose-cross, who have lately inhabited the City of Paris; with the History of their Manners, the Wonders worked by them, and many other particulars.*

These books sold well. Here is one account of their contents quoted in Charles Mackay's 1854 book *Extraordinary Popular Delusions and the Madness of Crowds:*

It was said in these volumes that the Rosicrucian society consisted of six-and-thirty persons in all, who had renounced their baptism and hope of resurrection. That it was not by means of good angels, as they pretended, that they worked their prodigies; but that it was the devil who gave them power to transport themselves from one end of the world to the other with the rapidity of thought; to speak all languages; to have their purses always full of money, however much they might spend; to be invisible, and penetrate into the most secret places, in spite of fastenings of bolts and bars; and to be able to tell the past and the future. . . . It was believed . . . that persons of a mysterious aspect used to visit the inns and hotels of Paris, and eat of the best meats and drink of the best wines, and then suddenly melt away into thin air when the landlord came with the reckoning. That gentle maidens who went to bed alone, often awoke in the night and found men in bed with them, of shape more beautiful than the Grecian Apollo, who immediately became invisible when an alarm was raised. It was also said that many persons found large heaps of gold in their houses without knowing from whence they came. All Paris was in alarm. No man thought himself secure of his goods, no maiden of her virginity, or wife of her chastity, while these Rosicrucians were abroad.

While this excitement continued, Mackay reported, another placard appeared: "If anyone desires to see the brethren of the Rose-cross from curiosity only, he will never communicate with us. But if his will really induces him to inscribe his name in the register of our brotherhood, we, who can judge the thoughts of all men, will convince him of the truth of our promises. For this reason we do not publish to the world the place of our abode. Thought alone, in unison with the sincere will of those who desire to know us, is sufficient to make us known to them, or them to us."

Mackay summarizes the mythology of the Rosicrucians as follows:

They said there were no such horrid, unnatural, and disgusting beings as the incubi and succubi, and the innumerable grotesque imps that man had believed in for so many ages. Man was not surrounded with enemies like those, but with myriads of beautiful and beneficent beings, all anxious to do him service. The air was peopled with sylphs, the water with undines or naiads, the bowels of the earth with gnomes, and the fire with salamanders. All these beings were the friends of man, and desired nothing so much as that [humans] should purge themselves of all uncleanness, and thus be enabled to see and converse with them. They possessed great power, and were unrestrained by the barriers of space or the obstruction of matter.

But these creatures were also said to be touchy and "revengeful" at times because they envied humans their souls, which the invisible beings supposedly did not have.

The parallels between the Rosicrucians' career and the modern UFO phenomenon are close and numerous. For example, the Rosicrucians had mysterious origins, became the subject of sensational books, caused public alarm, made cryptic theological references, allegedly practiced contact by thought, spoke many languages, reportedly practiced teleportation and apparent telepathy, delivered vague promises of blessings for humankind, had demonic associations, were the object of inconclusive official investigations, assured the public that their intentions were benevolent, and were said to be able to pass through material objects and travel great distances instantaneously. The Rosicrucians still exist, but are at low ebb.

See also ENCOUNTER PHENOMENA; OCCULTISM.

Roswell incident One of the most celebrated cases in the history of UFO studies, the so-called Roswell incident was the alleged discovery in 1947, near Roswell, New Mexico, of wreckage of a purportedly extraterrestrial spacecraft, along with the bodies of its occupants.

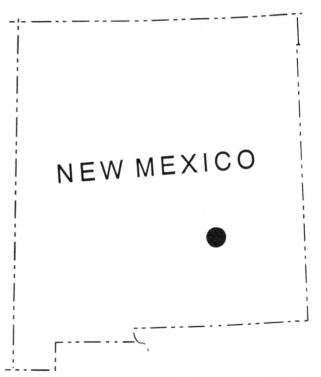

In the Roswell, New Mexico, incident, U.S. military allegedly recovered a crashed saucer. (U.S. Geological Survey)

A disc-shaped object was sighted over Roswell on the evening of July 2, 1947, moving northwest. The next day, wreckage, presumably from the flying object, was found scattered over a wide area some 75 miles northwest of Roswell. The military recovered some of the wreckage, which consisted in part of material resembling (but not identical to) tinfoil, as well as small lightweight and flexible beams bearing markings similar to hieroglyphics. A piece of metal foil found among the wreckage was very light but nonetheless so strong that it could not be dented with sledgehammer blows, one report said. The wreckage was ordered collected and shipped to Wright Field (now Wright-Patterson Air Force Base), Ohio, for study. At a press conference, the wreckage was described as the remains of a weather balloon and a tinfoil radar reflector attached to it. Besides this area of wreckage, there reportedly was another crash site near Roswell, and at this location the main body of a metallic vehicle was recovered, together with the bodies of its occupants. The beings were described as having round heads, small eyes and hairless bodies, with yellow or orange skin having a beaded texture like that of reptilian skin. The heads were much bigger than those of humans in proportion to the rest of the body. The bodies were clad in one-piece gray outfits without zippers, buttons or belts.

On the public record, however, there appears to be no proof that anything extraordinary was actually recovered at Roswell in July 1947, nor that any official cover-up of evidence took place. One report has it that a high-level group of experts within the United States government, called "MAJESTIC 12," was formed to study the evidence supposedly gathered from the Roswell "crash," but this story appears to be based on a document of questionable authenticity.

See also AZTEC INCIDENT; CRASHES; MAJESTIC 12.

rumors   The rumor mill has worked actively on the UFO phenomenon from the very beginning. Now a vast body of rumor surrounds the subject of UFOs. In many writings about UFOs, rumor has been cited as fact, and as a result the truth about many UFO-related incidents is difficult to determine. For example, numerous rumors circulate about alleged cover-ups designed to hide "the truth"—such as information on saucers and "extraterrestrial" bodies recovered after UFO crashes—from the public. Other widely circulated rumors include stories of a vast underground tunnel network connecting UFO-related facilities throughout the western United States; "aliens" working side by side with scientists in Nazi Germany to develop flying saucers for Hitler; extraterrestrials collaborating with American engineers to develop and test-fly anti-gravity spacecraft; laboratories where "hybrid" babies, half human and half alien, are supposedly harbored in great tanks of liquid; Antarctic bases where aliens process seawater for some valuable but mysterious ingredient; secret "deals" between the government and extraterrestrials, allowing aliens to abduct humans in return for access to the aliens' technology; and aliens both advising and masquerading as members of the federal government. The proliferation of rumors concerning UFOs may serve to bring order—even if a merely deceptive order—to the vast and often confusing body of information on UFOs.

See also ANTARCTICA; ANTI-GRAVITY; BASES; BENDER MYSTERY; CENTRAL INTELLIGENCE AGENCY; CHADWELL MEMORANDUM; CONSPIRACY THEORIES; CRASHES; HOAXES; PARANOIA; ROBERTSON PANEL; TUNNELS; UNDERGROUND INSTALLATIONS.

Russia   Russia has a long history of UFO sightings. Some reasonably well-documented reports are centuries old. Under the former Soviet Union, UFO research in Russia appears to have been both encouraged and discouraged at various times. Although the tightly controlled Soviet press was allowed to speculate on occasion about UFOs and the possibility of extraterrestrial life, official research into the UFO phenomenon appears to have been stifled, as in the case of the Stolyarov committee. Research continued under the Soviet regime, but on an unofficial level. Students of the UFO phenomenon met and corresponded in private, serving as an "invisible college" (in UFO investigator Jacques Vallee's words) to study the subject. Sometimes, speculation about UFOs took the form of science fiction stories. Science fiction writer Alexander Kazantsev, for example, used short stories to analyze the hypothesis that the great Tunguska explosion was actually the wreck of an extraterrestrial spacecraft.

Following the fall of communism, public discussion of the UFO phenomenon increased, as did published reports of sightings. Among the most famous sightings of the post-communist era in Russia were the Voronezh sightings, in which large humanoids were reported seen next to their spacecraft in a park. Russian investigators reportedly have used occult or quasi-occult methods to investigate UFO sightings and alleged landings. One such method is "biolocation," which appears to be merely the ancient occult practice of dowsing.

See also BIOLOCATION; ROBOZER INCIDENT; RYBINSK INCIDENT; ST. NILUS INCIDENT; STOLYAROV COMMITTEE; TUNGUSKA EVENT; VORONEZH SIGHTINGS.

Rybinsk incident, Russia   This incident involves a report of guided missiles being fired at, and evidently destroyed by, a giant UFO over Rybinsk, approximately 90 miles from Moscow, in the summer of 1961. The missiles were part of a new defense system installed around Moscow. A gigantic discoidal UFO reportedly appeared at about 12 miles' altitude, along with several smaller discoidal UFOs. A salvo of missiles was fired. All the missiles exploded about two miles from the target. Before more missiles could be launched, the smaller UFOs reportedly took action to neutralize all electrical equipment at the missile facility. The equipment resumed functioning when the small UFOs departed. This report bears certain similarities to the alleged destruction of an American Atlas missile by a UFO.

See also ATLAS INCIDENT.

S

S–4 A rumored U.S. government project involving the study of captured extraterrestrial spacecraft and bodies of aliens. One craft allegedly under study by S–4 was a disc about 40 feet in diameter, housing an anti-matter reactor. The tale of S–4 is an example of the numerous rumors surrounding the UFO phenomenon and the U.S. government's alleged involvement in research on UFO technology.

See also AREA 51; RUMORS; TECHNOLOGY.

Sadaim According to Hebrew lore, the Sadaim were beings intermediate between humans and angels. In Greek, the Sadaim were known as daimonas, or demons. The Sadaim were thought to possess extraordinary powers, including the ability to communicate with aerial beings.

See also DEMONOLOGY.

Sagrada Familia incident, Brazil In August 1963, a reported UFO encounter case from Brazil appeared to resemble the Voronezh sightings reported from Russia almost 20 years later. Three boys drawing water from a well near the town of Sagrada Familia allegedly witnessed a large sphere hovering over the treetops. From the sphere descended, on a pair of beams of light, a humanoid some 10 feet tall, wearing a transparent helmet. The being reportedly had what was described as an "eye" in the middle of its forehead. The entity moved as if preparing to seize one of the boys. Another boy picked up a rock to throw at the intruder but found himself literally paralyzed by the entity's gaze. The being then returned to the sphere on the twin beams of light. Very tall beings similar to the entity described in this case, as well as an account of paralysis and the detail

of the "eye" or similar structure in the forehead, were elements of the Voronezh sightings in Russia in 1989.

See also HUMANOIDS; PARALYSIS; THIRD EYE; VORONEZH SIGHTINGS.

Saint, Project An early space defense system, Project Saint (short for Satellite Interceptor or Satellite Inspector) would have used missile-launched interceptors to investigate and destroy enemy spacecraft. Project Saint was an early plan related to what would become the Strategic Defense Initiative, or SDI. Project Saint and SDI both have been interpreted, though with no persuasive evidence for such a view, as possible responses to a perceived national security threat from UFOs.

See also STRATEGIC DEFENSE INITIATIVE.

Saint Francis Convent sighting, New Jersey, United States Several weeks after the Wanaque reservoir sightings in New Jersey, another sighting of a UFO at low altitude was reported at the Saint Francis Convent near Wanaque. More sightings occurred in the area in October 1966. The sightings were part of an extraordinary UFO "wave" in 1966. One official explanation of the sightings attributed them to helicopters carrying bright lights.

See also WANAQUE DAM INCIDENT.

St. Nilus incident The spiritual literature of Russian Orthodoxy includes a story that sounds much like a modern UFO abduction case. Shortly after the death of St. Nilus of Sora in the 15th century, a certain priest and his son were living at a monastery that the saint had founded. According to the story, a mysterious stranger (actually a demon) kidnapped the boy from the monastery and carried him at great speed into a deep forest, where he placed the boy in a cabin. The priest and the monks prayed to St. Nilus for help in finding and recovering the youngster, and the saint released the boy by striking the window-frame of the cabin with his staff. The evil spirit who had kidnapped the boy was ordered to return him to the monastery, and did so. Then the kidnapping spirit vanished from sight. The experience is said to have had profound psychological effects on the boy, and the father was so frightened that he left the monastery with his son.

Saitama incident, Japan Reported from Japan's Saitama province on October 3, 1978, this incident involved a man who was driving his automobile up a mountain in the company of his young daughter. A beam of light allegedly was directed somehow onto the car and struck the girl. An orange glow then covered her body. The car's engine reportedly failed, and a small entity with large ears was seen at a window of the automobile. Then power returned to the automobile, and the man drove away. The man and his daughter both are said to have experienced minor physical symptoms such as headache following the incident, but they recovered. The various elements of this report—a beam of light, an engine failure, and an entity seen at a car window— are familiar to students of UFO encounters, and the description of the big-eared creature at the window resembles the account of beings reported seen in the Kelly–Hopkinsville incident in the United States.

See also JAPAN; KELLY–HOPKINSVILLE INCIDENT; VEHICLE EFFECTS.

Salandin incident, United Kingdom A reported near-collision between a Royal Auxiliary Air Force fighter plane and a UFO, the Salandin incident occurred on October 14, 1954, as Flight-Lieutenant J.R. Salandin was flying his Meteor Mk.8 aircraft near the Thames estuary. He saw two other Meteor fighters behind and above him, and watched them. The he saw two circular objects flying rapidly between the two fighters, in the opposite direction from them. One of the objects was silver and the other golden in color. Next Salandin saw a UFO directly in front of him, evidently on a collision course with him. He described it as resembling two saucers joined together, with a "bun" both above and below. The object was silver in color and appeared to extend beyond the edges of the fighter's windscreen. This information allowed a rough estimate of the object's size, because a Meteor fighter with a wingspan of 37 feet would exactly fill another Meteor's windscreen at a distance of 150 yards.

There was no collision; the object changed course and passed Salandin's plane on his port (left) side. Salandin reported the object was moving at "tremendous" velocity. The case has been discussed widely.

See also AIRCRAFT, UFOS AND.

Sambrot, William, American science fiction author (1920–) Sambrot's 1962 short story "Control Somnambule," published in *Playboy*, concerns an astronaut who apparently vanishes from his capsule while on a space mission. Later, under hypnosis, the astronaut relates how he was abducted from his capsule, examined by aliens on board their huge spacecraft, and released after being "marked" by an inscription inside his abdomen. Sambrot's story is identical in many respects to later reports of UFO abductions (including the use of hypnosis to "retrieve" memories of an abduction), although the story was published more than a decade before such abduction stories become widely reported in major media.

San Germán incident, Puerto Rico In this incident, dated November 16, 1988, a large, yellow, luminous UFO allegedly appeared over the community of San Germán and caused two jet fighters flying near the UFO to vanish. The individual planes' engine noise reportedly ceased at the moment each plane disappeared. After the disappearance of the jet aircraft, two smaller, luminous UFOs allegedly emerged from the original UFO and flew away rapidly. The large yellow UFO reportedly also departed at high speed afterward. This case is among the most widely publicized in the modern literature on UFOs and is one of several prominent reports allegedly involving the disappearance or "capture" of terrestrial aircraft by UFOs. The San Germán incident allegedly occurred within several weeks of another, similar incident at Cabo Rojo, Puerto Rico.

See also AIRCRAFT; CABO ROJO INCIDENT; MISSING PERSONS AND AIRCRAFT.

Sanskrit The written form of Old Indic, Sanskrit has figured prominently in the etymology of the UFO phenomenon. Gavin Gibbons's terminology for various configurations of UFOs, for example, is derived from Sanskrit.

See also VIDYA; VIMANA; VULYA; VUNU.

"Santa Claus" American astronauts reportedly have used the code expression "Santa Claus" to re-

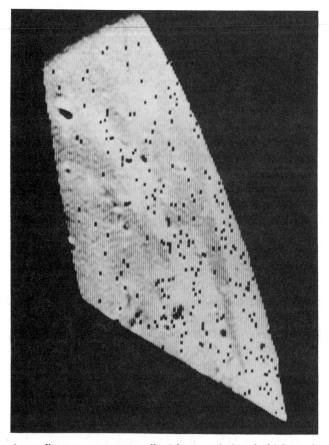

According to rumor, *Apollo 8* lunar mission (which took this photo of the moon from about 70 miles altitude) may have encountered "Santa Claus." (NASA)

fer to sightings of UFOs during manned space missions.

See also ASTRONAUTS, UFOS AND.

Santa Maria incident, Brazil Two reports from March 1954 concern one Rubem Hellwig, who allegedly encountered an ovoid craft about the size of an automobile on the ground. On investigation, he met two slender men of average height with brown complexions, one inside the craft, the other apparently gathering samples of grass outside. They addressed Hellwig in a language unfamiliar to him; yet he reportedly understood that they were requesting ammonia. He gave them directions to a town nearby. The vehicle then vanished noiselessly and at once, with a display of blue and yellow flame.

Hellwig reportedly encountered another unusual craft the following day. On this occasion he met a tall man of fair complexion, along with two women who allegedly had brown complexions, slanted dark eyes and long black hair. They were dressed in one-piece garments made of suede-like material. They described themselves to Hellwig as scientists and said they were surprised that he did not flee. One detail of this account is especially interesting, namely the configuration and hue of the women's eyes in the second encounter. Such slanted, dark eyes would become a commonly reported characteristic of alleged extraterrestrials in UFO reports.

See also HUMANOIDS.

Sassier incident, France Around 4:30 P.M. on October 11, 1954, two motorists driving near Sassier allegedly encountered a cylindrical object sitting in a nearby pasture, with several small humanoids beside the craft. The automobile's lights failed, and the men reported both an electrical "shock" and paralysis during the encounter. Such bodily effects (notably paralysis) and interference with automobiles' electrical systems are commonly reported in UFO encounter cases.

See also BODILY EFFECTS; PARALYSIS; VEHICLE EFFECTS.

satellites Since the launching of the first artificial satellite, the Soviet Union's *Sputnik 1*, in 1957, large and especially brilliant satellites have been mistaken for UFOs. An example is America's *Echo 1*, a passive telecommunications satellite that consisted of a huge plastic balloon that reflected back to Earth signals directed at it from a station on the ground. *Echo 1* was easily visible on clear nights.

Satellites re-entering the atmosphere create, in effect, artificial meteors that may be seen over wide areas and reported as UFOs. Rocket boosters burning up in the atmosphere may create similar displays in the skies and generate UFO sightings. A famous case of UFO sightings resulting from a booster's re-

Satellites such as America's *Echo I*, shown here, may be mistaken for UFOs. (NASA)

entry occurred after the launch of the Soviet *Zond 4* satellite in 1968.

See also ZOND 4 INCIDENT.

Saturn shape This configuration has been reported in many descriptions of UFOs and consists of a round or ovoid body bisected by a platform, in the manner of the planet Saturn and its rings.

Schirmer incident, United States One Sergeant Herman Schirmer, a law enforcement officer, reportedly encountered a UFO along a highway near Ashland, Nebraska, around 2:30 A.M. on December 3, 1967. At first, Schirmer saw two red lights and presumed they belonged to a truck. Then he saw that the lights originated from a saucer-like UFO. His next conscious recollection was that the object rose, emitting something resembling flames from its underside and a siren-like noise. He apparently suffered some kind of temporary paralysis and felt ill when he reached his office. His case was selected for review by the Condon committee, a UFO study group at the University of Colorado. When he visited Colorado to meet with the committee, Schirmer reportedly was introduced to a man who was identified as Dr. Edward Condon, head of the committee. During this meeting, however, someone addressed "Condon" by a name not even remotely similar to Edward or Ed, and Schirmer recognized this "Condon" as an impostor. During a psychological inkblot test at the university, Schirmer withheld his cooperation, because he thought any answers he might give could be used to discredit his testimony.

Schirmer met later with UFO investigator Jacques Vallee, an astronomer who has interpreted the UFO phenomenon as a tool for reshaping human belief systems. Schirmer said he had experienced a "tingling" sensation briefly and a localized pain behind his ear. At that particular location, Vallee reports in his book *Confrontations,* a welt with small holes appeared. For three years after the incident along the highway, Schirmer reportedly suffered from headaches, some of them evidently strong enough to awaken him from sleep. A psychologist who examined Schirmer added that Schirmer experienced symptoms including ringing in his ears before going to sleep, and "violent" disturbances of sleep. Schirmer also mentioned to Vallee that he had seen, in dreams, a bizarre landscape including mountains, UFOs and mysterious domes. Schirmer produced for Vallee a pencil sketch of one of the craft's occupants. The picture reportedly showed a man with a wrinkled forehead, a stern expression, and big, elongated pupils. Above the left ear was a round object with an antenna less than two inches in length. On one shoulder, the figure wore the insignia of a winged serpent. Schirmer said he had been removed from his patrol car and shown around the saucer. The saucer's occupant reportedly addressed Schirmer as "Watchman" and promised that one day Schirmer would "see the Universe." Vallee cites this incident as an example of "unethical" and "unprofessional" behavior on the part of certain UFO investigators.

See also CONDON REPORT; ENCOUNTER PHENOMENA; VALLEE, JACQUES.

"Secret Commonwealth" Coined to describe certain alleged supernatural phenomena, this expression also has been used to refer to certain elements of the UFO phenomenon. A Scottish clergyman named Robert Kirk published in 1691 a book entitled *The Secret Commonwealth of Elves, Fauns and Fairies,* describing alleged supernatural phenomena that resemble in some important ways modern descriptions of UFOs and their occupants and activities. Kirk claimed that the supernatural creatures could appear as material beings and could vanish from sight; were best visible around dusk; in many cases lived in subterranean dwellings; spoke in a curious whistling language but also were capable of communicating with humans in the languages of this world; often appeared dressed according to local fashion; could not be harmed by human weaponry; could fly; and mutilated cattle and other animals to obtain their "substance," which was necessary for the supernatural beings to survive.

All these attributes have parallels in modern reports and rumors of UFOs and their activities. The "aliens" allegedly appear as material beings, as in the celebrated accounts of "contactees" George Adamski and Truman Bethurum, and are often reported seen after daylight, as in the Kelly–Hopkinsville, Kentucky, incident. The belief in the underground dwellings of supernatural beings has a parallel in present-day suggestions that "extraterrestrials" are operating out of subterranean bases on Earth. UFO occupants have been reported speaking

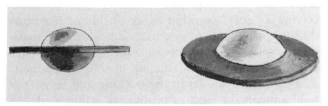

Saturn shape, shown here in profile and oblique view, is commonly reported UFO configuration. (D. Ritchie)

to one another in unintelligible languages, and speaking human languages on other occasions, sometimes in dialect. The "aliens" are believed to be capable of flying and impervious to attack by guns and other terrestrial weapons. Kirk's account of the mysterious beings attacking animals resembles modern reports of animal mutilations associated with UFOs, as well as current speculation that visitors from other planets are conducting tissue-sampling operations and various other medical procedures on abducted humans in order to obtain material for genetic manipulation.

See also ABDUCTIONS; ADAMSKI, GEORGE; ANIMALS, UFOS AND; BETHURUM INCIDENT; DEMONOLOGY; KELLY–HOPKINSVILLE INCIDENT; MYTHOLOGY.

Semjase A 330-year-old female extraterrestrial from the Pleiades supposedly contacted by Eduard Meier. She is described as a blue-eyed woman with amber, waist-length hair, delicate features, extremely pale skin and very high cheekbones. She addressed Meier in German and told him that the people of the Pleiades had not originated there, but rather somewhere in the constellation Lyra. A war there forced much of the population to immigrate to the Pleiades, the Hyades and a planet circling the star Vega. Since the Pleiadeans discovered Earth, she continued, two earlier terrestrial civilizations had arisen and been destroyed. The first civilization was founded by Pleiadeans who settled on Earth and mated with the native population. This civilization destroyed itself through warfare. The second civilization originated with a later Pleiadean expedition to Earth but was destroyed when war broke out again. The Pleiadeans visiting Earth in Meier's time, he was told, were non-warlike Lyrans who intended to help direct the spiritual development of humankind, with the aim of averting the mistakes of the two earlier civilizations on Earth. Semjase described her people as humans like those on Earth, but possessing knowledge and technology superior to our own. She told Meier that religion had had a "detrimental" influence on humankind and indicated that the life and death of every creature were governed by the "Creation," which she described vaguely as a set of "irrefutable" laws that would remain valid for eternity. These laws could be discerned in nature and supposedly would lead humans to "greatness" in spiritual growth. The "real" spirit, she implied, was antithetical to religion. Semjase added that "charlatans" on Earth were responsible for spreading an untruth that the Pleiadeans were angels dispatched by the Creation to bring peace and truth to Earth. This was a lie,

because the Creation does not issue commands, Semjase said. She described the Creation as "a law unto itself," to which every living thing is expected to conform and become a part. Semjase's ill-defined message about religion resembles in its vagueness other messages allegedly delivered by "extraterrestrials" about religion about about humankind's need for "spiritual" growth.

The reported war on the Pleiadeans' homeworld is also a widespread feature of science fiction. Semjase was only one of several beings identified as Pleiadeans who allegedly contacted Meier. They said their homeworld was called Erra, and Meier related some brief and highly generalized descriptions of it.

See also ASKET; ENCOUNTER PHENOMENA; ERRA; HOMEWORLDS; HUMANOIDS; HYADES; MEIER CASE; PLEIADES; RELIGION, UFOS AND; SFATH.

sentinel trick UFO investigator Jacques Vallee has described a pattern of UFO contact that he calls the "unsuspecting sentinel trick," in which a "saucer" appears to a small group of soldiers on lonely duty somewhere. A similar pattern is commonplace in reports of occult activity. A soldier on sentry duty looks up and is astonished to see a spectral figure advancing toward him. This pattern is a well-known feature of British ghost lore. Perhaps the most famous case in point is the opening of Shakespeare's *Hamlet*, in which sentinels at Elsinore are frightened by an appearance of the ghost of Hamlet's father. Certain appearances of "Spring-Heeled Jack," the apparition that terrified 19th-century Britain and resembled closely some "humanoids" reported in 20th-century close-encounter cases, followed a similar pattern.

See also APPARITIONS; SPRING-HEELED JACK; VALLEE, JACQUES.

sequential abductions In sequential abduction cases, an individual is said to have been abducted repeatedly, possibly starting in childhood and continuing into the adult years. Although imagination almost certainly plays a major role in such stories, they are numerous in the UFO literature and may be "revealed" by an alleged abductee under hypnotic regression. The sequential abductee may recall receiving a "scar" or other mark on his or her body during an abduction in childhood, although many other explanations are possible for scars on a child's body. The sequential abduction may be "explained" as a procedure similar to the tracking and tagging of wild animals on Earth. Accounts of multiple abductions resemble reports from the literature on demonology of children being "chosen" for special domination by the Devil early in life or even before they are born.

See also ABDUCTIONS; BODILY EFFECTS; CHILDREN, UFOS AND; DEMONOLOGY.

Serchio River incident, Italy On the night of July 24, 1952, a fisherman on the banks of Tuscany's Serchio River, near Vico, reportedly saw a discoid UFO some 60 feet in diameter hovering for 10 minutes over the river. The UFO allegedly had a set of propellers at its rear and was surmounted by a dome with structures resembling blades atop it. The UFO extended a hose into the water. The witness allegedly saw, through a window in the craft, a being wearing something like a diving helmet. The UFO directed a greenish "ray" at the fisherman, who felt an electric shock as the ray hit him. Then the UFO flew away eastward. Several days later, a mysterious stranger with a foreign accent reportedly contacted the fisherman and tried to intimidate him, in the manner of the "men in black" often associated with UFO sightings. This report also bears a strong similarity to certain other UFO reports in its description of the craft extending a hose into the river.

See also GEORGIAN BAY INCIDENT; STEEP ROCK LAKE INCIDENT.

sexual encounters Among the most lurid elements of UFO lore are reports of sexual encounters between human abductees and alleged extraterrestrials. In such encounters, an "alien" may have direct sexual intercourse with a human, or the aliens reportedly may extract semen or ova from the human captive. Cases of artificial insemination of human women by extraterrestrials also have been reported. Perhaps the most celebrated case of this kind is that of Antonio Villas-Boas, the farm worker who claimed to have gone aboard an alien spacecraft and had sexual relations with a red-haired woman.

Numerous other cases of sexual encounters have been reported in the literature on UFOs. The sexual encounter allegedly may occur with a figure identical to a human; a humanoid similar to, but distinct in some ways from, an ordinary human; or a humanoid but definitely nonhuman figure. The alien partner described in such cases may appear to be part amphibian or reptilian. The encounter may be cold and impersonal on the part of the "alien," and in some cases is said to involve brutality toward the human partner.

Various interpretations of these reports are possible. One interpretation is that the accounts of sexual activity with extraterrestrials are sheer fantasy. Another interpretation is that the stories represent distorted and embellished recollections of sexual abuse of children by adults. Hoaxes are another possibility. Then there is the chance that at least some of the sexual encounter reports really are accurate recollections of sexual contact between human abductees and highly intelligent, nonhuman entities.

There has been speculation that if UFO occupants were "extraterrestrial biological entities" (EBEs), or intelligent organisms from some other planet, then their interest in human sexual activity might represent an effort to collect human genetic material for breeding purposes or to "rejuvenate" (however one might define that verb) the genetic material of the extraterrestrials. Another suggestion is that extraterrestrials might be trying to create a "hybrid" race—half human and half alien—for some purpose. There is, however, no solid evidence to support either of these speculations.

Sexual encounters in UFO lore bear a strong resemblance to accounts, from the literature on demonology, of the activity of incubi and succubi. An incubus is an evil spirit that is capable of having sexual relations, as a male, with a human female, whereas a succubus appears in female form and has sexual intercourse with a human male.

It should be noted that many reports of sexual encounters with UFO occupants are related by subjects under hypnosis, which is a notoriously questionable way to retrieve "hidden" memories.

See also ABDUCTIONS; DEMONOLOGY; ENCOUNTER PHENOMENA; EXTRATERRESTRIALS, BEHAVIOR OF; INCUBI AND SUCCUBI.

Sfath One of the Pleiadean extraterrestrials who allegedly communicated with Swiss "contactee" Eduard Meier, Sfath is described as an elderly man whom Meier met aboard a metallic craft that landed in an isolated location where Meier had been told, by "telepathic" instruction, to wait. Sfath told Meier that he had been chosen to carry out a mission that would be made clear to him later. This interview with Sfath lasted about four hours. Although this allegedly was Meier's only meeting with Sfath, the being supposedly maintained telepathic contact with Meier for years afterward. Eventually he was succeeded as Meier's guide by a female entity named Asket.

See also ASKET; MEIER CASE; PLEIADES.

shamanism An occult discipline closely related in many ways to the UFO phenomenon, shamanism is a collection of practices in which a person undergoes an altered state of consciousness and allegedly travels to otherworldly realms where he may visit "superior" beings and/or communicate with spirits. The shaman enters this state at will. A retinue of "helping" spirits is said to follow the shaman and aid him in his work. A "guardian" spirit who supplies the shaman's power is also associated with the shaman. Shamanism makes extensive use of music, specifically chants and songs. The shaman also allegedly has the ability to take flight, sometimes in magical ships.

Numerous parallels exist between shamanism and the UFO phenomenon, particularly alleged UFO abductions and other "contactee" cases. The "contactee" may report an altered state of consciousness, in which perception is altered and ordinary intellectual functions are intensified somehow. Encounters may involve meetings with "advanced" intelligences that resemble disembodied spirits in their capabilities. The "ships" of shamanism have their parallel in the "spacecraft" described in UFO encounters. As a shaman does, the UFO contactee supposedly may enter into contact at will with the "aliens." The "helping" and "guardian" spirits associated with the shaman also appear to be roughly equivalent to the alleged extraterrestrials that reportedly pledge to help and enlighten certain UFO contactees.

The musical element of shamanism also has a significant parallel in the UFO phenomenon. As the shaman uses a song or chant to make contact with spirits, the modern UFO contactee may describe musical elements of close encounters. In Steven Spielberg's famed 1977 motion picture *Close Encounters of the Third Kind,* a five-note musical theme is used to communicate with extraterrestrials in what may be interpreted as a shamanistic experience.

The modern UFO abduction phenomenon resembles "involuntary election," a condition in which an individual becomes a shaman through an involuntary dream or trance in which spirits supposedly tell him that he has been selected to become a shaman. In 20th-century UFO abduction reports, the abductee may tell of a similar experience, with "extraterrestrials" taking the place of the shaman's spirit companions.

"Implants," or small artifacts said to be implanted in the bodies of abductees by alleged extraterrestrials, also have parallels in shamanism. In certain shamanistic societies, notably among the Aborigines of Australia and the Native American peoples of North America, certain objects symbolizing power, such as crystals or stones, are placed in the shaman's body during initiation rituals. These objects may be symbolically equivalent to implants reported in UFO abduction cases.

The shaman is commonly viewed in his own community as a leader. In similar fashion, the modern UFO contactee may become the leader of a large cult that looks to him for guidance and enlightenment.

In summary, the UFO phenomenon may be viewed as a shamanistic phenomenon, and particularly as an expression of "neo-shamanism," a movement that seeks to integrate elements of shamanism into modern Western society and culture.

See also CLOSE ENCOUNTERS OF THE THIRD KIND; CULTS; ENCOUNTER PHENOMENA; EXALTED ONES; HIGH STRANGENESS; IMPLANTS; MUSIC; OCCULTISM; PERCEPTION; PSYCHOLOGICAL EFFECTS.

Shambala Possibly the model for the fictional land of Shangri-La in James Hilton's novel *Lost Horizon,* Shambala is a legendary mystical kingdom in Tibet. According to legend, Shambala is hidden deep in the mountains and can be reached only by flying through the air with the aid of siddhis, special spiritual and paranormal powers related to kundalini energy. Residents of Shambala allegedly could master time, cure illnesses, practice telepathy, become invisible and exhibit precognition.

The legend of Shambala bears many parallels with 20th-century UFO lore and related beliefs, such as Tibet as a focus of UFO activity; flight through seemingly supernormal methods or "technology"; control over time; telepathic ability; precognition and invisibility; and kundalini energy, which has been suggested as one possible explanation for the power of alleged extraterrestrials to paralyze humans at a distance.

See also KUNDALINI; KUNDALINI GUN; TIBET.

Shasta, Mount, California, United States Located in northern California, and for many years a center for occult societies and their activities, volcanic Mount Shasta is known in UFO lore as a UFO base and as a stop along a huge, intricate network of tunnels said to link various UFO-related facilities in the western United States. Some observers of the UFO phenomenon see Mount Shasta as a symbol of the prominent link between occultism and the UFO phenomenon.

See also OCCULTISM; TUNNELS.

Shaver mystery Sometimes called the "Shaver hoax," this phenomenon played a part in the popularization of the UFO cult in the mid-20th century. The originator of the so-called mystery was Richard Shaver, a welder at an automobile plant in Michigan

According to UFO lore, California's Mount Shasta is said to be the site of vast underground city and UFO base. (U.S. Geological Survey)

during the Prohibition era in the United States. Shaver thought he heard voices trying to communicate with him through his welding apparatus, which he presumed was an "augmenter" of thoughts. He thought he heard talk of spaceships and space travel. Eventually, Shaver imagined that the Earth harbored a vast subterranean civilization of beings whom Shaver called "deros." The deros were thought to be much smaller than ordinary humans and committed to causing humankind as much trouble as possible by turning harmful rays on the unsuspecting surface dwellers. Shaver's visions were published in the American science fiction magazine *Amazing Stories*, edited by Raymond Palmer, in March 1945. Shaver's connection with the UFO phenomenon is largely the work of Palmer, who became interested in flying saucers following Kenneth Arnold's initial sighting near Mount Rainier in Washington state in 1947. In an effort to link UFOs with the hollow-Earth fantasies of Shaver, Palmer contended that flying saucers originated within the Earth and used holes at either pole of the Earth to travel from their underground home to the planet's surface. Although Shaver's and Palmer's ideas continue to circulate through the community of UFO enthusiasts, there appear to have been few converts to the saucers-from-underground hypothesis. Some elements of Shaver's tale, notably its image of the

deros as small humanoids, are common to many later reports of encounter phenomena.

See also ARNOLD INCIDENT; ENCOUNTER PHENOMENA; HOLLOW EARTH HYPOTHESIS; HUMANOIDS; LEMURIA; PALMER, RAYMOND.

Sherbrook incident, Canada   One night in December 1953, one Mrs. Orfei reportedly heard a knocking at her door late at night but received no answer when she inquired who was there. The heavy knocking continued. The woman's dog leaped at the door, then retreated in apparent terror and hid in the corner. Mrs. Orfei went upstairs and watched from a window as two "indescribable," shadowy beings left the vicinity of the house. Later, a large, round object took off from a point about 300 feet from the house, accompanied by blue-green light displays. A police investigation reportedly revealed bushes that had been broken as if by a tremendous weight. Of particular interest in this case is the reaction of the dog to the presence at the door. In this and other cases, dogs have been reported to lunge at an alleged extraterrestrial being, then retreat in great fear. Such fear among animals in "alien" encounter cases has a parallel in the behavior of dogs and other domestic animals said to have encountered evil spirits, as reported in the literature of demonology.

See also ANIMALS, UFOS AND; DEMONOLOGY.

Sierra Chica incident, Argentina   This incident is notable for its parallels with ghost lore and Japanese spirit lore. On July 2, 1968, a 15-year-old boy riding a horse near Sierra Chica, a town near Olavarria in the province of Buenos Aires, reportedly encountered two men with white hair, wearing red clothing, with an odd, unblinking gaze. The men's legs were partly transparent, and the boy could see through them to the grass behind the men. The men told the boy that someday they would take him to see the world and gave him a written message to that effect. Nearby, the boy also saw a silvery machine about six feet wide and two feet high resting on three landing legs. After delivering the written message, the mysterious men climbed aboard the object and flew away.

The boy rode home and told his family what had happened. The family and some neighbors went to the site of the encounter and found three holes in the configuration of an isosceles triangle where the three-legged machine reportedly had stood. Although the case was reported to the police, it met with skepticism. That evening, a party of merrymakers from a local social club decided to visit the site and conduct an investigation. A police sergeant armed with a revolver went with them. At the site, the men encountered a luminous object moving just above the ground, toward the spot where the strange machine allegedly had landed. The police sergeant was about to fire at the glowing object when another man in the group stopped him. The object traced a zigzag course across the landscape and eventually flew straight up and disappeared. This incident was part of a wave of UFO sightings in South America. The Sierra Chica incident resembles various incidents in ghost lore in which only the upper or lower half of a spectral figure is observed, the other half being diaphanous or nonexistent. Also, the detail of the mysterious men promising to take the boy on a tour of the world is reminiscent of a story from Japan about a tengu, or mountain goblin, carrying a boy on travels to distant lands.

See also APPARITIONS; TENGU; WAVES.

Sign, Project

Sign, Project   An early U.S. Air Force study of the UFO phenomenon, Project Sign reportedly concluded that UFOs might represent visitations by extraterrestrials in spacecraft. The project was closed down and replaced with Project Grudge, another UFO study that eventually became Project Blue Book. According to at least one report, Project Sign maintained liaisons with MAJESTIC 12.

See also BLUE BOOK, PROJECT; GRUDGE, PROJECT; MAJESTIC 12.

"signs and wonders"

"signs and wonders"   This biblical passage, from the gospel of Luke, refers to conditions on Earth immediately before Christ's return: "And great earthquakes shall be in divers places, and famines, and pestilences; and fearful sights and great signs shall there be from heaven." (Luke 21:11). The passage has been interpreted as a reference to the UFO phenomenon and to the launching of spacecraft in the late 20th century. Also pertinent to the UFO phenomenon is the second letter of Saint Paul to the Thessalonians. This letter describes conditions that are expected to prevail at the start of the Antichrist's reign and has been interpreted as referring specifically to UFOs. Paul writes:

Let no man deceive you by any means: for that day shall not come, except there come a falling away first, and that man of sin be revealed, the son of perdition; who opposeth and exalteth himself above all that is called God, or that is worshipped; so that he as God sitteth in the temple of God, shewing himself that he is God. . . . And then that Wicked shall be revealed, whom the Lord shall consume with the spirit of His mouth, and shall destroy with the brightness of His coming: even him, whose coming is after the working of Satan with all power and signs and lying wonders. (II Thessalonians 2:3–4, 8–9.)

This passage describes the reign of the demonic world ruler as characterized by impressive but false "signs" and "wonders," presumably including aerial wonders such as UFOs. Another biblical passage often cited with reference to this eschatological view of UFOs is Revelation 13:11–13, which describes the evil world ruler's capability to work "wonders" more specifically:

And I beheld another beast coming up out of the earth; and he had two horns like a lamb, and he spake as a dragon. And he exerciseth all the power of the first beast before him, and causeth the earth and them which dwell therein to worship the first beast, whose deadly wound was healed. And he doeth great wonders, so that he maketh fire come down from heaven on the earth in the sight of men . . .

(The "first beast" mentioned here is another monster described in Revelation 13:1–8 as having seven heads and 10 horns, with one head apparently "wounded to death.")

The distinguished Orthodox Christian theologian Father Seraphim Rose, in his analysis of the UFO phenomenon, suggested that luminous UFOs might represent the fulfilment of the prophecy about fire coming down from heaven at the beast's command. Father Seraphim went so far as to speculate that demonic "extraterrestrials" might even land on Earth at the appearance of the Antichrist, to worship their diabolical master and thus help lead humankind to accept the Antichrist's rule.

See also ANTICHRIST; CHRIST AND CHRISTIANITY; DEMONOLOGY.

Silence Group

Silence Group   A hypothetical and vaguely defined organization supposedly bent on suppressing discussion of UFOs, the Silence Group is a prominent part of UFO lore. On numerous occasions, "contactees" and other witnesses of UFOs and related phenomena have reportedly been visited by mysterious agents, apparently representatives of some official body, who advised them not to discuss the UFO-related incidents they had observed. There appears to be no agreement on what purpose such attempts at suppression might serve. In any case, the attempts (if they occurred at all) appear to have been largely unsuccessful, in view of the vast number of UFO observations reported and the widespread discussion of UFOs in popular literature. Stories about the Silence Group may be, in part, a manifestation of what has been called the "paranoid pseudocommunity," an imagined conspiracy of opponents perceived by an extremist group whose members believe they possess some powerful "truth."

See also ADAMSKI, GEORGE; CONSPIRACY THEORIES; MEN IN BLACK; OTTO INCIDENT; PARANOIA.

silent UFOs   One often-reported characteristic of UFO close-encounter reports is a strange silence that allegedly accompanies the encounters. Witnesses may report that sound seemed to be suppressed in the immediate vicinity during the encounter. Bird song, for example, reportedly may cease if the encounter occurs in or near a wood.

No exotic explanation involving alien technology is needed to account for such alleged silences. Close encounters are noted for their emphasis on the visual elements of perception. If a witness is preoccupied by visual stimuli, then his or her mind may simply ignore auditory stimuli during the alleged encounter, even though there is no cessation in bird song or any other sound in the vicinity.

There is also an easily understandable explanation for reports of silent UFOs flying overhead, as in the Hudson Valley sightings in New York state. Certain aircraft, which easily can be mistaken for "extraterrestrial" UFOs, emit little engine noise and are virtually silent to witnesses on the ground several hundred feet below, unless the witnesses happen to be directly under the planes' flight path. Such quiet aircraft are believed to have been used in a hoax that allegedly generated the Hudson Valley sightings.

See also ACOUSTICAL EFFECTS; HUDSON VALLEY SIGHTINGS.

Simonton incident, United States   One of the most widely cited close-encounter reports in the literature on UFOs, the Simonton incident allegedly occurred on the morning of April 18, 1961, when an American farmer named Joe Simonton discovered a saucer-like object some 30 feet wide and 12 feet high hovering near the ground on his property. Through an opening in the hull, Simonton reportedly saw three humanoids, about five feet tall, inside the craft. The beings had dark hair and swarthy complexions, and Simonton said they resembled "Italians." One of the beings allegedly presented Simonton with a jug to be filled with water, and Simonton complied. When he returned to the craft, he saw one of the beings cooking food on a grill within

the object. Simonton requested samples of the food and was given three objects like pancakes, each about three inches in diameter. Simonton ate one of the pancakes and said it tasted like "cardboard." After the UFO departed, Simonton presented the pancakes to a Federal food and drug laboratory for analysis. The laboratory reported that the pancakes were made of terrestrial constituents but contained no salt.

The Simonton incident is considered an example of "metalogic," in which a human witness to a UFO encounter is presented with a seemingly absurd situation that requires some explanation with bizarre, confusing information.

See also HUMANOIDS; "ITALIANS"; METALOGIC.

Sinistrari, Lodovico Maria (1622–1701)   Franciscan theologian Sinistrari studied reports of succubi, female demonic spirits capable of having sexual intercourse with men, and incubi, male demons that can have intercourse with women. Sinistrari's descriptions of these mysterious beings at work bear a close resemblance to modern accounts of UFO abductions and related phenomena. In his book *De Daemonialitate*, he tells the story of a woman named Hieronyma who reportedly encountered an incubus that appeared to her in the form of a small man and evidently tried to have sexual relations with her. The being approached Hieronyma in her bedroom; her husband appears to have slept through the entire incident. The incubus's visits allegedly occurred repeatedly over some years. The evil spirit started visiting her, according to the story, immediately after a cake had been delivered for some unknown reason to Hieronyma's house, and she had tasted it. The incubus reportedly subjected the woman to bodily abuse and on one occasion stripped her naked in public. Mysterious phenomena, including the levitation of a nursing baby and the destruction, disappearance and displacement of various objects in the home, also reportedly occurred in connection with the incubus's activities.

There are many similarities between this case and UFO encounters reported in our time. The visitor appears in the form of a small humanoid, and makes repeated visits, with the apparent aim of having sexual relations with a human. Physical abuse reportedly occurs. At one point in these ongoing encounters, the human subject is stripped naked. Finally, the arrival of the cake resembles elements of close-encounter incidents in which "aliens" present their human subject with something to eat or drink.

See also ABSURDITY; ANDREASSON CASE; DEMONOLOGY; ENCOUNTER PHENOMENA; INCUBI AND SUCCUBI;

ROSE, FATHER SERAPHIM; SEXUAL ENCOUNTERS; VIL-
LAS-BOAS INCIDENT.

skyquakes   These phenomena consist of powerful
explosive noises, comparable to sonic booms produced by aircraft, but with no proof that aircraft actually generated them. The shock waves from a
skyquake are intense and produce effects similar to
those of moderate earthquakes, such as vibrating
windows and shaking buildings. Skyquakes have
been reported in various parts of the world but most
notably in California, where one series of skyquakes
recorded at Caltech reportedly followed a pattern:
The skyquakes occurred on Thursday mornings and
were detected first over Catalina Island and then
over the San Bernardino Valley and San Gabriel Valley inland. The California skyquakes are widely
thought to be generated by a supersonic aircraft
known as Aurora, said to be capable of speeds up to
Mach 6, or six times the speed of sound. An aircraft
traveling at Mach 6 would have a velocity of approximately 4,000 miles per hour. Aurora is believed to
be a successor to the American SR-71 reconnaissance
and surveillance aircraft, which was retired in 1991
after some two decades of service.

See also AIRCRAFT, UFOS AND; TECHNOLOGY.

Slater study   A psychological study of nine alleged UFO abductees, conducted by Dr. Elizabeth
Slater and published in 1985, has been cited as evidence that abduction reports have their origins in
abnormal psychological states, at least in certain
cases. Slater found that the nine individuals she
studied could not be labeled as generally psychotic,
but neither were they normal. In "lay terms," Slater
said, some of the subjects probably would be considered "odd" or "eccentric." She also found them low
in self-esteem and sensitive to "fantasy." Under
stressful circumstances, she added, the subjects
tended to exhibit impulsive behavior—such as
"storms" of emotion or "acting out" behaviors—as
well as confused thought processes that she considered "bizarre." Again in lay terms, the individuals
in this study had difficulty telling the difference between fantasy and reality.

Slater was not told beforehand that the nine individuals were alleged UFO abductees. After learning
this information, she stated her opinion that the individuals, though not entirely "normal," were not
disturbed seriously enough to account for their tales
of abductions by extraterrestrials. It has been suggested that "dissociative states," conditions in between on a continuum of "normal" mental health

and more serious psychopathologies, might be responsible for some abduction reports.

See also ABDUCTIONS; DISSOCIATIVE STATES.

sleep   Numerous UFO encounters are reported as
the witness is either entering or emerging from
sleep. In this condition, between sleep and full
wakefulness, a person may be subject to hallucinations that have been interpreted as possible explanations of certain UFO encounter stories.

See also HALLUCINATIONS.

sleep paralysis   This phenomenon incorporates
many elements of UFO encounter reports and has
been suggested as a possible explanation for many
portions of the UFO phenomenon. The sleep paralysis syndrome is characterized by the inability to
move one's body at will while either awakening or
falling asleep. Other characteristics of the sleep paralysis syndrome include strange bodily sensations;
a feeling of paralysis; unfamiliar odors; tactile sensations, such as a feeling that something is touching a
part of one's body; odd noises, such as ringing or

**Sleep paralysis cases may involve visions of terrifying
monsters like those reported in certain UFO encounters.**

buzzing sounds; a feeling of floating upward, off one's bed; and the perception of a strange and terrifying presence in the same room with the percipient. These beings may be vague, dark shapes, or some strange humanoid or nonhuman creature. All the aforementioned elements are reported, in various combinations, in numerous UFO encounter reports, notably the so-called bedroom encounters, in which the "contactee" or "abductee" is approached at night, while trying to sleep. According to one estimate, 15 percent or more of the population as a whole may have experienced sleep paralysis and its accompanying perceptions at one time or another. If this estimate is accurate, then sleep paralysis may account for many alleged UFO encounters and for the estimated large numbers of such encounters.

See also ABDUCTIONS; BORDER PHENOMENA; HALLUCINATIONS; HUMANOIDS; IMAGINAL REALM; ODORS; PARALYSIS; PERCEPTION; REALITY; SLEEP.

Smith, Helene   This was a pseudonym of Catherine-Elise Müller, a 19th-century Swiss channeler who claimed to have contacted the planet Mars. In a trance state, she described Mars as having wheelless, horseless "carriages" that gave off sparks as they traveled; a yellow-green sky; pinkish-blue lakes; and inhabitants who looked exactly like humans and wore robes and sandals. The medium produced paintings that purported to show Martian houses, which looked like inverted pagodas or elaborate birdbaths. She also wrote and spoke in what she represented to be the Martian language. This "extraterrestrial" language, however, turned out to be a transliteration of French. The case is described in psychologist Theodore Flournoy's 1900 book *From India to the Planet Mars*. Flournoy's book appeared at approximately the same time as H.G. Wells's science fiction novel *The War of the Worlds*, which depicted a fictional Martian invasion of Earth. Müller's visions bear a certain similarity to those of alleged UFO contactees in the 20th century, such as American Truman Bethurum, who related stories of industrial facilities on Mars.

American unmanned space probes visited Mars some 75 years after the publication of Flournoy's book and revealed that the Martian sky was pink, not yellow-green; no lakes of any color were visible; and there were no Martians of any description, robed and sandaled or otherwise. The dream of life on Mars is by no means dead, however, and detailed photographs of the planet's surface actually have revived speculation about the possibility of intelligent life on Mars (albeit in the distant past).

See also AUTOMATIC WRITING; BETHURUM INCIDENT; CAPTAIN AURA RHANES; CHANNELING; FACE ON MARS; MARS; WAR OF THE WORLDS, THE; WELLS, H.G.

Snowbird, Project   This project is said to be, or to have been, an American attempt to test-fly a recovered extraterrestrial spacecraft. The project was supposedly started in 1972 and was rumored to have been involved with the test flight of a vehicle reported seen near Houston, Texas, in 1980. One witness was believed to have experienced serious bodily effects caused by radiation from the UFO.

See also CASH–LANDRUM INCIDENT.

societies, extraterrestrial   Alleged extraterrestrials in UFO close-encounter reports appear to be less than forthcoming about the character of societies on their homeworlds. As a rule, the alien societies and civilizations described in such encounters resemble those of humankind on Earth, only cleaner and better organized. The "aliens" commonly claim to have overcome such woes as war, hunger and pollution, although the result in many such accounts appears to be a society that subordinates the individual's interests to those of society and leaves individuals curiously lacking in personality. In this respect, the descriptions of extraterrestrial societies contain a strong element of Platonic thinking, in which the state's interests supersede those of the individual.

Some descriptions of alien societies on other planets, as relayed through UFO "contactees" such as George Adamski and Truman Bethurum, have turned out to be totally inaccurate when they could be verified by other means. Adamski, for example, described a highly advanced civilization to be found on Venus and the Moon, both of which were shown to be uninhabited when unmanned spacecraft visited and photographed them years later. Likewise, Bethurum's account of industrial facilities on Mars, as described by "Captain Aura Rhanes," turned out to be in error when U.S. space probes visited Mars and photographed its surface. In their details, many descriptions of imagined extraterrestrial societies are merely ridiculous, as in the case of the polka-dancing aliens to be found on Clarion, Aura Rhanes's alleged homeworld.

See also ADAMSKI, GEORGE; BETHURUM INCIDENT; CAPTAIN AURA RHANES; CLARION; HOMEWORLDS; MARS; VENUS.

Socorro, New Mexico, incident, United States
A widely publicized and carefully investigated close-encounter case, the Socorro incident reportedly oc-

curred on the afternoon of April 24, 1964, near Socorro, New Mexico. Lonnie Zamora, a policeman, was pursuing a speeding automobile when he reportedly heard a roar and saw flames nearby. Zamora thought a dynamite shack might have exploded. He drove his car off the road toward the site of the flames and encountered what he described later as an ovoid object resting on the ground. Two apparently humanoid beings in white coveralls stood beside the object. Zamora thought the object might be an overturned car and told the sheriff's office by radio that he was investigating an accident. Then he heard another loud noise, and the ovoid craft took flight with a great blast of flame, accompanied by a strange whine and roar. The UFO departed in horizontal flight, 10-to-15 feet above the ground. A New Mexico state trooper arrived at the scene soon afterward and examined the site with Zamora. They allegedly found indentations in the ground, as well as brush burning where the UFO supposedly had taken to the air.

J. Allen Hynek investigated the incident and described it as a "major" sighting. Famed UFO "debunker" Philip Klass also investigated the sighting, however, and found numerous discrepancies between Zamora's account and evidence at the site. For example, pictures taken at the site showed only minor burning on a bush and clumps of grass, rather than the extensive burning one would expect from the large blast of flame described on takeoff. Moreover, twigs that should have been burned or blown away by such an event could be seen lying undisturbed at the site. Klass suggested the Socorro case might have been merely a hoax designed to bring publicity and tourism to the town.

See also HOAXES; KLASS, PHILIP.

soda pop factor

This expression refers to the fact that humans sometimes do ordinary things in highly extraordinary situations, such as UFO contact cases. In one UFO contact story, when an "extraterrestrial" reportedly mentioned being thirsty, the human "contactee" went into a store and bought two sodas. Thus the "soda pop factor" got its name.

See also ABSURDITY; ENCOUNTER PHENOMENA.

soft object

This expression refers to a UFO with a particular set of characteristics. A soft object looks like a bright light or cluster of lights; usually is seen at night and appears to act as if directed by intelligence; and is not obviously solid. A soft object may emit bright beams of light like those from searchlights, thus giving the appearance of a "hard" object. A soft object may appear as a "ghost light" (a light sometimes seen in woods and remote areas, and linked with poltergeist activity), or even as a luminous humanoid. When seen by day, a soft object may take the form of a cloud and may even discharge seemingly solid material, such as "angel hair."

See also ANGEL HAIR; EARTH LIGHTS; HARD OBJECTS; HUMANOIDS; POLTERGEIST ACTIVITY.

Sonderborg incident, Denmark

At noon on June 19, 1951, a mechanic named Joseph Matiszewski allegedly encountered a UFO that landed in a meadow and was accompanied by a whistling noise. Matiszewski approached to within about 150 feet of the object, then became paralyzed. He noticed that this paralysis apparently extended to cows in the vicinity and that birds had ceased to sing. Four handsome male figures with brown skin reportedly emerged from the UFO, wearing shiny clothing. Other crew members appeared to be making repairs on the craft. Several additional objects were seen to emerge from the craft and hover over it. At last the UFO and its accompanying objects departed, and the witness was released from his paralysis. This report includes numerous commonly reported elements of UFO close-encounter stories, including handsome humanoids; suppression of sound in a UFO's vicinity; paralysis of the witness; and UFO crew members apparently performing repairs on the craft.

See also HUMANOIDS; PARALYSIS; REPAIRS.

Sonora Aero Club, United States

A mysterious, semi-secret aeronautical society reportedly founded in the 19th century in Sonora, California, the Sonora Aero Club involves reports of technology reminiscent of "airship" sightings of the late 1800s in America. What is known of the group and its activities comes from the writings of one C.A.A. Dellschau, who at his death left behind a manuscript in German describing exotic airships called "aeros." The craft had wheels for travel on land, paddles for propulsion on water, and motors for navigation in the air. The club's plans for airships were reportedly executed in great detail and included such modern features as searchlights, parachutes and retractable landing gear.

The club was said to have included some 60 members and to have been made up primarily of Germans and Englishmen. The society took pains to conceal its activities. Even portions of Dellschau's manuscript were written in a cryptic manner and had to be deciphered before translation into English. Funding allegedly was supplied by an even more mysterious source in the eastern United States, known only as "NYZMA." Dellschau said the operation of the club's bizarre machines was made possible by a gas called "NB" or "Supe," which reportedly had the potential to neutralize gravitation (or "weight," as Dellschau put it). Dellschau claimed that several airships actually were built and flown, then taken apart so that their workings would remain secret. Two of the craft, he wrote, were destroyed in a fire that swept the community of Columbia, California, some miles from Sonora. The technique for manufacturing "Supe" allegedly was lost in the 1860s after one Peter Mennis, a key figure in the organization, died. Dellschau indicated that Supe was made from a green liquid that combined with air and certain other substances and turned into a pink gas that was used to operate machinery on the airships. Apparently Mennis kept the secret of Supe's manufacture to himself, and his secretiveness caused discontent within the club. There is speculation that he was murdered in connection with a division in the club.

Dellschau moved to Texas in the 1870s and settled around 1880 in Houston. He left Houston for several months in 1890 and, on his return, exhibited a changed personality characterized by fear and anxiety. He worked thereafter as a janitor and, toward the end of his life, quit his work and lived virtually as a recluse, apparently because he feared being killed. During this last period of his life, he composed the written accounts of the club's airships. He attributed the deaths of some members of the club to careless talk or to attempts to use their knowledge of the airships for personal gain.

The case of the Sonora Aero Club bears on the "airship" mystery of the late 1800s in America, where numerous bizarre aerial craft were reported seen in the skies. There is, however, no proof that any of the airship sightings were connected in any way with airships actually built and flown by the club. The club and the experiences of Dellschau also contain important parallels with the UFO phenomenon in America during the following century. The unidentified character of "Supe" is reminiscent of the mysterious propulsion technologies claimed for flying saucers in our own time. Likewise, the extravagant claims made for the club's aircraft—claims unsupported by evidence beyond Dellschau's own account—resemble UFO reports of the 20th century. Even the name of the club's sponsor in the East, NYZMA, is much like the nonsensical, two-syllable

names given to "extraterrestrial" worlds in 20th-century contact cases, such as UMMO and Hoova. As in some modern contact incidents, Dellschau vanished from his regular activities for a while, then appears to have returned with serious psychological problems, such as fears for his life. Paranoia, as evidently exhibited in Dellschau's strange behavior after his return, is also a prominent component of the UFO phenomenon.

See also AIRSHIPS; ANTI-GRAVITY; ENCOUNTER PHENOMENA; PARANOIA; UMMO.

sorcery, UFOs and The practice of sorcery—that is, the performance of certain occult rites intended to summon the presence and/or aid of demons or other spiritual entities—has numerous parallels and associations with the UFO phenomenon. In certain close-encounter reports, the human contactee may be given a set of instructions for summoning the alleged extraterrestrials. The instructions may involve reciting a certain "magic" word or holding some kind of talisman (or "communication device") in one's hand. In UFO lore, music also may be used to make contact with extraterrestrials; this practice has its parallel in sorcery, in the form of chants and incantations. The practice of witchcraft also has been associated with various phenomena identical to certain UFO sightings, such as the passage of bright, luminous globes over areas where covens allegedly have practiced their rites. The numerous similarities between sorcery and certain aspects of the UFO phenomenon establish one of many links between UFOs and occultism.

See also DEMONOLOGY; FAMILIAR SPIRITS; OCCULTISM; WITCHCRAFT.

Soviet Union The former Soviet Union was the site of some notable reported UFO incidents, such as the Rybinsk incident. Because no free flow of information was permitted out of the Soviet Union concerning UFOs, many such incidents there probably went unrecorded and therefore are unavailable for study. Official policy on the reporting and public discussion of the UFO phenomenon appears to have varied over the years. At times there appears to have been a virtual blackout of news on the subject. There also have been times when UFO reports were made public, although at least some of these alleged sightings are believed to have been cover stories for tests of various military space systems. Although news reports of UFO sightings were not always allowed, it was permissible to treat the UFO phenomenon as a theme of fiction, and the Soviet science fiction writer Alexander Kazantsev suggested in two famous short stories that the Tunguska event, generally thought to have resulted from the collision of some celestial object (such as a comet nucleus) with the Earth, was actually the explosion of a nuclear-powered extraterrestrial spacecraft over Siberia.

The military threat posed by the Soviet Union influenced official U.S. government policy toward the UFO phenomenon in the years just after World War II. Wary of Soviet bomber attack, the U.S. government was concerned that spurious UFO reports might be used to overwhelm American air defenses in the event of a Soviet air assault. Moreover, the government saw controversy over UFOs as a potential threat to public trust in the government. For these reasons, the Robertson panel, an advisory committee convened by the government to study the UFO phenomenon, recommended (in effect) a "debunking" policy aimed at calming public fears about UFOs by trying to explain them as well-known terrestrial phenomena.

Since the fall of the Soviet system, numerous UFO sightings have been reported in the former U.S.S.R., including the famous Voronezh sightings, which were widely publicized in the West.

See also DEBUNKERS; ROBERTSON PANEL; RUSSIA; RYBINSK INCIDENT; TUNGUSKA EVENT; VORONEZH SIGHTINGS.

space brothers This expression usually refers collectively to alleged extraterrestrial entities "channeled" by mediums. Large numbers of such communications and entities have been reported. Some of the most famous cases involve entities called Ashtar, Orlon and Spectra. As a rule, channelers' reported contacts with "space brothers" are not taken seriously by the more reputable UFO investigators, partly because of the tremendous potential for fraud in such cases. Nonetheless, some degree of correlation has been observed among certain cases, notably Spectra, an alleged extraterrestrial intelligence that reportedly has been channeled by several practitioners independently of one another. The messages of "space brothers" tend to focus on imminent catastrophes supposedly facing Earth; the ability of "extraterrestrials" to rescue humankind from destruction; and the extraterrestrials' wish to see humankind adopt an essentially Hinduistic belief system with elements of pantheism and shamanism. Messages attributed to the space brothers also tend to be devoid of specifics and filled with references to the spiritual "evolution" of humankind.

See also ASHTAR; BELIEF SYSTEMS; CATASTROPHES; CHANNELING; COMMUNICATIONS; HINDUISM; HOAXES; MEDIUMISM; MESSAGES; METALOGIC; ORLON; SHAMANISM; SPECTRA.

Spectra This alleged entity is said to have been "channeled" on many occasions by various individuals and has been described as some advanced extraterrestrial intelligence from the future. The reported communications from Spectra illustrate how correlations sometimes can be found among separate encounter reports involving so-called extraterrestrials.

See also CHANNELING; CORRELATIONS; MEDIUMISM.

spheres One frequently reported element of UFO sightings is that of the sphere. Many UFOs, especially nocturnal lights, are described as spherical. For example, the "foo fighters" observed during World War II were said to be spheres; and in more recent years there have been numerous reports of spherical objects associated with UFOs and "aliens" in the recollections of UFO witnesses and "abductees." Perhaps it is significant that classical descriptions of spirits also ascribe spherical forms to the spirits' manifestations. In the following passage from his book *The Anatomy of Melancholy*, the 17th-century English scholar Robert Burton describes the alleged spherical forms of spirits: ". . . Angels [and] Devils . . . [must] be of some shape, and that absolutely round, like Sun and Moon, because that is the most perfect form, which has no roughness, angles . . . prominences, but is the most perfect among perfect bodies; therefore all spirits are corporeal . . . [and] in their proper shapes round." The sphere is therefore one element linking UFOs with spiritual phenomena.

See also DEMONOLOGY; FOO FIGHTERS.

Spitzbergen incident, Norway A mysterious UFO case from the early days of the Cold War, the Spitzbergen incident concerned the alleged discovery of UFO wreckage near Spitzbergen. In May 1952, the pilot of an aircraft of the Norwegian Air Force reported sighting what appeared to be debris of a crashed aircraft on an island. He alerted Norwegian rescue forces. Soon afterward, the Norwegian government reportedly announced that the wreckage found on the island belonged to a flying saucer. No further information was made available, except to say that the debris was being studied by the Norwegians, the Americans and the British. A later report surfaced, saying that the craft found on the island had actually been from the Soviet Union. This statement was denied later by the Norwegian government, which claimed that the wreckage could not have belonged to a craft that originated on Earth, and that the attempted analysis of materials used in its construction had been unsuccessful. It has been suggested that the wreckage may have been that of an American RB-36 bomber engaged in reconnaissance of the northern Soviet Union, and the flying saucer report was intended merely as a cover story.

See also CRASHES.

splitting   Some individual UFOs are said to split apart into two or more distinct segments, which then maneuver on their own and may rejoin later to form an apparently single object again.

See also LONDON–KENT SIGHTING.

Spokane, Washington, incident, United States

Around noontime on June 21, 1947, eight discoid objects, each estimated to be approximately the size of a house, allegedly were seen flying over Spokane in eastern Washington state. One witness said the objects dropped from the sky in the soon to be familiar "falling leaf" motion and fell to Earth along the Saint Joe River in Idaho. This sighting was reported three days before pilot Kenneth Arnold's famous sighting of UFOs near nearby Mount Rainier, and three days before the widely publicized "Maury Island incident," which reportedly occurred near Tacoma, Washington, and now is seen as a hoax.

See also ARNOLD INCIDENT; FALLING LEAF MOTION; MAURY ISLAND INCIDENT.

spook lights   These frequently reported phenomena, similar in many ways to certain UFOs, are small luminous objects that are said to appear at night, close to the ground, in locations reputed to be "haunted." An example from the United States is the "Hornet spook light" reported seen near the former community of Hornet along the Missouri–Oklahoma border. A gravel road some four miles long, known as Spook Light Road or the Devil's Promenade, is said to be the site of the spook light's appearances. The light allegedly varies in size from that of a baseball to that of a bushel basket, and behaves in much the same manner as a typical UFO. It may travel rapidly down the middle of the road and climb to the level of the treetops, or it may swing slowly up and down and from side to side, as would a lantern carried by a walking person. The light varies in color and, on at least one occasion, has been seen to explode and scatter sparks. The light has been said to chase vehicles and to vanish just before a pursuing car was about to make contact with it.

Various romantic tales have arisen to account for the spook light. According to one story, the spook light marks the movements of a ghostly moonshiner fleeing from federal agents. Other, more mundane explanations also have been put forward to account for the spook light. According to one explanation, the spook light is merely an effect of automobile headlights from nearby U.S. Highway 66, although the spook light allegedly was seen before the age of automobiles. The spook light also has been linked to the nearby New Madrid fault zone, an area of unstable crustal rock that was the location of the most powerful earthquakes in U.S. history, during the winter of 1811–1812. Lights in the sky are associated with areas of frequent and intense earthquake activity. "Earthquake light" is a glow often reported seen in the sky during, or near the moment of, earthquakes, and has been linked tentatively with certain kinds of UFO activity.

See also EARTHQUAKE LIGHTS.

Spring-Heeled Jack   The literature on encounter phenomena from the 19th century includes one of the strangest cases in British history, and one with many similarities with 20th-century encounter phenomena: the tale of "Spring-Heeled Jack," so called because of his prodigious jumping abilities. This ghostly figure appeared at various places in England over a period of almost 70 years, starting in the early 1800s. Described as a giant wearing what appeared to be an oilskin outfit under a dark cloak, with a "fishbowl" over his head, Spring-Heeled Jack reportedly turned up one evening in February 1837 on the doorstep of Jane Alsop, of Bearhind Lane, Bow. Responding to a loud knock at the front door, Alsop found herself facing a figure so tall that she had to lift up her candle to see his face. What she saw terrified her. She described her visitor later to police as having a "hideous" face with luminous eyes and fiery breath. His claw-like hands were said to be as cold as ice. Alsop's screams brought her father and sisters running to her aid. At this point the bizarre figure ran off.

Similar occurrences were reported at other locations. In one especially dramatic encounter, the monster reportedly was seen to leap easily over a wall 14 feet high. Additional reports contributed to public concern over the frightening figure, until in January 1838 the Lord Mayor of London made Spring-Heeled Jack's reign of terror a matter of public record by citing a letter from a resident of Peckham, who told of a fearsome specter that carried out extraordinary feats of leaping.

Jack appeared again in 1877 at an army installation at Aldershot, to the surprise of two sentries who fired at him at close range without apparent effect.

Again, the mysterious figure merely leaped away. Similar reports came in from Newport and Lincoln. Jack's last public appearance took place in Liverpool in September 1904. The apparition is said to have performed magnificent feats of jumping, leaping from housetop to housetop and sometimes covering 30 feet in a single bound. This farewell performance lasted some 15 minutes. Then Spring-Heeled Jack bounded over a row of houses and was gone for good. This incident coincided approximately with a wave of UFO reports and stories of animal mutilations in Britain.

Spring-Heeled Jack's appearances bear numerous similarities to close-encounter cases of the middle and late 20th century. Even the details of his apparel and performances—the "fishbowl" helmet, the glowing eyes and the remarkable acts of locomotion—would be replicated in reports of UFO encounters more than a century after Jack's first reported appearance.

See also ANIMALS, UFOS AND; EGRYN LIGHTS; ENCOUNTER PHENOMENA.

status inconsistency theory

This theory, advanced by sociologist Donald I. Warren, is based on the idea that paranoid thinking in individuals—the kind of thinking that is manifested in many ways in the history of the UFO phenomenon—has its origins in unpleasant social reversals. Warren's analysis of Gallup poll data, cited in UFO historian Martin Kottmeyer's study of paranoid elements in the UFO phenomenon, indicates that a person who is overeducated for the job that person holds is many times more likely to report a UFO sighting than another person whose status is higher. This inconsistency between education and actual status gives the status inconsistency theory its name.

See also PARANOIA.

Steep Rock Lake incident, Canada

On July 2, 1950, a man and his wife reportedly witnessed a saucer descend to the surface of a lake. Ten humanoids, slightly smaller than men and wearing shiny garments, allegedly emerged from the craft and walked about on its deck in a manner reminiscent of robots. The beings, whose faces were not visible, lowered a hose into the lake. Then the UFO departed. This incident resembles the Georgian Bay incident in Canada in 1914 and is one of many reports of UFO activity in or just above large bodies of water.

See also AQUATIC OBJECTS; GEORGIAN BAY INCIDENT.

Stolyarov committee, U.S.S.R.

The story of the Stolyarov committee is one of the many mysteries of UFO investigations. Although the committee allegedly was formed in 1967 to investigate Soviet UFO reports and placed under the leadership of Major General Porfiry Stolyarov, a retired Air Force officer, the Soviet Air Ministry is said to have denied the committee access to official reports of UFO sightings. In November of 1967, one of Stolyarov's colleagues, Dr. Felix Zigel, reportedly made a public appeal over Moscow television for details of UFO sightings but the committee was disbanded soon afterward. Why Zigel should have been allowed to make his appeal on television (presumably with official permission) when the committee was about to be disbanded, remains unexplained.

See also RUSSIA.

straight-line mystery See ORTHOTENY.

Strategic Defense Initiative

A plan to defend the United States against missile attack, the Strategic Defense Initiative (SDI) was proposed by then–President Ronald Reagan in 1983. Various designs for the controversial anti-missile system were proposed. Plans called for SDI to destroy enemy missiles and warheads by using a combination of interceptor missiles, ground-based and space-based lasers, and particle beam weapons. Although the stated aims of SDI were to deter Soviet attack and to neutralize any such attack should it occur, some observers saw in SDI a possible response to a perceived threat of invasion by extraterrestrials. This interpretation, however, was never widely accepted. The SDI program encountered strong political opposition and never advanced as far as deployment. By 1993, SDI was considered dead for practical purposes.

strawberry ice cream show

This derisive name was applied to a rumor involving an extraterrestrial who was supposedly taken into custody by the U.S. government and kept as a prisoner. The alien was said to be fond of various terrestrial foods including strawberry ice cream. This case is an example of absurdity in the literature on UFOs.

See also ABSURDITY; RUMORS.

Strieber, Whitley, American author (1945–)

Previously an author of horror stories, Whitley Strieber became known as a UFO "contactee" following publication of his 1987 book *Communion*, which was presented as an account of Strieber's meetings with extraterrestrials. Strieber described being abducted from the bedroom of his cabin in upstate New York one night and undergoing a frightening series of quasi-medical operations conducted by nonhumans. He reported feeling intense fear when he perceived that the "aliens" intended to perform some kind of operation on his brain. The operation, if it actually occurred, evidently was completed almost instantaneously and involved a loud noise and a flash of light. Strieber also reported being raped, in effect, by a foot-long, triangular object that was inserted into his rectum. After these experiences, he found himself back in bed. Strieber's accounts of his dealings with extraterrestrials have been analyzed and found to bear certain similarities to elements of his fiction.

See also ABDUCTIONS; INCUBI AND SUCCUBI.

suicides   Among the curious deaths associated with the UFO phenomenon are at least two reported suicides. One is that of Morris Jessup, the American astronomer whose book *The Case for the UFO* played an important part in the case of the Allende letters. Another is Dr. James McDonald, an American astronomer who testified before a Congressional hearing on UFOs in 1966 and considered the so-called extraterrestrial hypothesis the "least unlikely" explanation for the UFO phenomenon. McDonald's suicide is thought to have been incidentally related to his views on, and investigations of, UFOs. The circumstances of Jessup's apparent suicide remain mysterious. Jessup died in 1959, McDonald in 1971.

See also ALLENDE LETTERS; DEATHS; EXTRATERRESTRIAL HYPOTHESIS; JESSUP, MORRIS.

Sumpter–McLemore incident, Arkansas, United States   A notable report from the wave of "airship" sightings in the United States in the late 1800s, this incident involved two policemen, one Constable Sumpter and one Deputy Sheriff McLemore, of Hot Springs, Arkansas. The men allegedly were riding together on the night of May 6, 1897, when they saw a bright light high in the sky. The light disappeared, then appeared again, much nearer the ground, after the men had ridden about five miles. The men stopped and watched the light vanish behind a hill. After they had ridden another half mile, their horses stopped and refused to proceed. Approximately 300 feet ahead, the policemen saw two figures moving "with lights." Sumpter and McLemore drew their guns and ordered the figures to identify themselves and state their business. A man with a long, dark beard reportedly approached the policemen, holding a lantern, and said he and his party were traveling in an airship. Sumpter and McLemore reportedly saw the outline of a cigar-shaped craft about 60 feet long. The bearded man's companions appeared to be a young man and a young woman holding a parasol. The bright light, Sumpter and McLemore were told, came from a bril-

liant searchlight that consumed much of the airship's power. The policemen were invited to come aboard the craft for a ride, but declined. Sumpter and McLemore departed hastily. When they returned to the site some 40 minutes later, the airship and its occupants were no longer there. The men said they neither heard nor saw the airship depart. This incident demonstrates how UFO reports tend to reflect the available technology of the particular land and time, such as the lanterns.

See also AIRSHIPS; TECHNOLOGY.

S.W. incident   A case from the files of psychiatrist Dr. Carl Jung, this incident involves a female Swiss channeler identified as "S.W.," who believed she had seen an extraterrestrial seated near her on a railway journey. S.W. was extremely agitated after this encounter. She related her alleged knowledge of the star-dwellers. She claimed they had no souls such as humans have; had no science and philosophy such as ours; but were more advanced than humankind in technology and had been traveling in flying machines long before that technology was developed on Earth. The woman added that star-dwellers who visited Earth were not allowed to approach nearer than 75 feet of the planet's surface. Any star-dweller who violated this law was forced to remain on Earth and assume the appearance of a human, from which the being was freed only after the death of his human body. Star-dwellers confined to Earth, she said, were cold and cruel by nature and could be identified by their hairless and "eyebrowless" faces. Emperor Napoleon I, she explained, was characteristic of the star-dwellers.

Jung apparently was able to identify the alleged star-dweller on the train as a sour-faced, elderly businessman he knew. S.W.'s description of the star-dwellers is interesting nonetheless, because modern accounts of encounters with extraterrestrials—especially "grays"—often mention the cold and cruel manner and the hairless crania of the alleged aliens. Modern UFO lore also is filled with rumors of extraterrestrials living on Earth in the guise of humans. Jung took an intense interest in the UFO phenomenon and interpreted it as an expression of humankind's search for unity and wholeness in a fragmented world.

See also GRAYS; JUNG, CARL GUSTAV.

swamp gas incident   One of the most notorious incidents of the 20th-century UFO controversy in America, the swamp gas incident was related to a widely publicized series of UFO sightings in the area of Ann Arbor, Michigan, in March 1966. The UFOs reportedly moved across the skies at high velocities and displayed extreme maneuverability. One sighting near the community of Dexter, Michigan, on March 20 involved a "meteor" that allegedly landed in a swamp. A man and his son said they approached to within 500 feet of the object and described it as pyramidal, yellow in color and adorned with white and blue-green lights. The white light allegedly changed color, to red, as the witnesses watched. As the men drew near, the object disappeared. More than fifty persons claimed to have seen the UFO that night. The following day, additional witnesses said they had seen a similar object near Ann Arbor. Eighty-seven female students at a dormitory at Hillsdale College near Ann Arbor reported a sighting that night of an object that reportedly carried bright lights and flew about in a swampy area for approximately four hours. Other witnesses included a college official who had worked as a newspaper reporter. The object in this case was described as luminous and football-shaped and reportedly moved in an irregular, wobbling fashion.

The Michigan UFO sightings created such intense public interest that Project Blue Book, the U.S. Air Force's study group for the UFO phenomenon, was asked to investigate. The Air Force sent astronomer and UFO investigator Dr. J. Allen Hynek to Ann Arbor. Hynek found that conditions in the vicinity resembled "hysteria," and was unable to conduct an in-depth investigation. At a press conference, without definitely attributing any one explanation to the UFO sightings, Hynek suggested they might have been episodes of burning methane, or swamp gas. The news media responded with amused commentary about the Michigan incidents. Soon after the "swamp gas" incident, Michigan's Republican Congressman Gerald R. Ford (later to become president of the United States after the resignation of President Richard Nixon in 1974) called for a congressional investigation of the Michigan sightings.

See also ARMED SERVICES HEARINGS; BLUE BOOK, PROJECT; HYNEK, J. ALLEN; METHANE.

swastika   This occult symbol, consisting of a cross with its tips bent at right angles to the arms of the cross, in either a clockwise or counterclockwise direction, is involved in some UFO close-encounter and "contactee" reports, notably the alleged experiences of George Adamski. Written communications from Adamski's "extraterrestrials" featured the swastika, which, Adamski suggested, represented the rotation of the galaxy. Although the swastika's most notorious association is with Nazi Germany, the swastika also is an emblem used in Native American cultures.

See also ADAMSKI, GEORGE; OCCULTISM; SYMBOLISM.

Swedenborg, Emanuel (1688–1772)   Swedish visionary and author. Although Swedenborg lived before the age of the so-called UFO phenomenon, he appears to have had numerous "visions" and other experiences comparable in many ways to modern close encounters. A well-educated man, prolific author and member of Sweden's House of Nobles, he began to experience, in his middle years, what appeared to be visions of other worlds. At age 56, he devoted himself to exploring and writing about these previously unseen worlds, and continued doing so for the next quarter century. He described a "world of spirits," which he said was located midway between hell and heaven. His account of events following the death of one's body, and the separation of the soul from the body, match closely some 20th century reports of near-death experiences. He also claimed to have met inhabitants of Jupiter and other planets, as well as to have met Protestant reformer Martin Luther in "heaven" and converted him to Swedenborg's own beliefs. Swedenborg added that he also met Luther's colleague John Calvin there, but failed to change Calvin's mind about the doctrine of predestination.

Swedenborg's "mystical" experiences along this line followed years of preparation. While still a child, he began practicing what today would be called meditation techniques. Before long, he began to see a flame during his meditations, and he viewed the flame as an indication that someone or something approved of his activities and ideas. Swedenborg started to perceive the existence of a world of "spirits" around him. His contacts with these spirits resemble UFO close encounters, notably in their element of absurdity. For example, one evening after overindulging in food, Swedenborg reportedly saw darkness and a vision of reptiles crawling on the ceiling, followed by the vision of a man who said, "Don't eat so much," and then vanished. This experience frightened Swedenborg, but he interpreted it as beneficent because it provided "moral" advice. The same visitor returned later that night and identified himself to Swedenborg as God. He said he had selected Swedenborg to interpret the "spiritual" aspect of Scripture to humankind.

This entity, whom Swedenborg called "the Lord," would give Swedenborg frequent glimpses into the other world, where Swedenborg held conversations with "angels" and "spirits." Swedenborg described the "world of spirits" as a place where one prepares for residence in heaven through a process of education that lasts up to a year.

Heaven itself differed little from this place of preparation, and both were much like Earth, Swedenborg claimed. He described buildings, halls, gardens and parks, and reported that angels had bedrooms and large supplies of clothing. Government and laws also appeared to resemble those on Earth but were more "spiritual" in character. Swedenborg said churches existed in heaven, and clergymen delivered sermons in them. If anyone disagreed with a sermon, however, the clergyman would become confused. Many other earthly institutions were found also in Swedenborg's "heaven," including marriage, reproduction and schooling.

Several important parallels may be seen between Swedenborg's visions and modern close encounters. As in many UFO reports today, the "contactee," in this case Swedenborg, had experience in occult practices before starting to receive images of the "next world." His encounters with "God" began in a ridiculous manner, with a vision of reptiles and a warning to avoid overeating; likewise, absurdity is a major component of many alien contact reports today. The "heavenly" world that Swedenborg describes sounds merely like a more peaceful version of Earth. In similar fashion, alleged aliens describing their homeworlds to human contactees tend to depict decidedly Earth-like places, only more impressive. The description of the planet "Clarion," as delivered to contactee Truman Bethurum, for example, resembled a housing development on Earth. Even some minor details of Swedenborg's experiences have counterparts in UFO lore, such as his reported debates with Luther and Calvin, which are comparable to accounts of "aliens" arranging meetings between modern contactees and figures from the past. In short, Swedenborg's experiences of other worlds may be seen as part of a long series of encounter cases extending back for centuries before, but also including, the modern UFO phenomenon.

See also ABSURDITY; BETHURUM INCIDENT; ENCOUNTER PHENOMENA; METALOGIC.

Swift–Watson observations

A total eclipse of the Sun on July 29, 1878, was observed in the United States by astronomers Lewis Swift, director of the Warner Observatory, and James Watson, once director of the University of Michigan's astronomical observatory. Swift and Watson made their observations from sites some 185 miles apart. During the eclipse, both astronomers reported seeing discoid or planet-like objects, red in color and equal in apparent size to the planet Mercury or slightly smaller,

Swift–Watson observations involved search for hypothetical planet inside orbit of Mercury (shown here). (NASA)

close to the Sun. These objects were presumed to be planets inside the orbit of Mercury. The two astronomers saw the objects, however, at different positions. Watson saw them separated by perhaps two degrees of arc, whereas Swift saw them much closer together. (A separation of two degrees is considerable. The full moon, for example, subtends only about half a degree of arc.) In view of this discrepancy, other astronomers argued that Swift and Watson had merely seen stars and misidentified them. Such an error seemed improbable, because both observers were experienced astronomers and unlikely to make such an elementary mistake.

An intense controversy developed around the Swift–Watson observations, and no satisfactory resolution to the controversy was ever obtained. In an analysis of the observations, one Dr. C.H.F. Peters dismissed the possibility that the mysterious objects were planets within Mercury's orbit and argued that the two astronomers must have seen and misidentified stars, or else they actually had seen nothing at all.

Decades after the Swift–Watson observations, American astronomer Morris Jessup used Peters's analysis to support an argument that Swift and Watson might have seen UFOs. Jessup suggested the discrepancy between Swift's and Watson's observations was caused by "parallax," the shift in apparent position of a celestial object when viewed from two widely separated locations on Earth. Jessup imagined that the objects were both in outer space but close to Earth, 2,000 to 20,000 miles away. Jessup estimated that the larger and more distant of the objects was as much as a mile and a half in diameter, while the nearer and smaller object was only about 10 percent as wide. Jessup went so far as to apply the term "mother ship" tentatively to the larger object. The red color of the objects, Jessup explained, could have been due to their being in the penumbra, or shadow, of the Moon during the eclipse. Jessup suggested the objects were reflecting reddened light that had passed once through the Earth's atmosphere, again through the atmosphere by being reflected back out into space, and a third time through the atmosphere when the light was reflected off the two objects and observed on Earth by the astronomers.

See also ASTRONOMY; HARRISON INCIDENT; JESSUP, MORRIS.

sylphs Mythological beings once said to inhabit the air and travel in aerial vehicles, sylphs were described in terms almost identical to certain modern UFO abduction reports. On occasion, sylphs allegedly would abduct a man and give him an introduction to their civilization, then return the man to Earth. When the local populace saw one of these abductees alighting from one of the sylphs' "spacecraft," a mob was likely to form and haul the abductee away to be tortured and killed as a suspected sorcerer. In similar fashion, modern "abductees" may report receiving an overview of the alleged extraterrestrials' homeworlds and cultures,

and experience an unpleasant reception (though usually short of torture and execution) from other humans following the so-called close encounter. The Emperor Charlemagne is said to have believed in the sylphs' existence and pronounced heavy penalties against them.

See also ABDUCTIONS; ENCOUNTER PHENOMENA; MYTHOLOGY.

symbolism An important aspect of the UFO phenomenon, symbolism takes many forms in experiences involving UFOs. Psychiatrist Carl Jung, for example, saw in the familiar circular shape of UFOs a yearning for wholeness on the part of humankind, to whom the circle traditionally has stood for completeness and harmony. Occult symbolism is abundant in UFO lore. The triangle, a widely reported symbol in UFO sightings, is also a major element of occultist and New Age symbolism. The occult symbol of the swastika also features in some UFO encounter reports, notably those of American "contactee" George Adamski. Animal symbols are also widely reported in UFO encounter cases. Alleged extraterrestrials in some cases are described as resembling reptiles, age-old symbols of evil (as in the story of the serpent in Eden, in the biblical book of Genesis, and the great red dragon that symbolizes Satan in the book of Revelation). The phoenix, mythological symbol of death and rebirth, also has been reported seen in the alleged abduction experiences of Betty Andreasson Luca.

See also ANDREASSON CASE; DEMONOLOGY; JUNG, CARL GUSTAV; MANDALA; OCCULTISM; REPTOIDS; SWASTIKA; TRIANGLE.

syncretism Alleged messages from extraterrestrials urge listeners, in some cases, to adopt new, "syncretic" belief systems. "Syncretic" means assembled from a variety of sources. Spiritual belief systems endorsed by alleged aliens may include elements of Christianity, Buddhism, Hinduism and shamanism.

See also BELIEF SYSTEMS; COMMUNICATIONS; MESSAGES; RELIGION, UFOS AND.

T

talls This expression refers to certain alleged extra-terrestrials who are considerably taller in stature than the familiar "grays," which are said to stand about three to four feet tall. According to UFO lore, some hostility exists between talls and grays. This alleged animosity between talls and grays is an example of modern mythology surrounding UFOs.

See also GRAYS; HUMANOIDS; MYTHOLOGY; RUMORS.

Taupignac incident, France At about 7:30 P.M. on October 11, 1954, three men were driving near Taupignac when they reportedly saw a bright red sphere overhead and stopped to observe it. They also allegedly saw another UFO, estimated at about 18 feet in diameter, emitting red-yellow light, at a distance of about 600 feet and an altitude of 30 feet. This object was silent and stationary at first, then moved suddenly in a horizontal direction and landed. Two of the men went to investigate the landing and reportedly saw four small humanoids, about three feet tall, who appeared to be performing some kind of work on the machine. When the men approached within about 45 feet, the humanoids boarded the craft hurriedly. The craft emitted a dazzling, multicolored display of light, then departed vertically at great speed. Some elements of this report, such as the small humanoids apparently working on their craft in plain view of human witnesses, fit the pattern of UFO close encounters that, some students of the UFO phenomenon believe, are staged so as to give humans a close look at the craft and their occupants.

See also ENCOUNTER PHENOMENA; REPAIRS.

technology Technology described in reports of UFOs has tended to reflect the level of technological advancement in human society when the reports were made. In centuries past, for example, UFOs were described as dragging "anchors" that caught on buildings or on fences. Nineteenth-century UFO reports of mysterious "airships" were cast in the language of then-current technology, such as air brakes and propellers; moreover, 19th-century ignorance of aeronautics was reflected in the crude design of the alleged airships, which probably could not have flown even if they had been built. UFO sightings in Scandanavia immediately after World War II were attributed to rockets. Selected items of "alien" technology reported in the postwar period, from ray guns to humanoid robots, also have had parallels either in actual technology of the time or in fictional treatments of that technology, such as science fiction stories and motion pictures.

The technology of UFO sightings underwent a curious evolution following World War II. "Contactee" cases in the United States between 1945 and 1950 featured hardware that, although ostensibly alien, was already well-known in one form or another, such as the motion picture projector. As lasers and other new technologies were developed, these, too, began to turn up in UFO encounter stories. In the 1970s and 1980s, however, descriptions of UFO technology began to take a turn toward the magical and supernatural. Instead of flying into a witness's field of view and then departing in the manner of an airplane or helicopter, UFOs reportedly started simply appearing and disappearing at particular sites. Despite efforts to explain such performances in terms of "interdimensional gateways" and other theoretical constructs, witnesses described the events essentially in terms of supernatural phenomena. This emphasis represented a major change from the traditional assumption that UFOs represented material spacecraft visiting Earth from some other world. Now UFOs were coming to be seen more as psychic phenomena than as material objects.

Unsubstantiated rumors about alien technology in use on Earth have proliferated since 1945. These rumors include stories that the U.S. military has been trying for decades to test-fly captured extraterrestrial spacecraft; that transistors were derived from solid-state technology found on a crashed saucer in the southwestern desert of the United States immediately after World War II; that the aliens have perfected a "fuel-less" propulsion source, perpetual motion machine, anti-gravity device or other such technology; and that the Third Reich contacted extraterrestrials and learned from them secrets of alien technology, which were passed along to the United States following Germany's defeat. See also ANTI-GRAVITY; CRASHES; DIMENSIONS; INTERDIMENSIONAL GATEWAYS; PRECEDENTS; ROBOTS.

Teesdale inheritance   An example of the mystery and absurdity surrounding the UFO phenomenon, the Teesdale inheritance involved the estate of one "A.P. Teesdale, Esq.," in England. In 1988, alleged trustees of the estate placed an ad in a Paris magazine, trying to contact groups that might be able to satisfy the reqirements of Teesdale's will. Specifically, the groups should be engaged seriously in contacting and setting up relationships with extraterrestrials. The following year, at a meeting in Paris, Teesdale's "confession" was read. Supposedly, Teesdale, while serving as a soldier in World War I, underwent a near-death experience after a shell exploded near him. In this experience, he allegedly met a being that described itself as a "sentinel" and gave him a curious object with instructions to give it to scientists. In a later encounter, the sentinel told him that he would receive another object. Teesdale tried to interest other people in the objects, but without success, and finally left the disposition of the objects to the trustees of his estate. The inheritance was awarded to Claude Vorilhon, leader of the Raelians, a European movement devoted to contact with extraterrestrials. Vorilhon took possession of a cryogenic receptacle that presumably contained one or both of the objects. Reportedly, a large sum of money was also awarded to Vorilhon's group, but the money never was delivered, and the

Tehran incident, Iran, resembled certain alleged close-encounter cases in the United States. (U.S. Geological Survey)

firm handling the business turned out to be nonexistent.

See also ABSURDITY; HOAXES; NEAR DEATH EXPERIENCE; RAELIAN MOVEMENT.

Tehran incident, Iran   This incident allegedly occurred around 2:30 A.M. on October 8, 1954, when a witness standing on the balcony on the second floor of his home saw a white, luminous UFO about 60 feet away. Inside the craft, the witness reportedly saw a small humanoid wearing black clothing and a mask with a projection resembling an elephant's trunk. As he watched the object, the witness felt as if he were being attracted toward the object by magnetic influence. He shouted in fear and awakened his neighbors. Then the object flew away rapidly, giving off sparks, and was lost from view. Because of the time at which the incident reportedly occurred, one might be inclined to dismiss it as a dream or an hallucination.

See also HALLUCINATIONS.

Teilhard de Chardin, Pierre (1881–1955)   The French theologian and philosopher Teilhard de Chardin expounded a theory of "ultra-hominization," meaning the evolutionary advancement of humankind to some higher level of development. Similar thinking has led some students of the UFO phenomenon to presume—without proof, it should be emphasized—that alleged extraterrestrials are here on Earth to guide humankind toward ultra-hominization or some comparable condition. Ultra-hominization, at least when applied to the UFO phenomenon, is essentially an occult belief.

See also EVOLUTION; OCCULTISM.

telepathy Defined as the transfer of thoughts or information directly from one entity's mind to another, without the use of written or vocalized language or symbols to convey the information, telepathy has been reported widely in UFO encounter cases. Humans in these encounters may report that an "alien" entity conveyed messages to them by telepathy, and there are numerous reports of UFOs reacting to a person's thoughts as if the entity or entities controlling the UFO were reading the observer's mind. Sometimes reports of telepathic contact also mention unpleasant sensations such as headaches.

See also BENDER MYSTERY; ENCOUNTER PHENOMENA; WORLD CONTACT DAY.

telephone calls Among the most curious elements of the UFO phenomenon, mysterious telephone calls are associated with some UFO sightings. Within a day or two of a UFO sighting, the witness may be contacted by an anonymous caller who warns the witness against mentioning what he or she has seen. Such calls may arrive before the witness has discussed the sighting with anyone and may be placed to unlisted telephone numbers.

These telephone calls are examples of various kinds of harassment allegedly directed at witnesses following UFO sightings. Some witnesses are said to receive visits from sinister "men in black," who may threaten the witness with bodily harm if he or she talks about the sighting.

Such calls in UFO literature have parallels in the lore of occultism. "Telephone calls from the dead" have been reported frequently in ghost stories. The calls allegedly are made to living persons who were close relatives of, or shared some other strong association with, the deceased. A famous case involved actress Ida Lupino, who allegedly received a telephone call from her recently deceased father concerning the location of important papers required to settle his estate.

Various explanations have been suggested for these calls to UFO witnesses. One is that intelligence agencies or other organizations on Earth are attempting to suppress discussion of UFOs. If that is the case, then the technique appears to have failed, because public discussion of the UFO phenomenon is widespread.

Another hypothesis is that extraterrestrials place the calls, for unfathomable reasons, to silence witnesses. This explanation also has its flaws. Why, for example, should extraterrestrials visiting Earth in highly visible spacecraft wish to intimidate witnesses into silence when the spacecraft themselves appeared to be designed and operated to maximize their visibility?

A third explanation is that the phone calls are spiritual phenomena, executed by evil spirits to frighten and confuse humans. If true, this explanation would be consistent with many other elements of the UFO phenomenon that have been linked at least tentatively with demonic activity.

A fourth explanation, of course, is that the calls are hoaxes.

See also COMMUNICATIONS; DEMONOLOGY; ENCOUNTER PHENOMENA; MEN IN BLACK; MESSAGES.

teleportation This alleged phenomenon, which may be defined as the instantaneous bodily translocation of a person from one point to another, considerably distant point without any ordinary, real-time travel between the two points, has been discussed in the UFO literature, but its place in UFO lore is hard to ascertain. Astronomer Morris Jessup, an early analyst of the modern "flying saucer" phenomenon, examined several alleged instances of teleportation—including the case of Oliver Larch (identified as "Lerch" in Jessup's account), who supposedly was abducted from his family's farm near South Bend, Indiana, on Christmas Eve of 1889—and linked them tentatively to UFO activity. Jessup suggested that a fast-moving UFO might pick up a person at one location, then set the person down again on Earth quickly, not recognizing that the UFO and its human passenger had covered a great distance in the meantime.

See also JESSUP, MORRIS; LARCH INCIDENT.

Telos One of the more bizarre tales in UFO lore involves an imaginary "Lemurian" city called Telos, supposedly built beneath Mount Shasta in California. According to the myth of Telos, the city has a population of about 1.5 million and runs on a fantastic technology using force fields and partially "organic" computers. These technologies allegedly were developed in the lost land of Lemuria and were salvaged when the mythical ancient continent was destroyed. Telos is said to be part of a vast "Agartha network" of more than 100 subterranean cities and to be a UFO base. Tales of Telos, the Agartha network and its strange technologies are typical of the

Telos, an underground city and UFO base, is said to be located under California's volcanic Mount Shasta. (U.S. Geological Survey)

mythology that has arisen around the UFO phenomenon, especially in the last quarter of the 20th century.

See also BASES; LEMURIA; MYTHOLOGY; SHAVER MYSTERY; TUNNELS; UNDERGROUND INSTALLATIONS.

temperature effects   Humans in the vicinity of UFOs frequently mention sensing change in temperature. This change often takes the form of an intense chill, although extreme heat may be reported in some cases. Even when a UFO encounter is recalled through regression under hypnosis, a perception of coldness may turn up prominently in the subject's recollections. A similar feeling of cold is often reported in encounter cases involving occult phenomena, such as "hauntings."

Temperature effects like those reported in certain UFO encounters are related also in an anecdote about Eliphas Levi, the 19th-century French occultist. In 1854, when he attempted to call up the spirit of the ancient sorcerer Apollonius of Tyana, Levi reportedly felt great cold and fright as a shrouded figure appeared in front of him. One of his arms went numb at the elbow as something touched it.

Levi felt a profound weakness come over him and fainted. Afterward, the shaken Levi warned against such practices. He advised "the greatest caution" to anyone contemplating a similar experience, because the result could be exhaustion and illness.

Levi's experience resembles that of many UFO contactees, and not only in Levi's perception of cold. Like many contactees in our own time, he also was made numb and weak, and then driven to unconsciousness, by the presence of the spirit he had summoned. The parallels with UFO encounter cases and Levi's occultist doings are close and numerous. Except for a few details, Levi's experience is virtually identical to that of some modern UFO contactees who claim to have been immobilized by an "alien."

See also ENCOUNTER PHENOMENA.

temporal lobe epilepsy   A condition involving the temporal lobe of the brain, this variety of epilepsy has been suggested as a possible explanation for certain alleged UFO encounter cases. Individuals with temporal lobe epilepsy may experience visual and olfactory hallucinations comparable to those reported in many UFO encounter stories.

See also HALLUCINATIONS.

tengu   In Japanese folklore, the tengu (sing. tengu) are long-nosed, boastful goblins who are said to inhabit the mountains. A remarkable story involving a tengu, and bearing a strong similarity to many modern UFO abduction reports, is found in the writings of Hirata Atsutane, a Japanese physician and scholar of the late 18th and early 19th centuries. His 1828 work *Kokon Yomiko*, "A Study of Weird Beings, Ancient and Modern," contains an account of a boy named Torakichi, who claimed he had been carried off by a tengu and had visited the Moon as well as many foreign countries on Earth. An old man brought news of the boy Torakichi's experiences to Hirata in 1820, and Hirata went to meet Torakichi. Hirata was surprised to find that the boy provided specific information about the distant realms he supposedly visited. The boy said he had been authorized to reveal details of his travels and of conditions in the other world. Hirata agreed, figuring that because many other kinds of knowledge were coming to public attention just then, it was time for the message of the tengu to be revealed as well.

Torakichi said his involvement with the spirit world started at age seven, in 1812. Torakichi met a long-haired man who had with him a little jar of medicine. The man claimed to be able to fit himself into the jar. He proceed to do so. Then the jar sailed away into the sky. The following day, Torakichi and

Tengu, the long-nosed, boastful goblins of Japanese folklore, resemble "aliens" in many modern UFO reports. (NASA)

the mysterious man met again in the same spot. This time the man offered to take Torakichi along with him in the jar. Despite misgivings, Torakichi consented. They were transported to a mountaintop where Torakichi had heard that the tengu gathered. For the next several years, between ages 7 and 11, Torakichi made many such trips. Sometimes he stayed away from home for more than three months at a time, but no one in the family noticed he was missing.

At age 11, on the advice of his father, Torakichi became a Buddhist priest and joined a temple. He became known there as a spell-caster. In 1819, following his father's death, Torakichi resumed his supernatural travels and supposedly visited many foreign countries. He indicated that on one trip he had visited a cold land where the people worshipped images such as a man on a cross, and a woman holding a small child (apparently a reference to icons of the Crucifixion and of Mary, Christ's mother, holding the infant Jesus). Torakichi said he had asked his companion about them and was told they were images of Christianity, a "false" religion. Torakichi's companion reportedly spat on the images.

Torakichi also described a trip to the Moon. Torakichi reported that he felt intensely cold on the way

to the Moon, but once near the lunar surface felt comfortably warm. He indicated he had approached within 600 feet of the surface, and said the Moon had seas full of something that resembled mud. He also said that at one point on the surface, he observed several holes through which stars could be seen shining.

The similarities between Torakichi's testimony and modern UFO abductions and other encounter stories are considerable. Torakichi's abductions by tengu supposedly began when he was a child. He had an encounter with a mysterious being that was capable of changing its size and shape. That being entered a vessel and flew away into the sky, taking Torakichi with him. Torakichi had the ability to see into the future. He claimed to have visited another celestial body, his description of which turned out to be grossly inaccurate. He traveled great distances on Earth with a tengu's assistance. The boy also delivered a "religious," specifically anti–Christian message.

Torakichi's revelations came at a time when new knowledge was being disseminated widely, and a "new age," as a later generation would put it, was believed to be starting. Temperature effects were reported in Torakichi's alleged trip to the Moon. There is even an element of "missing time" (to use UFO researcher Budd Hopkins's term) in Torakichi's story, on the occasions when he stayed away from home for weeks at a time without anyone noticing his absence.

See also ABDUCTIONS; CHRIST AND CHRISTIANITY; DEMONOLOGY; ENCOUNTER PHENOMENA; MISSING TIME.

Terauchi incident   A widely reported sighting involving a Japanese civilian aircraft, this incident allegedly occurred on the night of November 17, 1986, when Japan Air Lines flight 1628 was approaching Anchorage, Alaska. Pilot Kenju Terauchi reportedly noticed several lights following the airliner and described one of the UFOs later as a walnut-shaped object twice the size of an aircraft carrier. The objects reportedly flew along with the jet for half an hour before disappearing. Terauchi was quoted as saying that the objects flew so quickly and stopped so abruptly that they might have an extraterrestrial origin.

See also AIRCRAFT; JAPAN.

Tesla, Nikola (1856–1943)   European-born American inventor. Tesla's career has played a small but interesting part in the UFO phenomenon. A highly eccentric man with an interest in the occult, Tesla invented the famous "Tesla coil," a spectacular piece of electrical equipment often demonstrated in science courses. Tesla also was partly responsible for the adoption of alternating current for use in household electrical systems. According to one story, Tesla was about to demonstrate a tremendous source of virtually cost-free electrical energy when his financier, industrialist J.P. Morgan, withdrew support form Tesla's work. Tesla's name has been applied to the "Tesla globe," an alleged photographic phenomenon associated with UFO activity. Tesla's name also has been invoked in pseudoscientific literature on alleged UFO technology and related subjects, such as anti-gravity.

See also ANTI-GRAVITY; PSEUDOSCIENCE; TESLA GLOBE.

Tesla globe This phenomenon is a luminous sphere or ovoid that appears on photographs taken at night but is not visible to the unaided eye, according to Ellen Crystall, a student of the Hudson Valley sightings in the United States. Crystall reports taking numerous photographs in an area of New Jersey where UFO sightings are reported frequently, and finding Tesla globes on many of her photos. Crystall claims to have photographed Tesla globes ranging in size from a house to a tennis ball. Tesla globes are named after the inventor Nikola Tesla.

See also EVIDENCE; HUDSON VALLEY SIGHTINGS; PHOTOGRAPHY; TESLA, NIKOLA.

third eye In the UFO phenomenon, occult teaching abut the "third eye" appears to be reflected in certain reports of encounters with "extraterrestrials." Ancient Egyptian teachings about the third eye describe it as a characteristic of Maat, goddess of truth. Later the third eye became an attribute of the warrior deity and Sun god Horus. Hinduistic teachings describe the third eye as a "chakra," or point of energy, on the forehead. In the modern New Age movement, the third eye is known as the Ajra Center. Christian doctrine, based upon the book of Revelation, maintains that the Antichrist will place his seal upon his followers either in this location or on the right hand. These teachings are reminiscent of descriptions of aliens in UFO encounters having a third eye or some similar feature in the middle of their foreheads. In some cases, alleged UFO abductees subjected to hypnotic regression may "recall" having a third eye emplaced somehow in the middle of the forehead.

See also ABDUCTIONS; ANTICHRIST; ENCOUNTER PHENOMENA; NEW AGE MOVEMENT; OCCULTISM; SAGRADA FAMILIA INCIDENT.

This Island Earth One of the first motion pictures of the postwar period to deal with the subject of UFOs and extraterrestrial visitors, *This Island Earth* (U.S., 1954) concerns the efforts of alien scientists on Earth to enlist help from humankind in saving their besieged planet, Metaluna. A man and woman from Earth travel to Metaluna by flying saucer and arrive in time to see the planet destroyed by hostile aliens who bombard Metaluna with large meteorites. Among the aliens were bizarre humanoids with huge, exposed brains and crab-like claws. The film was a lavish production for its time and was released by Universal Pictures. The cast included Faith Domergue, Jeff Morrow and Rex Reason.

See also MOTION PICTURES.

"Three suns" In the third part of Shakespeare's play *Henry VI*, the Prince of Wales and the Duke of York witness what appear to be three suns in the sky. The Duke of York describes the scene as follows:

> Three glorious suns, each one a perfect sun;
> Not separated with the racking clouds,
> But sever'd in a pale clear-shining sky,
> See, see! they join, embrace, and seem to kiss,
> As if they vow'd some league inviolable;
> Now they are but one lamp, one light, one sun,
> In this the heaven figures some event.

This account has been widely interpreted as a sighting of several luminous UFOs and bears some resemblance to aerial phenomena reported in connection with certain alleged apparitions of the Virgin Mary.

See also MARIAN APPARITIONS.

Thunderbird This mythical animal features in the lore of Native Americans and is said to have been a giant bird capable of carrying off deer and humans. The myth of the Thunderbird resembles in some respects modern accounts of UFO abductions. The Thunderbird story also brings to mind certain 19th-century reports of humans who apparently were snatched off the ground at night and carried off into the sky by an entity or entities unknown.

See also ABDUCTIONS; LARCH INCIDENT.

Thutmose incident, Egypt Pharaoh Thutmose III, who reigned over Egypt between approximately 1500 B.C. and 1450 B.C., reportedly witnessed a fiery circle in the sky. The object gave off a foul smell. Thutmose appears to have ordered an official study of the phenomenon. Soon after this initial sighting, many other fiery objects, brighter than the sun, are said to have appeared in the skies over Egypt. This report is believed to be a modern hoax derived from the story of the Old Testament prophet Ezekiel.

See also EZEKIEL.

Tibet   A minor but possibly significant element of the UFO phenomenon is the importance of Tibet in the narratives of UFO "contactees." In some accounts, Tibet is said to be, or have been, a gathering place for UFOs, as well as a base for their occupants. Associations with Tibet permeate UFO lore, largely because of the UFO phenomenon's association with occultism, which traces many of its various branches to Tibet. George Adamski, for example, belonged to a cult in California called the royal Order of Tibet; Alexandra David-Neel, whose paranormal experiences paralleled those of modern UFO contactees, performed an intensive study of Tibetan occultism; and the founder of theosophy, Madame Helena Petrovna Blavatsky, whose thinking influenced the modern UFO phenomenon, had strong links with the occultism of Tibet.

See also ADAMSKI, GEORGE; BEN MACDHUI; BLAVATSKY, HELENA PETROVNA; MILAREPA; OCCULTISM; SHAMBALA; TULPA.

time barrier   One obstacle to interstellar flight—and consequently to the "extraterrestrial hypothesis" that UFOs represent material spacecraft bearing intelligent organisms from other star systems—is that interstellar travel at velocities slower than light would take a very long time. Because relativity theory has established that no physical object can travel faster than light, and because light requires many years to travel to Earth even from stars in our vicinity, travel to and from nearby stars might require hundreds of years. Even an organism with a life span measured in centuries might be too short-lived to survive a trip from its postulated homeworld to Earth under such circumstances.

This "time barrier" has been discussed extensively among UFO observers, and several hypotheses have been proposed to circumvent it. One hypothesis is that extraterrestrials might use some natural phenomenon or trick of technology to travel faster than light. "Wormholes," or portals between distant points in space, are one widely cited (though purely imaginary) mechanism for overcoming the time barrier. According to this hypothesis, an extraterrestrial

spacecraft might use a "wormhole" to travel directly from a remote part of our galaxy to Earth, without the need for extended travel through space. In another hypothesis, an alien spacecraft might travel so close to the velocity of light that relativistic time effects would allow passengers on the spacecraft to complete a voyage to Earth in only a few years as measured by clocks on the ship, even though hundreds or thousands of years might pass as measured by timepieces on Earth. A third hypothesis has it that UFOs might not represent extraterrestrial spacecraft at all, but rather time-traveling machines from Earth's own distant past or future. This hypothesis simply eliminates the need to overcome the interplanetary "time barrier" by eliminating the need for travel between star systems. All of these hypotheses are, of course, mere speculation, and likely to remain so for the indefinite future.

See also DIMENSIONS; EXTRATERRESTRIAL HYPOTHESIS; TIME TRAVEL.

time effects   One frequently reported element of UFO close-encounter stories is that "extraterrestrials" seem able to manipulate time, or at least the perception of time. Thus, what impresses an "abductee" as a relatively brief encounter, lasting only minutes or hours, may be found to have taken much longer when the incident is over. The witness may report afterward that time seemed to "stop" during the encounter. This perception is common to UFO encounter reports and many incidents from mythology and folklore.

See also FOLKLORE; MISSING TIME.

time travel   Numerous fantasies have been written about travel through time, meaning travel at will, through specialized technology, either backward or forward in time. Among the most famous fictional treatments of this subject is H.G. Wells's 1895 story *The Time Machine*. Time travel has been suggested as a possible explanation for certain UFO reports in which a "spacecraft" is said to materialize or dematerialize in a given location, without visible movement to or from the site. Fanciful accounts of future civilizations visiting our age through time-traveling UFOs have a colorful place in UFO literature, as do speculations about visitors from imagined "advanced" civilizations of the distant past (Atlantis, for example) dropping in on the modern world through similar means. There is, however, no substantial evidence to support the hypothesis of such time travel by UFOs.

See also ATLANTIS; WELLS, H.G.

Tlon A fictional world imagined by the Argentine writer Jorge Luis Borges, Tlon figures in his short story "Tlon Uqbar Orbis Tertius," written in 1947. In the story, an American financier underwrites the compiling of a huge encyclopedia about the imaginary planet. Behind the scheme is a secret order called Orbis Tertius. The information about Tlon is made public, but only in small installments. Borges speculates that as belief in Tlon's existence spreads, the myth eventually will displace reality, and Orbis Tertius, in effect, will have conquered the world.

Borges's fantasy planet is reminiscent of descriptions that some UFO "contactees" have provided of other worlds. Time as we understand it is a meaningless concept on Tlon. Past, present and future all intermingle. Moreover, on Tlon, every ordinary object has a double, called a "hronir." If the original object is lost, its hronir can be located by a seeker who believes the lost object can be regained. In the story, hronir can be created through the beliefs of their discoverers. In theory, as more and more imaginary hronir are found, their existence will take priority over the real world in the minds of humans, so that eventually Earth will turn into Tlon. Astronomer and UFO investigator Jacques Vallee has pointed out parallels between Borges's story and the UFO phenomenon. Vallee cites the UMMO hoax as a real-life example of hronir being fabricated out of fantasy.

See also UMMO.

Tomakomai incident, Japan The Tomakomai incident was reported in July 1973 and involved a luminous UFO that allegedly extended a tube and drew water from a bay. After the UFO had collected water, it flew toward the shore and was described as resembling a large drum with windows, in which entities of some kind could be seen. A number of other glowing objects appeared in the sky near the large UFO and were drawn inside it before the UFO departed. The incident was witnessed by a security guard. The reported behavior of the UFO resembles that of another UFO allegedly sighted at Steep Rock Lake, Ontario, Canada, on July 2, 1950. This UFO also was said to extend hoses into the lake and apparently withdraw water from it. In this case, entities were also reported seen: robot-like figures three to four feet tall, wearing blue or red caps. These incidents fall into a curious category of UFO sightings associated with bodies of water.

See also WATER.

Topcliffe incident, United Kingdom During a North Atlantic Treaty Organization (NATO) exercise on September 19, 1952, a UFO was reportedly seen at the Royal Air Force's Topcliffe facility after a Meteor jet that was preparing to land at a nearby base. The object was circular and silvery, at an estimated altitude of 10,000 feet, some five miles behind the jet. As the object descended, it described a pendulum-like motion in the air, from left to right. Then the object stopped, appeared to rotate, and finally departed at great velocity. Observers described the object as solid, and clearly not a vapor trail or smoke ring. The "pendulum" motion described in the report resembles the "falling leaf" motion mentioned in many other UFO reports.

See also FALLING LEAF MOTION.

transients A proposed explanation for certain UFO sightings, transients are thought to be short-lived zones of natural radiation that form and then dissolve in the atmosphere. A person caught in a transient supposedly might experience visions such as balls of light (commonly reported in UFO encounter cases) and sensations such as tingling skin (also a common element of such reports). Other postulated effects of a transient include loss of consciousness and amnesia, which also are associated with UFO reports.

transitivity UFO investigator Jacques Vallee has cited transitivity as a particular fallacy in the investigation of UFOs. Transitivity may be described in general terms as follows: A person makes an assertion, A, then makes a second, seemingly strange statement, B, when asked to prove the truth of A. For example, imagine that someone says, "Extraterrestrials exist and have contacted me." This would be assertion A. When asked for proof or at least solid evidence of the truth of this assertion, the person says, "The extraterrestrials gave me the ability to levitate this book off the table." He proceeds to make the book rise off the table somehow. An observer might conclude, erroneously, that the "contactee" in this case had proven his assertion that extraterrestrials exist and had contacted him. In fact, no such thing has been proved. The "contactee" merely demonstrated that he can make the book rise off the table by some means. Fallacies such as this are widespread in the UFO phenomenon and may be used by charlatans to "prove" assertions about alleged extraterrestrials by mere trickery and legerdemain.

See also DECEPTIONS; HOAXES.

triangle The triangle as a geometric form appears often in the literature on UFOs. Triangular UFOs are reported frequently, in cases such as the Belgian sightings of 1989–90, and in the Hudson Valley sightings in the United States. Triangular emblems also occur elsewhere in the UFO phenomenon. In the celebrated "Dr. X" case in France, for example, Dr. X and his young son both allegedly were "branded" on their bodies with the imprint of a triangle. Some students of the UFO phenomenon see in the triangle motif a connection between UFOs and occultism, because the triangle is a widely used occult symbol.

See also DR. X INCIDENT; OCCULTISM; SYMBOLISM.

trickster Sometimes cited in the literature on UFOs, this figure of mythology is described as a player of pranks, a being that may appear in many different forms, including those of animals such as dogs and birds. The alleged extraterrestrials in some UFO encounter cases exhibit trickster-like traits, including a mischievous sense of humor and the ability to appear in many different guises.

See also POLYMORPHY; PROTEUS.

Tripoli incident, Libya Described by investigator Jacques Vallee as the "perfect landing," this incident allegedly occurred around 3:00 A.M. on October 23, 1954, near Tripoli. According to the report, a farmer saw an ovoid UFO land near him, with its long axis horizontal. The object was about 18 feet long and nine feet wide. Its lower half appeared to be metallic, while the upper portion was transparent, with bright white light inside. The craft allegedly made a noise like that of a compressed-air machine for inflating automobile tires. The UFO also had an external ladder and landing gear with six wheels.

Inside the UFO, the farmer saw six men in coveralls, wearing gas masks and working at instrument panels. One of the men removed his mask to exhale into a tube. The man's face looked like that of an ordinary human. The farmer walked up to the machine and put a hand on the ladder but was knocked to the ground by a powerful shock. One man inside the craft gestured to the farmer as if warning him to keep his distance.

The encounter lasted some 20 minutes. Then the object took off noiselessly, rose to about 150 feet altitude, and left at high velocity toward the east, leaving behind imprints on the ground from the wheels on its undercarriage. Vallee has suggested that this incident was some kind of three-dimensional "hologram" designed to be witnessed and reported.

See also BODILY EFFECTS; ENCOUNTER PHENOMENA; HUMANOIDS; VALLEE, JACQUES.

Jupiter—or rather its astrological symbol—played a small but interesting part in the Tujunga Canyon case. (NASA)

Tübingen incident, Germany On December 5, 1577, objects resembling large hats reportedly appeared in the skies over Tübingen. Most of the "hats" were said to be black, but others allegedly were red, green and blue in color.

Tujunga Canyon case, California, United States This widely reported case involved two young women who allegedly were abducted from their home in southern California by extraterrestrials in 1953. Under regressive hypnosis, the women told of their alleged capture and a medical examination at the hands of the aliens. One of the women claimed to have been marked on her back by the aliens with a symbol resembling the astrological glyph for the planet Jupiter. She thought the mark was meant to help the aliens identify and track her through successive "incarnations" on Earth.

See also ABDUCTIONS; ASTROLOGY; JUPITER; REGRESSIVE HYPNOSIS; REINCARNATION.

Tulli papyrus A nonexistent document, the so-called Tulli papyrus was said to describe a fleet of UFOs that appeared over Egypt some 3,500 years ago during the reign of Pharaoh Thutmose III. The papyrus was said to have been part of the collection of one Professor Tulli and to have been translated by one Prince de Rachelwitz. Supposedly, the document was kept in the Vatican archives. A U.S. government investigation of the papyrus, however, revealed that the Vatican had no record of the Tulli papyrus; Tulli was dead; and neither Tulli nor Rachelwitz was considered a qualified authority on the Thutmose story. Careful study of the story has indicated that it originated in modern times and is adapted from the story of the prophet Ezekiel in the Old Testament.

See also EZEKIEL; HOAXES; THUTMOSE INCIDENT.

tulpa   In occultism, a tulpa, or "thought form," is an entity that lacks material form and is created by thought. A famous case involving an alleged tulpa is that of Alexandra David-Neel, an occultist active in the late 19th and early 20th centuries. David-Neel reportedly created a tulpa during an investigation of Tibetan occultism. David-Neel originally envisioned the tulpa as a good-humored figure, and that indeed was the tulpa's manner at first; but then its character and behavior turned malevolent, and the tulpa began touching her and rubbing against her. David-Neel tried to rid herself of the tulpa but did not succeed for some six months.

The similarities between such a tulpa and manifestations of demonic activity are considerable. Certain "Bigfoot" sightings, a phenomenon associated with UFO activity, have been attributed to tulpas. Tulpas are associated with black magic, especially as practiced by the monks of Tibet. The link between tulpas and UFO activity remains mysterious, but both phenomena have roots in the occult.

See also BIGFOOT; DEMONOLOGY; HUMANOIDS; OCCULTISM; TIBET.

Tunguska event   On June 30, 1908, a great explosion occurred in mid-air over Siberia and caused tremendous damage. More than 700 square miles of forest were blown down, and humans and animals were reported burned many miles from the explosion, although no fatalities were reported. Investigations at the site revealed no crater, as one would have expected to find if a very large meteorite had struck the Earth. The effects of the blast resembled those of a modern nuclear explosion, although the first such device was not exploded for more than 35 years after the Tunguska event. Moreover, the yield of the Tunguska blast was estimated later at some 30 megatons, or equivalent to the explosion of 30 million tons of TNT. That yield was many times greater than the yield of the first nuclear explosions, which were only in the range of several kilotons (thousand tons) of TNT.

Eyewitnesses to the Tunguska event said a brilliant object had sailed across the sky just before the explosion, and some accounts said the object had changed course at one point in mid-flight. Various explanations, none of them completely persuasive, have been offered to account for the peculiar pattern of effects observed in the Tunguska case. One suggestion is that a very small "black hole" or a bit of anti-matter collided with the Earth. Another explanation says a comet nucleus entered the Earth's atmosphere and exploded with tremendous violence in mid-air. Some students of the UFO phenomenon have suggested that an extraterrestrial spacecraft developed trouble with its atomic power plant while visiting Earth and exploded in flight. This idea formed the basis for two widely read science fiction stories by Soviet writer Alexander Kazantsev. A nuclear explosion (or anti-matter explosion, if one prefers to imagine a spacecraft with a propulsion system that derives its energy from anti-matter) would account for many features of the Tunguska event.

One problem with the extraterrestrial-spacecraft explanation of the Tunguska event, however, is that it is hard to imagine how a competently designed spacecraft, especially one created by an extraterrestrial race with technology far advanced over our own, could blow up in flight. Nuclear propulsion technology as understood and practiced on Earth simply is not built for producing explosions. Portions of a nuclear reactor may melt in certain malfunctions, but the reactor will not explode in the manner of a nuclear bomb. It is conceivable that a reactor powered by the annihilation of anti-matter could explode in an event like that witnessed at Tunguska, but here one enters the realm of fantasy. Whatever the cause of the Tunguska explosion, it has added considerably to speculation about extraterrestrial spacecraft visiting Earth.

See also ANTI-MATTER; BLACK HOLES.

tunnels   One colorful rumor from modern UFO lore involves a vast underground network of tunnels said to connect alleged UFO-related facilities and subterranean "bases" in the western United States. This putative network is said to link sites including Vandenberg Air Force Base, California; Los Alamos, New Mexico; and Mount Shasta, California. Perhaps it is significant that Mount Shasta has long been known as a center of occult activity, since occultism is a major element of the UFO phenomenon.

See also BASES; OCCULTISM; RUMORS; UNDERGROUND INSTALLATIONS.

Twilight Bar, The   Written by Arthur Koestler in 1933, the play *The Twilight Bar* deals with the landing of a huge craft resembling a meteor in the sea near an island where a war is about to begin. The craft's passage causes a blackout. Two occupants of the craft, dressed in white coveralls, emerge to warn humankind that it has only three days in which to improve its behavior, or else face destruction. Should humankind fail to mend its ways, the visitors explain, the Earth will be repopulated with another species after being cleared of humans. The play incorporates many elements of UFO encounters reported later in the 20th century, such as the power failure and the humanoid aliens wearing coveralls. The theme of humankind facing annihilation by aliens for its crimes became a prominent theme of science fiction about UFOs, notably the motion picture *The Day the Earth Stood Still*. A staunch anti–communist famed for his novel *Darkness at Noon*, an indictment of Stalinism, Koestler became interested in the paranormal later in his life. Attraction to the paranormal is commonly associated with interest in UFOs.

See also DAY THE EARTH STOOD STILL, THE; HUMANOIDS; POWER FAILURES, UFOS AND.

Twin Falls, Idaho, incident, United States   On August 13, 1947, two boys and their father at Twin Falls, along the Smoke River Canyon in Idaho, allegedly saw a blue object shaped like an upside-down plate, about 300 feet away and 75 feet above the ground. The object, estimated at some 21 feet wide and 10 feet thick, apparently was agitating treetops beneath it, and made a "swishing" noise. Red flame reportedly issued from the top of the object. This report was part of a notable series of UFO sightings in the northwestern states of the United States in 1947.

See also ARNOLD INCIDENT; MAURY ISLAND INCIDENT.

2001: A Space Odyssey   Stanley Kubrick's 1968 motion picture depicted humankind's first contact with extraterrestrials and dramatized the discovery of a huge black monolith placed by extraterrestrials on the Moon. The extraterrestrials supposedly had intervened in the evolution of prehuman apes to produce human intelligence, although this presumption was not stated explicitly in the film.

This particular element of the film—alien intervention in human evolution—has been a prominent feature of UFO lore. At the end of the film, a human astronaut captured by the extraterrestrials is transformed into an apparently hybrid "star child," half human and half alien, and is seen returning to Earth in the final frames of the movie. The "hybrid" offspring of humans and aliens also has been a familiar element of UFO lore in recent years. *2001* may have had an effect on UFO contact reports through its highly detailed spacecraft models; after the film was released, alleged extraterrestrial spacecraft described in some contactee reports tended to have similar configurations and levels of detail, as distinct from the comparatively simple flying discs described by earlier contactees. The giant black monoliths depicted in the movie, however, apparently did not appear in contactee reports following the film's release, despite the picture's tremendous popularity.

See also EVOLUTION; MOTION PICTURES.

U

"UFO," British television series (1969–70) Intended for children, "UFO" was created by Gerry and Sylvia Anderson (previously known for the puppet science fiction series "Thunderbirds" and later for the series "Space 1999") in collaboration with Reg Hill. Stories dealt with the activities of a government agency formed to counteract hostile activities by alien spacecraft.

UFO phenomenon, history of Although unidentified objects have been reported seen in the skies for many centuries, the modern UFO phenomenon originated in the late 19th century, when observers in the United States and elsewhere began sighting what appeared to be powered aerial craft, or "airships." These reports contained many details that would become familiar elements of the UFO phenomenon in the 20th century, including unexplained origins, technology comparable to that of the witnesses' land and time, and unpredictable and often absurd behavior on the part of "airship" occupants.

The airships were succeeded by sightings of "ghost aircraft." These unexplained aircraft sightings were followed during World War II by the "foo fighter" phenomenon. Foo fighters were said to be mysterious silvery objects or balls of light that would pace military aircraft in flight for a time and then depart. Immediately after the war, "ghost rockets" were sighted in large numbers over Scandinavia. The "rockets" in this case were streaks of light that resembled meteors but performed maneuvers that were impossible for meteors and beyond the capabilities of known rocket technology at that time.

In 1947, the expression "flying saucer" entered the English language after pilot Kenneth Arnold, flying his private aircraft near Mount Rainier in Washington state, reported seeing several shiny objects in flight. He compared their motion to that of saucers skipped across a pond. Press reports of the sighting made it sound as if the objects themselves resembled saucers, and thus the expression "flying saucers" originated. The Arnold sighting was only one of many reported in the United States, and especially in the Pacific Northwest, about this time.

The first flying saucer sightings occurred at an especially uneasy time for the United States. World War II had just ended. America was squaring off against the Soviet Union for domination of the postwar world. An aerial assault from the Soviet Union seemed possible, even likely, in the near future. Maintaining U.S. air defenses was therefore an important priority, and flying saucers appeared to pose a challenge to those defenses. If the saucers were material aircraft or spacecraft of some unknown kind, their occupants evidently had no fear of being shot down. The saucers seemed to move through American airspace at will, and U.S. interceptors were powerless to stop them. At the same time, flying saucers quickly became a national obsession, and sightings of them were so numerous that the U.S. armed forces feared reports of saucer sightings might overwhelm and neutralize air defense in the event of an actual bomber attack from the Soviet Union. For these reasons, the government launched its own investigation of the UFO phenomenon and how to deal with UFOs. The investigation apparently concluded that flying saucers presented no clear threat to the national security of the United States. There did appear to be a threat from public

 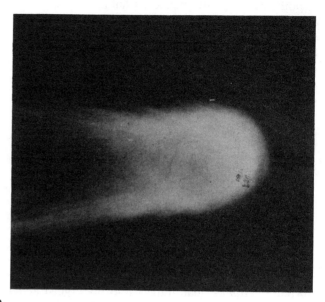

Untrained observers might mistake comets for UFOs. (NASA)

fear of UFOs, however, and so the government decided to implement a policy of "debunking" UFOs, or presenting them as misinterpretations of ordinary phenomena, so as to allay public fears of flying saucers. This policy remained in effect for some two decades. Although no conclusive evidence exists that the U.S. government has tried to suppress "proof" that extraterrestrials are visiting Earth, numerous conspiracy theories have circulated to the effect that such proof is in the government's possession, and that official statements concerning UFOs amount to a huge "cover-up." (Conspiracy theories are viewed as an expression of the paranoia that is widespread within the UFO movement. Indeed, the UFO phenomenon may be viewed as little more than an expression of paranoid thinking.)

By the early 1950s, the UFO phenomenon entered a new phase with the emergence of "contactees," individuals who claimed to have encountered UFOs on the ground in remote locations and received messages from the UFOs' occupants, who were presumed to be beings from other planets. The most prominent contactees included George Adamski, Truman Bethurum and Daniel Fry. Many other alleged contactees came forward at this time, telling stories that bore many elements in common, such as reports that the imagined space folk were benevolent and wished to help humankind solve its problems, such as the threat of nuclear warfare.

The contactees gave the UFO phenomenon the atmosphere of a circus. This situation tended to discourage serious research into UFOs. In reaction to the absurdities of the contactees, serious students of UFOs in the 1960s tried to emphasize the scientific study of the phenomenon, in hopes of making UFO research more legitimate and respectable. The "scientific" approach to UFO studies in the 1960s was based upon the "extraterrestrial hypothesis." According to this hypothesis, UFOs represented visitations to Earth by intelligent biological organisms from other star systems, traveling in material, "nuts-and-bolts" spacecraft. The extraterrestrial hypothesis was based on the following reasoning: because humans are intelligent biological organisms who travel in material vehicles, any visitors Earth may receive from intelligent nonhumans also will be similar beings in comparable vehicles. The extraterrestrial hypothesis and the assumptions underlying it reflected the prevailing opinion in the scientific and engineering communities of the developed nations at that time.

It soon became evident, however, that the extraterrestrial hypothesis was inadequate to account for the observed characteristics of UFOs. Many UFOs were seen performing extraordinary maneuvers that would be impossible for any material spacecraft and any biological entity inside it. Such maneuvers would have required the postulated spacecraft, in effect, to be massless and free from inertia: an impossible set of conditions for a material spaceship. Moreover, such maneuvers would have killed any reasonably large and complex organism such as a human. Another shortcoming of the extraterrestrial hypothesis was investigators' failure to discover, after years of examining thousands of UFO reports, any substantial and unequivocal piece of material evidence for the existence of extraterrestrial spacecraft visiting Earth. If such craft were visiting Earth, then one would expect them to leave behind at least a few such traces of their presence here. Yet by the early 1960s, there still was (as indeed there still is) no such evidence. There was no doubt that UFOs existed, but they appeared to be nonmaterial objects, in many cases at least.

Therefore, investigators began to consider a paranormal explanation for the UFO phenomenon. A traditional scientific approach to UFO studies was inadequate to explain the true nature of the phenomenon, because UFOs appeared to be paranormal phenomena as much as anything else. UFO reports shared many features with such well-known paranormal events as "hauntings" and poltergeist activity, and in some cases actually were associated with such phenomena. Moreover, some of the paraphernalia of occultism, such as the Ouija board or an equivalent device, already had been used to investigate the UFO phenomenon and the alleged extraterrestrial entities behind it.

At the same time, the "abduction" phenomenon was entering UFO studies. In abduction stories, humans were said to be taken aboard UFOs against their will and subjected to bodily examinations (sometimes in brutal fashion) and to strange, quasi-medical "operations" that tended to concentrate on the head and on the genital and anal areas. One of the earliest abduction reports dated from 1961 (although it was not made public until 1966) and involved a New England couple, Betty and Barney Hill, who allegedly were taken aboard an alien spacecraft and subjected to something like a physical examination by extraterrestrials. The Hill case represented a departure from previous close-encounter cases involving alleged face-to-face meetings with aliens. Unlike previous "contactees" who became known as cranks and publicity seekers, the Hills were a quiet, respectable couple who did not appear to seek publicity or personal gain from reporting their experience. Other abduction reports followed, and within a few years of the Hill incident it was almost fashionable to report that one had been abducted by a flying saucer.

By the late 1960s and early 1970s, the "ancient astronauts" phenomenon was encroaching on UFO studies. This particular school of thought was based on the assumption that the "gods" of earlier ages were extraterrestrials who visited Earth and impressed our ancestors with their seemingly supernatural feats of engineering. Among the most famous popularizers of the ancient astronauts phenomenon was Swiss author Erich von Däniken, who in a series of highly successful books used dubious evidence and equally questionable reasoning to support the equation, "extraterrestrials = gods."

The result of these various approaches to the UFO phenomenon was confusion. The ancient astronauts phenomenon struck serious students of UFOs as absurd, as did many alleged abduction cases. Yet the extraterrestrial hypothesis was scarcely more tenable. By 1977, it remained unsupported by solid evidence after some 30 years of investigation.

Meanwhile, the "paranormal" approach to UFO study was so unscientific that it seemed unlikely to yield any useful information at all about the UFO phenomenon. Nonetheless, in the late 1970s and afterward, the paranormal view of UFOs began impressing itself successfully on public thinking about the UFO phenomenon. Various elements of the so-called New Age movement, an essentially occultist belief system incorporating faith in the paranormal, began infiltrating the UFO phenomenon, which in turn became an element of New Age belief. Thus it became acceptable in many circles for one to profess belief in reincarnation and practice mediumism in connection with one's faith in visitations by "extraterrestrial" UFOs.

This embrace of occult belief dismayed serious students of the UFO phenomenon but allowed less critical minds to accept belief in benevolent aliens while finding an excuse to dismiss powerful evidence against the claims of alleged contactees and abductees. George Adamski, for example, claimed to have met visitors from Venus. Yet when space probes visited Venus, they revealed that Venus has surface temperatures and atmospheric pressure far too high to support intelligent life as we know it. Occult beliefs provided a way to reconcile such discrepancies. The credulous could maintain belief in benevolent "space people" even in the face of such evidence, by invoking occult notions such as that of the "etheric realm," an imagined, habitable universe existing parallel to this one and connected to it by some kind of gateway that allowed travel between them. According to this belief, Venus might be inhabited in the etheric realm even though uninhabitable in our universe. Such intellectual legerdemain has had a wide following among UFO enthusiasts and has allowed "contactees" to build successful careers by lecturing about their reputed contacts with extraterrestrials from planets that we know to be uninhabitable.

Messages supposedly delivered by extraterrestrials have undergone a significant change since the days of the first "contactees." In the 1950s, aliens visiting Earth were said to be preoccupied, as humans themselves were then, with the threat of nuclear warfare. Many alleged messages from space concerned the danger that humankind would annihilate itself in a nuclear exchange. This theme diminished in importance by the 1970s, when new themes of environmental awareness and spiritual "evolution" began to dominate messages from the so-called extraterrestrials. Public perception of UFOs and "aliens" changed too. UFOs and the intelligences thought to be associated with them were perceived as agents of a "higher consciousness" that sought to unite humankind with itself, or at least to correct numerous errors in human thinking.

"Alien" intelligences were widely thought in the 1970s and 1980s to be benevolent, despite anecdotal evidence to the contrary. In some encounter reports, extraterrestrials were said to be friendly. Yet, other reports, especially certain well-publicized abduction cases, described extraterrestrials as hostile. Aliens were said to abduct humans, violate them sexually and subject them, in effect, to torture. Here, believers in the extraterrestrial hypothesis found themselves trying to reconcile two mutually exclusive points of view. Were the alleged extraterrestrials friendly to humankind or hostile? One attempted explanation was that several different "races" of extraterrestrials, some benevolent and some unfriendly, were visiting Earth. According to another viewpoint, the motivations of the alleged extraterrestrials were simply beyond human comprehension and could not be interpreted by ordinary human standards of judgment.

Theological interpretations of the UFO phenomenon have tended to concentrate on perceived similarities between alleged extraterrestrials and angels, particularly the fallen angels, or demons. Some observers of the UFO phenomenon have noted numerous similarities between UFO-related phenomena and reported manifestations of demonic activity. These similarities include untruthfulness on the part of the "extraterrestrials"; a perception of intense cold in their presence; and reports of brutal assault (often of a sexual character) by extraterrestrials during abduction cases. Among the principal exponents of this interpretation of "aliens" as demons was the American-born Russian Orthodox theologian Father Seraphim Rose, who found reports similar to modern UFO encounter stories in the lives of Orthodox Christian saints.

The potential for hoaxes in the UFO phenomenon is tremendous. Numerous hoaxes have been uncovered, and many additional hoaxes are thought to have been perpetrated for every one that has been revealed. Some hoaxes are extremely elaborate.

Another prominent characteristic of the UFO movement is pseudoscience, meaning the selective use of data to support a preconceived hypothesis. Pseudoscience has been used to support the extraterrestrial hypothesis, for example, in the absence of substantial evidence in favor of that hypothesis.

In recent years, some UFO investigators have come to view the UFO phenomenon as an effort to redirect human belief systems. This process is believed to involve "metalogic," a practice of using contradictory, absurd and seemingly inexplicable information in an attempt to confuse observers. Trying to interpret this puzzling information, the mind becomes more receptive to whatever explanation eventually is provided. Thus human belief is redirected through metalogic. There is no universal agreement on whom or what might be responsible for such an effort to alter human belief systems, but several distinct themes have been perceived in alleged messages from "extraterrestrials." For example, humankind has been urged to trust that the "aliens" are benevolent, wise and committed to leading humankind toward some higher level of spiritual and social "evolution," despite tales of non-benevolent behavior and motives on the part of the so-called extraterrestrials.

Numerous cults have arisen within the UFO phenomenon. Many of these cults are active today and may involve belief in an anticipated day of "salvation" when benevolent extraterrestrials are expected to land on Earth and deliver humankind from its troubles.

See also ABDUCTIONS; ADAMSKI, GEORGE; AIRSHIPS; ANCIENT ASTRONAUTS; ANGELS; ARNOLD INCIDENT; BELIEF SYSTEMS; BENDER MYSTERY; BETHURUM INCIDENT; CHADWELL MEMORANDUM; CHRIST AND CHRISTIANITY; COLLECTIVE DELUSION; COMMUNICATIONS; CONSPIRACY THEORIES; CULTS; DEALS; DEBUNKERS; DECEPTION; DEMONOLOGY; DISSOCIATIVE STATES; ETHERIC PLANE; EVIDENCE; EXTRATERRESTRIAL HYPOTHESIS; EXTRATERRESTRIALS, BEHAVIOR OF; GHOST AIRCRAFT; GHOST ROCKETS; GOOD AND EVIL; HALLUCINATIONS; HUMANOIDS; ILLUSION; IMAGINAL REALM; INCUBI AND SUCCUBI; MEDIA, UFOS IN THE; MESSAGES; METALOGIC; NEAR-DEATH EXPERIENCE; NEW AGE MOVEMENT; OCCULTISM; OUT-OF-BODY EXPERIENCE; PARANOIA;

UFOs, characteristics of

So many different kinds of UFOs have been reported that an entire book would be required to describe their putative characteristics in detail. Here is a brief summary of alleged characteristics of UFOs, especially those sighted in the latter half of the 20th century.

Number. Although many UFOs are reported singly, large formations of UFOs, sometimes encompassing dozens of individual craft, have been sighted on occasion.

Size. UFO reports describe objects in a great range of sizes, from several inches in diameter to dimensions larger than aircraft carriers. A typical diameter for the familiar, discoid "flying saucer" is perhaps 30 to 45 feet.

Color. UFOs have been reported in virtually every color, from dull gray to brilliant, luminous white. In many cases, a UFO is said to display multicolored lights, sometimes blinking on and off in rapid succession.

Luster. Various UFOs are described as dull in luster, like dirty metal, whereas others show such brilliant luminosity that one reportedly can read a newspaper at night by their illumination.

Formations. Dozens of different formations of UFOs in flight have been described, including circles, crosses and **V** formations.

Shape. The classic "flying saucer" is a disc shaped like one dinner plate inverted on top of another, with perhaps a hemispherical cabin on top and another below the main body of the disc. Many other shapes have been reported, however, including spheres, ovoids, cylinders, and bell, walnut and cigar shapes. The "Saturn shape," a sphere with a round, horizontal, planar "deck" running through its midsection, is also commonly reported. In some reports, UFOs are said to alter their shape while in flight.

Velocity. Here again, a wide range of estimates is reported. Some UFOs are said to move at very slow velocities (perhaps only a few miles per hour), whereas others have velocities estimated at thousands of miles per hour.

Behavior. UFOs tend to exhibit high maneuverability and reportedly can make abrupt 90-degree turns in flight without apparent deceleration—behavior that appears to violate the laws of physics as we know them, presuming the UFOs are material objects with more than negligible mass. On some occasions, UFOs reportedly have behaved as if they were material objects, being displaced slightly by bullet impacts or punching holes in objects they struck. Other UFO reports, however, emphasize the seemingly non-material character of the objects, some of which allegedly pass directly through material structures such as walls with no difficulty. UFOs may appear and disappear (or "materialize" and "dematerialize," if one prefers) at a given location, rather than fly into the vicinity from elsewhere and then depart in lateral or vertical flight.

Waves. One curious aspect of the UFO phenomenon is that unusually large numbers of UFO reports tend to occur at certain times. These "waves" of sightings may last for several months before subsiding.

Sounds. UFOs are commonly associated with a humming, whistling or whining noise, but numerous sounds have been reported in UFO sightings, including music.

Odors. A frequently reported characteristic of UFOs in close-encounter reports is an unpleasant smell, such as that of sulfur or of rotten organic material.

Landings. There are many reports of UFOs seen on the ground. In some cases, witnesses allegedly have approached landed UFOs closely and received bodily harm. Reported UFO landings also are associated with various alleged items of physical evidence, such as scorched ground and/or vegetation; depressions like those one would expect landing gear to make in soil; and flattened areas of grass, crops or reeds, including the now-famous "crop circles."

Material evidence. Alleged material evidence of UFO encounters has a strange way of "disappearing" before skeptical investigators can examine it. Often the so-called evidence turns out to be obviously fraudulent, or else a misidentification of something commonplace. Claims of some UFO enthusiasts to the contrary, there appears to be no unequivocal material evidence of any close encounter between humans and UFOs.

Photographs. Numerous faked photographs of UFOs have been presented as genuine. Such pictures can be fabricated in numerous ways, from photographing crude models suspended on strings to using computer graphics to generate sophisticated composite pictures of UFOs in flight or on the ground. No known photograph of an alleged UFO has been accepted as proof that an extraterrestrial spacecraft's visit to Earth actually was recorded on film.

Occupants. Some close-encounter reports include descriptions of the alleged occupants of UFOs. These figures may be humanoid or nonhumanoid, dwarfish or gigantic, evidently friendly or manifestly hostile.

Technology. The technology of reported UFOs tends to reflect the technological advancement of the society where a report is made. In America during the "airship" wave of the 1890s, for example, UFO reports featured descriptions of propeller-driven aerial machines. Rocket-like UFOs were widely reported during the late 1940s, when rocket technology was becoming a subject of popular interest. By the 1970s, descriptions of UFO technology in U.S. encounter cases had advanced to laser-like devices, as such equipment came into widespread use for various military and civilian applications. Speculations on the technology of UFOs have ranged in character from the sober to the ridiculous and have included pseudoscientific discussions of "anti-gravity" and other chimeras of physics.

Communications. UFO occupants reportedly have communicated with "contactees" by speech, telepathy, radio, gestures, flashing lights, music, photographic images and diagrams. Some communications allegedly have been delivered by radio and others by the occultist practice of "automatic writing." Messages delivered in these communications have tended to be vague, confusing and banal, although some common elements have been noted in various alleged messages from so-called space people. Many of these messages have concerned some unspecified but supposedly imminent cataclysm that is expected to befall Earth. Just as technology in UFO reports tends to reflect the technological progress of humankind, so does the content of UFO communications tend to reflect preoccupations of human society. In the 1940s and 1950s, for example, alleged communications from "extraterrestrials" often mentioned the danger of global nuclear war; some 30 years later, as the threat of nuclear war diminished, the emphasis of such "alien" messages had changed to concern over the deterioration of Earth's environment.

Harm to observers. Despite reported messages in which the so-called aliens profess to love humankind, there are numerous reports of human witnesses suffering serious bodily and psychological harm in encounters with UFOs. In some cases, the physiological effects are said to resemble symptoms of overexposure to hard radiation, including burns on the skin; psychological effects may include depression, disorientation and loss of appetite, as well as amnesiac symptoms that are sometimes described as "missing time," the inability to account for a period of hours or days when the subject allegedly had an ongoing encounter with extraterrestrials. Extreme changes in personality may be reported after a person allegedly experiences a close encounter with a UFO.

Abductions. Among the most dramatic elements of the UFO phenomenon, alleged abductions of humans by "extraterrestrials" have received extensive coverage in the popular press. Abduction stories commonly include details such as a quasi-medical examination on board an alien spacecraft; extraction of ova or semen from abductees; artificial insemination of female abductees and subsequent harvesting of "hybrid" babies; surgery on the abductee's head; and implantation of small artifacts resembling BB shot in the nasal passages or other parts of the abductee's body. According to such stories, the abductee may be "tagged" with mysterious glyphs on the skin. In some accounts, the abductees may be stripped naked and forced to engage in sexual activity with human or nonhuman aliens. Alleged visions of the future may be presented to abductees, who also may be instructed to perform certain tasks following their release. There is considerable disagreement about how to interpret abduction stories. One interpretation is that such tales are purely imaginary. Another view is that the abduction reports are distorted recollections of traumatic events in abductees' lives. A third interpretation is that prompting or leading questions by interviewers may encourage the subject to invent—perhaps without conscious intent to deceive—fictional elements for the story. A fourth interpretation has it that the events of the abduction story actually occurred just as described. Much about abduction stories is confusing and contradictory information; and even when two witnesses report the same abduction experience simultaneously, each witness may describe a markedly different version of events during the abduction.

Vehicle effects. Vehicles present at some close encounters with UFOs are said to undergo engine trouble and stop running when the alleged UFO is nearby. Such effects are said to result from powerful electromagnetic fields supposedly surrounding UFOs, but more mundane explanations are possible.

Time effects. "Missing time"—the inability to recall events during a period when a subject is said to have encountered a UFO—is a widely reported element of UFO reports. One explanation of missing time is that aliens, for some reason, induce amnesia in abductees. According to some reports, time is experienced in a different-than-usual way during an abduction; the abductee may think he or she has spent only a few minutes or hours inside an extraterrestrial craft, then emerge to find that a much longer period has elapsed. Even when no abduction is reported, a person describing an alleged encounter with a UFO and/or its occupants may claim later that time seemed to "stop" or decelerate during the encounter.

Altered perceptions. Human witnesses to close encounters with UFOs may recall afterward that their perceptions changed during the experience. A witness may have felt groggy, or unusually alert. Reports of altered perceptions may be linked with beverages allegedly served to the witness by the "extraterrestrials."

Animal behavior. Wild and domesticated animals are said to display unusual behavior during close encounters with UFOs. Animals may exhibit great fear and flee. An ordinarily aggressive animal may act intimidated. Dogs reportedly seem especially sensitive to the presence of UFOs and other manifestations of paranormal activity.

Animal mutilations. Mutilated corpses of animals sometimes are reported found in areas where intensive UFO activity is said to have occurred. Many such incidents of animal mutilation, notably involving cattle, have been reported in the United States.

Geographical distribution. UFOs have been reported seen in almost all parts of the world, but certain areas known as "windows" appear to be focal points for UFO sightings. UFO windows have been identified in countries including the United States, Australia, Japan, France, Brazil, Argentina and the United Kingdom.

Deception. This is a prominent element of the UFO phenomenon. "Extraterrestrials" are said to deliver grossly inaccurate information about conditions on other planets. Hoaxes and what appear to be well-organized disinformation campaigns about UFOs add to the confusion and deception surrounding the subject of UFOs.

Absurdity. The element of the absurd is pronounced in many UFO close-encounter reports. The witness may claim to have received from aliens, or given to them, something ridiculous, such as pancakes or bottles of carbonated drinks. Absurd messages are commonplace in close-encounter reports.

Parallels with mythology and demonology. These are numerous. Many myths, such as those of the "lost lands" of Atlantis and Lemuria, have been woven into the mythology of UFOs, and alleged contacts with extraterrestrials bear many close resemblances to manifestations of evil spirits in cases from the literature on demonology.

Link with occultism. The occult element can be strong in the UFO phenomenon. In many cases, such as that of famed "contactee" Albert Bender, close encounters with UFOs and their alleged occupants are believed to follow witnesses' involvement in occultism. Moreover, the paraphernalia of occultism, such as the divining rod and the Ouija board or their equivalents, have been used to contact "extraterrestrials" and investigate UFO sightings. The occult practice of "channeling," or mediumism, also is used to contact putative extraterrestrials.

See also ABDUCTIONS; ABSURDITY; ACOUSTICAL EFFECTS; ANIMALS, UFOS AND; ATLANTIS; BELIEF SYSTEMS; BENDER MYSTERY; BODILY EFFECTS; CIGARS; CLOUD CIGARS; COMMUNICATIONS; DECEPTION; DEMONOLOGY; DIVINING ROD; ENCOUNTER PHENOMENA; EVIDENCE; GRAYS; HUMANOIDS; INSECTOIDS; LEMURIA; LIGHT EFFECTS; MESSAGES; METALOGIC; MISSING TIME; MYTHOLOGY; OCCULTISM; ODORS; PHOTOGRAPHS; PSYCHOLOGICAL EFFECTS; REPTOIDS; SEXUAL ENCOUNTERS; SPHERES; TECHNOLOGY; VEHICLE EFFECTS; VIDYA; VIMANA; VULYA; VUNU; WAVES; WINDOWS.

Ulrich incident This case, involving three alleged simultaneous deaths by mysterious means, has been cited in the UFO literature, even though no UFO was actually reported in connection with the incident. On April 7, 1938, at 1:14 P.M. in the local time zone just west of Ireland, the helmsman of the steamship S.S. *Ulrich,* one John Greeley, allegedly was found burned to a cinder in the wheelhouse, although there was no other evidence of fire on the spot. At about the same time, in the next time zone to the east, police in the English community of Upton-on-Chester in Cheshire reportedly found the burned remains of George Turner, the driver, in the cab of his truck, but did not see any other signs of combustion in the cab. The clock on the dashboard allegedly was found stopped at 2:14 P.M. local time, or the same moment Greeley was alleged to have perished on the S.S. *Ulrich.* Meanwhile, a third victim, William Ten Bruik, was said to have died at the very same time (3:14 P.M. local time), under similar circumstances, in his Volkswagen in Nijmegen, The Netherlands. Noted UFO "debunker" Philip Klass investigated this set of incidents, reported in the book *The Flying Saucers Are Hostile* by Brad Steiger and Joan Whritenour. In his book *UFOs Explained,* Klass reports that he contacted the U.S. Maritime Administration in Washington, D.C., and asked if the office had any record of a ship called S.S. *Ulrich* traveling the seas in 1938. No ship under that name could be found in the Lloyds of London register for that year, nor in any other year between 1928 and

1940, Klass was informed. Similar searches of the American Shipping Register and the U.S. Customs Department's Merchant Marine list turned up no record of the S.S. *Ulrich,* Klass reported. Klass also contacted police in Nijmegen and Upton-on-Chester to check the other two reports mentioned in this case. The Nijmegen authorities told Klass that pertinent records from 1938 had been destroyed in World War II and could not be consulted. Klass was informed, however, that Volkswagens such as the one supposedly involved in the incident were not introduced into the Netherlands until 1947, years after the alleged combustion of William Ten Bruik. Moreover, Volkswagens had not even entered production in April of 1938; the cornerstone for the first Volkswagen plant was not laid until the following month. Klass also was told by the constabulary in Cheshire that a truck driver actually was found burned to death in his vehicle in April of 1938, but the man's name was given in a local newspaper's account of the event as Edgar Beattie rather than George Turner; the incident took place around 5:00 P.M., not 2:14 P.M.; and the entire truck was destroyed by fire after it struck a bridge. Klass's investigation makes the so-called Ulrich incident appear dubious, if not a complete fabrication.

See also DEBUNKERS; KLASS, PHILIP.

ultra-hominization The postulated evolutionary advancement of humankind toward some vaguely defined but supposedly higher level of development. In various formulations, this idea has played an important part in UFO lore by providing a rationale for the presence of alleged extraterrestrials on Earth, to "guide" humankind in its progress toward ultra-hominization.

See also TEILHARD DE CHARDIN, PIERRE.

UMMO Widely believed to be a hoax, the UMMO phenomenon is based in French and Spanish UFO lore and concerns messages allegedly received from an extraterrestrial "federation" of planets. The messages are said to originate from a planet called UMMO, circling a star named IUMMA, identified by terrestrial astronomers as Wolf 424. The UMMO phenomenon fits the familiar pattern of UFO hoaxes in that it contains abundant detail but none of the detail is substantiated. The alleged extraterrestrial names in this case also match the two-syllable, seemingly infantile, pattern observed in many other reported "communications" from extraterrestrials. A symbol associated with UMMO—three vertical lines transfixed by a single horizontal line—was reported seen on a UFO in the former Soviet Union during the famous Voronezh sightings. The UMMO symbol in that instance is thought to have been added for the sake of "verisimilitude," if that word can be applied in such a case.

See also HOAXES; NAMES.

Unarius Foundation Based in San Diego, California, the Unarius Foundation is led by one Ruth Norman (also known as "Uriel") and is based on the expectation that interplanetary spaceships will land in San Diego in 2001.

underground installations A recurring set of rumors in the UFO phenomenon concerns mysterious underground installations supposedly used by extraterrestrials in their operations on Earth. The "aliens" are believed to have set up vast subterranean installations to serve as bases on this planet for spacecraft. In some cases, such bases are thought to have been constructed and to be operated with the knowledge and cooperation of government authorities. With no evidence to support them, lurid tales have circulated about underground installations and

Underground bases figure prominently in UFO lore. (D. Ritchie)

what may be happening therein. The "Shaver mystery," for example, was based on the presumption that a race of malignant beings was operating out of subterranean facilities and afflicting humans on the planet's surface with all manner of ills and calamities. Other accounts of UFO activity in the late 20th century, such as some concerning the Hudson Valley UFO phenomenon in the United States, have tried to convince the public that construction is under way on underground installations for the use of aliens. UFO investigator Jacques Vallee has disposed of one such fantasy by asking: "Who takes out the garbage?" A huge underground installation, Vallee pointed out, would produce correspondingly great amounts of trash, which would have to be carted away and deposited somewhere. It would be difficult to conceal such activity. Roads would have to be constructed leading to the facility, and their existence could not be hidden. Moreover, a large underground base would generate considerable heat and therefore would be visible on satellite photos taken in infrared wavelengths. Despite such rebuttals, rumors of underground UFO bases on Earth have persisted and probably will continue to do so.

See also BASES; CONSPIRACY THEORIES; HUDSON VALLEY SIGHTINGS; MYSTERIANS, THE; SHAVER MYSTERY.

unidentified flying object (expression) The expression "unidentified flying object," or "UFO," is though to have originated with Air Force Captain Edward Ruppelt, who introduced it in his 1956 book *The Report on Unidentified Flying Objects* to replace the expression "flying saucer."

United Kingdom, UFOs in The United Kingdom has been a hotbed of UFO activity for decades and is the location of several "windows" where UFO sightings are reported on an especially frequent basis. Many familiar elements of the modern UFO phenomenon are prominent in British UFO reports, including stalling of automobile engines in the vicinity of UFOs. British UFO lore contains numerous parallels with ghost stories and occult folklore of the British Isles. Among the most famous UFO reports in British history is the Bentwaters incident, which has been interpreted as a possible experiment in psychology aimed at determining how military personnel would respond to an actual UFO landing. Alleged UFO encounters in Britain apparently tend to be peaceful, with little or none of the violence reported from certain other countries. Crop circles,

widely associated in popular lore with UFOs, have been found in many locations in Britain.

See also BENTWATERS INCIDENT; BLACK HANDS; BURTOO INCIDENT; BYLAND ABBEY INCIDENT; CHIPPING WARDEN INCIDENT; CRADLE HILL HOAX; CROWLEY, ALEISTER; CROP CIRCLES; DYFED, WALES; EGRYN LIGHTS; E.K. INCIDENT; ELIDOR; HOOK INCIDENT; "LITTLE BLUE MAN" INCIDENT; LONDON–KENT SIGHTING; SALANDIN INCIDENT; WEST FREUGH INCIDENT; WINDOWS; WOODBRIDGE INCIDENT.

United States, UFOs in American leadership in the 20th century has encompassed UFOs as well as political and military power. For most practical purposes, the UFO phenomenon of the latter 20th century originated in the United States, with the initial "flying saucer" sighting by pilot Kenneth Arnold near Mount Rainier in Washington state in 1947. Hundreds of notable UFO encounters have been reported from the United States since then, and even before. If one includes the numerous "airship" sightings of the late 19th and early 20th centuries as part of the UFO phenomenon, then UFOs have been on the minds of Americans for a century or more. The first of the modern "contactees," namely George Adamski, announced his alleged meetings with extraterrestrials in the southwestern desert only a few months after the Arnold sighting. Many other Americans in the 1950s followed Adamski's lead and reported their own face-to-face meetings with alleged space travelers; Truman Bethurum, for example, claimed to have encountered a UFO and its beautiful female captain, one "Aura Rhanes," in the Nevada desert.

The American entertainment media did much to inflate early saucer sightings into a UFO cult. Soon after the Arnold incident, Hollywood began turning out motion pictures on the theme of extraterrestrials visiting Earth. Television programming took up this theme, and by 1960 the image of the "flying saucer" piloted by a small, humanoid extraterrestrial was implanted firmly in American popular culture. America's fascination with television programs and motion pictures about UFOs and imagined extraterrestrials continued through the 1960s and 1970s and led to several highly influential programs and films, including the NBC-TV series "Star Trek" and Steven Spielberg's celebrated 1977 motion picture *Close Encounters of the Third Kind*, which depicted the arrival of a fictional UFO at Devil's Tower, Wyoming.

The print media in the United States generally have been more restrained in their treatment of UFOs than have motion pictures and television, but the press has done its part nonetheless to promote the UFO cult and disseminate its mythology. UFOs are a favorite topic of American tabloid newspapers, which favor fantastic stories embellished with crudely faked illustrations. Much of the UFO mythology of our century originated in American magazines specializing in science fiction or the occult. Editor Ray Palmer, for example, helped generate much of modern UFO mythology through his magazines *Fate* and *Amazing Stories.*

Some of the most prominent figures in the UFO phenomenon have been American. These include Dr. J. Allen Hynek, who coined the expression "close encounters" to describe UFO sightings; various "contactees" such as Adamski and Bethurum; journalists such as Donald Keyhoe and Frank Edwards; and "debunkers," including aerospace journalist Philip Klass and Harvard University astronomy professor Donald Menzel. Numerous organizations devoted to studying UFOs also have been established in the United States, such as the National Investigatory Committee on Aerial Phenomena and the Mutual UFO Network.

Although UFOs have been reported seen virtually everywhere in the United States, a few parts of the country have emerged as prominent UFO "windows." Among these are the Pacific Northwest (Oregon and Washington); California; Texas and the other Gulf Coast states; and the Hudson Valley, including portions of New York State, New Jersey and New England.

The connection between politics and the UFO phenomenon has been complex in the United States. In the years immediately after World War II, UFOs were viewed as objects of mystery and terror, partly because they were widely suspected of being "secret weapons" originating in the Soviet Union. That particular fear subsided by the 1960s and was replaced by an uncritical fascination with UFOs that bordered, in some cases, on worship of extraterrestrials. In the 1980s and 1990s, popular belief in UFOs and extraterrestrial life melded with the New Age movement to produce an essentially occultist belief system that incorporates faith in global salvation by benevolent aliens. Numerous UFO cults have arisen in the United States, offering their adherents a dubious hope that benign aliens are prepared to intervene in human history soon and provide solutions for the political and social problems of humankind.

See also ADAMSKI, GEORGE; BETHURUM INCIDENT; DEBUNKERS; EDWARDS, FRANK; GULF BREEZE SIGHTINGS; HUDSON VALLEY SIGHTINGS; HYNEK, J. ALLEN; KEYHOE, MAJ. DONALD; KLASS, PHILIP; LUBBOCK LIGHTS; MENZEL, DONALD; MOTION PICTURES; MYTHOLOGY; OCCULTISM; PALMER, RAYMOND; PASCAGOULA INCIDENT.

V

Valens incident   A story from the ancient spiritual literature of Orthodox Christianity, the tale of Valens the Palestinian contains many close parallels with modern UFO encounters. Valens was a monk who became so proud and deceived by evil spirits that the Devil appeared to him in a form similar to that of Christ, accompanied by phantoms in "chariots and carriages of fire." The demons told Valens that Christ admired his life and works. The monk also was commanded to worship a figure he thought to be Christ (actually the Antichrist) seated in a luminous "chariot" about a mile away. When Valens saw this being, he fell down and worshipped it. Soon Valens became so deluded that he walked into church and proclaimed that he did not need to partake of the offering, for he had "seen Christ Himself." Valens was confined for about a year and eventually was cured of his delusions.

Besides the obvious parallel with modern UFO close-encounter reports, namely the "chariots of fire," Valens's case resembles UFO contacts in other ways as well. The encounter was designed to mislead Valens; in similar fashion, deception is a major element of many modern UFO contactee cases. The Devil appeared to Valens in a form resembling that of Christ; in modern UFO contactee reports, an alien entity may take on the appearance of an "exalted one." The encounter with the Devil encouraged Valens to view himself as a specially favored person; likewise, modern UFO contactees may come away from their "extraterrestrial" encounters convinced that they are uniquely blessed in some way.

Valens's great pride is consistent with the psychological profiles of certain modern UFO contactees, as described in the "status inconsistency theory" of UFO contact cases. This theory is based on the idea that paranoid thinking in individuals, the kind of thinking that is manifested in many ways in the history of the UFO phenomenon, has its origins in unpleasant social reversals. A proud, well-educated person stuck in a job for which he or she is overqualified appears many times more likely to report a UFO sighting than another person whose status is higher. Likewise, Valens, out of pride, thought he had been granted a vision of Christ and therefore had special privileges. There was a great inconsistency between Valens's high opinion of himself and his actual status as a member of the community.

See also ANTICHRIST; CHRIST AND CHRISTIANITY; DECEPTION; DEMONOLOGY; ENCOUNTER PHENOMENA; STATUS INCONSISTENCY THEORY.

Valensole incident, France   One of the most famous cases in UFO lore, the Valensole incident allegedly involved an encounter on July 1, 1965, between a farmer named Maurice Masse and two "extraterrestrials" in Masse's lavender field at Valensole. Masse reportedly saw an ovoid object about 15 feet wide resting in his field, and went to investigate. Near the object, he allegedly encountered two small humanoids, about four feet in height and wearing what looked like green ski outfits. The beings were said to have oversized heads and large, slanted eyes, much in the manner of "grays" reported in American close-encounter cases. One of the beings aimed a rod at Masse and paralyzed him temporarily. Then the humanoids boarded their craft and flew away. After the encounter, Masse allegedly had trouble staying awake and found he required about 12 hours' sleep per day, compared to only five or six hours before the incident. In contrast with Americans, who often report feelings of terror connected with such encounters, Masse apparently experienced a peaceful feeling during his encounter. Ground traces reportedly were found at the landing site.

See also ENCOUNTER PHENOMENA; FRANCE; HUMANOIDS; PARALYSIS.

Valentich case

One of the most celebrated of all UFO encounters, the so-called Valentich case was reported in 1978 and is said to have involved the disappearance of Frederick Valentich and his Cessna 182 aircraft during an encounter with a UFO over the Bass Strait between Australia and Tasmania. The flight occurred on October 21, 1978. While in flight, Valentich reported to the Melbourne Flight Service Unit Controller that he had seen a "large" unidentified aircraft with four bright lights, which Valentich compared to landing lights. Valentich said the strange craft appeared to be playing a "game" with him. Evidently the craft traveled at great velocity; Valentich said he could not determine how fast it was traveling. His description of the craft was vague, except that it had bright lights, a "long shape" and a "metallic" exterior. At one point, he claimed the object was "orbiting" on top of him, and that it had a green light. The last reported statement from Valentich said that the object was "not an aircraft." At the end of Valentich's final transmission, his microphone allegedly remained open for 17 sec-

The Valentich incident allegedly occurred above the Bass Strait between Australia and Tasmania. (U.S. Geological Survey)

onds, as a strange metallic sound was heard. The Australian Department of Aviation's Bureau of Air Safety reported in 1982 that the incident was presumed fatal to Valentich, and that no reason had been determined for the disappearance of the pilot and aircraft.

See also AIRCRAFT, UFOS AND; AUSTRALIA, UFOS IN; ENCOUNTER PHENOMENA.

Vallee, Jacques, French-born American astronomer and UFO investigator (1939–)

One of the most prominent investigators of the UFO phenomenon, Vallee has written numerous books on the subject and has suggested that UFOs constitute a "control system" for governing human belief. He also has investigated the elements of deception and absurdity in the UFO phenomenon and has written on the role of "metalogic" in alleged UFO encounters.

Vallee has questioned the modern interpretation of UFOs as extraterrestrial spacecraft and has pointed out that UFO sightings are too numerous to be explained in all cases as sightings of alien spaceships. He adds that the alleged extraterrestrials described in UFO contact reports resemble humans too closely to be considered genuine extraterrestrials. There is also a serious discrepancy, he points out, between the advanced technology one would expect space-traveling aliens to use, and the crude equipment and techniques that "aliens" in many close-encounter cases are said to use. One possible explanation of the UFO phenomenon, Vallee has suggested, is that some "alien" but Earth-based intelligence may be trying to modify human behavior.

See also ABSURDITY; BELIEF SYSTEMS; DECEPTION; EXTRATERRESTRIAL HYPOTHESIS; METALOGIC.

vehicle effects

In many close-encounter cases involving UFOs, interference with the operation of motor vehicles is reported. An automobile's ignition and lights may fail, for example, at the approach of a UFO. Other interference with the operation of automobiles may be reported, up to and including the levitation of a vehicle from the highway, or the teleportation of a vehicle and its occupants to some distant location. When a vehicle is halted, according to many reports, entities from a nearby UFO may take that opportunity to approach and investigate the occupants of the car or truck. Sometimes marked temperature effects, such as a dramatic heating of the air inside the vehicle, are reported. On occasion, occupants of an automobile have been reported seen signaling to UFOs overhead with their car's headlights. Interference with the operation of aircraft in flight also has been alleged, notably in the Valentich incident over Bass Strait between Australia and Tasmania. From the viewpoint of physics, no completely adequate explanation of UFOs' alleged interference with the engines and electrical systems of motor vehicles has been proposed, although a powerful electromagnetic field, in theory, could accomplish such interference. The energy output of some UFOs might suffice for such interference.

It is worth noting that interference with the operation of motor vehicles is also an element of ghost lore and the literature on demonology. British ghost lore, for example, contains numerous reports of large, disembodied, hairy hands appearing before motorists along a certain stretch of highway. Another notable report of vehicle interference occurred in connection with an exorcism that took place in Iowa in 1928. A woman named Emma Schmidt was afflicted by several evil spirits and was brought to a convent to undergo exorcism. After one of the evil spirits threatened a priest assisting in the exorcism, that priest was summoned to perform the last rites for a dying woman. As he was on the road, a thick, black cloud reportedly descended on his vehicle, and the car wound up wrecked on a bridge. The priest was uninjured. Afterward, one of the evil spirits revealed that the priest's patron saint had prevented any bodily harm from coming to him. An extensive account of this incident may be found in *Haunted Heartland*, by Beth Scott and Michael Norman. Arthur Myers, in his book *The Ghostly Register*, also cites an incident of vehicle interference connected with alleged supernatural manifestations.

See also "BLACK HANDS"; DEMONOLOGY; ENERGY ESTIMATES.

Venado Tuerto incidents, Argentina   In September 1978, a series of notable UFO incidents was reported in the small community of Venado Tuerto, Argentina. One case involved a 12-year-old boy named Oscar, whose family operated an *estancia*, or ranch. Oscar was riding his horse on the morning of September 6, 1978, when he allegedly saw several objects congregate overhead and start maneuvering. The objects emitted light of various colors. The horse was frightened and started to run away, but the boy brought the animal under control. Oscar reported the incident to his father, who sent the boy back to complete his original errand, which was to round up a herd of horses. On returning to the site of his encounter with the UFOs, the boy found a craft landed there. The herd of horses fled in panic, and Oscar's horse again became frightened. From the landed UFO emerged a figure more than seven feet tall, wearing a helmet and gloves. The figure asked Oscar to come inside the craft. Oscar tied his horse to a ladder extended from the craft and climbed up the ladder to look inside the object. There he saw what appeared to be a robot cutting up the bones of animals, possibly cattle. Oscar prepared to leave and asked the tall being for one of his gloves to take back as evidence of what he had seen. When the figure gave him a glove, Oscar noted that the being's hand was green, with blue metallic claws. The being used one claw to prick Oscar on the right arm close to the shoulder. Oscar said the prick felt like the bite of a mosquito. On the way home with the glove, Oscar was pursued by two flying objects that pulled the glove away from him.

Over the next few days, the boy lost his appetite and would wake up screaming at night. At the spot where the giant's claw pricked him, Oscar developed a small depression in his arm. UFO investigator Jacques Vallee, discussing Oscar's case in his book *Confrontations*, adds that Oscar's father had discovered the body of a cow, minus its ribs and hindquarters. The man apparently thought it unlikely that thieves were responsible for the death and mutilation of the cow, because they would have been expected to steal the hide as well. Vallee adds that the family did not own a television set at the time of Oscar's encounter.

Oscar's case involves numerous commonplace elements of close-encounter reports, including bodily and psychological effects, animal mutilation, and panic on the part of domestic animals at a UFO's appearance. The pattern of a tall alien accompanied by a robot also occurred several years later in reports from Voronezh in Russia.

See also ANIMALS, UFOS AND; BODILY EFFECTS; ENCOUNTER PHENOMENA; VORONEZH SIGHTINGS.

Venus   Once thought to be a possible home for extraterrestrial life, Venus is perhaps best known among UFO investigators for its part in the tales of UFO contactee George Adamski, who claimed to have been visited by space travelers from Venus. Exploration of Venus by American and Soviet unmanned space probes, however, revealed that intense heat and tremendous atmospheric pressure on Venus would make intelligent life there highly unlikely, if not impossible. Exploration of the Moon and Mars likewise has virtually eliminated them as candidates for extraterrestrial homeworlds.

See also ADAMSKI, GEORGE; HOMEWORLDS; MARS; MOON.

Vianney, Jean-Marie-Baptiste (1786–1859)

Better known as the Curé d'Ars, Vianney was a Roman Catholic clergyman who served in the village of Ars in France and is famous for his reported encounters with evil spirits. Some of these encounters sound much like modern accounts of close encounters with "extraterrestrials." Displays of light that occurred in Vianney's presence resemble reports of UFOs and related phenomena. Vianney's biographer, Abbé François Trochu, described one incident in December 1826 in which Vianney started out before dawn, on foot, for Saint-Trivier-sur-Moignans, where he was expected to preach. "Sinister" lights appeared to fill the air around Vianney; the air itself looked as if it were ablaze, and bushes alongside the road appeared to be on fire. Trochu attributed these phenomena to the Devil and suggested that Satan was trying to intimidate Vianney, who nonetheless kept walking to his destination.

Other reported incidents of diabolical activity in Vianney's life also resemble details of modern UFO encounters. Vianney's experiences included strange sounds as well as (evidently) visual manifestations of demonic activity, such as bats hanging from the curtains of Vianney's bed. Bizarre noises were reported too, including that of a prancing horse. As in many modern UFO encounters, Vianney was especially troubled by such occurrences at night, in his bedchamber. Sometimes he would report that the "grappin" (Vianney's derisive name for the Devil, meaning "pitchfork" or "dung-fork") had kept him awake all night.

One incident from Vianney's life bears an interesting similarity to some UFO landing reports in which clearly defined areas of scorching are described. On either February 23 or 24, 1857, Vianney was hearing confessions at an earlier hour than usual and was about to leave the confessional to say Mass when he was told his room was on fire. Vianney made a joke to the effect that since the Devil could not get the bird, he would try to burn the cage. An investigation reportedly showed that the fire displayed mysterious effects. The bed and everything near it burned up, but the fire stopped in front of a reliquary atop a chest of drawers. The blaze allegedly consumed everything on one side of the reliquary but left everything on the other side untouched.

The case of the Curé d'Ars is significant to students of the UFO phenomenon not only because it resembles in so many particulars the close-encounter stories of the 20th century (such as mysterious lights; hostile activity on the part of "extraterrestrials"; and close encounters that are initiated at night, when the human subject is in bed and sleeping), but also because its resemblance to such stories highlights the apparent links among demonology, occultism and UFO reports.

See also DEMONOLOGY; ENCOUNTER PHENOMENA; OCCULTISM.

Viborg incident, Russia

A curious report from the former Soviet Union concerned a rocket-like object that reportedly was discovered in the northwestern U.S.S.R. in or around 1967. The object allegedly was found near Viborg and was recovered by military units and placed under guard. The object was described as resembling the American space shuttle, although smaller, about 45 feet long, 15 feet wide and eight feet high. Although wingless, the object reportedly had two streamlined swellings on either side of its fuselage, with a third, smaller swelling on top. The object reportedly had a smooth finish and was gray to tan in color. The rear of the object looked as if it was "chopped off" abruptly. No landing gear could be seen, and the underbelly of the craft was said to be totally smooth. Three small triangular windows allegedly were set in the nose of the craft. The cockpit was said to be too small for adult humans and to have two separate seats. Apparently there were no controls such as exist on present-day spacecraft. When military personnel tried to remove portions of the craft for analysis, they reportedly experienced thermal burns on their hands, although the men wore gloves. This story may have been a case of disinformation. Another possibility is that the military actually did recover an unusual craft of some kind, but one that originated on Earth rather than on some other world. The mysterious object described in this report bears a strong resemblance to the "kosmolyot" or spaceplane that the Soviet Union allegedly tried to develop in the 1970s. It is conceivable that a dummy vehicle based on the spaceplane's design was planted by the Soviet government in the northwestern U.S.S.R. as a test to see how military personnel would react to an encounter with an actual alien spacecraft. Although no proof exists that any such experiment was planned or conducted in this case, it has been suggested that at least one other reported close encounter with a UFO or related object has been staged to investigate the reactions of armed forces to the arrival of an alleged extraterrestrial spacecraft. Another possibility is that the Viborg report is merely a hoax originating in the West.

See also HOAXES; RUSSIA; WOODBRIDGE INCIDENT.

vibrations

The pseudoscientific character of the UFO phenomenon makes itself plain in many ways, including its misuse of terms from physics. A case in point is the expression "vibration." Technically, a vibration is a periodic, resonant motion of an object, such as a violin string or tuning fork. Alleged communications from aliens, however, use "vibrations" in a highly imprecise and inappropriate manner, often to describe some upcoming change that is expected to alter the character of human society. In this case, "vibrations" may refer to changes in social structure or religious belief, or to some emotional or psychic influence upon society and the individual. This misapplication of "vibrations" in UFO lore appears to parallel the misuse of that expression in popular American usage. In the 1960s, sympathetic or hostile emotional reactions came to be known respectively as "good vibrations" or "bad vibrations." If this usage was indeed the origin of "vibrations" as applied to the UFO phenomenon, then this case would be an example of cultural influence on the UFO phenomenon.

See also CULTURAL FACTOR; CULTURAL TRACKING; PSEUDOSCIENCE.

vidya Small, unmanned vehicles of various shapes and sizes, vidyas are said to be used for reconnaissance, including (UFO authority Gavin Gibbons suggests) scanning the thoughts in human minds.

See also VIMANA, VULYA, VUNU.

Villas-Boas incident One of the most famous cases in the literature on UFO close encounters concerns one Antonio Villas-Boas, a Brazilian who at the age of 23 reportedly was abducted by extraterrestrials and underwent a sexual encounter with a mysterious woman aboard an alien craft. According to the report, Villas-Boas was plowing a field on his tractor on the night of October 15, 1957, when an ovoid, luminous object landed in front of him. The tractor's engine died and its lights failed. Although Villas-Boas abandoned his tractor and tried to flee, he was overpowered and hauled aboard the craft by several small figures that wore gray clothing and helmets that left only their eyes exposed. Villas-Boas reported seeing five of the small beings altogether. Aboard the craft, Villas-Boas was stripped completely of his clothing and given a sponge bath with a transparent liquid. Then the room began filling with a gray smoke. Villas-Boas became nauseated and felt as if he was being suffocated. After he vomited, he was able to breathe more easily. Next, a naked woman, with a beautiful body but of short stature, entered the room. He described her as having pale skin, strangely slanted blue eyes, and bright red hair in her armpits and pubic region. Without speaking words, she embraced him and proceeded to have sexual intercourse with him. During their encounter, Villas-Boas said, the woman emitted strange, animal-like grunts that he found unpleasant. Before departing, the woman smiled, pointed at her belly, and then pointed upward. Following this experience, Villas-Boas reportedly underwent a medical examination and was found to have symptoms—including nausea, headaches, loss of appetite and pains all through his body—consistent with a diagnosis of radiation poisoning. These symptoms bear some likeness to those reported in the Falcon Lake incident in Canada.

Villas-Boas reportedly said later that he had the impression the beings were using him as a "stallion" for breeding purposes. In its "breeding" aspect, the Villas-Boas case resembles certain abduction cases of later decades, in which humans supposedly were abducted for purposes of reproduction and/or genetic experimentation by extraterrestrials. The incident also exhibits close parallels to reports, from the literature on demonology and the supernatural, of incubi and succubi, evil spirits capable of having sexual relations with humans.

See also BODILY EFFECTS; BURTON, ROBERT; DEMONOLOGY; FALCON LAKE INCIDENT; GENETIC MANIPULATION; INCUBI AND SUCCUBI; RADIATION; RADIATION EFFECTS; SEXUAL ENCOUNTERS; VEHICLE EFFECTS.

Vilvorde incident, Belgium In December 1973, one of the most famous humanoid sightings in the literature on UFOs reportedly occurred in the town of Vilvorde, Belgium, about eight miles from Brussels. The witness, a 28-year-old man, looked out into the garden of his home around 2:00 A.M. and allegedly saw a small humanoid, slightly over three feet tall, wearing a one-piece suit that appeared to give off a greenish glow. The being wore a transparent helmet with a tube connecting it to some apparatus on his back. A halo of some kind appeared to surround the humanoid, who held in his hands a device that resembled a carpet sweeper or mine detector. The humanoid moved slowly and deliberately and apparently was unable to turn his head on his neck, for he reportedly had to turn his entire body to look in a given direction. The being had a dark face and pointed ears, but no mouth or nose could be seen. The eyes were bright, oval in shape, and yellow in color, with green edges. The mysterious being allegedly turned to look straight at the witness, made the **V** sign with the index and third fingers of one hand, and then departed in a peculiar fashion: he walked straight up the brick wall at the

Vilvorde humanoid: Artist's conception of the small humanoid reportedly seen at Vilvorde, Belgium. (D. Ritchie)

end of the garden, then over the top and (presumably) down the opposite side, as if untroubled by gravitation. Several minutes after the little humanoid climbed over the wall, the witness heard a faint noise comparable to a cricket's chirping and saw a round UFO about 15 feet in diameter rise from the opposite side of the wall. The UFO's upper half was luminous and orange in color, with a cupola atop it giving off a greenish glow. Inside the dome, the humanoid could be seen. Just below the cupola, the witness allegedly saw an emblem that looked like a dark circle with a stylized yellow lightning bolt overlying it. The lower half of the object had a dark reddish hue with three lights—red, yellow and blue—flashing on and off in sequence, in a horizontal line. Around the UFO's periphery, where the luminous upper portion joined the dark lower half, the witness saw outbursts of sparks. The UFO rose to an altitude of about 60 feet, then accelerated and rose vertically out of sight, leaving a glowing trail behind. The witness claimed he felt no fear during the encounter. An investigation the next morning revealed no physical traces of the humanoid's alleged visit;

not even any footprints. Despite an invitation to come forward, no other witnesses reported seeing the humanoid or the UFO on this occasion.

The witness apparently had seen another UFO some months earlier along the Belgian coast at Westende, while walking along the shore with his wife, cousin and sister-in-law. The sighting allegedly occurred around midnight. This UFO moved along the water's surface. The object was described as flat, red and rectangular, and perhaps 15 to 18 feet long, with dim lights resembling illuminated portholes along its underside. When a flashlight beam was directed at it, the object's lights went dark. The UFO rose into the air to clear the breakwater, then dropped back to the water's surface again.

The Vilvorde humanoid sighting bears numerous similarities to other close encounters involving humanoids, including the markedly stiff movements of the humanoid; the being's small stature and large eyes; the one-piece suit with helmet; and the strange "halo" that appeared to surround the entity.

See also AQUATIC OBJECTS; EMBLEMS; ENCOUNTER PHENOMENA; EYES; HALOES; HUMANOIDS.

vimana   In a classification system widely used in the early days of the modern UFO phenomenon, a vimana is the classic "flying saucer," a disc-shaped vehicle roughly the size of a private jet, that carries several occupants and is capable of landing on the Earth. The name vimana, Gibbons says, comes from the Sanskrit and means "chariot of the sky." Alleged UFO lore from India says that ancient Indians possessed plans for three varieties of vimanas. Thirty-two "secrets" were involved in flying a vimana, and mantras—names and syllables pronounced in occult rituals—were required to supply certain "spiritual" powers needed to build indestructible aircraft. One "secret" allowed the vimana to be made invisible. Other techniques supposedly allowed the pilot to transform the appearance of the vimana, to make it appear terrifying, assume the shape of an animal (such as a tiger or lion), and even appear as a beautiful woman adorned with jewels and flowers. Yet another secret allowed the vimana to project a "poison" influence that would render persons at a distance insensible and even comatose. Still other secrets allowed the vimana to assume the appearance of a cloud, and to fly on a zigzag course.

This account of the alleged secrets needed to build a vimana has many parallels in observations of UFOs. Certain UFOs have been seen to move in a zigzag pattern, notably the famous "falling leaf motion"; they allegedly have the ability to paralyze and even render unconscious humans who come too close to them; one category of UFO sightings is known as "cloud cigars," or curiously shaped clouds; sightings of terrifying entities and beautiful, female "extraterrestrials" are commonplace features of UFO reports; and certain sightings indicate that UFOs are able to become invisible under some circumstances.

The reported ability of vimanas to take on the appearance of animals, such as large cats, is intriguing in view of the curious reports of "pumas" seen in England and associated with UFO activity. The alleged spiritual character of the vimana's motive power is consistent with the modern presumption that UFOs actually constitute a spiritual phenomenon as well as a psychological one. Virtually everything about this account of the vimanas' operation and construction is consistent with the analysis of the UFO phenomenon provided by the 20th-century American Orthodox theologian Father Seraphim Rose, who wrote at length about the Hinduistic roots of that phenomenon and its essentially spiritual character.

See also BODILY EFFECTS; CLOUD CIGARS; FALLING LEAF MOTION; HUMANOIDS; KUNDALINI GUN; OCCULTISM; POLYMORPHY; ROSE, FATHER SERAPHIM; SANSKRIT; VIDYA; VULYA; VUNU.

Vins-sur-Caramy incident, France One of the most thoroughly investigated and documented UFO cases, the Vins-sur-Caramy incident allegedly occurred in 1957. One afternoon, two women were walking along a road and heard a loud noise, turned around and saw an object like an inverted cone, apex pointing toward the ground, flying nearby, only a few feet above the ground. The object was perhaps four feet high and three feet in diameter and was topped by a set of what appeared to be antennae. The "antennae" vibrated rapidly, as did road signs when the object passed overhead. Another witness said the object appeared metallic. Observers in the nearby village of La Moutonne also reported seeing the object. This incident was noteworthy because it occurred in daylight; because the object was seen close to the ground, so that its size could be estimated accurately by comparison to nearby objects; and because the incident was witnessed by many observers. The Vins-sur-Camary incident resembles sightings in 1964 in Georgia in the United States.

See also FLYING TOP.

volcanoes Especially in the United States, volcanic mountains occupy a special place in UFO lore. Famous UFO sightings have occurred in the vicinity

Volcanoes figure prominently in UFO lore. Crater Lake in Oregon, shown here, is near site of first "flying saucer" sighting in 1947. (H.R. Cornwall/U.S. Geological Survey)

of such mountains. A case in point is the Arnold incident near volcanic Mount Rainier in Washington state in 1947, when pilot Kenneth Arnold saw the UFOs that made "flying saucer" a familiar expression. Various natural phenomena, such as "mountain-top glows" and perhaps small eruptions, may account for certain UFO reports involving volcanoes. Because UFOs also are associated with areas of high seismic activity (that is, earthquake potential), the areas of intense earthquake activity around many volcanoes also may play a role in UFO sightings by creating conditions favorable for unusual luminous phenomena in the skies. Certain volcanoes have particular prominence in UFO lore, notably Mount Rainier and California's Mount Shasta, which is said to sit atop a huge underground city and UFO base called Telos. Such modern myths concerning volcanoes and UFOs are reminiscent of certain volcanoes' reputation as sites of ritual occult activity. Mount Shasta in particular has such a reputation.

See also ARNOLD INCIDENT; BASES; EARTHQUAKE LIGHTS; EARTHQUAKES; METHANE; MOUNTAIN-TOP GLOWS; MYTHOLOGY; SHASTA, MOUNT; TELOS; TUNNELS; TRANSIENTS.

Von Däniken, Erich (1935–) Swiss author. One of the most prominent and controversial figures in the UFO phenomenon during the 1970s, Erich von Däniken wrote several books based on the premise that the "gods" of human antiquity were in fact extraterrestrial astronauts who visited Earth millennia ago and had a profound impact on the evolution of the human species and the emergence of human civilization.

Von Däniken argued that the spectacular engineering achievements of ancient civilization, such as the monuments of Egypt, were beyond the capabilities of humans at that time and indicated that extraterrestrials using advanced technology had been responsible for building these structures. Von Däniken even suggested that a visit by extraterrestrial space travelers had resulted in the emergence of *Homo sapiens*.

Von Däniken's first book in this genre, published in German as *Erinnerungen an die Zukunft* (Memories of the Future) in 1968 and in English as *Chariots of the Gods?* in 1969, is credited with setting off the public enthusiasm for "ancient astronauts" that was so marked in the United States during the early 1970s. His subsequent books on this same theme included *Gods from Outer Space* (1968) and *The Gold of the Gods* (1973). Von Däniken's writings provided the basis for motion pictures and television specials, and were followed by the publication of dozens of popular books on "ancient astronauts."

To support his contentions, von Däniken cited numerous pieces of alleged evidence from various corners of the world, notably ancient Egypt, where, he claimed, a sophisticated civilization appeared (as it were) fully formed, without any detectable prehistory. One skeptical commentator on von Däniken's works, Ronald Story, pointed out in his book *The Space-Gods Revealed* (1976) that Egypt did indeed have a history of civilization before the construction of the famous pyramids. Story cited two cases of earlier pyramid-building projects that were apparently experiments that taught the Egyptians valuable lessons to be applied later in building the great pyramids. Story added that Egyptologists have worked out a sequence of prehistorical events in Egypt beginning with farming operations in approximately 5000 B.C. Story and other "debunking" authors also disposed of many additional claims by von Däniken.

Although his evidence and arguments have been largely discredited, von Däniken contributed greatly to public interest in the subject of UFOs and, through his quasi-theological speculations, used the hypothetical extraterrestrial astronauts to put forward an alternative belief system to traditional Judeo–Christian faith. Story interprets von Däniken's writings and public fascination with them as rooted in certain currents in theology during the 1960s, notably the "God is dead" school of thinking, which discouraged the centuries-old belief in an all-powerful deity active in human history and responsive to human needs and prayers. The "ancient astronauts" hypothesis of the origins of humankind and human civilization supplied a belief system attuned more closely to the understanding and priorities of 20th-century First World cultures than traditional faiths had been.

See also ANCIENT ASTRONAUTS; MYTHOLOGY; PSEUDOSCIENCE; RELIGION, UFOS AND.

Voronezh sightings, Russia   The city of Voronezh, located some 300 miles south of Moscow, was the site of several widely publicized UFO reports in the autumn of 1989. A local press story described an encounter involving several teenagers and alleged extraterrestrials on September 27. The teenagers were playing soccer in the park when a red or pink light was seen in the sky. The light became a red sphere some 30 feet wide and descended to within about 40 feet of the ground, then landed. From the UFO emerged a humanoid described as being about 10 feet tall and wearing a silver coverall and boots of a bronze hue. The creature appeared to have three eyes, including one in its forehead. The eyes reportedly glowed. The being had a companion that appeared to be a robot having a cuboid body with arms and legs, as well as knobs on the front of its body. At one point the alien appeared to adjust a control on the robot, and the robot started walking around. When the alien made a sound, a luminous patch about four feet long and two and a half feet wide was seen on the ground. The luminous patch then disappeared, apparently at a spoken command from the tall being. The sphere and the alien disappeared, then reappeared several minutes later. This time, the alien carried a tube approximately four feet long and pointed the tube at a nearby teenager. The boy vanished. Then the alien went back into the UFO and flew off. As the UFO departed, the boy reappeared. The incident was allegedly witnessed by several dozen individuals and apparently was part of a UFO "wave" that had affected the Voronezh area for several days previously.

UFO investigator Jacques Vallee visited Russia soon after the Voronezh sightings and reported that three different kinds of beings were said to have been seen in incidents at Voronezh. In addition to the three-eyed giants and the robot, a third category of "alien" was reported seen, having a gray-green face and two eyes, and wearing clothing resembling a raincoat.

One interesting aspect of the sightings in the park at Voronezh was a symbol displayed on a reconstruction of the craft. The symbol, three vertical strokes joined by a horizontal bar through their midpoints, was that of UMMO, the subject of a series of contactee reports that were regarded (Vallee writes) as a hoax. Vallee suggested that someone had known of the UMMO symbol and its UFO associations beforehand and had included it in the reconstruction in the hope of making the report seem more credible. The effect, Vallee noted, was actually to diminish its credibility.

An examination of the alleged landing site in the park allegedly revealed an oblong area of flattened grass, as well as a circular area of slightly increased radioactivity surrounded by four rectangular imprints. Beside one of the imprints were two smooth vertical holes 15 inches in depth. One estimate of the pressure required to produce effects observed at the landing site placed the weight of the object at approximately 11 tons. The alleged UFO landing sites at Voronezh also were studied by "biolocation," a technique similar to the occult practice of dowsing.

Physical traces reportedly were left in another UFO sighting in the Voronezh area at about this time. A UFO seen taking off allegedly left behind a circular imprint in the grass, which was bent in a pattern similar to that reported in "crop circles," a phenomenon tentatively linked to UFO activity, in various other countries.

Vallee also cites the case of one M.N. Polyakov, a 56-year-old factory worker and alleged eyewitness to a UFO close encounter involving vehicle effects and bodily effects. Polyakov was one of a party traveling by car through Voronezh in late September when his group reportedly encountered a UFO in the city's southern suburbs. The car's electrical system malfunctioned. The driver stopped on the shoulder of the road and got out to examine the engine. A yellow-pink sphere estimated at 30 feet in diameter was seen hovering above the road several hundred feet away. The object emitted a beam of light that moved across the ground toward the automobile. Polyakov said he felt frightened as the beam approached. When the beam touched the car, Polyakov said

"something" alien and invisible occupied the driver's seat. Polyakov imagined he could reach over and touch the unseen being, but he found himself unable to move his arm. As the ray moved away from the car, the automobile's electrical system resumed functioning, and the driver was able to restart the engine. When Polyakov questioned the driver about the incident, the driver seemed unable to recall either the UFO or the stop alongside the road. Polyakov noticed a tingling sensation in his fingers, as from a cramp. He reported suffering from a headache until noon of the following day. He also said he was subjected to two strong electrical shocks following the UFO encounter. The first shock occurred when he reached for a door handle, and the second when he inserted a key into a keyhole at home.

The park encounter resembles another case investigated by Vallee, involving a boy in Venado Tuerto, Argentina. The boy claimed to have seen a landed UFO along with a gigantic being and a robot.

See also BIOLOCATION; BODILY EFFECTS; HOAXES; KIEV INCIDENT; RUSSIA; UMMO; VEHICLE EFFECTS; VENADO TUERTO INCIDENTS.

vulya UFOs in this category, part of a classification system widely used in the early years of the modern UFO phenomenon, are very large discs, hundreds or even thousands of feet in diameter, which supposedly carry large crews and are used on interstellar missions.

See also VIDYA; VIMANA; VUNU.

vunu This is a once popular term for cigar-shaped UFOs, several hundred feet long, that allegedly are carried on vulyas, or giant discs, and serve as "mother ships" for small scout ships.

See also VIDYA; VIMANA; VULYA.

W

Wales One of several widely publicized UFO "windows" in the United Kingdom, Wales has been the site of numerous outstanding UFO reports in the latter part of the 20th century, including a widely publicized "wave" of sightings in 1977.

See also DYFED, WALES; UNITED KINGDOM, UFOS IN; WAVES; WINDOWS.

Walton incident, United States The alleged abduction of Travis Walton on November 5, 1975, has become one of the most widely publicized and debated UFO close-encounter cases in history. The abduction reportedly occurred in a forest in Arizona and was witnessed by six people. Walton allegedly was knocked unconscious by a beam of light from a UFO hovering overhead and was taken aboard the craft. There, according to the story, he encountered three humanoids slightly under five feet tall, wearing coveralls. Walton was placed on a table, and something resembling an oxygen mask was placed on his face.

According to his account, the next thing he recalled was awakening on the ground near Heber, Arizona, as a circular UFO arose from a highway and left the scene. Five days had passed since his disappearance. Walton's story became the basis for a 1993 American motion picture called *Fire in the Sky*. UFO debunker Philip Klass has labeled the Walton story a hoax, partly on the basis of a polygraph (lie detector) exam that Walton reportedly failed.

The Walton abduction report bears many similarities with other such reports, including the small, bald-headed humanoids; the table on which Walton allegedly was placed; and the element of five days' "missing time."

See also ABDUCTIONS; HOAXES: HUMANOIDS; KLASS, PHILIP; MISSING TIME; ABDUCTIONS; POLYGRAPHY.

Wanaque dam incidents, New Jersey, United States A series of UFO sightings at the Wanaque reservoir near Wanaque, New Jersey, in January 1966 was part of a wave of sightings that occurred in 1965 and 1966 and illustrates an apparent association between UFO sightings and bodies of water. A patrolman at the reservoir allegedly saw a bright white light moving slowly over the dam. The object changed color from white to red and then to green, and finally returned to white. The patrolman reported the sighting by radio. Soon other police units arrived at the scene and witnessed the UFO, which was estimated to be about 30 feet in diameter. The object moved only a short distance above the reservoir and reportedly displayed a pendulum-like motion in flight. Suddenly, the UFO rose to an altitude of several hundred feet and allegedly directed a strong beam of light downward onto the ice covering the reservoir. The light flashed on and off intermittently for an hour, after which the object climbed rapidly into the sky and was lost from sight. A few minutes later, the UFO returned, or else some other luminous, unidentified object was sighted. This time the object was described as resembling a group of several bright stars. This sighting lasted only a few minutes before the object departed. Several nearly circular holes—apparently melted—allegedly were discovered in the ice at the northern part of the reservoir, where the unidentified object was said to have directed its beam of light down onto the reservoir. Other unidentified, luminous objects were reported seen in the vicinity of Wanaque on several following nights. The objects were described as circular or ovoid and of various colors. The Wanaque incidents resemble numerous other sightings in which UFOs are associated with bodies of water, such as reservoirs and lakes. Alleged extraterrestrials' interest in water is a widely reported element of the UFO phenomenon.

See also WATER; WAVES.

wands　In close-encounter cases, some alleged extraterrestrials confronting human witnesses reportedly use a hand-held device like wand, rod or tube to paralyze the witness. This device bears a strong resemblance to the "magic wand" of folklore. Various interpretations of the "wand" are possible. One interpretation is that it represents an actual piece of technology used to immobilize a person by interfering with the activity of nerves and muscles. According to another possible interpretation, the "wand" is merely an illusion created somehow in the mind of the observer. A similar element of science fiction stories is the "ray gun" or other, comparable device used to stun or kill animals or adversaries. The presence of a "wand" apparently is not necessary for paralysis to occur, because paralysis is reported in some close-encounter cases where such a tool is not in evidence.

See also ENCOUNTER PHENOMENA; KUNDALINI GUN; PARALYSIS; TECHNOLOGY.

Wang Chih incident, China　A story from Chinese folklore, this incident involves one Wang Chih, a Taoist who was gathering firewood in the mountains one day when he encountered several elderly men playing chess in a grotto. He put down his ax and stopped to observe their game. One of the elderly men gave him something resembling the pit of a date and told him to put it on his tongue. Wang Chih found that the object eliminated thirst and hunger. Later, one of the chess players said Wang Chih had been there a long time and ought to return home. When Wang Chih went to retrieve his ax, he found that the handle had crumbled into dust. After leaving the grotto, he discovered that hundreds of years had elapsed. This story is reminiscent of the "missing time" element in modern UFO close-encounter reports and resembles folklore and literature of other lands, notably the story of Rip van Winkle in America.

See also MISSING TIME; TIME EFFECTS.

warfare　The threat of warfare has been a significant element of the UFO phenomenon in the second half of the 20th century. In the years immediately

Martian "War Machines" invaded Earth in H.G. Wells's novel *The War of the Worlds*. (D. Ritchie)

after World War II, the United States and other nations were concerned that UFOs, such as the "ghost rockets" sighted over Scandinavia, might represent a Soviet weapon or some other military threat to their security. The fear of Soviet weaponry appears to have been unjustified in this case, but apprehension continued concerning UFOs and their perceived potential for warfare. Invasion from other planets became a theme of popular entertainment in the 1950s, with the planet Mars (named for the Roman god of war) being a common choice for the invading aliens' homeworld. Treatments of the invasion-from-space theme were sometimes crude, as in the 1953 American film version of H.G. Wells's novel *The War of the Worlds*, which depicted Martians laying waste Earth's major cities; and sometimes more subtle, as in the 1955 American film *Invasion of the Body Snatchers*, which concerned invading aliens assuming the bodily forms of humans in a small town. Warfare among extraterrestrial races has been another prominent theme both in UFO contact reports and in fictional treatments of the subject. On occasion, alleged extraterrestrials are said to have contacted humans in the hope that such contact can prevent humans from self-destruction through atomic warfare. In some cases, the "aliens" reportedly claim that such warfare devastated their own civilizations and forced their people into space. An alternative scenario is that a vast war on Earth among ancient civilizations devastated the planet and forced some of the technologically advanced peoples of that age into space, where they migrated to other worlds. It would appear that extraterrestrial (or ancient terrestrial) races with such a warlike history are poorly qualified to advise humankind on the ways of peace, but that thought is not widely expressed among UFO enthusiasts.

See also MEIER CASE; MOTION PICTURES; WAR OF THE WORLDS, THE.

War of the Worlds, The

This novel by British science fiction author H.G. Wells was published in 1898 and describes a fictional invasion of Earth by Martians. Some 40 years after its publication, the novel was dramatized in a famous radio broadcast by Orson Welles' Mercury Theater. Later the story was made into a 1953 motion picture starring Gene Barry. Although Welles's radio adaptation of the story caused widespread panic on the night of its broadcast in the United States, it apparently did not generate any flurry of UFO sightings, unlike some later motion pictures and television productions that were credited with giving rise to numerous UFO reports.

See also MEDIA, UFOS IN THE; MOTION PICTURES; PRECEDENTS; WELLS, H.G.

Washington, D.C., sightings, United States

Part of a "wave" of UFO sightings in 1952, the Washington incidents involved both reported radar and visual sightings of UFOs. The first of two incidents began at 11:40 P.M. on July 19, when air traffic controllers at National Airport in Washington reportedly detected seven slowly moving objects on radar screens. The objects appeared to be about 15 miles distant from the airport and moving at a velocity of 100 to 130 miles per hour. Identical images allegedly were picked up on radar at nearby Andrews Air Force Base in Maryland. The Air Force's Air Defense Command learned of the radar contacts at 3:00 A.M. and sent two radar-equipped fighter aircraft to investigate. The aircraft detected nothing unusual in the skies above the airport and left. After the aircraft departed, the images reportedly reappeared on the radar screens and remained until dawn. One week later, on July 26, radar at National Airport allegedly detected another set of several unidentified objects.

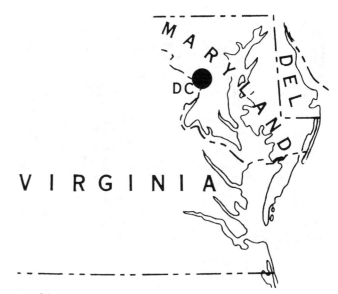

Washington, D.C., UFO sightings caused a stir in the nation's capital. (U.S. Geological Survey)

Again, Andrews Air Force Base also had picked up the radar returns. Moreover, in this case, the pilots of aircraft arriving and departing through National Airport also reported sighting unusual objects. Jets were dispatched again to investigate the reports, and the pattern of the earlier incident repeated itself. The radar returns reportedly vanished from the screens when the jets arrived, then reappeared after the jets departed. The incidents eventually were dismissed as the result of temperature inversions.

The Washington sightings were covered extensively in the local news media and appear to have parallels in popular entertainment. The sightings occurred one year after the release of Robert Wise's celebrated motion picture *The Day the Earth Stood Still*, in which an extraterrestrial spacecraft is detected on radar and then lands in Washington, D.C., bearing an alien emissary who warns humankind about the dangers of nuclear weaponry. Four years after the Washington sightings, the nation's capital became the scene of another spectacular motion picture, *Earth Versus the Flying Saucers*, in which brilliant special effects sequences by Ray Harryhausen show disc-shaped saucers attacking the District of Columbia.

The Washington sightings of 1952 occurred only days after another widely publicized incident in which a set of luminous red UFOs were reported seen over the Norfolk, Virginia, area.

See also DAY THE EARTH STOOD STILL, THE; EARTH VERSUS THE FLYING SAUCERS; NASH–FORTENBERRY INCIDENT; RADAR.

Some UFOs appear to be attracted to bodies of water, such as lakes and reservoirs. (D. Ritchie)

water According to numerous reports, UFOs show a marked attraction to bodies of water, such as rivers, lakes and seas. UFOs often are described as diving into, emerging from or hovering just above the waters. UFOs commonly are described as directing beams of light into the water, as if searching for something. In at least one case, a famous "contactee," Albert Bender, claimed that extraterrestrials were here on Earth to extract some valuable commodity from the planet's oceans.

See also BENDER MYSTERY; HUDSON VALLEY SIGHTINGS; MYSTERIANS, THE; PASCAGOULA INCIDENTS; PEROPAVA RIVER INCIDENT.

waves UFO sightings sometimes occur in "waves," which consist of large numbers of sightings reported in a given country or region within a period of a few days or weeks. Numerous UFO waves have been recorded in the latter half of the 20th century, although earlier waves have been reported. Some waves have involved only sightings of unknown objects in the skies, whereas other waves have included reports of personal encounters with "animated" beings purported to be extraterrestrials. Major waves appear to have occurred about every two years on the average. Some major waves of the mid-20th century, for example, include waves in 1946, specifically involving the "ghost rockets" sighted over Scandinavia; June and July 1947, centered in the western United States; July and August 1952, in the eastern United States; October 1954, in France; November 1957, in the midwestern and southwestern United States and in South America; June through August 1959, in Australia and other locations in the western part of the Pacific Ocean ba-

sin; May through August 1962, in Argentina; and a global wave that occurred between the summer of 1965 and the spring of 1966. This last wave appears to have begun in the American Midwest and spread to the eastern United States, giving rise to the famous sightings at Wanaque, New Jersey, and Exeter, New Hampshire. Other national and regional waves were reported in 1965 and 1966 from various portions of Africa, Asia, Australia and Europe. Numerous other waves have been reported in the last third of the century, including the 1973 wave that produced the famous Pascagoula, Mississippi, sighting in the United States, supposedly involving the abduction of two fishermen.

There is no universal agreement on the origins of UFO waves. Misinterpretation of natural phenomena, such as the "opposition" periods in which the planet Mars appears to be unusually bright in the night sky, may be responsible for some UFO waves. "Mass hysteria," or conditions when the population is uneasy and more than usually suggestible, may account for some other waves. Deliberate propagation of rumors is another possible origin.

Moreover, one should not discount the possibility that unidentified, intelligent beings actually are producing unusual phenomena in the skies. It has been suggested that if intelligent extraterrestrials are indeed responsible for certain UFO sightings and waves, with the aim of influencing human belief systems, then the recurrent waves are a useful technique for reinforcing public interest and belief in the UFO phenomenon.

An interesting parallel exists between the "wavelike" character of UFO sightings and recurrent sightings of Marian apparitions. During the so-called miracle of Fatima, for example, an entity alleged to be the Virgin Mary appeared in a series of "visitations" in Portugal. The alleged entity pledged to reappear at various times, and these recurring apparitions helped to augment public belief in, and response to, the visitations. So successful was this approach that thousands of visitors to the apparition site claimed to have seen wondrous phenomena there, and the "miracle" eventually won the official sanction of the Roman Catholic church.

Although the news media appear to play some part in the propagation and perpetuation of waves, by publicizing or even trying to initiate UFO reports, there are many occasions where waves appear to have occurred without the stimulus of media coverage. There are, for example, reports of waves that occurred long before the mass media began to exercise their current level of influence on public opinion. Also, the mass media have presented news reports and fictionalized treatments of encounters with "extraterrestrials" that have not generated large numbers of UFO reports. A case in point is Orson Welles's famous radio broadcast of a dramatized version of H.G. Wells's novel *The War of the Worlds,* which caused widespread alarm in the United States but evidently did not engender any UFO "wave." Likewise, Stanley Kubrick's highly popular motion picture *2001: A Space Odyssey,* with its depiction of huge, mysterious "monuments" emplaced in our solar system by some extraterrestrial intelligence, did not appear to set off any wave of "monument" sightings.

In summary, the UFO wave phenomenon is complex and cannot be dismissed easily by simple explanations such as mass hysteria or misidentification of familiar natural and man-made phenomena and objects in the skies.

See also ABDUCTIONS; ARNOLD INCIDENT; EXETER, NEW HAMPSHIRE, INCIDENTS; FATIMA, "MIRACLE" OF; FLAPS; GHOST ROCKETS; HALLUCINATIONS; KLASS, PHILIP; KNOCK INCIDENT; MARIAN APPARITIONS; MARTIAN OPPOSITIONS; MASS HYSTERIA; MEDIA, UFOS IN THE; PASCAGOULA INCIDENT; PERCEPTION; PRECEDENTS; UFO PHENOMENON, HISTORY OF; WANAQUE DAM INCIDENTS; WAR OF THE WORLDS, THE.

Wells, H(erbert) G(eorge) (1866–1946)

British science fiction writer H.G. Wells is responsible for some of the modern fascination with UFOs and extraterrestrial life. His novel *The War of the Worlds* depicted an invasion of Earth by Martians who traveled in spacecraft fired by cannon from Mars. On Earth, the Martians used huge, tripodal war machines and a laser-like "heat ray" to devastate cities. Wells's novel exercised, and still does exercise, a powerful influence on readers' imaginations, either directly or through radio, movie and television adaptations. There are several notable parallels between Wells's story and certain elements of the UFO phenomenon. The aliens are described as hostile, as in certain modern UFO encounter stories. The Martians' technology includes a powerful "ray," as in modern encounter stories that mention incapacitating rays directed against humans. At one point in the story, a character speculates that Wells's nonhuman, vaguely octopoid Martians might be able to transfer their brains into various kinds of bodies as needed; this capability parallels the "shape-shifting" characteristics reported in many UFO close encounters with alien "humanoids." The Martian origin of Wells's fictional invaders also parallels the correla-

H.G. Wells's fictional Martians had huge brains but atrophied bodies. (D. Ritchie)

tion observed between UFO "waves" and Earth's oppositions with the planet Mars.

Wells's other work also contains parallels with elements of the modern UFO phenomenon. In his 1901 novel *The First Men in the Moon,* Wells describes a fanciful anti-gravity device that two British explorers use to reach the Moon in a home-built spacecraft. One of the explorers remains on the Moon, while the other escapes to Earth in the spaceship. On the Moon, the Britons encounter a society of "selenites." These are frail, insect-like creatures ruled by a being called the "Grand Lunar," who is little more than a mammoth brain with tremendous intellectual capabilities. The Grand Lunar is horrified to hear accounts of warfare on Earth, and the explorer who remains on the Moon is murdered by the selenites. In similar fashion, modern reports of contacts with extraterrestrials mention "insectoid" aliens as well as "exalted ones," beings of vast intellect who resemble in many ways Wells's fictional Grand Lunar. As in many 20th-century contactee stories, Wells's selenites have a peaceful society and are distressed over violence on Earth. The fantastic "anti-gravity" technology described in Wells's story also has counterparts in UFO lore. Finally, UFO contact reports from the latter half of the 20th century sometimes describe violent and even murderous behavior on the part of alleged extraterrestrials who disapprove of human nature and society, as in Wells's novel.

See also ABDUCTIONS; BENDER MYSTERY; BETHURUM INCIDENT; ENCOUNTER PHENOMENA; EXALTED ONES; HUMANOIDS; INSECTOIDS; MARS; MARTIAN OPPOSITIONS; MOTION PICTURES; PROTEAN-PSYCHOID PHENOMENA; TECHNOLOGY; WAR OF THE WORLDS, THE; WAVES.

West Freugh incident, United Kingdom

The Royal Air Force's (RAF) West Freugh facility in Scotland reportedly tracked an unidentified target at an altitude estimated at 60,000 feet on April 4, 1957.

The object apparently was never identified. A weather balloon was released from another RAF facility in Ireland shortly before the West Freugh incident and might have reached the Scottish coast at about the time the unidentified object was detected, but the UFO allegedly moved so quickly and at such a high altitude that a balloon could not be held accountable.

windows   These are localized areas where large numbers of UFO sightings are reported. Numerous UFO windows have been identified around the world. Several of the best-known windows are in the United Kingdom, notably at Lothian and Luce Bay, Scotland; Dyfed, Wales; the Pennine Hills; and Warminster, Wiltshire. Other widely publicized UFO windows have been located in Texas, Florida, the Pacific Northwest and the Hudson Valley in the United States; Puerto Rico; Brazil; Argentina; France; Italy; Spain; Norway; the Canary Islands; and Malaysia. In Japan, the northern island of Hokkaido has been identified as a UFO window. Australia has several alleged UFO windows, including Cairns, Queensland; Kempsey, New South Wales; the Nullarbor Plain; and the Bass Strait, which was the site of the famous disappearance of pilot Frederick Valentich and his private aircraft. There appears to be no clear correlation between population density and the existence of a UFO window. Some windows have been identified in densely populated areas, such as the Hudson Valley in the United States, whereas other windows occur in relatively empty areas, such as the Nullarbor Plain in Australia. Apparently there is a notable absence of UFO windows in Africa.

See also ARGENTINA; AUSTRALIA, UFOS IN; BRAZIL; CANARY ISLANDS; FRANCE; HESSDALEN VALLEY; ITALY; JAPAN; UNITED KINGDOM, UFOS IN; UNITED STATES, UFOS IN; VALENTICH CASE.

winged beings   Some UFO encounter reports involve alleged meetings with winged beings. For example, a report from Hythe, Kent, England, on November 16, 1963, described a dark, headless, humanoid being with batlike wings, sighted emerging from a cluster of trees after a pair of unusual lights, one reddish-yellow and the other golden, were observed at Sandling Park. The winged being in this incident resembles Mothman, the headless, large-winged being reported seen in West Virginia on several occasions in late 1966 and often cited in literature on UFOs.

See also MOTHMAN; SPRING-HEELED JACK.

Winthrop incidents, Massachusetts, United States   In his journal of 17th-century Boston life, Massachusett's governor John Winthrop mentioned several incidents of apparent UFO sightings. The first reportedly occurred in March 1639, when one James Everell and two other men in a scow were crossing Muddy River in what is now the Back Bay district of Boston. The time was about 10:00 P.M. The men saw a bright light appear in the sky above them. The light appeared to be square or oblong in shape and was estimated to be about nine feet wide. The object held stationary at first, then darted across the Charles River to Charlestown, and then returned. This back-and-forth motion reportedly continued for two to three hours. Eventually, the light vanished. After it disappeared the men discovered that their scow apparently had been moving against the tide during this period; although the tide had been going out, and the men had been too terrified to attempt escape, the boat was farther upstream than it had been when the light appeared. Winthrop added that the light was reported seen by other witnesses later, at approximately the same place.

Winthrop also told of another apparent UFO sighting five years later, on the night of January 18, 1644. Observers on the Boston waterfront reportedly saw a mysterious light approximately as big as the full Moon rise above the northeast horizon around 8:00 P.M. Another light, similar in appearance, was seen some minutes later approaching from the east. The lights met above the harbor, in the vicinity of Noddle's Island, and maneuvered energetically for a while, emitting small flames or other displays of light. The lights finally descended behind a hill and were lost from sight. While this display was happening, another curious event reportedly happened to several individuals on the water between Dorchester and Boston. These witnesses said they heard, as if speaking from the sky, a "dreadful" voice speaking the words "boy" and "come away," over and over. The voice sounded as if it came from a long distance and from various directions. A week later, the lights reappeared. A week after that, the voice was heard again, this time near Noddle's Island, site of the lights' first appearance.

Winthrop evidently tried to explain these strange phenomena in terms of black magic. He noted that the site of the mysterious lights, Noddle's Island, was near the spot where the pinnace of one Captain Chaddock had blown up several weeks before, when gunpowder in its hold was ignited. Chaddock was rumored to practice necromancy and was suspected of having committed murder in Virginia.

Chaddock's body allegedly was never recovered, although the bodies of crewmen killed in the blast had floated ashore. One interpretation of this incident is that Winthrop thought the Devil had visited Boston that night, in the company of lesser demons, to claim Chaddock's soul.

New England has a long history of mysterious, UFO-like objects reported seen in the skies.

See also NEW HAVEN SPECTER SHIP; PALATINE LIGHT; PUTNEY HILL GLOBES.

wise baby dreams This expression refers to encounters in which alleged female abductees are said to meet and hold the "hybrid" infants—half human and half "extraterrestrial"—produced with the women's genetic material. These women may presume they were impregnated somehow by the aliens, and the hybrid baby then was taken from them. The women may report feeling that the baby was highly intelligent. The experience may be unpleasant for the woman, especially if she has the impression that there is something "wrong" or deficient about the baby.

See also ABDUCTIONS; GENETIC MANIPULATION; SEXUAL ENCOUNTERS; WOMEN, UFOS AND.

witchcraft Although this particular branch of the occult is not widely associated in the public mind with the UFO phenomenon, substantial ties are believed to exist between UFOs and the practice of witchcraft. Definitions of witchcraft differ, but in a broad sense witchcraft represents a body of rituals and paraphernalia intended to bring the practitioner into contact with disembodied spirits, for a great variety of purposes. The boundaries between witchcraft and other occult practices are not always clear, and there is a certain degree of overlap between witchcraft and other phenomena such as divination and manifestations of UFOs.

Accounts of witchcraft from the 17th century contain references to phenomena similar to elements of modern UFO encounter reports, such as paralysis affecting persons targeted by witches' spells. Records of witch trials in Salem and Andover, Massachusetts, in 1692 mention other alleged phenomena similar to those reported in many UFO close-encounter cases, including humanoid "specters" and animal mutilations.

The association of UFOs with witchcraft and other occult practices in modern times is evident when one examines popular literature on the UFO phenomenon. Publications devoted to UFOs often contain advertisements for so-called psychics, spell-casters and other practitioners of the occult. These advertisements may offer for sale a selection of occult texts and paraphernalia, such as guides to black magic and talismans said to bring success in such fields as romance and gambling.

Witchcraft and the UFO phenomenon both may be seen as points, so to speak, on a continuum of "paranormal" phenomena associated with occultism.

See also ANIMALS, UFOS AND; BIOLOCATION; BODILY EFFECTS; DEMONOLOGY; DIVINING ROD; HUMANOIDS; OCCULTISM; UFOS, CHARACTERISTICS OF.

women, UFO and The female experience of alleged UFO encounters tends to differ significantly from that of men. Many reported close encounters between "extraterrestrials" and women are said to involve some kind of sexual violation or extraction of ova. Some women who claim to have had abduction experiences say later that they believe they were impregnated by extraterrestrials, and that the resulting "hybrid" child—half human, half alien—was taken by the aliens. Some women say they were given an opportunity to see and hold their hybrid babies later; these experiences commonly are called "wise baby dreams" and involve a feeling that the baby is unusually intelligent or that something is "wrong" about the child. Some of the most famous abduction reports have involved women, notably American "abductees" Betty Andreasson Luca and Betty Hill. Although alleged extraterrestrials usually are described as masculine, if they appear to have any gender at all, female "aliens" are reported on some occasions, as in the case of Truman Bethurum, who claimed to have met a female extraterrestrial named "Captain Aura Rhanes." Sometimes an impressive, apparently female apparition is seen in circumstances not related directly to, but nonetheless strongly resembling, UFO encounters.

See also ABDUCTIONS; ANDREASSON CASE; BETHURUM INCIDENT; ENCOUNTER PHENOMENA; GENETIC MANIPULATION; HYBRIDS; FATIMA, "MIRACLE" OF; HILL INCIDENT; MARIAN APPARITIONS; SEXUAL ENCOUNTERS; WISE BABY DREAMS.

Woodbridge incident, United Kingdom One of the most mysterious and controversial incidents in the history of the modern UFO phenomenon, this sighting allegedly occurred in December 1980 when a UFO was sighted on the ground in Rendlesham Forest near the gate of the Woodbridge air base complex operated by the Royal Air Force and the United States Air Force. There is no unanimity about what reportedly was sighted in the forest that night, but according to one account, a pair of security guards saw unidentified lights near the gate and thought an airplane might have crashed. Three men were sent to investigate and, in this version of the story, found a triangular UFO about six feet high and nine feet wide in the forest, emitting a powerful white light. The object either was resting on landing gear or hovering a short distance above the ground. Some descriptions of the object say it bore red and blue lights, and that it was not triangular at all, but huge and shaped like a saucer. Nonhuman entities were reported seen at the site, inside the UFO. Conflicting accounts of the alleged incident have made investigation difficult, and various interpretations of the case have been proposed. One suggestion is that the incident was some kind of experiment designed to test how military personnel would react to the landing of an actual extraterrestrial spacecraft.

See also ENCOUNTER PHENOMENA; UNITED KINGDOM, UFOS IN.

World Contact Day   An early experiment in contacting extraterrestrials by telepathy, World Contact Day reportedly took place on March 15, 1953. The procedure, as described by famed "contactee" Albert Bender, was to memorize a brief message to be directed telepathically to the aliens, then repeat the message silently in one's mind. The message, addressed to occupants of interplanetary spacecraft visiting Earth, included an invitation to make an appearance on Earth, to help humankind with its problems, and to provide some sign that the message had been received. At one point, the message actually requested a "miracle." This experiment was coordinated as an event in which hundreds of potential participants in the experiment were asked to attempt telepathic contact with extraterrestrials. The experiment was coordinated so that, if all went as planned, the message would be recited by participants all over the globe at the same moment, 6:00 P.M. eastern standard time.

Bender reported a highly unpleasant experience in connection with the experiment. After he had repeated the message three times in his mind, starting at 6:00 P.M., Bender was subjected to an intense chill and experienced a tremendous headache. He also detected a foul odor like that of burning sulfur or rotten eggs. What he described as small lights, blue in color and blinking like the lights of an ambulance, appeared to him. Bender had the impression that he was floating somehow on a cloud, with a peculiar weightless feeling. He emphasized later that he felt

extremely cold, as if he were lying nude on a block of ice in the Antarctic. What Bender reported next resembled a classic "near-death experience" or "out-of-body experience." He perceived himself hovering several feet above his own body. Next he received a message from a voice that nonetheless was not in audible speech. The voice spoke in the first person plural and advised Bender to quit investigating the universe's "mysteries." The being or beings sending the voice also threatened to make an appearance if Bender (and, presumably, his colleagues in UFO investigations) disobeyed the warning. Bender asked why the entities seemed unfriendly, since the humans meant them no harm. The voice replied simply that the aliens had a mission to perform and did not wish to be disturbed. Bender was told that the alien entities were on Earth and were watching his every move. Then Bender felt a sensation of falling, and he found himself in bed. He thought the room was filled with yellow mist. Nearby, he perceived a shadow similar to that of a man, but the shadow vanished as Bender prepared to rise from bed. Bender felt nauseated. He checked the clock and found that five minutes had elapsed since he began the experiment.

The details of Bender's experience are familiar to students of UFO contact cases, notably the sensation of intense cold and the perception of a threatening presence, as well as the presence of a humanoid form standing near one's bed. These perceptions also are common to reports of contact with evil spirits. Bender's description of a foul odor resembles the accounts of unpleasant smells detected at exorcisms.

See also BENDER MYSTERY; DEMONOLOGY; NEAR-DEATH EXPERIENCE; OUT-OF-BODY EXPERIENCE; TEMPERATURE EFFECTS.

wormhole   A concept in theoretical physics, the wormhole is a passageway—a "short cut," one might say—that (in theory) would allow a spacecraft to travel almost instantaneously from one point in the universe to a far distant point, thus eliminating the need for a lengthy journey between the two points in real time. Because the velocity limit imposed on interstellar travel by relativity theory, specifically the velocity of light, means that travel between star systems would take many years or even centuries to accomplish, supporters of the "extraterrestrial hypothesis" have suggested that wormholes might serve as a means for postulated aliens to travel to Earth from other solar systems in much less time. That suggestion is mere speculation, however, and is likely to remain so indefinitely.

Worth, Patience   A celebrated case from occult lore, the Patience Worth phenomenon involved a St. Louis woman named Pearl Curran who supposedly channeled the spirit of a woman named Patience Worth, starting in 1913 and continuing for more than a decade. "Worth" was supposed to be the spirit of an Englishwoman who was born in Dorsetshire in 1649, immigrated to America in her later years and was killed there in a massacre by Native Americans. The spirit allegedly dictated some four million words in historical novels, short stories, poems and other literary output to Curran through automatic writing. The novels are considered authentic in historical detail, although the vocabulary is considerably different from what one would expect of a 17th-century Englishwoman. Curran used a Ouija board for a time but later abandoned it in favor of automatic speech.

The Worth case has numerous elements in common with the modern UFO phenomenon, particularly mediumistic communications from alleged extraterrestrials. The mediumistic technique of automatic writing, for example, was used by George Hunt Williamson and his companions to "channel" messages from "extraterrestrials" in 1952. For this project, Williamson and company, in effect, reinvented the Ouija board. In the 1980s and 1990s, channeling has become a widely practiced approach to contacting putative aliens.

See also AUTOMATIC WRITING; CHANNELING; COMMUNICATIONS; MESSAGES; OCCULTISM; OUIJA BOARD; TELEPATHY.

Y

Yoritsume incident, Japan The Japanese general Yoritsume allegedly saw lights maneuvering in the sky on the night and early morning of September 24, 1235. An investigation, reflecting the erroneous astronomical knowledge of the time, concluded that the general had seen stars swaying in the wind.

See also JAPAN.

Z

Zeta Reticuli The stars Zeta 1 and 2 Reticuli, located in the constellation Reticulum (the Net), are located approximately 30 light-years from Earth and have become prominent in UFO lore as a result of the reported experiences of Betty and Barney Hill. Betty Hill recalled seeing what appeared to be a star map, shown to her by one of the entities she claimed to have encountered. Her description of the map made possible a tentative reconstruction of it. On the strength of this evidence, it has been suggested that the "aliens" in the Hill incident originated from a planet around Zeta 1 or 2 Reticuli. There are serious questions about the value of this evidence, however, because the so-called star map evidently was very crude, included no scale and was unfit for use in any kind of navigation.

The "Reticulans" are presumed to be humanoids approximately four feet tall, but there is disagreement on their other characteristics. Some students of the UFO phenomenon think Reticulans are equivalent to grays, the big-headed humanoids reported seen often in the United States. Other observers, however, argue that there are considerable differences between "grays" and "Reticulans."

Reticulans figured prominently in a 1978 alleged contact case in South Carolina. The contactee, one Bill Herrmann, reportedly was told no fewer than four times that the putative aliens were from a system with two suns. The entities encountered by Herrman were said to have been well-mannered and kind. This information stands in sharp contrast to reports of indifferent or even cruel behavior on the part of "aliens" toward humans in some other contact cases. According to the report, the Reticulans once took control of a home computer in a store and displayed a message, ZETA 1 RETICULI, ZETA 2 RETICULI, followed by Herrmann's name. The "aliens" also are said to have told Herrmann that they had contacted a couple in 1961 who had received excessive attention; presumably this reference was to the Hills. The postulated Reticulans have been implicated in various other cases, notably the Aztec and the Roswell incidents. See also AZTEC INCIDENT; CRASHES; GRAYS; HILL INCIDENT; HUMANOIDS; ROSWELL INCIDENT.

Zond 4 incident, eastern U.S. The re-entry of a Soviet booster rocket into the atmosphere over the eastern United States on March 3, 1968, was mistaken for a brilliant UFO by numerous witnesses in the U.S. An investigation by UFO "debunker" Philip Klass revealed that the booster re-entered the atmosphere along a trajectory that carried it from southwest to northeast across the states of Tennessee, Ohio, Pennsylvania and New York. The booster broke apart into many glowing fragments. Many independent witnesses of this phenomenon reported it as a UFO and even described it in (inaccurate) detail; although the disintegrating booster was miles in altitude and many miles distant from the observers, one witness estimated the diameter of the "UFO" at some 1,000 feet, despite the fact that the diameter of such an object would be difficult or impossible to estimate accurately under such conditions. One report described the UFO as a giant metallic saucer with numerous windows illuminated from within. In another report, the alleged UFO took the form of a cigar-shaped object with windows and an exhaust like that of a rocket. Even an animal's reaction to the UFO was reported. A science teacher, who described the re-entering rocket as three UFOs flying in formation and apparently under "intelligent" direction, said her dog appeared to be frightened by the UFO. Later, it was learned that the teacher had taken her dog outside for a walk on a cold night when the sighting occurred; her dog disliked the cold, and its displeasure was interpreted as a reaction to the UFO when in fact the animal was merely chilly. The *Zond 4* incident demonstrated how unreliable eyewitness testimony in UFO sightings can be and how easily exotic explanations can be applied to everyday phenomena, such as a pet's aversion to cold weather.

See also ANIMALS, UFOS AND; CONSTRUCTIVE PERCEPTION.

Selected Bibliography

The literature on UFOs is huge, and this bibliography represents only a tiny fraction of that literature.

Barclay, David, and Therese Marie Barclay. *UFOs: The Final Answer?* London: Blandford, 1993.

Bergier, Jacques, and the editors of *INFO*. *Extraterrestrial Intervention: The Evidence*. Chicago: Henry Regnery, 1974.

Berlitz, Charles, and William L. Moore. *The Roswell Incident*. New York: Putnam, 1980.

Binder, Otto. *What We Really Know about Flying Saucers*. Greenwich, Conn.: Fawcett, 1967.

Conroy, Ed. *Report on Communion: The Facts Behind the Most Controversial True Story of Our Time*. New York: William Morrow, 1989.

Crystall, Ellen. *Silent Invasion*. New York: Paragon House, 1991.

David, Jay, ed. *The Flying Saucer Reader*. New York: New American Library, 1967.

Druffel, Ann, and D. Scott Rogo. *The Tujunga Canyon Contacts*. New York: New American Library, 1989.

Fawcett, Lawrence, and Barry J. Greenwood. *The UFO Cover-up*. Englewood Cliffs, N.J.: Prentice-Hall, 1974.

Friedman, Stanton T., and Don Berliner. *Crash at Corona*. New York: Paragon House, 1992.

Good, Timothy. *Above Top Secret: The Worldwide UFO Cover-up*. New York: William Morrow/Quill, 1988.

———. *Alien Contact*. New York: William Morrow, 1993.

Hall, Richard. *Uninvited Guests: A Documented History of UFO Sightings, Alien Encounters and Coverups*. Santa Fe, N.M.: Aurora Press, 1988.

Hough, Peter, and Jenny Randles. *Looking for the Aliens: A Psychological, Scientific and Imaginative Investigation*. London: Blandford, 1991.

Hynek, J. Allen. *The UFO Experience: A Scientific Inquiry*. New York: Ballantine Books, 1974.

Hynek, J. Allen, Philip J. Imbrognio and Bob Pratt. *Night Siege: the Hudson Valley UFO Sightings*. New York: Ballantine Books, 1987.

Jacobs, David. "UFOs and the Search for Scientific Legitimacy," in Howard Kerr and Charles Crow, eds., *The Occult in America: New Historical Perspectives*. Urbana and Chicago: University of Illinois Press, 1983; pp. 218–232.

Kinder, Gary. *Light Years: An Investigation into the Extraterrestrial Experiences of Eduard Meier*. New York: Atlantic Monthly Press, 1987.

Klass, Philip. *UFO Abductions: A Dangerous Game*. Buffalo, N.Y.: Prometheus Books, 1989.

Leslie, Desmond, and George Adamski. *Flying Saucers Have Landed*. New York: British Book Centre, 1953.

Lindeman, Michael, ed. *UFOs and the Alien Presence: Six Viewpoints*. Santa Barbara, Calif.: The 2020 Group Visitors Investigation Project, 1991.

Lore, Gordon I.R., Jr., and Harold H. Deneault. *Mysteries of the Skies: UFOs in Perspective*. Englewood Cliffs, N.J.: Prentice-Hall, 1968.

Randle, Kevin D., and Donald R. Schmitt. *UFO Crash at Roswell*. New York: Avon Books, 1991.

Randles, Jenny. *Alien Abductions: The Mystery Solved*. New Brunswick, N.J.: Inner Light Publications, 1988.

———. *From Out of the Blue*. New York: Berkley Books, 1993.

———. *The UFO Conspiracy.* New York: Barnes and Noble, 1987.

Rose, Father Seraphim. *Orthodoxy and the Religion of the Future.* Platina, Calif.: Saint Herman of Alaska Brotherhood, 1977.

Spencer, John, ed. *The UFO Encyclopedia.* New York: Avon Books, 1993.

Steiger, Brad, ed. *Project Blue Book.* New York: Ballantine Books, 1976.

Thompson, Keith. *Angels and Aliens: UFOs and the Mythic Imagination.* Reading, Massachusetts: Addison-Wesley Publishing Company, 1991.

University of Colorado. *Scientific Study of Unidentified Flying Objects.* Boulder: University of Colorado, 1969.

Vallee, Jacques. *Anatomy of a Phenomenon: UFOs in Space.* Chicago: Henry Regnery, 1965.

———. *Confrontations: A Scientist's Search for Alien Contact.* New York: Ballantine Books, 1991.

———. *Passport to Magonia: On UFOs, Folklore and Parallel Worlds.* Chicago: Contemporary Books, 1993.

———. *Revelations: Alien Contact and Human Deception.* New York: Ballantine Books, 1991.

———. *UFO Chronicles of the Soviet Union.* New York: Ballantine Books, 1992.

Vallee, Jacques, and Janine Vallee. *Challenge to Science: The UFO Enigma.* Chicago: Henry Regnery, 1966.

INDEX

Boldface page numbers indicate main topics;
italic page numbers denote illustrations.